The Pentateuch

The Biblical Seminar
39

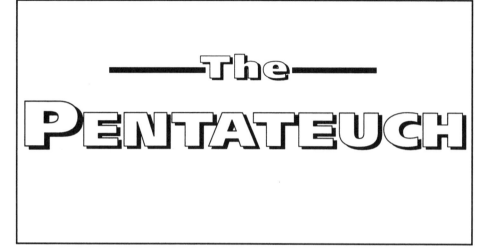

The
PENTATEUCH

edited by
John W. Rogerson

Sheffield
Academic Press

Published by Sheffield Academic Press Ltd
Mansion House
19 Kingfield Road
Sheffield S11 9AS
England

Printed on acid-free paper in Great Britain
by The Cromwell Press
Melksham, Wiltshire

British Library Cataloguing in Publication Data

A catalogue record for this book is available
from the British Library

ISBN 1-85075-785-2

CONTENTS

ABBREVIATIONS

AB	Anchor Bible
AnBib	Analecta biblica
ANET	J.B. Pritchard (ed.), *Ancient Near Eastern Texts*
AnOr	Analecta orientalia
AOAT	Alter Orient und Altes Testament
ArOr	*Archiv orientálni*
ATANT	Abhandlungen zur Theologie des Alten und Neuen Testaments
BA	*Biblical Archaeologist*
BARev	*Biblical Archaeology Review*
BBB	Bonner biblische Beiträge
BETL	Bibliotheca ephemeridum theologicarum lovaniensium
Bib	*Biblica*
BJPES	*Bulletin of the Jewish Palestine Exploration Society*
BJRL	*Bulletin of the John Rylands University Library of Manchester*
BK	*Bibel und Kirche*
BKAT	Biblischer Kommentar: Altes Testament
BTB	*Biblical Theology Bulletin*
BWANT	Beiträge zur Wissenschaft vom Alten und Neuen Testament
BZ	*Biblische Zeitschrift*
BZAW	Beihefte zur *ZAW*
CBQ	*Catholic Biblical Quarterly*
GKB	Gesenius–Kautzsch–Bergsträsser, *Hebräische Grammatik*
HSM	Harvard Semitic Monographs
HTR	*Harvard Theological Review*
HUCA	*Hebrew Union College Annual*
IB	*Interpreter's Bible*
ICC	International Critical Commentary
IDBSup	*IDB*, Supplementary Volume
Int	*Interpretation*
JAAR	*Journal of the American Academy of Religion*
JANESCU	*Journal of the Ancient Near Eastern Society of Columbia University*
JBL	*Journal of Biblical Literature*
JCS	*Journal of Cuneiform Studies*
JJS	*Journal of Jewish Studies*
JNES	*Journal of Near Eastern Studies*
JNSL	*Journal of Northwest Semitic Languages*
JPOS	*Journal of the Palestine Oriental Society*
JSOT	*Journal for the Study of the Old Testament*

JSOTSup	*Journal for the Study of the Old Testament*, Supplement Series
JSS	*Journal of Semitic Studies*
JTS	*Journal of Theological Studies*
MVAG	Mitteilungen der Vorderasiatisch-ägyptischen Gesellschaft
NCB	New Century Bible
NICOT	New International Commentary on the Old Testament
OBO	Orbis biblicus et orientalis
Or	*Orientalia*
OTL	Old Testament Library
OTP	*Old Testament Pseudepigrapha*
OTS	*Oudtestamentische Studiën*
RA	*Revue d'assyriologie et d'archéologie orientale*
RB	*Revue biblique*
SB	Sources bibliques
SBLDS	SBL Dissertation Series
SJLA	Studies in Judaism in Late Antiquity
TDOT	G.J. Botterweck and H. Ringgren (eds.), *Theological Dictionary of the Old Testament*
ThWAT	G.J. Botterweck and H. Ringgren (eds.), *Theologisches Wörterbuch zum Alten Testament*
TRev	*Theologische Revue*
TS	*Theological Studies*
TynBul	*Tyndale Bulletin*
UF	*Ugarit-Forschungen*
VT	*Vetus Testamentum*
VTSup	*Vetus Testamentum*, Supplements
WO	*Die Welt des Orients*
WTJ	*Westminster Theological Journal*
ZA	*Zeitschrift für Assyriologie*
ZAW	*Zeitschrift für die alttestamentliche Wissenschaft*

LIST OF CONTRIBUTORS

Lyn M. Bechtel teaches at Moravian Theological Seminary, Bethlehem, PA.

Dan E. Burns lives in Carrollton, TX.

David J.A. Clines is Professor of Biblical Studies in the University of Sheffield.

Robert L. Cohn is Philip and Muriel Berman Professor of Jewish Studies in the Department of Religion, Lafayette College, Easton, PA.

Mary Douglas is retired Professor of Anthropology and Honorary Fellow of University College, London.

Lyle Eslinger is Professor in the Department of Religious Studies at the University of Calgary, Calgary, Alberta.

Bernard S. Jackson is Professor in the Faculty of Law at the University of Liverpool.

James M. Kennedy is Assistant Professor of Religion at Baylor University, Waco, TX.

Seth Daniel Kunin is Lecturer in the Department of Theology at the University of Nottingham.

Victor H. Matthews is Lecturer in the Department of Religious Studies at Southwest Missouri State University, Springfield, MO.

A.D.H Mayes is Erasmus Smith's Professor of Hebrew in the School of Hebrew, Biblical and Theological Studies at the University of Dublin.

Eckart Otto is Ordinarius for Old Testament Theology at Ludwig-Maximilians-Universität, Munich.

Rolf Rendtorff is Professor Emeritus at Ruprecht-Karls-Universität, Heidelberg.

Alexander Rofé is Professor of Bible at the Hebrew University of Jerusalem.

G. Savran teaches at the Rothberg School for Overseas Students in the Hebrew University of Jerusalem.

H.H. Schmid is Rector of the University of Zürich.

Lieve Teugels is Lecturer in Jewish Studies in the Faculty of Theology at the University of Utrecht.

Thomas L. Thompson teaches in the Institute of Biblical Exegesis, Copenhagen University.

Richard Whitekettle is Assistant Professor of Religion and Theology at Calvin College, Grand Rapids, MI.

INTRODUCTION

In selecting nineteen of nearly seventy articles on the Pentateuch that appeared in *JSOT* from its inception in 1976, I have concentrated on two types of contribution: those that initiated or were important instances of new approaches in their particular fields, and those that illustrate the many different methods that are now commonplace in Biblical Studies.

When *JSOT* was launched in 1976, Brevard Childs had yet to give the lecture at the 1977 IOSOT Conference in Göttingen that officially launched 'canonical criticism' (*JSOT* would later devote issue 16 [1980] to canonical criticism), modern revision of the Documentary Hypothesis, including the post-exilic dating of the 'Yahwist', was only just beginning, and the impact of ethno-archaeology upon writing the history of ancient Israel had yet to be felt. Literary readings of biblical texts were in their infancy.

It is for this reason that the first articles to be chosen illustrate how paradigms were beginning to change in the late 1970s. The contributions by Rolf Rendtorff and Hans Heinrich Schmid were forerunners or seminal works that would change the face of Pentateuchal studies, while Thomas Thompson's use of such things as environmental geography and social anthropology indicated a coming of age for the application of archaeology to Old Testament Studies. David Clines's pioneering study in 'final form' criticism (the inverted commas were his!) and Robert Cohn's use of a canonical perspective also indicated the new directions that Old Testament Studies were taking intertextual, structuralist and cultural anthropological approaches are illustrated respectively by the articles by Dan Burns, James Kennedy, Lieve Teugels, G. Savran, Seth Kunin and Victor Matthews.

An author who has made a considerable impact on Old Testament Studies in the past twenty years is the Social Anthropologist Mary Douglas, especially through her *Purity and Danger* (London: Routledge & Kegan Paul, 1966). It is therefore a pleasure to be able to include her article on 'The Forbidden Animals in Leviticus', together with Richard

Whitekettle's article on Leviticus, which engages critically and construc-
tively with Mary Douglas's work. Another important feature of recent
Old Testament Studies has been the use of social and political theory to
inform judgments about the setting and purpose of Old Testament
books. Andrew Mayes's article on Deuteronomy illustrates this.

The articles that have yet to be mentioned are those by Alexander
Rofé on warfare in Deuteronomy, Lyle Eslinger on Exodus 1–15 and
Lyn Bechtel on Genesis 34. I have chosen them because they deal with
difficult topics of general interest. Any reader of Deuteronomy will be
struck by the contrast between the imperatives to be gracious to fellow
Israelites and the harsh instructions about waging war. Rofé's article
traces the origin and purpose of Deuteronomy's war traditons, while
Eslinger considers whether Exodus 1–15 can be read in a non-triumphalist
way. Bechtel offers a striking alternative reading of the story of the rape
of Dinah.

I have tried various ways of grouping the articles, none of which has
satisfied me. I have therefore decided that they should appear in order of
date of publication.

JSOT 3 (1977), pp. 2-9

THE 'YAHWIST' AS THEOLOGIAN?
THE DILEMMA OF PENTATEUCHAL CRITICISM*

Rolf Rendtorff

Recent Old Testament research shows a notable change in the assessment
of the 'sources' of the Pentateuch. Earlier generations of scholars were
concerned to examine, as carefully as possible, the *literary* demarcation
between the individual, written sources, to study their use of language,
to determine the date of their origin and finally to describe the process
of editing and compilation. In more recent times, it is remarkable how all
these problems have fallen into the background. Instead, there predom-
inates a strongly marked interest in the *theology* of the written sources
of their authors. Indeed, the characteristic element of the written sources
is frequently seen in the fact that they are theological works. Even so,
the traditional terms 'Yahwist', 'Elohist', 'Priestly Writing' are used, and
the traditional arguments are referred to in making the distinction. This
shows that many scholars are not fully aware of the change in the way
the question is now being put.

In fact, a fundamental change in the formulation of the question is
involved. At the beginning of this century, in spite of all the care taken
to achieve an exact distinction between the sources of the Pentateuch,
there was frequently discernible an obvious scepticism whether this
distinction could be carried through precisely and reliably, and particularly whether a clear profile of the individual Pentateuchal sources could

---

*   Since this article first appeared, my *Das überlieferungsgeschichtliche Problem
des Pentateuch* (BZAW, 147; Berlin: de Gruyter, 1977) has appeared in English
translation: *The Problem of the Process of Transmission in the Pentateuch* (trans.
J.J. Scullion; JSOTSup, 89; Sheffield: JOT Press, 1990). I would also refer readers
to my article 'The Paradigm is Changing: Hopes–and Fears', *Biblical Interpretation*
1 (1993), pp. 34-53.

be made out. For example, Hermann Gunkel, in the introduction to his
commentary on Genesis, described the 'sources' as 'collections which
do not come from *one* mould and which cannot have been finished at
one time, but which *have evolved in the course of history*'.[1] From this
he deduces: '"J" and "E" are *not individual authors, but schools of
narrators*'.[2] Gressmann went a step further when he wrote in *Mose und
seine Zeit* (1913): 'In many cases J and E are nothing more than labels
that can be changed at will'.[3] Numerous similar quotations could be
made from other scholars.

In view of this scepticism, how can it have come about that nowadays
there is again so great an interest in the authors of the different sources
as *personalities*? The decisive reason for this is the fact already mentioned, that the authors of the sources are thought of as *theologians*, and
that accordingly it is their respective theological concepts that attract
interest. But how did this new perspective come about? If I am right,
one of the most significant factors was the new conception of the
growth of the Pentateuch (or Hexateuch) developed by Gerhard von
Rad. In his book *Das formgeschichtliche Problem des Hexateuchs*
(1938)[4] he represented the growth of the 'Hexateuch' as a great work
of composition, in which a quite new unity was produced out of numerous, originally separate complexes of tradition. This composition came
about, in von Rad's view, as the result of quite distinct theological
principles and consequently is to be understood as the theological product of an individual.

At this point it must be stressed that this thesis of von Rad involves a
fundamentally new approach to the solution of the problems of the
Pentateuch (or Hexateuch), which has nothing in particular to do with
the question of distinguishing the sources, let alone with its answer. The
business of distinguishing the sources starts from the *final* form of the
Pentateuch and poses the question of the literary unity of the text we
have in front of us today. In this way a solution is offered in the shape of

---

1.   H. Gunkel, *Genesis übersetzt und erklärt* (Göttingen, 3rd edn, 1910; 7th
edn., 1966), p. lxxxiv.

2.   Gunkel, *Geneis*, p. lxxxv.

3.   H. Gressmann, *Mose und seine Zeit: Ein Kommentar zu den Mose-Sagen*
(Göttingen, 1913), p. 368.

4.   Reprinted in H.W. Wolff (ed.), *Gesammelte Studien zum Alten Testament*
(Munich, 4th edn, 1971[1958]), pp. 9-86; ET; *The Problem of the Hexateuch and
Other Essays* (Edinburgh and London, 1966), pp. 1-78.

the 'classical' documentary hypothesis, according to which all the material of the Pentateuch is divided into several extensive, parallel *horizontal sections*, each of which is supposed to have included, to a greater or lesser extent, a complete presentation from the creation (or at least from the patriarchal history) to the settlement (or at least to the death of Moses). Von Rad poses an entirely different question. He specifically bypasses the question of parallel strands, each of which extends throughout all the material, and examines instead the complexes of tradition, each containing *one* theme or range of themes. When these complexes are brought together, who emerges with a new, comprehensive theme? In this way von Rad once more wanted to understand the Pentateuch as a unified work, conceived as a whole and with a strong theological motivation behind its formation.

It was not immediately clear that the type of question now being asked was fundamentally different. Perhaps even von Rad did not fully realize it himself. The reason why the difference was not grasped was apparently because von Rad was too much a child of his own time and could not easily free himself from the traditional view of the division of the sources. So when he had to choose a name for the theologian who had carried out this work of composition, he spoke quite naturally of the 'Yahwist'. Von Rad evidently never saw any problem in this, although his 'Yahwist' had hardly anything to do with the 'Yahwist' of the documentary hypothesis. Most significant of all, von Rad's 'Yahwist' is not *one* of several authors of the sources. Quite the contrary. Von Rad has said himself, quite clearly, that the traditional division into sources has no place in his view.

> Not that the conflation of E and P with J would now appear to be a simple process, nor one that could be altogether explained to one's satisfaction. The problem of the origin and purpose of these two works, the nature of their genesis, and the readers for whom they were destined, is as much an open question now as it was before, and will probably remain so. But these problems are generically different from the ones we have been dealing with in our present study.[5]

In a word, the existence of different sources side by side disturbed von Rad's perspective and was really incompatible with it.

It follows, in my opinion, that it was a historical accident that von Rad ascribed the final formation of the Pentateuch (or Hexateuch) to someone

---

5.　Wolff, *Gesammelte Studien*, p. 81 (ET; p. 74).

he described as the 'Yahwist'. He could just as well—or better and more appositely—have chosen another, less loaded name. Apart from anything else, he would not then have had to adopt along with this name the whole uncertainty of the traditional source-critical hypothesis.

There has been an interesting shift of ground in subsequent scholarship. Martin Noth indeed adopted von Rad's basic thesis, but he altered it crucially in that he allowed the Yahwist a much smaller part in the formation of the Pentateuch. In spite of that, he firmly maintains that the Yahwist is primarily a theologian. But he now sees his theological contribution essentially at the beginning of his work, in his prefixing of the primeval history and in the formulation of the passage Gen. 12.1-3.

> In what follows he (J) then held firmly—almost without exception—to the received material of the Pentateuchal narrative, without intervening into its substance by way of modification or expansion. He was content to have said plainly at the beginning how he intended everything beyond that to be understood.[6]

Like Noth, many scholars look for the theology of the 'Yahwist' in what he *said*—quite differently from von Rad, for whom the Yahwist's theological achievement lay in the formation and composition of the entire Pentateuch out of the different complexes of tradition. Thus the question of *literary* differentiation and characterisation has almost wholly disappeared in the search for the 'theology'. This applies especially to the 'Yanwist'. Repeatedly, elements which might belong to the 'Priestly Writing' and to the 'Elohist' (or the 'Elohistic fragments') are simply excised; the rest then belongs, in a greater or lesser degree, to the 'Yahwist' (so far as yet another source is not assumed). By such a process of subtraction, whatever is left over is the 'Yahwist's'. The question about his literary characteristics is scarcely asked. On the contrary, it is often said that the Yahwist definitely cannot be thought of as a single *literary* figure, but rather that he was a compiler and that therefore, the style of presentation frequently changed. But how can the theology of the 'Yahwist' be determined until literary criteria can be advanced on the basis of which material can be identified as his?

This is where the dilemma of more recent Pentateuchal criticism appears. Most of all it lies in the fact that two modes of questioning have been combined which cannot be combined. More and more, literary

---

6.   M. Noth, *Überlieferungsgeschichte des Pentateuch* (Stuttgart, 1948), p. 258; ET; *A History of Pentateuchal Traditions* (Englewood Cliffs, NJ, 1972), p. 238.

criticism has shown the lack of unity within the 'sources'. Nevertheless, these same entities undergo examination on the basis of their supposed unified theological conception. Correspondingly, the result is unsatisfactory, as is shown by the fact that recent writers have presented quite different answers to the question of what the theology of the 'Yahwist' was. Obviously, that is a question to which the accepted method of enquiry can give no plain answer.

What conclusions are to be reached from this analysis of the current situation? It is clear that current interest is centred in the *theological* formation of the material in the Pentateuch. This interest is undoubtedly justified, but we must look for better and more appropriate ways to deal with the questions that are thereby raised.

If it is correct to say that the 'source documents' do not possess an inner unity because they comprise a variety of material, then one must look for their theological purpose in the editing of this material. First of all, this 'editing' could consist simply in the arrangement and composition of the material. But we have many examples in the Old Testament which show that redactors were not satisfied with that kind of compositional activity. Rather, they disclosed their particular theological outlook unmistakably. So we have to ask whether we can recognize in the Pentateuch clear traces of planned, theological editing.

Once this line of enquiry is followed up, we soon find traces of quite different kinds of editorial activity in various areas of the Pentateuch. So we are brought back to complexes with an individual theme as developed by von Rad. The theological treatment of the patriarchal tradition is clearly of a quite different kind from that of the Moses or Exodus tradition, and that is again quite different from the Sinai tradition or the tradition of Israel in the wilderness. So we must pay attention to these separate complexes of tradition.

In the limited space of this lecture, I will now confine myself to a few observations about the theological editing of the patriarchal narratives in Genesis. It immediately becomes apparent that theological statements here are made largely in the form of divine *promise speeches*. Accordingly, it is in them that we are likely to find traces of theological editing.

As is well known, the promise speeches are various, diverse and many-layered in both their themes and their form. Claus Westermann has made an important contribution to the clarification of this problem in his study of kinds of narrative in Genesis.[7] We can accept his results

7.   C. Westermann, 'Arten der Erzahlung in der Genesis' (1964), in his

and go on from there. The main contents of the promise are: the land, the succession, the blessing—and, in my opinion, 'guidance' is also an independent theme of the promise. The forms in which the promises are expressed and the ways in which the themes are combined are various, and it appears extremely difficult to recognize a system in this variety. But it is possible to make certain particular observations. I now confine myself to the question of the arrangement and framework of the patriarchal narratives.

In the story of Isaac there are two promise speeches, one at the beginning and one towards the end of the collection (26.2-5, 24). Neither has any close connexion with the narrative context and so they obviously belong to a particular editorial layer. Both are introduced with the formula, 'There Yahweh appeared to him'; both contain an assurance of 'guidance' ('I will be with you'); at the beginning there is a whole collection of promise themes, with the promise of the land in the emphatic central position; at the end there is only the promise of numerous descendants. Clearly, the promise speeches have been placed here as a systematic means of providing a framework and theological interpretation of the story of Isaac.

In the story of Jacob the promise of guidance runs through the whole collection of narratives. At the first decisive turning point, when Jacob is in Bethel fleeing from Esau, the promise is stated in the terms: 'I will be with you, and I will protect you wherever you go' (28.15); before Jacob's decision to flee from Haran the narrative sequence is interrupted by a short oracle of Yahweh which again contains the promise of guidance (31.3); and finally, Jacob once more receives the promise of guidance right at the end of his story of his life, before his journey to Egypt (46.2-4). Again with Jacob, as with Isaac, the promise of the land stands at the beginning (28.13) contained within a complex speech of promise, and towards the end of the collection there is once more the promise of numerous descendants (35.9-12, esp. 11f.) in an emphatically presented promise speech, which is independent of the narrative context.

Finally, in the story of Abraham, the promise of the land forms a central theme, being especially frequent in the first part of the collection (12.7; 13.15, 17; 15.7). Then at the end, in a promise speech attached to the narrative of the sacrifice of Isaac, stands once more the promise of

Forschung am Alten Testament, Gesammelte Studien (Munich, 1964), pp. 9-91. (Originally published as 'Der "Jahwist" als Theologe? zum Dilemma der Pentateuchkritik', VTSup, 28 [Edinburgh Congress Volume; Leiden: Brill, 1975], pp. 158-166.

numerous descendants (22.17), exactly as with Isaac and Jacob.

Yet it is just here that another element appears: the promise of the operation of blessing for all peoples. It is taken up again here at the end of the story of Abraham: 'In you all nations of the earth shall find blessing' (22.18), although this promise has already been given an emphatic position at the beginning of the story (12.3). But it does occur both in the story of Isaac and in the story of Jacob—and significantly only once, with emphasis, at the beginning (26.4; 28.14). Consequently, it is possible to see in this element signs of a unifying and comprehensive theological editing of all three patriarchal stories.

Further, I would here like to point out an interesting detail. The promise of blessing is recognisable in two different grammatical constructions—in the *niphal* and the *hithpael*. The two *niphal* constructions occur in 12.3 and 28.14 as: 'in you all *families of the earth* shall be blessed'. On the other hand, the *hithpael* forms in 22.18 and 26.4 have 'all peoples of the world'. The oracle of Yahweh cited in 18.18 takes a middle position. Now here is something of the first importance: in 12.3, the first occurrence of this formula is addressed to Abraham himself, '*in you* they will find blessing', just as in 18.18 '*in him...*'; in 28.14 the second case in the *niphal*, it again begins, '*in you* all families of the earth shall find blessing', but then there is added '*and in your seed*'. This quite clearly indicates that here we have to do with a later addition. Where the *hithpael* is used, it is quite a different matter. Here it says in both cases: '*in your seed* all peoples of the world shall find blessing'. Obviously, the material has here undergone a further development. First of all there is the promise to the patriarch himself, then the 'seed' is added, and finally this takes the place of the patriarch, so that now it is no longer the patriarch himself, but rather the 'seed' only that is the recipient of the promise.

The same development in the promise speeches of the patriarchal stories can be clearly seen in other places. At this stage I must confine myself to *one* example only. In the promise of the land we frequently read 'To you I will give the land', for example at 15.7 and 13.17; in some cases this is then extended to include the 'seed', as in 13.15, 28.13; 35.12; and finally, in a number of cases, such as 12.7; 15.18; 24.7, it says, 'To your seed I will give this land'. Here then the promise to the patriarchs themselves has been displaced by a promise to their progeny, 'the seed'. Clearly this is a development which has taken place *within* the theological editing of the patriarchal stories. Therefore, this editing does not occur at one stroke. Rather, there are indications within the editing itself of different stages or strata. However, I must content myself with these few examples.

At any rate, it is perfectly clear that the promise speeches are one element in the systematic, theological editing of the patriarchal stories—and this is evident not only in the arrangement and framework of all the individual patriarchal stories, but also in the fact that all these patriarchal stories are brought together under one comprehensive, governing, theological principle. In the light of our thesis, the question now arises whether this applies to an editing which embraces the whole Pentateuch.

The answer to this question is quite obviously negative. The element of the promise speeches that plays such a significant role in the patriarchal stories, has nothing corresponding to it in the subsequent theme complexes of the Pentateuch. The contents of the promise are not even expressed in some other form. This is particularly noticeable in connection with the promise of the land which plays a central role in the patriarchal stories, pointing to its future fulfilment. So it is all the more surprising that, within the whole cycle of the Exodus tradition, in the older strata of the text, there is not a single word which refers to this promise. On the contrary. When the land is first mentioned, in the announcement of the Exodus from Egypt, it is referred to as though the promise tradition was completely unknown: 'I will bring you into a fine, broad land, into a land flowing with milk and honey, to the cities of the Canaanites, Hittites, Amorites, Perizzites, Hivites and Jebusites' (Ex. 3.8). Not a word about the patriarchs. Not a word about the patriarchs already having lived in this land for generations, nor about God having promised to give this land to them and to their progeny as a lasting possession. It is indeed a good and fruitful land but it is also an unknown, strange land, in which many foreign nations live. (The later, priestly stratum, is the first to mention God's 'oath' to the patriarchs about giving the land to them, Ex. 6.2ff.)

Once we are aware of this fact, yet more becomes apparent: neither the patriarchs nor the promises addressed to them are mentioned in either Exodus or Numbers in any place which, in traditional source criticism, has been regarded as being definitely a part of one of the older sources—except in the formulaic expression: the 'God of the fathers'. It can hardly be demonstrated more clearly that the patriarchal stories are not combined with the subsequent theme complexes in a common, comprehensive work of theological editing. If there had been a

'Yahwist' who was responsible for the compilation and theological editing, then surely the traces of his work must have been recognizable here. It is absolutely unthinkable that a theologian of such rank as the 'Yahwist' must have been, according to the prevalent view, should have displayed the promise speeches so prominently in the patriarchal stories, and then later on not have mentioned them at all. The fact that the Exodus from Egypt is not represented as a return to the land of the patriarchs, leads to only one conclusion—namely, that the two accounts were conceived and theologically edited independently of one another, and also that they were not brought into relation to one another theologically before the phase of the final, priestly redaction.

Clearly, there is no room here for the idea of the 'Yahwist' as a theologian. There is no such person. But it is also clear that for their part the patriarchal stories have been subjected to a very intensive theological editing, obviously composite in nature—an editing of which it cannot be possibly said, as Noth said of his 'Yahwist', that it sufficed him to have said plainly at the beginning how he intended everything beyond that to be understood. Anyone who wants to grasp the theological intentions which stand behind the collection and editing of the material of the Pentateuch must rather examine these editorial traces in very exact detail. In this way one will come across various important theological statements, but will not meet the authors of the 'sources' as understood in the classical documentary hypothesis.

The dilemma of the recent phase in Pentateuchal criticism lies in the fact that an attempt is being made to answer the newly emerged question about the *theological* intentions of the collection and editing of the old traditions, by a method that was developed to answer entirely different kinds of questions and which therefore proves to be totally unsuitable. If the question about theological intentions is to be put seriously, it must be freed from these traditional methods, and new, adequate methods must be developed. In this way a new phase could be introduced into the study of the Pentateuch.

JSOT 3 (1977), pp. 33-42

IN SEARCH OF NEW APPROACHES IN PENTATEUCHAL RESEARCH*

H.H. Schmid

R. Rendtorff calls sharply into question, in the article here being reviewed[1] and principally in his book *Das überlieferungsgeschichtliche Problem des Pentateuch* (*The Problem of the History of the Transmission of the Pentateuch*),[2] the documentary hypothesis (source theory) of Pentateuchal criticism in the present century. He demonstrates that Pentateuchal study stands in need of a fundamentally new change of mind and that the approaches it employs must be thought out again *de novo*. In order to remove at the beginning any doubt about the starting point of the following contribution to the discussion, let me say: I regard Rendtorff's critique of Pentateuchal research and his demand for a fundamentally new beginning as compelling in broad principle. Of course, in matters of detail questions may be raised and emphases may be placed somewhat differently. But the time has passed for disputations upon the usual basis of the differentiation of sources. Such debates could only be rearguard actions, which have become irrelevant in view of the way the question of fundamentals has become urgent.

The background to this agreement with Rendtorff is provided by the results of my own investigation, *Der sogennante Jahwist* (*The So-called Yahwist*),[3] which led, independently of Rendtorff and in part on the basis of different presuppositions, to very comparable results and postulates. In the light of this basic agreement with Rendtorff, I intend in what

* Translated from the author's German by D.J.A. Clines.

1. See above, pp. 2-10 of this volume (the article is hereafter cited as 'Yahwist').

2. R. Rendtorff, *Das überlieferungsgeschichtliche Problem des Pentateuchs* (BZAW, 147; Berlin, de Gruyter, 1977); hereafter cited as *Problem*.

3. H.H. Schmid, *Der sogennante Jahwist* (Zürich: Theologischer Verlag, 1976); hereafter cited as *Jahwist*.

follows not to offer a critique of Rendtorff's criticism; the interest will rather, in conversation with Rendtorff, revolve about the question of the direction in which the proposed new approaches to Pentateuchal criticism should now develop. I believe that fruitful observations may result from the tension between agreement and difference in our two studies. In view of the limited space at my disposal in the present context, I must limit myself to a selection of a few aspects, and even these I can only sketch in broad outline.

Rendtorff proposes that, before dealing with the question of the development of the Pentateuch as a whole, the 'larger units' (Primeval History, patriarchal narratives, exodus narratives, wilderness wandering, Sinai pericope, occupation of the land), which are only loosely connected with one another, should be studied with respect to their separate development and their individual growth. He can produce good reasons for this proposal: once one frees oneself from the presuppositions of the source theory, it becomes apparent that the connection of the individual 'larger units' took place only at a relatively late stage, prior to which the individual 'units' had already undergone a quite lengthy process of transmission and redaction. His observations on the patriarchal narratives,[4] which he intends to be taken as paradigmatic for the other Pentateuchal 'units', illustrate the manner and result of such a process. I can only agree with Rendtorff in this suggestion; my own investigation also called for a basically similar procedure. Nevertheless, from these conclusions it seems to me that the programme mapped out by Rendtorff is not quite extensive enough, not thoroughgoing enough and conceived at a still insufficiently fundamental level.

My own study took as its starting point the question of dating that Pentateuchal layer in which the various 'larger units' were for the first time united into a whole. The result is in agreement with that reached by Rendtorff: all indications point to the circle of Deuteronom(ist)ic thought.[5] Except for that—and especially in view of the pre-history of the 'larger units'—Rendtorff brackets out, from the beginning, questions

---

4.   Rendtorff, 'Yahwist', pp. 16-19 of this volume; *Problem*, pp. 29-65.
5.   Briefly, in Schmid, *Jahwist*, p. 167; cf. Rendtorff, *Problem*, pp. 160-71. In 'Yahwist', p. 19 of this volume, Rendtorff still proceeded from the assumption that the collecting of the 'larger units' took place in the phase of the 'priestly' final redaction; in *Problem*, pp. 162-63, he has corrected this decision, as indicated above.

of dating[6] and enquires primarily about the 'actual process(es)'.[7] At the same time it is striking that in Rendtorff's statements on the patriarchal narratives virtually no texts from the rest of the Old Testament are introduced into the interpretation. In both cases, in my view, Rendtorff imposes a somewhat premature limitation upon himself. If both these aspects are brought into the investigation from the beginning, modifications and precisions would be made, according to my conclusions, to a whole series of details as well as to the basic method of approach.

As an example of the modifications of detail I would choose the promises to the patriarchs, treated in detail by Rendtorff. According to Rendtorff, the promise to the patriarchs is located in the redaction which provides a framework for, and an interpretation of, the individual traditions or groups of traditions. At the same time he shows that the individual passages are composed of many layers, and have passed through a complex development of transmission or redaction, both in their formulation and in the combination of the various contents of the promises, before the (initial) total redaction of the Pentateuch. This being so, it becomes clear that it is not the final stage of this development that points to a Deuteronom(ist)ic sphere, but a context closely related to the Deuteronom(ist)ic sphere. Even these oldest elements have no parallels in the remainder of the text of the Old Testament that is prior to the Deuteronom(ist)ic writing, but they find in this relatively late context, from the point of view of religion and theology, their obvious and, indeed, necessary function (and that for the first time, in my opinion).

The *promise of land* first plays a role—apart from a few Pentateuchal passages which are clearly not pre-Deuteronomic[8]—in Deuteronomy.[9] It is to be understood 'from a time when the possession of the land began to be a matter of doubt for Israel',[10] and the traditional understanding of the land as Yahweh's gift, transformed now into a promise, was expressly maintained in the new historical, spiritual and religious circumstances prevailing now that the possession of the land was open to question. The

6. Rendtorff, *Problem*, pp. 169-73.

7. Rendtorff, *Problem*, p. 171.

8. Exod. 13.5, 11; 32.13; 33.1; Num. 11.12; 14.16, 23; cf. 32.11. Cf. Schmid, *Jahwist*, p. 142.

9. Schmid, *Jahwist*, pp. 138-43.

10. H. Gunkel, *Genesis übersetzt und erklärt* (Göttingen: Vandenhoeck & Ruprecht, 4th edn, 1964), p. 176 on Gen. 13.17, a passage which according to Rendtorff (*Problem*, p. 42), contains the most original form of the promise of land.

promise of increase is attached to the pledge of a son, and extends it.[11] The transition can be observed particularly well in Gen. 15.1-6[12] in a passage which is certainly not to be dated prior to the classical prophets. For the context of that promise of increase which promises that the patriarch will become a (great) people we must have recourse again to Deuteronomy, where the 'great people' first appears as a theological theme—at a time when the formerly great nation was in danger of shrinking to a tiny remnant.[13] As for the promise of blessing, it is well known that it is secondary to the unmediated, direct pronouncement of blessing;[14] if one looks for parallels to the transition from direct pronouncement to more indirect promise, once again no passage prior to Deuteronomy can be pointed out.[15] Once more also the historical situation offers an intelligible framework; it was a time when all visible sign of the divine blessing was in danger of being lost. From the point of view of the history of tradition, the primary recipient of blessing, in the Old Testament as well as in the ancient Near East, was not a patriarch but a king. The transference of the royal formulation of Ps. 72.17 to Abraham in Gen. 12.3 and elsewhere occurs most probably after the crisis in the function of the king as the maintainer of order, and is connected with the considerable freedom now in evidence compared with the obviously strong connections between institution and speech-form apparent in the period of the early monarchy.[16] So it is probably no accident that a similar transference (of the royal oracle of salvation) to Abraham in Gen. 15.1-6[17] occurs in a passage which, as has been already mentioned, belongs to a relatively later setting.

When these observations are taken together, the result is a well founded supposition that the redactional process in the patriarchal narratives pointed out by Rendtorff cannot be attributed simply to any setting one cares to mention, but must be brought, as regards both time and content, into a connection (yet to be specified more exactly) with the

11. C. Westermann, *Forschung am Alten Testament* (TBü 24, 1964), pp. 19ff., 32f.; Rendtorff, *Problem*, pp. 45-46.

12. Schmid, *Jahwist*, p. 128; what is here skilfully woven together appears in 16.10-12 in a simple redactional addition and is in 21.8-21 worked into a narrative (cf. on the last passage Westermann, *Forschung*, p. 21).

13. Schmid, *Jahwist*, pp. 130ff.

14. Westermann, *Forschung*, pp. 25-26; Rendtorff, *Problem*, p.48.

15. References in Schmid, *Jahwist*, pp. 137-38.

16. Cf. Schmid, *Jahwist*, pp. 133-36.

17. Cf. Schmid, *Jahwist*, pp. 121ff.

Deuteronom(ist)ic process of tradition and interpretation, which itself still needs differentiation. This, however, means that the separation, which Rendtorff effects implicitly at least, between the 'Deuteronomically-influenced' combination of the individual 'larger units' and the preceding phases of the redaction is inappropriate. Redaction and combination are aspects of one and the same process of interpretation—in which indeed various stages may be distinguished, but which in fact is coherent. This process of interpretation does not have attached to it in a particular phase 'Deuteronomically-influenced' elements, but stands as a whole in parallel to and in connection with the Deuteronom(ist)ic process of tradition.

This conclusion is confirmed by investigating the narratives of the Exodus[18] and of the wilderness journeyings.[19] Their theological redaction likewise occurred in more than one phase, but in a similar way it is not free, even in its earliest formations, from parallels to the Deuteronom(ist)ic process of tradition. The case is somewhat different in the Sinai pericope,[20] but here too it can be shown that the theological outworking of the Sinai tradition, so significant for the Old Testament, is very closely related to the Deuteronomic formation of tradition.

If this modification and extension of Rendtorff's view is correct, important indications result from the new question of the development of the Pentateuch as a whole. In view of the closeness of the Pentateuchal process of redaction to the Deuteronom(ist)ic formation of tradition it can be supposed that the development of the Pentateuch can be described in very similar terms to that of the Deuteronom(ist)ic work.[21] At least two observations central for Rendtorff's argument come at this point into a new light.

Rendtorff shows that the theological redaction in the various parts of the patriarchal traditions occurred in different ways. While in the realm of the Isaac stories the promises show no direct connection with the narrative context, the links are somewhat stronger in the Jacob stories, but especially so in the Abraham narratives; here we also encounter promise-speeches that do not have simply the nature of a framework.[22] Thus the degree of editorial interference with the traditional material

18. Cf. Schmid, *Jahwist*, pp. 19-53.
19. Cf. Schmid, *Jahwist*, pp. 61-82.
20. Cf. Schmid, *Jahwist*, pp. 83-118.
21. Similarly (but formulated as a question), Rendtorff, *Problem*, p. 168.
22. Rendtorff, *Problem*, pp. 57-61.

differs. This phenomenon is repeated in the Deuteronomistic History and in the Deuteronomistic redaction of the book of Jeremiah.[23] It is obvious that this parallelism is of great importance in respect both of method and of interpretation.

A further observation is of importance for Rendtorff, namely that the individual 'larger units' must have been theologically worked out separately for rather a long time and have been brought together only at a relatively late period. Once again, a glance at the Deuteronom(ist)ic work shows that there too things are not essentially different. Thus only the later and latest layers of the many levels in the redaction of Deuteronomy[24] evidence explicit parallels with the Deuteronomistic portrayal of history, in fact for the first time at the stage of the polemical heightening of Yahweh's claim to exclusiveness and the concentration of the Deuteronomic commandments upon the first commandment. It is fairly well agreed that the stereotyped framework of the old traditions both in Judges and Kings belongs to the Deuteronom(ist)ic sphere. Nevertheless, in spite of all linguistic and theological connections, they each reflect an individual process of redaction. Yet the Deuteronomic redaction in Joshua and Samuel followed a different procedure: the similarity and dissimilarity to the rest of the Deuteronomistic work are obvious. Clearly the situation is more complicated than that portrayed by Noth;[25] important reservations are today being expressed against his picture of a relatively unified Deuteronomistic History.

To be sure, not all problems are by any means solved by demonstrating the affinity of the process of Pentateuchal redaction to that of the formation of the Deuteronom(ist)ic tradition. The questions about more precise datings still open concerning the Deuteronomistic History, which Rendtorff also refers to,[26] also remain open concerning the

23. Examples: Deuteronomistic framework or expansion without apparent intrusion into the traditional material: Judg. 3.11b-30; 1 Kgs 3.2-3; Jer. 18.1-12; Deuteronomistic intrusions into pieces of traditional material: Judg. 6.11-24; 1 Kgs 3.4-15; Jer. 7.1-15; Deuteronomistically composed narratives (partly with the use of traditional motifs) : Judg. 3.7-11; 1 Kgs 11.1-13; Jer. 11.1-8.

24. Cf. M. Seitz, *Redaktionsgeschichtliche Studien zum Deuteronomium* (BWANT, 93 [1971]); M. Rose, *Der Ausschliesslichkeitsanspruch Jahwes. Deuteronomische Schultheologie und die Volksfrömmigkeit in der späten Königszeit* (BWANT, 106 [1975]).

25. M. Noth, *Überlieferungsgeschichtliche Studien* (Darmstadt: Wissenschaftliche Buchgesellschaft, 2nd edn, 1957), pp. 3-110.

26. Rendtorff, *Problem*, pp. 170-71.

Pentateuch.[27] Nevertheless, I can see no objection to my primary large scale dating, but only a stimulus to the development of yet more precise criteria for dating. I, too, see very clearly the danger of a pan-Deuteronomism occasionally held up before me by colleagues because of my conclusions. Nevertheless, that is no reason for concealing the state of affairs in exegesis; it is only to emphasize the task of reaching still more differentiated distinctions, as is in part already being done,[28] within the Deuteronom(ist)ic sphere which is obviously becoming more and more comprehensive. The parallelism between the nature of the problem and the attitude to the problem in the Pentateuch and in the sphere hitherto termed the Deuteronom(ist)ic is in no sense an obstacle, but on the contrary opens up the possibility of new approaches, which should prove productive for the investigation of both fields simultaneously.

Thus I am, in sum, of the view that in investigating the process of the Pentateuchal redaction attention should be directed much more resolutely than appears to me to have been the case in Rendtorff's study to the rest of the Old Testament—and indeed not only to the Deuteronom(ist)ic lines of tradition. Similarly informative is an investigation of the relationships between the Pentateuchal redaction and the prophetic traditions. The fruits of such a study go far beyond the matter of a lack of influence by Pentateuchal traditions upon large stretches of pre-exilic prophecy, a lack which is indeed confirmed by Rendtorff and which is clearly significant.[29] Thus it can be shown that large passages of the narrative of the call of Moses,[30] of the story of the plagues,[31] and also of the narratives of the wilderness journeyings[32] presuppose, form-critically speaking, prophecy that has already become written, and in many parts (*horribile dictu!*) are strikingly connected to the Deuteronomistic picture of the prophets. Furthermore, a form-critical examination of the Pentateuchal redactional elements, which again goes beyond the approach of Rendtorff, opens up many new aspects. Of course this redaction, which was no doubt a largely literary procedure,

27. Cf. Schmid, *Jahwist*, pp. 168-69.
28. Cf. also Rendtorff, *Problem*, p. 165.
29. Rendtorff, *Problem*, pp. 171ff.; in a more broadly conceived context: Schmid, *Jahwist*, pp. 154-66.
30. Schmid, *Jahwist*, pp. 19-22, 31-35.
31. Schmid, *Jahwist*, pp. 44-48.
32. Schmid, *Jahwist*, pp. 58, 70-75.

contains no *Gattungen* of oral tradition in Gunkel's sense; yet it can be shown that it makes use in many cases of free transpositions of formulations which were originally bound up with particular *Gattungen*. Such transpositions not only offer pointers to questions of dating, but also permit one to venture some remarks concerning the spiritual background of this work of redaction.[33]

This leads to a final point: Rendtorff forcefully attacks, in his critique of Pentateuchal research, the attempt to establish the theology of the Yahwist before its textual content is sufficiently proved by literary indications.[34] This warning clearly deserves to be taken seriously in the light of the new presuppositions. At the same time, however, we have to realize that exegetical study can never be permitted to jump out of the circle of the mutual interdependence of literary and theological analyses and decisions, since literary processes in the Old Testament have taken place virtually without exception on the basis of theological processes. From the point of view of method, this means that literary hypotheses should always be tested by their theological implications and the probability of the latter. Thus the processes of redaction and growth within the Pentateuchal tradition could not be investigated without the accompaniment of the question of their place in the history of theology and of their theological function. (The pessimism expressed by Rendtorff[35] about the possibility of dating the separate stages of redaction has a certain justification in the light of Pentateuchal research hitherto,[36] but I believe that I have in my study developed, at least in approach, with the means I have indicated, a whole series of dating criteria, which could be further refined and made more specific.) I have attempted to show in detail in my book that, as a whole, the description of the redactional processes in the Pentateuch as parallel to the formation of the Deuteronom(ist)ic tradition can indeed be confirmed from other spheres of Old Testament theology and makes sense when

33. Cf. also the further form-critical backgrounds of Exod. 3–4, pp. 19-41, the forms that stand behind Exod. 14.13-31 (pp. 54, 60); or the previously mentioned reshaping of old Gattungen in connection with the promise of blessing, pp. 133-38.

34. Rendtorff, 'Yahwist', p. 14 of this volume; *idem*, *Problem*, pp. 103-109.

35. Rendtorff, *Problem*, p. 169.

36. Cf. also M. Noth, *Überlieferungsgeschichte des Pentateuch* (Darmstadt: Wissenschaftliche Buchgesellschaft, 2nd edn, 1960), p. 248: 'Sure clues for the precise dating of the individual sources are far fewer than people commonly want to believe' (ET; *A History of Pentateuchal Traditions* [trans. B.W. Anderson; Englewood Cliffs, NJ: Prentice-Hall, 1972], p. 229).

closely related to that historical situation and its religious problems—so that here I need only refer to it.[37] Nonetheless, that means that together with the question of the development of the Pentateuch, the comprehensive question of our total view of the Old Testament, of the history of Israelite religion, and of Old Testament theology, is under discussion.[38]

Personal postscript: In his book Rendtorff mentions my name in connection with the later dating of the Yahwist currently proposed by various writers, in response to whom he writes: 'Also, the discussion, recently kindled, over the dating of the Pentateuchal sources, especially of the 'Yahwist', merely sets these efforts on another plane, but is in my opinion a matter of chasing a phantom'. Rendtorff here refers to an unpublished draft of my book, which was thoroughly revized and expanded for publication. It is correct that my investigation starts with the question of the dating of the Yahwist. However, it stands out clearly, and not for the first time in the printed version, that my result differs greatly from the usual picture of the Yahwist and from the traditional source theory. The fact that I (still) retained the term 'Yahwist' is because I did not wish to sever completely the links with previous Pentateuchal study and because I wished to enquire, by means of this study, about what is presumably the oldest total redaction of the Pentateuch—even though I was reaching it by means of conclusions of a different shape, and all the more so when a whole series of observations in older Pentateuchal study provided (in part quite contrary to the intention of such study) arguments for my own perspective. Thus the restrictive title 'The So-called Yahwist' is meant to express both a continuity and a discontinuity with previous research. So I stand much closer to Rendtorff's position than that footnote would suggest.[39]

37. Cf. also H.H. Schmid, *Altorientalische Welt in der alttestamentlichen Theologie* (Zürich: Theologischer Verlag, 1974).
   38. Rendtorff, *Problem*, p. 150 n. 6. Cf. also pp. 170, 173.
   39. Cf. in addition to the above considerations, Schmid, *Jahwist*, pp. 168-74.

JSOT 9 (1978), pp. 2-43

THE BACKGROUND OF THE PATRIARCHS:
A REPLY TO WILLIAM DEVER AND MALCOLM CLARK

Thomas L. Thompson

The changes which have occurred during the last decade in publications dealing with the historical background of the patriarchs, beginning with Morton Smith's presidential address to the Society of Biblical Literature in 1968 and the publication in English of Benjamin Mazar's article 'The Historical Background of the Book of Genesis' in 1969, have dramatically altered our perspective on both the pentateuchal tales (cf. Thompson 1974, 1977a, 1977b) and the late pre-history of Palestine. The recent articles by William Dever and Malcolm Clark in the new Hayes and Miller *Israelite and Judaean History* (1977) admirably reflect this change. While both authors show respect for the ambiguities of early historical and archaeological data, both also attempt to mark off clearly the considerable grounds of agreement which now exist among scholars, and to suggest guidelines for possible future consensus on a number of far-reaching problems.

So comprehensive is their representation of current scholarship that one can hardly object to the general conclusions drawn from their survey. Nevertheless, it is clear in both articles that a consensus on a reconstruction of the historical context of the patriarchal stories is not yet achieved, but only cast in the future. The present situation, in fact, is immensely unstable and fraught with new methodological problems and assumptions which had not been apparent in earlier discussions (as, e.g., in Weidmann 1968; de Vaux 1971; Thompson, 1974). The concurrent uncertainties in pentateuchal criticism (cf. Schmid, Rendtorff) add a complexity and depth to discussions about the patriarchs which also had not existed a decade ago.

1. *The Patriarchal Narratives as Israelite Traditions*

In discussing the 'date and setting of the patriarchal traditions' Clark sets out four important rules (1977: 143): (1) Extra-biblical data must be accurately and independently evaluated; (2) such data should not be arbitrarily selected on the basis of preconceptions about the biblical narratives; (3) the biblical text should be examined, prior to any comparison, to avoid harmonization; and (4) in comparing similarities between the biblical and extra-biblical materials differences as well as likenesses must be candidly dealt with. Although these four principles essentially outline the methods which I used in re-examining the so-called 'Nuzi parallels to patriarchal customs' (1974: 196-297), I cannot wholeheartedly agree with them as proposed by Clark. My hesitation is not due to any objection to the rules themselves, but only to their limitations. Such rules are best applicable where a clearly defined 'parallel' is in question, and a direct affirmation or negation is sought, such as in the cases of the Nuzi contracts or early West Semitic names. For a general methodology, however, Dever's call for a divorce between the disciplines of archaeology and biblical studies seems more appropriate. Dever recommends an independent historical discipline dealing with analogues and 'sociological models'. Procedures leading to the affirmation or negation of identifications as outlined by Clark play a very secondary role to that of grasping the essential, comprehensive, and contextual significance of what is basically fragmented, pre-historical data.

Of course, the point of departure of the questions being asked by Dever and Clark are vastly different. Dever, as an historian, is writing the early history of Palestine, and discussing its possible association with the pre-history of Israel. Clark, as an exegete, is interested rather in an interpretive context for understanding the origin and development of the Genesis narratives. These two types of inquiries have frequently been assumed to proceed in tandem. To this writer, they increasingly appear to be wholly unrelated (cf. Irvin and Thompson 1977; Thompson 1978a; Thompson 1979).

Dever (1977: 120) sees more clearly than Clark the primacy of determining the historiographical character of narratives before asking historical questions of them; for if the patriarchs do not represent something more than themselves—ancestral heroes in tales—then there is nothing that archaeological research can say to biblical studies.

Archaeology and historical criticism can only engage the Genesis narratives directly if these tales can be related to the historical realities and problems of the historical entity Israel in some form. This is also the central issue—and not that of dating the narratives to either the ninth or sixth centuries—on which point J. Van Seters' approach radically diverges from my own. I have expressed elsewhere (1978a: 76-79) my doubt that the setting and date of the patriarchal narratives is important to either exegesis or history. Once it has been shown that there is nothing historically known which can directly associate the narratives with the historical and archaeological data of the second millennium— and that much has not generally been conceded—these narratives can be of only marginal interest in the positive alternative task of writing a comprehensive early history and prehistory of Palestine. The tenth–ninth-century dating which I have given the narratives (1974: 324-26; cf., however, 1978a) is essentially an ethnic identification of the tales as Israelite. Tales themselves cannot be dated; only their bearers. We know as fact that Israel and Judah existed as self-conscious political and national entities from at least the tenth century BCE. To the degree that these traditional narratives were transmitted as specifically Israelite or Judaean, then this literature should be dated within the known chrono-logical limits of those bearers, unless there is positive indication that this constitutive context—i.e., the existence of Israel and Judah—does in fact go beyond these limits. If, on the other hand the narrative traditions, as such, can not be shown positively to be either pre-Israelite or extra-Palestinian, then, my suggested dating 'that the stories were taken up into the Yahwistic tradition directly from the contemporary Canaanite/ Israelite milieu' (1974: 326), is not only acceptable, but is patent!

Traditional narratives (cf. Irvin 1977, 1978) can persist, in one form or another, for millennia. What we are dealing with, however, is a specific tradition, and the question of the cultural identity, continuity, and coherence of the tradition's formation. In principle, our ability to give an early dating to our narratives is limited to the ability to uncover the origins, not of the narratives at all, but of the historical Israel, whether or not that origin is reflected within the traditions. Prior to some form of the historical Israel, there were no traditions which were relevant to it. To identify the traditions as Israelite, and to relate them specifically to the monarchy as the first coherent and unequivocal historical reality which can be meaningfully identified with Israel, is the as-yet-earliest date which is entirely legitimate, since a priori, the myriad, potential pre-

Israelite variations of our tradition and its components, before it reached
its canonical form, leads well beyond the confines of both Palestine and
the Iron and Bronze Ages. Formulae, motifs, episodes, and tale types
have a persistence and mobility—to the best of our knowledge—as great
as humanity's.

Dever is most correct, in the early part of his essay, when he insists
that archaeology has only a modest role to play in questions of biblical
criticism (1977: 74-75). The independence of Palestinian archaeology,
which he advocates, is the more to be welcomed, however, because it is
to archaeology, *rather than to biblical studies*, that the question of the
origin of the people of Israel and Judah—independently of questions
relating to the interpretation of the Pentateuch or of Joshua and Judges
(cf. Irvin and Thompson 1977)—is to be directed. The changes which
brought about the settlement in villages and towns of the regions
occupied by the states of Israel and Judah, and caused to form a
geographical and cultural unity, are events that are essential to understanding the origin of Israel, and are also the ultimate possible context
for the formation of our origin traditions. The explication of these changes
is a question which is addressed exclusively to Palestinian archaeology. It
is, moreover, a question which now seem largely answerable, given
Dever's recommendation of a greater involvement of Palestinian archaeology in ecological, anthropological, and sociological concerns.

2. *'Dimorphism' in Mesopotamia*

Dever makes a strong case for a 'new' archaeology with an anthropological orientation (1977: 72-79; cf. the similar arguments of Martin
1976: 114). Only a few years ago, Peter Parr complained (1972: 805-10)
that Palestinian archaeology has paid only occasional attention to those
comprehensive hallmarks of prehistorical archaeology such as settlement
patterns, urban planning, and technological adaptations to environment,
which are the key to any meaningful large-scale historical reconstruction,
and which form the basis for analyzing those social, economic and
political relationships of which Dever speaks. It is to emphasize this new
concern, that in discussing my 1974 book on the patriarchs, Dever
points to my failure to address the new 'ethnographic and anthropological' studies of the Early West Semites of ancient Mesopotamia
(Dever 1977: 117). He suggests in his critique that such a concern would
have given a comprehensiveness to my analysis which, without it,

remains essentially a negative appraisal of 'earlier admittedly dated models'. Specifically, he finds my book on the patriarchs to fail in its analysis of the Early West Semites, in that I did not offer an alternative model by which 'nomadism and socio-political change' could be understood.

Although a comprehensive and positive treatment of the Early West Semites in Mesopotamia is more complex and formidable than Dever believes, he is, nevertheless, essentially correct in his criticism. Though I worked on the basis of the analyses of Kupper (1957), Moscati (1956), and the earlier studies of Klengel (1958, 1962), and had responded favorably to the limited analogous use of the Mari texts in relationship to the origin of the Israelites (1974: 87-88) by Weippert (1967: 106-110), Mendenhall (1962, 1969; cf. however, Thompson, 1978b), and especially Rowton (1967), I nowhere attempted a comprehensive treatment of either the Early West Semites or the question of nomadism. Hardly exhaustive, my treatment of the texts from Mesopotamia had very limited, *but not entirely negative*, goals. These were as follows:

(a) I questioned the basis for the common comparison between the patriarchal tales and cuneiform historical texts relating to the Early West Semites. Alternative interpretive 'models' or analogues were offered in my suggestion that the biblical tales be compared rather with ancient Near Eastern narratives than with historical materials. In more recent publications, I have made this alternative much more explicit (cf. Irvin and Thompson 1977; Thompson 1978a; Thompson 1979; for systematic treatments, cf. especially Irvin 1977, 1978).

(b) I denied any direct historical continuity between the Early West Semites of Mesopotamia and the population of Palestine, a connection which had been maintained by Albright, Noth, Kenyon, Dever (now 1977: 82-84), and others. This denial has much in common with the more specialized studies of Luke, Rowton, Haldar, Klengel (1972, 1977), de Geus (1976; 1971), and especially Liverani (1973). An alternative interpretation to hypothetical migrations of 'Amorites' was offered in my 1974 study (1974: 89-117, 144-71), namely that Early West Semites were indigenous to Palestine (so also, Haldar 1971; Liverani 1973; and de Geus 1976). This alternative hypothesis has subsequently received additional support from new texts discovered at Tall Mardih (cf. Fronzaroli 1977), which indicate an established Early West Semitic presence in western Syria and Palestine in the Early Bronze Age.

Dever (1977: 94-95) seems unaware of how inseparable the migratory aspect of the old 'Amorite hypothesis' is from the biblical story—indeed it is only in Genesis that any indication of a migration from the Euphrates region can be found. It is, moreover, fundamental to Albright's methodology that no single part of an historical synthesis is substantiated independently of the other components of a reconstruction.

(c) I also concluded that the Early West Semitic groups in the cuneiform sources were—in spite of their related language(s)—unrelated economically, politically, sociologically, and historically; that is to say, there was no comprehensive whole to be described, but only historically distinct groups (cf. Renger 1973: 264). I had maintained that to view them primarily from the perspective of their potentially ethnic designation was to distort rather than to clarify our texts (so also, Haldar 1971, and especially Liverani 1973, 1976a, 1976b). A comprehensive alternative interpretation could hardly have been attempted within the structure of a book dealing essentially with Palestinian tales. Indeed, there certainly is serious doubt that a comprehensive interpretation of the society of Mesopotamia, and with it the many roles played by Early West Semitic groups and individuals, can be achieved today. Particularly with the kind of sociological and anthropological analysis as recommended, for example, by Rowton (*passim*), Liverani (1973), and others, it is impossible to proceed critically without a much greater data base than has been used at present (cf. Thompson 1978b, and Gottwald 1978). Regarding Mesopotamia: though written sources are considerable during some periods, the archaeological basis for such a study is wholly inadequate. Rowton and Liverani, themselves, are fully aware of this difficulty. The situation for western Syria, however (cf. Haldar 1971; Liverani 1973), and especially for Palestine (cf. Thompson 1975; 1978c), is archaeologically far more promising.

A comprehensive view of the history of Palestine which could serve as an alternative to the earlier harmonizing and theologically oriented hypotheses of 'biblical archaeology' cannot be attempted without first developing methods whereby largely unrelated and accidental finds can be given interpretive structures, which would enable us to create needed interrelationships of function and change, and give meaning to fragmented data. Dever's stress on the attempts of Rowton and others to develop such interpretive structures goes to the heart of the current uncertainty in the historiography of the Bronze Age. In the past, discoveries relating to the Bronze Age in Palestine had been given coherence and historical meaning largely through biblical studies. Now that this is no longer possible, it has become necessary to develop a specifically archaeologically-based interpretive structure. The use of sociological and anthropological 'models', however, particularly when these 'models' are borrowed from Mesopotamian studies as recommended by Dever, raises as many problems as it solves.

Sociological analysis, or what used to be understood as the study of historical background, of social 'context' or 'setting' (*Sitz im Leben*), can help the historian, by means of analogies, to an intimation of the complex variability in the forms of society, and of the diversity of economic and historical factors implied by social forms. With a 'sociological-anthropological approach', our always very limited data can be amplified with a variety of possible implications, significances, and contexts. 'Models' do give us structures, but they do not do away with the necessity of having something to structure. They are rather related to the writing of history as tools. They are constructs of the analyst, not of the ancient societies which we study; they are not real. Sociological forms are essentially configurations of language. Their usefulness is in direct proportion to their ability to classify actual data and enable us to recognize patterns in the actions of individuals and groups. However, the patterns which are defined are not abstract universals. All concrete reality is essentially distinct; so all societies of the past are different, and conclusions drawn from one region or society are not transferable to the history of another region and the analysis of its society (cf. Adams 1971: 572). In applying such methods to the study of the ancient society of Palestine, three very concrete determinative factors, which form the structures of any society, must inform our analysts, namely, the environment, the economy, and change (similarly, Smith 1972: 409-426; Wittfogel 1971: 559; Adams 1971b: 591-93; Gottwald 1975: 172-74).

For these reasons, it is disconcerting to find that Dever (1977: 102-17) borrows the concept of 'dimorphism' for Palestine, and, on the basis of a single MB II site, described as a 'satellite village', attempts to portray the background of the patriarchs as a dimorphic society of the MB II period. This is unfortunate. The concept 'dimorphism' has been used in very different ways in discussions in the Mari texts by both Luke and Rowton to facilitate independently conceived radical departures from earlier, no longer tenable, concepts of nomadism. Although Rowton's usage is more widely known and has been adopted by Liverani and

others, Dever's understanding of the term as relating to Mari seems to
be drawn essentially from Luke's unpublished dissertation. Though, to
this reader, Luke's thesis misunderstands both Kupper and the Mari
texts, his description of some of the Early West Semitic groups at and
near Mari as having been 'dimorphically' both sedentary and transitory,
both farmers and pastoralists, is acceptable as a description of some of
these groups (cf. Weippert [ET] 1971: 117-18; Thompson, 1974: 71). It
does appear correct to speak of such groups as the Haneans as a single
socio-political entity, with however two distinguishable patterns of life:
sedentary and transitory, largely dependent upon the in-this-region
separable, but integrated, economic functions of agriculture and animal
husbandry. However, this description does not fit all of the West Semitic
groups, and can certainly not be used to describe the society of Mari.
The city itself, and most of those agricultural towns and villages
dependent on the irrigation works administered from Mari, can hardly
be described other than as sedentary. Luke's description is applicable to
those on the periphery of Mari's society. However, one must doubt the
entire appropriateness of the term 'farmer-shepherd' as used by Dever
and applied to such groups, however applicable this term might be to
some of the more sedentary agriculturalists here and elsewhere in the
Near East. It oversimplifies. Very different small groups live on the
periphery of Mari: some entirely pastoral; others entirely agricultural;
some perhaps with a pastoral, more transitory past; yet others following
a pattern of patch cultivation in a mixed economy with seasonal
migration. Moreover, the situation current among these peripheral
groups at the time of the Mari texts was not of their own making, but
rather the direct result of specific historic actions taken by the Mari
administration to settle into *ālānu* and *kuprātum*—for purposes of
control and taxation—some of the migratory steppe dwellers within the
Mari domain (cf. Weippert 1971: 117-23; similar action against the
steppe dwellers was taken by Idrimi of Alalakh, cf. Pritchard 1975: 98).
Sociologically speaking, the marginal agriculture and sedentary character
of many of these groups is a direct effect of the groups' subordination to
the state bureaucracy and military. I do not mean to imply that agriculture had been previously foreign to these groups, but wish only to
underline that the uniquely mixed economies reflected in the Middle
Bronze texts from Mari are related to quite specific historical actions,
and that the social structures resulting from such actions can be used
properly as analogues only in situations where similar actions have been

taken by great states in an attempt to control subordinate groups.

Rowton's concept of 'dimorphism' offers a much more satisfying interpretive structure for understanding the steppe dwellers of Mesopotamia. Rowton restricts his description of 'dimorphic societies' largely to those belonging to the great Syrian steppe: generally that region apart from the irrigated portions of the Euphrates valley, which lie in areas which receive between 200 and 400mm of rainfall annually. Unlike Luke and Dever, Rowton contrasts such societies, among whom would be the Ubrabeans, the Amnanites, and the Rabbeans, with the society of Mari (Rowton 1973b: 204). 'Dimorphism' for Rowton is a conceptual tool used to analyze forms of *nomadic* society which are peculiar to the Near East, and dependent upon the manner in which the steppe abruptly meets the agricultural zones under irrigation. A major weakness of his concept, however, and in direct contradiction to his own often repeated axiom that history begins in topography, is his assumption that this concept 'dimorphism' is applicable to the entire Near East and to most historical periods (1976b: 29). Moreover, the polarities and dichotomies of Rowton's analysis are applied from the perspective of the subordinate, less sedentary, sheep-herding groups, and not from that of the Mesopotamian society as a whole. Granted that every partial entity within a whole deals symbiotically with either the centralizing authority or with some or all of the other groups within the whole, to describe the polarity of such relationships as 'dimorphic' is to suggest an analysis which is not objectively descriptive, but one which proceeds from the very limited perspective of a single entity, and of the impact of its relationship with a central power or other groups, upon its own circumscribed economic and political structures. Rowton's analysis is useful primarily as a tool for studying subordinate societies belonging to marginal regions, during those periods which knew a significant occupation of the steppe zone.

Rowton's analysis proceeds in terms of polar abstractions:

(1) urban (= sedentary) ↔ nomadic (= transitory); (2) agricultural ↔ pastoral; (3) state (= sovereignty) ↔ tribe (= autonomy).

These abstractions allow for a concentration of the analysis upon the variety in the forms of settlement, economy, and political structure which might occur in the concrete within the range of the extremes, providing us with a wide choice of possible interpretations for our archaeologically and textually derived data (cf. also, Tringham 1972: xxiii). This strictly analytical approach (cf. Martin 1976: 16-18) also

allows Rowton to shift the analysis away from the steppe region and its
'dimorphic societies', to include other areas under a concept of 'dimorphic *structures*' insofar as nomadism, animal husbandry, and tribal
associations play a role in these areas. Though Rowton is aware of the
distinctiveness of these three analytical spectra, there is a strong
tendency in his writings to merge them into one single polarity of urban/
agricultural/state nomadic/pastoral/tribal—the occurrence of a single
characteristic being accepted as indicative of the others (1973a: 251-52;
1973b: 202-203). This prevents rather than enhances our ability to
structure concrete historical data where such distinctions are essential
(similarly, Binford and Binford 1968: 13; also cf. Liverani's limits on the
use of some of these concepts in Palestine: 1976a). The three spectra are
conceptually independent and coalesce only under quite specific
historical and geographical circumstances. Nomadism does not of itself
imply pastoralism (contra Rowton 1973a: 252); pastoralism is only one of
the many economic forms, frequently and often causally associated with
nomadic peoples (Thompson 1978b). Nomadism is one of many types of
territorial occupation which has a large variety of forms of dwelling
structures, which need to be analyzed along a continuum according to
their stability or transitoriness. This continuum ought properly also to
include the immense variety of what is often globally understood as
sedentary (city, town, village, hamlet, homestead, etc.), all of which have
sociologically considerable transitory elements in their society (cf. the
valuable discussion of Adams 1972: 735). Although animal husbandry is
frequently a mainstay of nomadic economies in modern societies
'nomadic' or 'transhumance' pastoralism, as reflected by some of the
groups living on the Mesopotamian steppe during the Mari period, was a
relatively new economic development which was dependent on and
subsidiary to the large-scale state irrigation networks. Nomadism, as
such, in earlier prehistoric and even Bronze Age times has been more
typically associated with a variety of hunting and food gathering
economies, as well as with forms of swidden and patch agriculture.
Animal domestication, on the other hand, is indigenous, not to the
steppe zones generally associated with Bronze Age nomadic groups, but
to the agricultural zones with a Mediterranean climate (cf. Butzer 1971:
214-15; also Luke 1965). In Palestine and Syria, animal husbandry is
from very early times associated with intensive forms of agriculture and
is necessary to the heavy cropping systems of agriculture typical of
Palestine since at least as early as the early Bronze Age. Indeed, it is

extremely doubtful that nomadism, as a form of society, played any significant role in the Palestinian economy, though shepherding frequently has taken the form of a specialized trade (cf. further below).

It is also not indicated by historical evidence that tribal political structures can be understood as peculiarly nomadic (contra Rowton 1976a: 17; cf. Klengel 1971: 163). Well known examples of sedentary tribes can be cited from south Arabia (de Geus 1976: 129), modern Africa, as well as ancient Israel. Nor has it yet been shown clearly that even the pastoral groups at Mari were tribal societies (so Rowton 1967: 121), though this failure may be due to inadequate sources (so Thompson 1974: 85). Finally, it must be doubted that agriculture is wholly equatable with sedentary forms of occupation (Flannery 1972: 23; also see the discussion on nomadic huts and compounds: 30-31). Not only do most nomadic groups practice some form of agriculture (cf., e.g., Marx 1967), but forms of swidden agriculture frequently *require* very transitory forms of settlement (cf. Harris 1972).

Rowton not only has difficulty in maintaining systematic distinctions throughout his analysis, but he is inclined to view the essentially abstract poles of his paradigmatic structures as dichotomous, and this is perhaps an inevitable result of what is finally a misuse of the word 'dimorphic'. Though undoubtedly contiguity and symbiotic associations lie at the base of most class stratification, social oppositions, and conflicts (Layton 1972: 380), and though they can even be understood as determining the form of some historical upheavals they do not themselves generate the dichotomies characteristic of such conflicts. Moreover the binary concepts 'state ↔ tribal' and 'agricultural ↔ pastoral' are not true polarities or opposites as is the structure 'sedentary–nomadic'. Rather they are *distinct types*, among many, of political structures and economies. Within Rowton's analysis of Mari, the functions 'tribal' and 'pastoral' are not truly dimorphic, but relate to forms which are subsidiary to the state and to its primary economy of agriculture, as are other political and economic subgroups. There are many autonomous groups within a sovereign state; as there are many specialist trades associated with large-scale irrigation agriculture.

The methodological leitmotif of the above criticisms of the studies of Luke and Rowton is that form is not an alternative to content, nor structures to data. Methods must be made appropriate to the materials studied, and conclusions must be drawn from evidence (cf. Gottwald and Frick 1975: 172).

3. *Shepherds and Farmers in Palestine*

Given the precariousness of these sociological analyses of the Mari letters, it is important to stress against Dever that the behavior of the Early West Semites of Mari has no direct relevance to either Palestinian or biblical studies, and can at best be used as one among many analogies of the essentially quite different events of Palestine (Thompson 1974: 87-88). Dever's suggestion that the studies of the society of Mari are directly related to the study of Palestine, yet still 'analogous', is inappropriate, contradicting the first principle of Rowton's analysis, that history begins in topology (1973a: 248). It is not accidental that Rowton's analyses of 'dimorphic' aspects of society are most satisfying in the discussion of the Mesopotamian steppe regions, since it is from the perspective of the steppe, as it abuts directly on some of the most densely populated agricultural zones of the ancient world, that his analogy was originally built (cf. 1976a: 31). It is specifically this environment of the great Syrian steppe which both limits and legitimizes Rowton's study. Mari is a border state, but it is not agriculturally marginal. It is rather built on an intensively cultivated irrigation plain, supporting tens of thousands of people (cf. Wittfogel 1971: 560).

The environmental topography of Palestine is so radically different as to require a completely independent analysis (as I have previously argued: 1978b). Environmentally, Palestine is a conglomerate of many different ecological zones of dramatic contrast. These essentially geographical differences in the subregions of Palestine are reflected in the patterns of settlement, as well as in economic and historical development.

Since early in 1970, I have been engaged on a project in which, through a comprehensive collection of the sources for the Bronze Age remains of Palestine, the Negev, and Sinai (over half of which have never before been published), I was able to establish a catalogue of approximately 2500 separate, often excavated, sites in these regions. After a systematic collation of the sources for each site, I distinguished, not only their names, location and chronological history within the Bronze Age but whether they were clearly defined archaeological sites, scattered remains, cave dwellings, or burial sites, as well as their location in relation to valleys, hills, slopes, sources of water, or ancient mines, their relative size, the quantity of finds from a given period, and whether the site had been excavated or known only from surface examination.

When any site had been previously published, I was able to give the relevant literature. I then charted this systematically differentiated data cartographically, using separate maps for each of the major periods ot the Bronze Age (EB, EB IV/ MB I, MB II, and LB). On the basis of these maps, and with the aid of maps and studies on the geomorphology, soils, water resources, climate, and agriculture of Sinai and Palestine, I was able to write the first, albeit schematic, ecological history of these regions, including some discussion of the nature and economics of the various regional settlements. Publication of my site lists and commentaries was begun in 1975 with *The Settlement of Sinai and the Negev in the Bronze Age*. The much larger and more detailed *The Settlement of Palestine in the Bronze Age*, involving over 1700 individual sites and several hundred excavations is now in press and will be published shortly (1978c). Seven maps in the scale of 1:500,000 and 1:1,000,000 will appear in the forthcoming *Tübinger Atlas des vorderen Orients* (TAVO), for which the entire project had been undertaken. The following discussion is my first attempt, on the basis of these earlier studies, to explore writing an archaeologically based 'history' of the Palestinian Bronze Age.

In sharp contrast to Mesopotamia, the steppe zones of Palestine are peripheral, and for the most part geographically isolated from regions of great population density, and from areas of large-scale irrigation agriculture. Only in the Jordan rift, i.e., in Beth Shan Valley and immediately to the south, does one find, during the Bronze Age, a close contiguity of steppelands with irrigation fields of major significance (1978c: 27-32). However, large-scale irrigation works involve only one area of the Beth Shan Valley. This irrigated area was apparently very densely settled, and the regional occupation was probably continuous throughout the Bronze Age. Yet, this irrigation zone is quite separate from most of the very large sites of the valley, including the great Tall Bēsan. It is only with great difficulty that the maintenance of the hydraulic works, or the large-scale irrigation and drainage networks of the valley used throughout the entire Bronze Age, can be associated with any of the valley's largest towns or cities. It seems rather more appropriate to suggest forms of federated cooperation among the many smaller settlements of the irrigation plain, which are directly dependent upon this form of agriculture. The nearby Jordan flood plain also supported a considerable population in this region. Its farming, however, was based on seepage agriculture, and small-scale drainage systems, needing no large-scale centralized planning. The larger settlements of the Beth Shan Valley are found on higher ground, in well drained areas of rich soils, with abundant groundwater. In these areas, small-scale irrigation and drainage seem quite sufficient to maintain a considerable population. The comparatively large size of these sites may well reflect the agricultural richness of the areas in which they are found. The settlement pattern of the valley does not suggest any movement towards political central-ization or regional authorities throughout most of the Bronze Age. By the beginning of the Late Bronze period, however, there is a decided reorganization of the settlement along the western slopes of the Beth Shan valley. Site clusters disappear, and the area is divided into zones, each dominated by one of the major tells—now apparently larger than during previous periods. This transition—found in many of the areas of the heaviest Bronze Age settlement in Palestine (cf. Thompson 1978c: *passim*)—seems to relect a rapid increase in the number of what is a peculiarly Palestinian form of 'city-state': an organisation of settlement which has its roots in history more than in economics, with a function which is primarily military and defensive. These fortified towns dotting the landscape of Late Bronze Palestine are certainly not to be confused with the great hydraulic states of Mesopotamia, with economic bases in state property and land and water control. No significant new large-scale irrigation projects are opened up during the Late Bronze period. Rather, some previously intensively settled areas, such as the great triangular plain between the Jordan and the Yarmūk, just south of the Sea of Galilee, are abandoned. A fundamentally different understanding of the proliferation of the 'city-state' in Palestine must be developed than what might be appropriate for Mesopotamia (cf. further, below: section 5).

Just as the agricultural zone of the Beth Shan is significantly different from that of Mari, so the steppe which meets the Beth Shan Valley to the south must be distinguished topographically from the great Syrian steppe of Mesopotamia. The Jordan Valley is much more arid, its rainfall falling rapidly from an average of about 250mm near the Beth Shan Valley to less than 100mm near the Dead Sea. Its climate ranges from semi-steppe to desert, and much of the area is given over to badlands. Significant agriculture or herd grazing is largely limited to the fans of the wadis and streams, descending from the hill country. In the desert climate of the extreme southern Jordan Valley, it is largely limited to oases. The Valley develops pockets of settlement, separated, not by steppe grazing lands, but by far less hospitable desert. Though grazing of flocks is certainly to be assumed in these regions, it could not have involved more than a small number of people, and the economy, and even less the society as a whole, can hardly be described as mixed or 'dimorphic'. It rather appears to follow the pattern of agricultural and irrigation regions. The steppe zone here is very small and, to our knowledge, largely unoccupied. The Judaean desert to the south and southeast forms a barrier between the southern Jordan Valley and the grasslands of the northern Negev. The small size of the area involved does not seem to allow the development of an indigenous society, distinct or separable from the sedentary population of Palestine, in the manner that such groups did develop in Mesopotamia. What grazing there was seems far more easily explained as a subordinate trade of the agriculturalists themselves, providing fertilizer, wool, milk, cheese and meat as a supplement to the area's agricultural products. Sheep and goat herding, seen as one trade among many—such as cattle herding, bee keeping, weaving, transport, and in other areas, fishing, shipping, dyeing, textile production, mineral extraction, etc.—may be appropriate for most of Bronze Age Palestine. Not only is most of Palestine's arable land separated from a relatively small steppe region, but Palestinian agriculture is dependent upon animal husbandry for the maintenance of its intensive cropping systems. Nor is there evidence that Palestine had developed distinct ethnic groups specifically associated with sheep and goatherding as did the Mesopotamian hydraulic states, who had consigned this industry to groups associated with the steppe zones, and as Old Kingdom Egypt had, confining so much of its shepherding to the more 'Asiatic' Delta (Adams 1971b: 599). Part of the reason for this surely was that, in Palestine, much agriculture, particularly the majority small-scale dry agriculture of the major plains and valleys, was carried out within short distances of grasslands within the Mediterranean climate, which could be grazed over long periods of the year (see my discussion of the Wādī l-'Amûd, the Northern Jordan Valley, the Jezreel, and the coastal plain in 1978c). That is, the primary areas of shepherding in Palestine were within the agricultural zone, with the likely consequence that individuals and families, not peoples, carried out the bulk of this trade.

The hill country of Palestine was not heavily settled and appears to have been largely wooded during the Bronze Age. Though deforestation began at least as early as the Early Bronze Age, it does not seem to have been irreversible in most areas until the Iron Age. Although most settlements in the hills, particularly during the EB and MB II periods, were associated with agriculturally oriented valley and enclosure terracing (cf. Ron 1966), a number of dwellings, some of which were in caves, are probably to be associated with less sedentary economies such as herding.

However, those areas which border on the steppe and desert lands of the east and south, developed essentially distinctive patterns of settlement, both in relation to their more arid climate, and, ultimately, in the forms of their economies. The coastal area south of Ashqelon, and the 'Arad Basin, and the Beersheva plain, with their semi-arid climate and rich steppe grasslands, form a continuous, and historically the most significant, steppe zone in Palestine. It is an area of transition between the Sinai desert to the south and southwest and the Palestinian hill country and coastal plain to the north. Because of aridity and the irregularity of rainfall, permanent settlement during the Bronze Age throughout this extensive area is unstable (cf. Thompson 1975: 5-11; 1978c: 7-9, 60-62). Villages and towns are confined almost exclusively to the areas·of highest agricultural potential and usually are to be found in the northern part of the region, along the major drainage wadis. There is some possibility that at least the larger of these border towns were not as dominantly agricultural as towns in the rest of Palestine, but were much more economically dependent upon grazing. A substantial investment in animal husbandry would give greater stability to what must have been otherwise a precarious agricultural economy. This would also add to the towns a much greater area of economic exploitation than would otherwise be allowed them with such severely limited farmlands. In addition, it is possible that these settlements were markets and centers for a much larger population than had lived within the towns. If so these would have been non-sedentary groups grazing flocks within the plains, and in the hills of central Sinai and the Negev, whose economy was perhaps supplemented by patch agriculture, carried out in the smaller wadi beds of the upland regions. On the basis of such a mixed economy of the towns of the northern Negev and the southern coast, as well as the necessary symbiotic political and social relationships which would have resulted from such an economy, one might describe the social structure as 'dimorphic', signifying, not that farmers were also shepherds, but that the economic importance of shepherding was such that it supported significant transitory groups, who, having developed distinctive social and political traits appropriate to their way of life, dealt symbiotically with the sedentary population of the border towns of Palestine, which, in turn, developed a significant dependence on the non-sedentary groups. The lack of direct evidence of such groups, however, makes such an interpretation arbitrary, and, since the towns are oriented towards the most fertile arable lands and conceivably independent for long periods of time, it ultimately rests upon a concrete analysis of the historical changes in the settlements of this region (cf. below, section 5).

A similar interpretation might be applied with more conviction to the Bronze Age settlement of the southern part of Transjordan between the Wādī l-Ḥāsā and the Wādī l-Wālā, some ten kilometers south of Amman. This area is bordered on the east by a 10-30 km strip of steppelands just west of the watershed. Though large areas are barren, much of this area is grasslands. Permanent settlement during the Bronze Age was confined to the hill country within a narrow zone of Mediterranean climate. This region is sharply broken by deep gorges, and, on the plateau north of the Wādī l-Mūǧīb, by intermediate steppe zones which form excellent grazing areas but hardly support agriculture other than occasional patch cultivation. The known settlement of south Transjordan is very limited thoughout this region during all periods of the Bronze Age. Broken up into isolated agricultural pockets, regional groupings among these settlements could have been neither strong nor very large. Individual settlements generally require some form of larger social and political context (cf. however, Wittfogel 1971: 565), and the marked isolation of these Bronze Age sites may well suggest that the proper context is to be found in connection with the steppe. The higher mountains to the south, not too far distant from the grasslands of the steppe, could support a form of transhumance pastoralism in limited numbers, which could find markets and supplementary agricultural products from the villages. The interpretation, however, is hypothetical and, at best, possible.

The essential requirement of historical evidence is finally satisfactorily met with by the settlements of the central Negev during the EB IV/MB I period (cf. Thompson 1975: 13-24). The several hundred settlements in the central Negev from this period have been found in two economically distinct environmental zones. The largest number of settlements and dwellings, and all of the large villages, lie on the northwestern slopes of the central hills, and in spite of the desert climate (less than 100mm rainfall) were supported by an agriculture based on a system of wadi terracing in which arable fields were kept under cultivation with the aid of run-off water. The necessary maintenance of the wadi terracing suggests an intensive form of cultivation, rather than the patch or swidden agriculture more typical of arid regions. This, in turn, suggests long-term, perhaps continuous, occupation (cf. Cranstone 1972: 487; Harris 1972: 245). Several large sites, with a long history of occupation, such as Tel Yaroḥam, confirm this. The most typical form of housing structure—apparently small round huts (reflected in the remains of circular stone foundation walls, generally ranging from 3–7m in diameter), related in homestead-like clusters, and distinguished one from the other by separate functions (cooking, storage, sleeping, hospitality, etc.)—has been found in other cultures, periods, and climates to be associated with both sedentary and transitory forms of dwelling (Cranstone 1972). In the Negev of the EB IV/MB I period, large numbers of the same type of dwelling structures were found in areas where there appear to be insurmountable obstacles to any form of agriculture beyond occasional patch cultivation. Most of these have been found in the high-lying regions of Ramat Maṭred, Har Romẹm, Naḥal Ṣin and the upper Naḥal Nisảnả. In these regions, considerable long-term winter grazing is available, and the economy of these settlements is undoubtedly oriented to animal husbandry. I have suggested elsewhere (1975) that the settle-ment of the central Negev as a whole during this period was based on some form of mixed economy of agriculture and grazing. There does seem, therefore, some reason to describe this mixture as 'dimorphic'. Nevertheless, a form of 'transhumance' may perhaps be more probable, since two distinct environments have been exploited (cf. Allan 1972: 221), with the long-term grazing of flocks through the winter growing season and a return to the lower northwestern slopes for the dry summer season grazing on the post-cropping stubble of the agricultural fields. After the first autumn rains, the wadi terraces are planted and the flocks grazed in the unfarmed gullies and on the nearby sparse hillside vegetation. When this gives out, the flocks are moved by some of the community to the highlands in the south to winter over. The settlement patterns of the south suggest the possibility that groups were confined to specific areas and that grazing rights were in force. In the spring the flocks are returned to the fields for the harvest. The summer is spent in repairing the agricultural terraces, sheep-shearing, spinning and weaving (for an analogous use of this region, cf. Marx 1967). Agriculture provides a home base, and produces grains, fruits, vegetables, nuts, oils, and summer feed for the flocks. The herds produce wool and dung fertilizer, milk, butter, cheese and meat (Adams 1971b: 596), and some protection from the undoubtedly frequent crop failure in this marginal area.

The area as a whole is isolated from the southern border of Palestine by a 30–35km stretch of sand desert, and is open to Sinia in the west. If this occupation of the Negev had lasted for any considerable time, one might expect the development of social and political structures appropriate to a life of transhumance. However, such settlement occurs during the Bronze Age only during EB IV/MB I, and during that period perhaps only for a short duration.

4. *The EB IV/MB I Settlement of Palestine*

Dever has argued (1977: 86) that the non-sedentary West Semitic groups of Mesopotamia are to be understood as living in a symbiotic relationship with the settled population; that is, as forming an integrated part of the Mesopotamian economy. He nevertheless argues that the EB IV/MB I period in Palestine was the result of these same 'Amorites infiltrating Palestine', coming 'from a semi-nomadic culture'. This claim appears arbitrary unless it can be shown with some concrete evidence that (1) the culture of EB IV/MB I in Palestine was indeed of a 'semi-nomadic' type, and (2) that it did derive from the Syrian steppe. Historians now generally agree (Haldar 1971; de Geus 1976: preface; Liverani 1973; Fronzaroli 1977) that the population of Palestine and Syria is already predominantly West Semitic before the end of the Early Bronze Age. Furthermore, the overwhelming conviction of Palestinian archaeologists is that the the Palestinian EB IV/MB I pottery tradition is essentially derived from indigenous EB forms (cf. Prag 1974; Dever 1977). The term 'semi-nomadic' is notoriously ambiguous, and Dever, in outlining current possible points of unanimity among scholars about EB IV/MB I (1977: 84), uses the term 'semi-sedentary'. Much more importantly, he refers to Prag's description of this period as essentially in agreement with his own. Prag, in her very important study, stresses some of the evidence for 'both permanent villages and well-established campsites' (Prag 1974: 102), and summarizes much of the evidence known from excavations about agriculture during the EB IV/MB I period, and concludes that her study differs from previous studies principally in pointing out 'a degree of sedentary existence and agriculture' (1974: 103). Although I am unable to accept her suggestion that a 'secondary wave of West Semitic people' caused the transition from EB to EB IV/MB I, the evidence she gives of sedentary occupation in some areas, and of more transitory long-term encampments in others, is based on sound observation and should form the starting point for any interpretive analysis of the period as a whole. Prag's study is also of immense importance in that it is the first major interpretation of this period by a field archaeologist, which, in attempting to reconstruct the origin, economy, and social structures of this people, is built on the basis of what has been found rather than on negative evidence (cf. Thompson 1974: 144-71).

The variety of climates in the many regions of Palestine makes it extremely difficult to use the discoveries from one site or from one type of region for all of Palestine. This is particularly true of the Bronze Age, and especially of the EB IV/MB I period, when Palestine did not share a historical development throughout the entire region. Furthermore, much of the evidence for the settlement of Palestine during this period is published either in Hebrew only or not at all and is unavailable to many western scholars. As a result, many interpretations are based on the limited excavations at EB IV/MB I levels (undertaken mostly within the hill country of Palestine), on the surface explorations of Nelson Glueck, and on brief reports in the archaeological journals (for a more comprehensive, but still very incomplete collection of sources, cf. Thompson 1975, 1978c). This inaccessability of the sources for a regionally oriented history of Palestine during EB IV/MB I has led to an understanding of this period which is essentially based on tradition. As Prag seems fully aware, this traditional picture is the inverse of reasonable expectations. Marginal areas (the Transjordan, the Negev) are occupied with permanent villages, while the agricultural heartland of Palestine is occupied by semi-nomadic pastoralists. With the long dominance of this essentially topsy-turvy understanding, it has been only a very short step to an invasion hypothesis (mitigated by some to an 'infiltration') in order both to explain what was thought to be an excessively transitory form of settlement during the period as well as to provide efficient cause for the end of the Early Bronze cities (Thompson 1974: 160-61). Prag's article is a major step towards a re-evaluation, and was formed independently of both biblical views of semi-nomadic patriarchs and undifferentiated, sociological concepts about flock-herding nomadism.

My own understanding of this period is that the population is essentially indigenous to Palestine and that the form of settlement is basically in continuity with that of the Early Bronze Age. An economy based on sheep and goatherding pastoralism, independent of a sedentary agricultural population, is foreign to the Bronze Age of Palestine.

During the EB IV/MB I period, the heaviest concentration of settlements was not in the Transjordan, nor was it in the Negev. The settlement pattern of EB IV/MB I was rather similar to and largely continuous with the EB occupation, concentrated in those regions where rich and extensive agricultural fields are found in connection with plentiful water with the greatest population near fields under irrigation: the northern Jordan Valley, the Beth Shan Valley and the Jordan Plain to the north, the Naḥal Ḥarod, the Jezreel Valley and the Wadi l-Fāri'a. Typical of both EB and EB IV/MB I in these areas—and apparently uninterrupted—were small unwalled villages and hamlets, directly oriented to the cultivated fields of the area. Such settlements of course did raise pigs, cattle, sheep, and goats, and were dependent upon them to maintain soil fertility, but it is unlikely that they can be legitimately described as pastoral.

Other major areas of considerable EB IV/MB I village settlement were the coast of Palestine and the northern Transjordan. The settlement patterns of each, however, vary considerably. Along the coast, to the north of the Haifa Bay, the EB IV/MB I occupation follows a pattern similar to that found for EB, but the settlements are fewer and are restricted to areas near the banks of streams and springs (Thompson 1978c: 52), suggesting the possible use in this area of simple irrigation techniques. The restriction of settlements to these well-watered zones suggests that, if grazing had been carried out in the plain, it did not develop any form of society or settlement separate from the agricultural villages. If shepherding was a subordinate function of the villages, the climate and topography of this region is such as to make it unlikely that grazing was either seasonal or migratory. A small number of EB IV/MB I sites along the shore in the Haifa Bay area, near Atlit, and along the central coast (Thompson 1978c: 54, 56, 58), suggest that some fishing and perhaps sea trade was carried out during this period. The extensive occupation of the central coast (p. 58) is largely confined to the banks of the major rivers, again suggesting a decided preference during this period for

irrigable lands. The area of greatest EB settlement, the broad alluvial
plain near the eastern hills which was probably developed by dry farming
techniques and intensive cropping, and where also heavy grazing is
possible, is abandoned during the EB IV/MB I period. As one moves
further to the south, into the more arid zones of the coast, the restriction
of EB IV/MB I settlement to well watered regions is even more marked.
Near the Nahal Soreq, where rainfall is close to 500mm, settlement is
still intensive, though restricted to the river banks. South of this river,
however, as the steppe zone is approached, settlement gives out almost
completely—in contrast to all other Bronze Age periods. The rich
grazing lands of the wide southern coast lies beyond the fringe of EB
IV/MB I settlement.

The area of northern Transjordan is another area of Mediterranean
climate with extensive agricultural settlement during EB IV/MB I. Here,
the sedentary character of settlement has never been in doubt, and is
primarily based on dry-farming techniques. Attempts to date these settlements chronologically earlier than those of western Palestine have been
so far unconvincing (cf. Martin 1976: 85). As during the subsequent MB
II and LB periods, the center of EB IV/MB I settlement was the Irbid
depression (Thompson 1978c: 18-20). The pattern of settlement within
this area reflects an intensive agricultural occupation which was relatively
stable throughout the Bronze Age. In the higher area of the Aglun, a
rugged area with plentiful rainfall (more than 600mm), a large number
of EB sites have been found, typically situated on isolated flat-topped
bluffs and ridges. Most of these settlements are small and relatively
unstable. Few sites survive the EB period, and the regional settlement is
limited and sporadic during all subsequent Bronze Age periods. A
similar pattern is found (except in the more stable area just to the south
of Wādī l-'Arab) in the extreme northern area of Transjordan, just south
of the Yarmūk: a large number of relatively small EB settlements in
isolated, rugged terrain, which is followed by a collapse of the regional
settlement and widespread abandonment of the area.

In western Palestine, very similar changes in settlement appear to have
occurred in the very rich agricultural plain of the isolated Carmel coast.
After a very intensive EB settlement, on the basis of irrigation agriculture, with a number of cave dwellings in the eastern hills probably
based in animal husbandry, the plain is largely abandoned by the end of
the EB period and during all subsequent Bronze Age periods (Thompson
1978c: 56-57). Similar patterns of the collapse of EB occupation of

agricultural regions are also noticed in the hill country of western Palestine. In the—for the Bronze Age—agriculturally marginal Allonim hills (pp. 41-42), EB settlement is limited to the isolated valleys of Naḥal Hillázon and Naḥal Ṣippori, where settlement is supported by rich soils and available spring water. However, these isolated regions are abandoned during the EB period, and remain unsettled during EB IV/MB I. A similar pattern is followed in the isolated Biq'at Bet Natofá. This pattern is in strong contrast to the stable and regionally continuous occupation of the well-watered, easily accessible and relatively unified regions closer to the Jordan Valley and the Sea of Galilee, especially along the Wādī 'Amūd, the Biq'at Yavna'ẹl, and the Naḥal Távor (p. 42). In the Carmel range, EB sites are usually restricted to small villages, possibly supported by valley terracing, along the lower, westward draining streams. The relative isolation of these sites, and the consequent precariousness of settlement here, undoubtedly affected the collapse of the region which did not begin to recover until the LB period. In the more accessible and well-watered areas along the Naḥal Dáliyá and the Naḥal Tanninim, however, regional settlement is maintained and is relatively continuous through subsequent periods. In the Saḥl 'Arrāba, just north of the hills of Samaria, the EB occupation is very large, proportionate to the occupation of the major valleys of Palestine. Settlement is continued, however, during EB IV/MB I at very few sites (1978c: 45), suggesting a very marked demographic collapse in this region. The Bronze Age settlement of the central hills is dispersed, because of the restriction of agricultural settlement to a few hilltops, plateaus, and, more frequently, to the valleys. In spite of these limitations, the EB settlement is nevertheless impressive, particularly in the higher altitudes. The collapse of these settlements and the abandonment of the entire central hills is nearly complete until the MB II resettlement. The marginal character of the few quite small settlements that have been found from EB IV/MB I suggests that these settlements had a mixed economy and were less dependent on the more sedentary form of agriculture than the settlements of this period in the great valleys (p. 47).

In the more arid, but more coherent, Judaean hills, the EB IV/MB I settlement, largely confined to areas near the watershed, reflects a collapse in the *size* of the population and the area of displacement (pp. 49-50) rather than an outright regional abandonment as in the north. A number of cave settlements suggests some transitory occupation. However marginal the association with agriculture, the sparseness of settlement throughout the Judaean hills would allow for considerable dependence on shepherding. Excavated sites near Hebron suggest a combined economy of agriculture and shepherding, similar to the settlements of the more marginal regions of the southern Transjordan and the lower Jordan Valley (cf. above, section 3, and especially Prag's discussion of Tall Umm Hamad: 1974: 96-97). In these areas, however, the EB IV/MB I occupation, *in common with* that of the whole of the Bronze Age, is obviously a response to the regional climatic and environmental conditions. In the Judaean hills, the EB IV/MB I settlement pattern is *in contrast* to the rest of the Bronze Age, and has its cause in the events which brought about such catastrophic changes in so many regions of Palestine late in the EB period.

In spite of major destructions in many fortified cities known to us from excavation reports, the agricultural continuity of most of the most populated regions of Palestine was maintained from the EB through the MB II period. In addition to city destructions (which began as early as the end of EB II: Thompson 1974: 161), there were essentially two types of region that were either abandoned or in which the size of the population dramatically collapsed late in the EB period, where recovery was not achieved until the MB II period, or, in some areas, much later. Most typically in the hill country, there were the relatively isolated, regionally fragmented, far-flung villages which lacked adherence to larger groups, and were consequently vulnerable to political and economic instability. In spite of the Mediterranean climate and the people's proven technological ability to settle these regions, they were unable to sustain their populations. In addition to these areas, the regions most affected were the more arid, agriculturally marginal areas, bordering on and lying within steppe climates—areas where water resources were precarious, with fragile soils which were subject to devastating effects from drought or overpopulation. Surprisingly, however, the semi-arid and arid zones of Palestine reflect an extremely mixed response to the catastrophes which struck so many areas. In southern Transjordan, where only a very small population was supported throughout the Bronze Age (cf. above, section 3), almost no change can be noticed during EB IV/MB I, either in the pattern or size of the occupation, though there was some possible growth in population. In the southern Jordan Valley, the general instability of settlement is probably to be explained by its marginal ecological context alone, rather than by any major transregional upheaval at the end of the EB period, since there is here no marked change in the regional settlement of EB IV/MB I. In the central Negev, on the other hand, there is an almost total absence of evidence for any EB exploitation of this region; yet, during the EB IV/MB I period there were several hundred new settlements, with a number of very large villages, occupying the area on the basis of the mixed economy described above in section 3. The contrast provided by this region is even more striking when seen over against the less arid steppe zones of the northern Negev and the southern coastal plain. The farmed areas of the southern coast during EB seem to have extended at least as far south as the banks of the Wādī Ġazza, where the rainfall falls below 300mm. It is also possible that some farming was carried out as far south as the Wādī l-ʿArīš (Thompson 1978c: 7-8, 60-61). During EB IV/MB I, however, settlement was abandoned throughout the entire area south of Naḥal Śoreq, just 10 km south of Tel Aviv. In the Beersheva and Arad Basins, aridity (200–300mm) generally restricted agriculture (at the level of Bronze Age technology) to areas where ground water was plentiful and stable; that is, to the fields along the banks of the Wādī Ġazza which drained the plain to the Mediterranean. The settlements along the northern arm of the Wādī Ġazza (the Naḥal Garar) were very large and stable, showing occupation during all periods of the Bronze Age. In the more arid south, however, the EB settlement concentrated around the major springs, the ʿAin aš-Šallāla and the ʿAin al-Fāriʿa. By the end of this period, those villages are abandoned, and almost the entire Beersheva plain south of the Naḥal Gerar is empty. The area west of the modern city of Beersheva and the ʿArad Basin is similarly affected, and given over to wilderness.

The overwhelming observation drawn from both excavation reports and settlement patterns (for bibliography, cf. Thompson 1978c: Part II), is that the end of the Early Bronze Age was catastrophic, involving destructions of cities, widespread impoverishment, dramatic shrinkage of population, abandonment of large regions which were normally capable of supporting considerable populations by either agriculture or grazing, and the dispersal of population into areas which earlier had been wilderness and which were technologically difficult to farm. Explanations which depend upon the assumption of vast numbers of landless pastoral peoples invading or immigrating into Palestine are very unsatisfactory (Thompson 1974; Martin 1976: 61; Haldar 1971: 49, 66). The disruptions of the Early Bronze period occur over a span of half a millennium!

Moreover, the hallmark of the most intensively settled regions during the EB IV/MB I period is able water exploitation: a continuation of the Early Bronze irrigation networks, and the opening of new areas based on wadi terracing and run-off collection systems. Conversely, the inability of the people to maintain settlement in Palestine's best grazing regions hardly gives us confidence in a description of them as 'pastoralists'. Nor is there any reason to see this period as involving any substantially new population. Indigenous burial traditions (Prag 1974: 99-102; Meyers 1969), the ephemeral character of so many of the settlements, the widespread frugality, and the population decline require quite other explanations.

The roots of the disaster which overcame the Early Bronze period in Palestine lie within the period itself, in its large cities and its prolific population. The prosperity of EB II is not just a counterpoint to the poverty of EB IV/MB I; it is perhaps its ultimate cause. EB II witnessed an unprecedented expansion of population in Palestine. Cities of over 20 dunams (1 dunam = 1000m^2), with thousands of inhabitants, were found everywhere in the more fertile regions of Palestine. Small villages and hamlets proliferated throughout the agricultural regions. Settlement expanded, through enclosure and wadi terracing, up into the more difficult hill country, wherever good soils and water were abundant. But the population of EB II also eventually expanded beyond these regions— into steppe zones capable of supporting over long periods of time only limited populations. The one near constant of history, namely demographic growth (cf. Adams 1971b: 591), however, made these settlements in marginal lands precarious, and, with their growth, ever more dependent on favorable weather and soil conditions. Also with growth, grazing and cropping intensified: longer fallows gave way to shorter, and ever more marginal land was brought under cultivation. In the primary agricultural zones, once maximum population density was approached, pressure for migration mounted, not only to the newer regions—into the hills and the steppe—but equally into the cities and into non-agricultural economies, increasing yet more the market for the agricultural sector, which was becoming less capable of meeting the demands made on it. With the burgeoning of the cities, and consequent inflation, the potential for eventual catastrophe was available. In the marginal regions, collapse may have been inevitable. In these areas, where agriculture depends largely on dry-farming techniques, even normal climatic variations can result in crop failure in dry years. Long-term drought or frequently recurring dry-spells can cause not only crop failure, but a lowering of the water table and the loss of springs and wells. With ever larger areas opening up to relatively simple methods of cultivation, the already poor lands necessarily must fail to produce consistently high yields. With compensation through a shortening or even abandonment of fallow systems, much of the land increasingly becomes subject to salinization. In heavily overpopulated marginal regions such as the 'Arad Basin, drought can result not only in agricultural failure but overgrazing and a consequent denudation of the soils (for analogies, cf. Smith 1969; Young 1972; Harris 1972; and Allan 1972).

Once serious food shortages began to occur, the danger of widespread famine increased and brought about a dramatic growth in the political and military importance of the cities in order to stabilize and regulate limited resources, however incapable they may have been of dealing with the causes of the shortages. Even short term famines, if spread over large regions, could, once the stores of the cities were threatened with depletion, bring about political conflict and warfare between towns. Such conflicts, however, might be contained for considerable periods of time, with only episodic warfare and the occasional destruction of villages and weaker cities. Nevertheless, a long period of instability, involving frequent hostilities between major regions, has also the capability of so disrupting normal life as to cause an internal collapse of the economy of a region and the abandonment of areas where settlements were relatively isolated and consequently insecure and incapable of fielding an adequate defensive army. Such collapses, even when regionally contained, create large numbers of refugees, straining further already limited supplies and increasing insecurity through the formation of robber bands.

In the early Bronze period destructions of major cities and the abandonment of settlements within the agricultural heartland of Palestine began already during EB II, and the last part of the Early Bronze period witnesses recurrent destructions of the fortified cities. By the EB IV/MB I period, whole regions had been given up, and the agriculture of most of the hill country and the outlying, marginal lands of Palestine had collapsed. The population, now massively diminished through starvation, warfare, and emigration, was concentrated in the very richest and largest agricultural zones where continuous fertility was supported through irrigation. Yet, the economy was frugal, village oriented, and isolated

from the world beyond Palestine. The lack of major fortifications, however, suggests a return to military stability and an absence of population
pressure. The steppe zones, ecologically the most fragile, were perhaps
the first areas to be given up. New settlements were undertaken by
immigrants and refugees in the agriculturally more difficult, but also
more viable, Central Negev. The mixture of the economy there, and
heavy dependence on herding, undoubtedly provided a satisfactory
margin against periodic drought. Similarly, the stability of the marginal
areas of the southern Transjordan and the lower Jordan Valley, in
contrast to more prosperous regions of Palestine, may be understood, if
we assume there a mixed economy of agriculture and grazing.

Numerically, the population of Palestine did not recover until the
prosperity of MB IIB, a period of rapid economic and demographic
growth.

5. *The City in Palestine*

In section 3 above, a number of possible variations of the herding
economy in Palestine were explored, and the difficulties of dealing
historically with non-sedentary forms of occupation were mentioned in
passing. I argued, on the basis of the nature of Palestinian agriculture
and of the relationship of Palestine's settlements with its environment,
that nomadic pastoralism, in its variety of forms, was a phenomenon
which played a major role on the borders and in the steppe zones of
Palestine, but was insignificant, perhaps nonexistent, within the heartland.

Dever, in discussing 'dimorphism' as a potential key to the interpretation of Bronze Age Palestine, refers to the recent archaeological
excavation of a small site near Tall r-Rumēla (commonly identified with
Beth Shemesh; map coordinates, Palestine grid: 1477.1286) as archaeological evidence for a 'dimorphic society' (Dever 1977: 111-12).
Excavations show that the 'dimorphic' site was a small agricultural
hamlet occupied during the MB IIB period (possibly site no. 1412.06 in
Thompson 1978c). The homogeneity of the pottery suggests to Dever
that the settlement was relatively brief. This factor, and the unwalled
character of the settlement, lead him to draw the conclusion that it was a
'satellite village' of Tall r-Rumēla, and, consequently, 'dimorphic'. This
is a very important observation for Dever, in the context of his argument, since this site is used as a paradigm for what he feels may be
typical of MB II, and is at the heart of his subsequent argument that

patriarchal society is both 'dimorphic' and to be dated to the MB II period (cf. Dever 1977: 112-20). Though in this initial discussion Dever's argument is not entirely coherent, it seems to center essentially on his understanding of Palestine during this period (MB II) as progressively urbanized. The MB II period as a whole tends to be understood in terms of the prosperous, heavily fortified town, described as a 'city-state' (Dever 1977: 84-89).

Tall r-Rumēla is in an area which is sparsely settled during the Bronze Age, and its potential involvement with less sedentary pastoral-ists—if they did in fact then live in this area—is quite apparent. However, is the existence of an agricultural hamlet *evidence* for pastoralism and hence 'dimorphism'? The town dwellers of Tall r-Rumēla may have been as likely to herd sheep as the farmers living in the hamlet. An unwalled site, though perhaps archaeologically ephemeral, is not obviously representative of a less sedentary form of life. Much more importantly, the one factor which permits the interpretation of a 'dimorphic' form of society—the agricultural limitations of the greater region for intensive Bronze Age settlement—is an ecological indication that the economy of Tall r-Rumēla and neighboring settlements cannot be used as a paradigm, as Dever would, for other, quite different, environmental regions. The understanding of this hamlet as a 'satellite village' is at first attractive. Another nearby site, perhaps also dated to the MB II period, might be similarly described (cf. Thompson 1978c, site no. 1513.07). However, the issue of interpretation is complex, and depends on much more than relative size and duration of settlement. Are there also economic or historical reasons for assuming, as Dever does, a relationship of dependence? During the EB period, there were several such small sites near Tall r-Rumēla (cf. Thompson 1978c, sites 1413.06.09 and 1412.01.04), including one (1412.03) which may have been occupied for a considerable length of time. Yet, since the EB occupation of Tall r-Rumēla was apparently quite small (cf. the bibliography for site no I.1412.05: Thompson 1978c), it is unlikely that we can understand the surrounding hamlets of that period as 'satellites'. Moreover, if the existence of a 'city-state' was not necessary for the maintenance of these settlements during EB, what grounds do we have in the evidence from MB II for assessing the political subordination implied in the terms 'city-state', and 'satellite', rather than a more neutral, but also politically possible, description such as 'agricultural hamlet' and nearby 'market town'? In fact, a relative independence and less centralized ownership of land might be suggested, failing historical indications to the contrary, by the direct relationship in many areas of this type between small-scale agricultural techniques and production and wealth. Particularly in the labor intensive dry farming, typical of the hill country of Palestine, land ownership, and with it political control, may be decentralized efficiently (cf. also Allan 1972: 221). Small—even temporary—settlements may be indicative merely of new lands open to production, or a desire to be closer to the fields under cultivation. The independent settlement may be indicative of a separate region being exploited. Potential military functions provided by the fortified town may find reciprocity in the villages in taxes or personnel. This might also historically be used as a basis for political subordination. On the other hand, the lack of political subordination might be one cause for the more frequent abandonment of so many such sites (on this, further below).

A brief survey will place the issue in sharper focus. In many regions, there appears to be an *inverse ratio* historically between the growth of the larger, fortified cities and the frequency of occurrence of the smaller, open sites. There are at least five major regional variations or patterns during the latter part of the Bronze Age (for a collection and summary of the archaeological data discussed below, cf. Thompson 1978c).

(1) The most widespread type of settlement in Palestine is the regionally very stable occupation of environmentally circumscribed agricultural zones where both large and small, but usually isolated, villages occur. At times a small number of settlements together, perhaps dominated by a larger town, are found within very limited regions. This is the pattern of areas such as the Upper Galilee, Mount Carmel, the Lower Galilee, the southern Jordan Valley, the Judaean hills, the steppe zones of the southeast, as well as most of the Transjordan. Though each of these regions of course has significant local variations, most representative of this type are those of the Upper Galilee, where one finds very small hamlets as well as very large towns (e.g., Tall Qadas measures 100 dunams) in regional isolation, on top of large hills or plateaus, near springs and in the larger valleys. Economically, the relative importance of a site and its economy is based on the wealth and stability of the narrow environmental context: the larger the area under cultivation, the larger the potential political influence. Regional hegemony, if it had existed, appears to have been more the result than the cause of size and wealth. Beyond individual and small regional organizations, there is every reason to suppose that there were only fragmented

and transient political organizations. Stability of settlement within these regions is very high throughout the entire Bronze Age, and changes in the economic and political structures in these areas are not notable. The possibility of major economic and political involvement with nomadic pastoralists, particularly in the more arid regions, would of course increase the environmental context of these sites. Yet, this would only affect their political structure marginally, since both the size of the steppe zones, and the numbers of nomads potentially involved are very limited (cf. above, section 3). Similarly, in the more Mediterranean climates, other industries, particularly those of fishing and logging, alter the geographical and economic context of sites of this type considerably. Such militarily weak regions are vulnerable to imperial forms of exploitation for taxes and for personnel. However, the lack of regional centralization makes the cost of imperial control over such isolated and largely frugal settlements prohibitive. Not until the Iron Age, and the immense increase of population of these regions at that time through an expansion of terracing technology beyond the Bronze Age valleys, hill-tops, and occasional spring-fed slope, to an intensively productive dry agriculture on the newly terraced slopes of the hills, do these regions become larger, centralized, economic units. First then does their regional importance become significant and find expression in the nation states of the first millennium.

(2) The second type of region consists of the most stable and important areas of Palestine and includes the Jezreel Valley, the lower Ḥulà basin and the Jordan Valley north of the Sea of Galilee, the Irbid depression, and the interrelated valleys of the central hill country in the immediate vicinity of Tall Balāta. These are large, open, intensively settled, and prosperous regions. These areas witness long continuous settlement, with many large tells showing occupation remains throughout the whole of the Bronze Age. There are also a number of small settlements, usually occupied only for short periods. The displacement of the largest, usually fortified, towns suggests that the larger valleys may have been regionally subdivided, with each subdivision dominated by a major settlement. A variety of possible coalitions of subdivisions may have developed pyramids of considerable political power and permanence, such as at Megiddo and Taanach. In some of the smaller, but still environmentally rich, regions, entire geographic areas tend to be dominated by single great tells, such as Qedeš and Hazor in rime lower Ḥulà area, or Shechem in the central valley of the hills of Samaria. These are the sites,

more than any others, which best fit the popular understanding of 'city-state', as the term is used of ancient Palestine: states consisting of a geographically limited region which is dominated by a single city, which possibly has subject towns or villages. That the political structure of such settlements can be described as 'feudal' may well be doubted. The primary agricultural economy, and hence land ownership in these areas, is only marginally dependent on centralized control. Irrigation, for the most part in these regions, is on a small scale, and much of the agricultural production can be maintained through the labor of individuals and families. The trade routes on the other hand, and the strategic importance of many of the largest towns, would certainly have demanded centralization, and the control of these strategic cities played a major historical role over the centuries in foreign imperial plans to control and exploit Palestine.

Though these cities were occasionally destroyed, regional settlement is remarkably continuous. During the Late Bronze period, there is a marked increase in the size and the importance of the very largest towns. Also during this period, many fewer small unfortified hamlets or villages are occupied than in any of the earlier periods. This is a possible indication of long-standing military insecurity during this period. The basic pattern of settlement, however, with the marked dominance of large towns, established already since the Early Bronze period, is also not noticeably changed during the early Iron Age.

(3) A very interesting variation of this pattern of settlement occurs primarily in some of the coastal regions. The pattern is most clearly pronounced in the northern and central coastal areas. Essential to this type is the interrelation of two adjacent but ecologically distinct zones: the largely agricultural and grazing lands of the coastal plain on one hand, and the western coastal area near the shore with its broad mixture of economies (fishing, shipping, mineral extraction, occasional grazing, agriculture in the valleys and deltas, etc.) on the other. Most typical of the earlier periods is a proportionately large number of fortified towns, regionally spaced along the agriculturally rich eastern edge of the coastal plain. In the central coastal areas, fortified cities are also found along the major river valleys, where the richest agricultural contexts are found. A number of smaller, largely ephemeral, unfortified settlements are also found in the neighborhood of the fortified towns; however, these are usually settlements of short duration. Some pyramiding of power through the subordination of neighboring settlements by many of the

larger cities was certainly a recurrent historical phenomenon, given the lack of geographical barriers. Such centralization may have been particularly frequent in regionally distinctive subregions, such as along the banks of the major rivers. In this respect, the pattern of settlement is much like that of type (2). In contrast, however, one finds, after the beginning of MB II, an increasingly large number of settlements along and near the shore, at considerable distances from the major cities. They are of mixed size, and some of them may be industrial rather than dwelling places. In the central region, there occur a large number of small unwalled hamlets, scattered in the alluvial pockets between the great river valleys. In the Haifa Bay area, the coast itself is settled by large port cities, geographically spaced along the shore line, while the less favorable agricultural plain is occupied during the LB period by small villages or hamlets, set on high ground to the east of the plain.

These patterns are severely sharpened at the end of the MB II period and during LB. The settlement on the shore continues to expand, with an ever larger number of settlements. In the areas of the great tells, however, the LB occupation is largely confined to the fortified cities, which grow in size. In the central coastal areas, there is some indication of serious long-term disturbance. Several regions are abandoned at the end of MB II, particularly along the swamp-prone lower Naḥal Ḥᵃdẹra and Naḥal Polẹg.

Politically, the coastal regions are obviously dominated, like type (2) above, by the large towns. However, though many of the richer agricultural towns, and the Haifa Bay port cities, could be understood as independent 'city-states', the continued spread of largely unprotected villages and hamlets in adjacent areas during a period of considerable disturbance may indicate larger, transregional, political structures such as federations of cities or the like, where military defense is less localized but rather dependent on strategic coalitions, border defenses and police networks. In a federation of political units, or a regionally based state, the defensive requirements for new settlements does not require site-by-site fortification, but only area-wide pacification.

A transregional orientation of defenses may conceivably explain much that is unusual in the southern coastal area and along the border between coastal Palestine and Sinai. As typical of settlements in marginal lands, most villages and towns here are situated in the alluvial oases of the wadis which drain towards the Mediterranean. They have the appearance of independent villages and hamlets, possibly loosely

organized in sub-regions such as the neighborhood of major springs or
areas where the water table is high. Large sites are found near rich soils
and abundant water, and appear to be—even when fortified—large
villages. The political hegemony of the larger towns over smaller
settlements is difficult to assume, except perhaps those few within their
immediate environs. It is possible, however, that they provide markets
for a very large area (cf. above, section 3). Their proximity to the North
Sinai trade route (cf. Thompson 1975: 9-13) would certainly strengthen
this function. The separateness of these sites, however, may be
misleading. The largely unsettled, but rich, grasslands of this region, with
the opening to Sinai in the south and the southwest, suggests the
possibility that the larger border towns such as Tall l-'Aǧǧūl and Tall
Ǧamma may have formed, during some periods, symbiotic associations
with pastoralists and other non-sedentary groups of the Negev and Sinai
(cf. the exciting discoveries of Oren 1973, in coastal Sinai; also
Thompson 1975: 12). Similarly, the many fishing villages and instal-
lations along the southern coast, in areas where agriculture was unlikely,
must have developed a symbiosis with the larger agricultural towns. The
long-term political disturbances at the end of the MB II period and
throughout the LB is also here marked, especially along the Naḥal
Šiqmá which is abandoned in the open plain. In other areas, large and
fortified sites increase in relative importance and size. Along the coast,
however, settlement is maintained, and small unfortified hamlets and
villages survive. Presumably they are under the protection of major
fortifications beyond their immediate regional context. The apparent
importance and remarkable size of the southernmost settlements might
then also find explanation as border towns of a military region, unified
through political coalitions or federations.

(4) The three types of sedentary political organization discussed
above, representing independent isolated villages, regionally dominant
towns, and regional federations, supported the most stable areas of
Palestine. The following types of settlement pattern were far less stable.
Type (4) includes the regions of the upper Jordan Valley just south of
the Sea of Galilee, the Beth Shan Valley, and Naḥal Ḥárod, and possibly
the Wādī l-Fāri'a, and takes in some of the agriculturally most
productive and most densely settled regions of Bronze Age Palestine.
The variety of agricultural production is great, even within very small
areas: there is to be found large-scale irrigation, seepage agriculture,
irrigation from abundant fresh water springs, dry farming, and at least

some enclosure terracing. The largest towns are outside the flood plains, and most directly associated with dry farming and spring and river fed irrigation systems. Between the EB and MB II periods, very large tells are typically found in areas of great fertility immediately adjacent to other equally large settlements. Regional spacing or the polarization of the larger towns as in the Jezreel Valley is not noticeable here. Smaller villages and hamlets—and there are many hundreds—seem to result from either the exploitation of limited, circumscribed regions, or, in some cases, the extension of larger settlements. Some sub-regions (e.g., the Jordan Graben) are settled primarily by small hamlets; others (e.g., the Wādī l-Fāriʻa) mostly by large villages. A pattern of centralization or subordination is difficult to identify in these regions before the end of MB II. Moreover, very many of the small hamlets are impressively stable, and appear to have occupation histories comparable to the largest tells. Although considerable centralization and even state ownership of some lands must be supposed in the areas of the major irrigation networks, autonomy ought to be assumed for the other regions (perhaps tempered by coalitions and, occasionally, military control from the more powerful towns).

The impact in these regions of the disruptions at the end of MB II and during LB was substantial. The settlement of whole areas collapsed. Large numbers of small villages and many larger towns, with histories of settlement going back to the Early Bronze period, were abandoned and remained unsettled throughout the LB period. At the expense of the countryside, a 'balling' of the population occurred into the well-fortified cities, with a consequent abandonment of many farms far from the cities. During the Late Bronze period, many of the large towns are spaced out in the valleys, suggesting a political polarization during this period, and perhaps independent sovereignty—a pattern in sharp contrast with that of earlier periods. This change is especially noticeable in the Wādī l-Fāriʻa, which is now dominated by only three very large and fortified towns situated at great distances from each other. The abandoned territories, not far from large settlements, becoming permanently insecure areas and inappropriate for agricultural settlement, form a possible basis for the development of an autonomous nomadic society of refugees and displaced persons, turning to animal husbandry and pastoralism, and developing independent living patterns (cf. Adams 1972: 744, for an analogy).

(5) The problem of displaced persons or refugees created by the

large-scale abandonment of settlement becomes even more acute when we describe our fifth type of settlement pattern. Slaughter in war, enslavement, and resettlement in the cities, may well account for the majority of people displaced by the collapse of settlement in the major valleys; the population of the 'insecure' territories need not be assumed to be very great. However, in the central hill country (excluding the ecologically distinct Shechem enclave) the disaster is more complete.

In the synclinal trough of the Carmel range, lying between the Naḥal 'Iron and the 'Emeq Dotàn, a gently rolling plateau is formed that is open to both the coast and the Jezreel. The easy slopes, good communications, deep rich soils, large number of springs and adequate rainfall (more than 600mm) make this a prosperous and important agricultural region. As might be expected, the settlement of the area is extensive, especially during the EB and MB II periods, and is found along the streams and on the watershed, near springs, and on the slopes above the Jezreel. The absence of large springs, and the cyclic drying up of springs in summer, prevented large settlements, and the intensive MB II settlement consists primarily of a very large number of hamlets and small unfortified villages on the central rolling plateau. These were, apparently, independent subsistence-farming communities, without major forms of political centralization, regional control, or substantial military protection. Their open, unprotected state made them particularly vulnerable to the disruptions at the end of the Middle Bronze Age. Almost the entire area, except for a very few sites along the Naḥal Dàliyà and the Naḥal Tanninim, is abandoned. This disruption of an area without major settlement (except, of course, Tall 'Ara, protecting the east–west trade route to the Jezreel) undoubtedly created large numbers of homeless people, and added substantially to the subsequent prevailing insecurity of the region.

A very similar catastrophe overtook the settlements of the central hills of Samaria. The earlier settlement pattern here resembles that of the Galilee (above, type [1]). There were many both large and small settlements in the small western valleys, along the gentler slopes of the hills, and especially in the many basins of the north. Given the technological limitations of methods of terracing and water storage during the Middle Bronze Age, the size of individual settlements and the density of regional occupation was in proportion to agricultural possibilities. Particularly in the larger basins, many towns were quite large, and, at times, fortified. The area as a whole was not unified, but was rather divided into many, probably independent, subregions, each with its own autonomy. Unlike the settlements of the Upper Galilee and of type (1) generally, however, most of the settlements of the central hills, particularly those in the western valleys, were not greatly isolated, and they were not protected from the dislocations of the end of the MB II period. Quite the contrary, most of the settlement of this vast and complex area is abandoned by the beginning of the Late Bronze period. outside the large unified region around Tall Balāta, LB settlement is largely restricted to a few small ephemeral sites near springs in the south.

The disruption in this region is more extreme than anywhere else in Palestine. Recovery is also noticeably slow. General pacification of the region seems to be restored and the settlement of many areas re-established by Iron I. However, many potentially prosperous areas are apparently not resettled until Iron II, when the settlement of the region as a whole experiences widespread expansion everywhere with the increased use of slope-terracing.

The analysis of settlement patterns offers significant access to a large number of historical problems. There is a pressing need, however, to integrate the archaeological data, and interpretations drawn from archaeologically derived reconstructions, with what we know of the history of Palestine from written sources. On one hand, the cause of the initial disruptions and destructions of the MB II settlement of Palestine needs clarification, as does the nature of the continued insecurity of some regions, particularly the central hill country. On the other hand, the political nature of the final pacification of disturbed regions, and the causes of a surge of new settlements, culminating in a unification of the hill country by Iron II, is obviously at the heart of the question of the origin of the nation states which gave unity to these regions, but needs much more specific definition. The origin of Israel can be observed archaeologically, since it is the unification of settlement in the hill country of Palestine which constituted that origin. However, our observation is still oblique. The specific causes of pacification and surge to new settlement is not yet explicit. Moreover, the exact nature of the continuity and discontinuity of this settlement with that of the Bronze Age—that is, the indigenous quality of this new settlement—needs much more critical reflection.

I would like to return in conclusion to the question of dating the origin of Israel's pentateuchal traditions, which has been dealt with above in section 1 of this paper. The recognition of an agricultural, potentially indigenous, Palestinian origin of the Iron Age population of the territory of Israel (cf. Thompson 1978b), makes it critically important to recognize that a 'history of Israel' prior to the Iron Age with its implication of the existence of an entity or concept—of an 'Israel' with national implications—is not only as yet unidentified (contrary to what has been implied in Clark's arguments), but is no longer to be seriously considered! For if 'Israel' is the political structure which gives *definition* to the unification of the hill country, it cannot exist independently of the settlement and unification of that territory. Its traditions, as traditions about Israel's ancestors (Thompson 1974: 326), also find meaning first here. One cannot posit the existence of a tradition without the concomitant existence of the bearers of that tradition.

WORKS CONSULTED

Adams, R.McC.

1971a   'Development Stages in Ancient Mesopotamia', in *Prehistoric Agriculture* (ed. S. Struever; Garden City, NY: Natural History Press): 572-90.

1971b   'Early Civilizations, Subsistence, and Environment', *Prehistoric Agriculture* (ed. S. Struever; Garden City, NY: Natural History Press): 591-614.

1972   'Patterns of Urbanization in Early Southern Mesopotamia', in *Man, Settlement, and Urbanism* (ed. G.W. Dimbleby *et al.*; London, Gerald Duckworth): 735-49.

Albright, W.F.

1957   *From the Stone Age to Christianity* (Garden City, NY: Anchor).

Allan, W.

1972   'Ecology, Techniques, and Settlement Patterns', *Man, Settlement and Urbanism* (ed. G.W. Dimbleby *et al.*; London: Gerald Duckworth): 211-26.

Binford, L.R., and S.R. Binford

1968   *New Perspectives in Archaeology* (Chicago: Aldine Press).

Butzer, K.W.

1971   'Agricultural Origins in the Near East as a Geographical Problem', in Struever (ed.), *Prehistoric Agriculture*: 209-35.

Clark, W.M.

1977   'The Patriarchal Traditions. 2: The Biblical Traditions', in *Israelite and Judaean History* (ed. J.H. Hayes and J.M. Miller; Philadelphia: Westminster Press): 120-48.

Cranstone, B.A.L.

1972   'Environment and Choice in Dwelling and Settlement: an Ethnographical Survey', in Dimbleby *et al.* (eds.), *Man, Settlement, and Urbanism*: 487-501.

Dever, W.G.
1977   'The Patriarchal Traditions. 1: Palestine in the Second Millennium B.C. The Archaeological Picture', in Hayes and Miller (eds.), *Israelite and Judaean History*: 70-120.

Flannery, K.V.
1972   'The Origins of the Village as a Settlement Type in Mesopotamia and the Near East: a Comparative Study', in Dimbleby *et al.* (eds.), *Man, Settlement, and Urbanism*: 23-54.

Frick F.S., and N.K. Gottwald
1972   'The Social World of Ancient Israel', in *Society of Biblical Literature, Seminar Papers I* (Missoula, MT: Scholars Press): 165-78.

Fronzaroli, P.
1977   'West Semitic Toponomy in Northern Syria in the Third Millennium B.C.', *JSS* 22: 145-66.

de Geus, C.H.J.
1971   'The Amorites in the Archaeology of Palestine', *UF* 3: 41-60.
1975   'The Importance of Archaeological Research into the Palestinian Agricultural Terraces, with an Excursus on the hebrew Word *gbi*', *PEQ* 107: 65-74.
1976   *The Tribes of Israel: An Investigation into Some of the Presuppositions of Martin Noth's Amphictyony Hypothesis* (Studia Semitica Neerlandica, 18; Assen/Amsterdam: Van Gorcum).

Gottwald, N.K.
1978   'The Hypothesis of the Revolutionary Origins of Ancient Israel: A Response to Hauser and Thompson', *JSOT* 7: 37-52.

Gottwald, N.K., and F.S. Frick
1975   'The Social World of Ancient Israel', *Society of Biblical Literature, Seminar Papers I* (Missoula, MT: Scholars Press): 165-78.

Haldar, A.
1971   *Who were the Amorites?* (Monographs of the Ancient Near East, 1; Leiden: Brill).

Harris, D.R.
1972   'Swidden Systems and Settlement', in Dimbleby *et al.* (eds.), *Man, Settlement and Urbanism*: 245-62.

Irvin, D.
1977   'The Joseph and Moses Narratives. 3: The Joseph and Moses Stories as Narrative in the light of Ancient Near Eastern Narrative', in Hayes and Miller (eds.), *Israelite and Judaean History*: 180-209.
1978   *Mytharion: The Comparison of Tales from the Old Testament and the Ancient Near East* (AOAT, 32; Neukirchen–Vluyn: Neukirchener Verlag).

Irvin, D., and T.L. Thompson
1977   'The Joseph and Moses Narratives. 4: The Narratives about the Origin of Israel', in Hayes and Miller (eds.), *Israelite and Judaean History*: 210-12.

Kenyon, K.
1966   *Amorites and Canaanites* (London: Oxford University Press).
Klengel, H.
1958   'Benjaminiter und Hanäer zur Zeit der Könige von Mari' (Dissertation, Berlin).
1962   'Zu einigen Problemen des altvorderasiatischen Nomadentums', *ArOr* 30: 585-96.
1972   *Zwischen Zelt und Palast* (Vienna: Schroll).
1977   'Nomaden und Handel', *Iraq* 39: 163-69.
Kochavi, M. (ed.)
1972   *Judaea, Samaria, and the Golan: Archaeological Survey 1967–1968* (Jerusalem: Carta Jerusalem).
Kupper, J.R.
1957   'Les Nomades en Mésopotamie au temps des rois de Mari' (Bibliothèque de la Faculté de Philosophie et Lettres de l'Université de Liège, fasc. 142).
Layton, R.
1972   'Settlement and Community', in Dimbleby *et al.* (eds.), *Man, Settlement and Urbanism*: 377-82.
Liverani, M.
1973   'The Amorites', *POTT*: 100-33.
1976a   Review of H. Klengel, *Zwischen Zelt and Palast*, *OrAn* 15: 68-73.
1976b   Review of R. de Vaux, *L'Histoire ancienne d'Israel* I.II, *OrAn* 15: 145-49.
Luke, J.T.
1965   'Pastoralism and Politics in the Mari Period: A Re-examination of the Character and Political Significance of the Major West Semitic Tribal Groups on the Middle Euphrates, ca. 1828–1758' (Dissertation, University of Michigan).
Martin, M.E.
1976   'The Appraisal of Argument in Biblical Archaeology' (Dissertation, Leiden).
Marx, E.
1967   *Bedouin of the Negev* (Manchester: Manchester University Press).
Mazar, B.
1969   'The Historical Background of the Book of Genesis', *JNES* 213: 73-83.
Mendenhall, G.E.
1962   'The Hebrew Conquest of Palestine', *BA* 25: 66-87.
1969   Review of M. Weippert, *Die Landnahme*, *Bib* 50: 432-36.
Meyers, E.M.
1969   'Jewish Ossuaries and Secondary Burials in their Ancient Near Eastern Setting' (Dissertation, Harvard University).
Moscati, S.
1956   *I Predecessori d'Israele* (Studi Orientali publicati a cura della scuola orientale, IV, Rome).

Noth, M.
1953   'Mari und Israel. Eine Personennamenstudie', *Festschrift A. Alt*: 127-
           52 (Aufsätze II: 213-33).
Oren, E.
1973   'The Overland Route between Egypt and Canaan in the Early Bronze
           Age', *IEJ* 23: 198-205.
Parr, P.J.
1972   'Settlement Patterns and Urban Planning in the Ancient Levant: the
           Nature of the Evidence', in Dimbleby *et al.* (eds.), *Man, Settlement,
           and Urbanism*: 805-10.
Prag, K.
1974   'The Intermediate Early Bronze–Middle Bronze Age: An Interpretation
           of the Evidence from Transjordan, Syria, and Lebanon', *Levant* 6: 69-
           116.
Pritchard, J.B.
1975   *The Ancient Near East*, II (Princeton: Princeton University Press,
           1975).
Rendtorff, R.
1977   *Das überlieferungsgeschichtliche Problem des Pentateuch* (BZAW,
           147; Berlin: de Gruyter).
Renger, J.
1973   'Who are All those People?', *Orientalia* 42: 259-73.
Ron, Z.
1966   'Agricultural Terraces in the Judaean Mountains', *IEJ* 16: 33-49 and
           111-22.
Rowton, M.B.
1967   'The Physical Environment and the Problem of the Nomads', *RAI* 15:
           109-21.
1973a   'Autonomy and Nomadism in Western Asia', *Orientalia* 42: 247-58.
1973b   'Urban Autonomy in a Nomadic Environment', *JNES* 32: 201-15.
1976a   'Dimorphic Structure and Topology', *OrAn* 15: 17-31.
1976b   'Dimorphic Structure and the Problem of the 'Apirû–'Ibrîm', *JNES*
           35: 13-20.
Schmid, H.
1976   *Der sogenannte Jahwist: Beobachtungen und Fragen zur Pentateuch-
           forschung* (Zürich: Theologischer Verlag).
Seters, J. Van
1975   *Abraham in History and Tradition* (New Haven: Yale University Press).
Smith, M.
1969   'The Present State of Old Testament Studies', *JBL* 88: 19-35.
Smith, P.E.L.
1972   'Land-Use, Settlement Patterns, and Subsistence Agriculture: A
           Demographic Perspective', in Dimbleby *et al.* (eds.), *Man, Settlement
           and Urbanism*: 409-26.
Thompson, T.L.
1974   *The Historicity of the Patriarchal Narratives: The Quest for the
           Historical Abraham* (BZAW, 133; Berlin: de Gruyter).

1975	*The Settlement of Sinai and the Negev in the Bronze Age* (BTAVO, Reihe B, Nr 8; Wiesbaden: Dr Reichert Verlag).
1977a	'The Joseph and Moses Narratives. 1: Historical Reconstructions of the Narratives', in Hayes and Miller (eds.), *Israelite and Judaean History*: 149-66.
1977b	'The Joseph and Moses Narratives. 2: The Joseph-Moses Traditions and Pentateuchal Criticism', in Hayes and Miller (eds.), *Israelite and Judaean History*: 167-80.
1978a	'A New Attempt to Date the Patriarchal Narratives', *JAOS* 98: 76-84.
1978b	'Historical Notes on "Israel's Conquest of Palestine: A Peasant Rebellion"', *JSOT* 7: 20-27.
1978c	*The Settlement of Palestine in the Bronze Age* (BTAVO, Reihe B; Wiesbaden: Dr Reichert Verlag).
1979	'The Jacob-Esau Conflict Narratives', *Semeia*.

Thompson, T.L., and D. Irvin

| 1977 | 'The Joseph and Moses Narratives. 4: The Narratives about the Origin of Israel', in Hayes and Miller (eds.), *Israelite and Judaean History*: 210-12. |

Tringham, R.

| 1972 | 'Introduction: Settlement Patterns and Urbanization', in Dimbleby *et al.* (eds.), *Man, Settlement, and Urbanism*: xix-xxviii. |

Vaux, R. de

| 1971/1974 | *Histoire ancienne d'Israël* I, II (Paris: Gabalda). |

Weidmann, H.

| 1968 | *Die Patriarchen und ihre Religion im Licht der Forschung seit Julius Wellhausen* (FRLANT, 94; Göttingen: Vandenhoeck & Ruprecht). |

Weippert, N.

| 1967 | *Die Landnahme der israelitischen Stämme in der neueren wissenschaftlichen Diskussion* (Göttingen: Vandenhoeck & Ruprecht). |
| 1971 | *The Settlement of the Israelite Tribes in Palestine: A Critical Study of Recent Scholarly Debate* (SBT, 11/21; London: SCM Press). |

Wittfogel, K.A.

| 1971 | 'Developmental Aspects of Hydraulic Societies', in Streuver (ed.), *Prehistoric Agriculture*: 557-71. |

Young, T.C., Jr

| 1972 | 'Population Densities and Early Mesopotamian Urbanism', in Dimbleby *et al.* (eds.), *Man, Settlement, and Urbanism*: 827-42. |

JSOT 13 (1979), pp. 33-46

THE SIGNIFICANCE OF THE 'SONS OF GOD' EPISODE
(GENESIS 6.1-4) IN THE CONTEXT OF THE 'PRIMAEVAL HISTORY'
(GENESIS 1–11)*

David J.A. Clines

Most studies of the 'Sons of God' pericope (Gen. 6.1-4) have busied themselves with the narrower exegetical problems within the pericope itself as an independent, not to say intrusive, piece of 'heathen mythology'[1] or as a partly demythologized 'foreign particle'[2] within the biblical text. My purpose here is to examine, via the exegetical problem of the identity of the 'sons of God' and via the backward and forward links between the material and its surroundings, the function of the pericope within the larger whole of the 'Primaeval History'. Without calling into question the consensus of opinion that the material of the piece derives from a pre-Israelite myth, I am concerned here essentially with the 'final form of the text'.[3]

1. *The Identity of the 'Sons of God'*

Concentration on this particular interpretational crux can, I think, point us to a solution of the larger problem of the function of the whole pericope within its present setting.

*   This paper was originally written in early 1972 and has been circulated in unpublished form. It has recently been thoroughly revised, with some account being taken of the more recent literature.

1. H. Holzinger, *Genesis* (KHAT, 1; Tübingen: J.C.B. Mohr, 1898), p. 64.

2. B.S. Childs, *Myth and Reality* (London: SCM Press, 2nd edn, 1962), pp. 57ff.

3. See J.F.A. Sawyer, 'The Meaning of אלהים בצלם ("In the Image of God") in Genesis I-XI', *JTS* 25 (1974), pp. 418-26 (pp. 418-19); *idem*, 'The "Original Meaning of the Text" and Other Legitimate Subjects for Semantic Description', *BETL* 33 (1974), pp. 63-70; D.J.A. Clines, *The Theme of the Pentateuch* (JSOTSup, 10; Sheffield: JSOT Press, 1978), esp. pp. 10-11, 82.

Three chief interpretations of the identity of the 'sons of God' have been advanced:

(i)   The 'sons of God' are the Sethites (cf. 5.1, 3), while the 'daughters of humans' are from the Cainite line.[4] In favour of this view is the division of the human race into two lines of descent in the previous chapters (4.17-5.32), but against it are the arguments that since 'humanity' (הָאָדָם) is used in v. 1 of humankind generally, it is unlikely to mean only one section of humanity in v. 2,[5] and that 'sons of God' does not appear as a collective term for the Sethites, either in these chapters or elsewhere.

(ii) The 'sons of God' are male heavenly beings,[6] who mate with earthly women. In favour of this interpretation is the regular use of the term 'sons of God' for the heavenly court that surrounds Yahweh (e.g. Ps. 29.1; 89.7; Job 1.6). There is a *prima facie* case for supposing that both the Nephilim and Gibborim of v. 4 are to be regarded as the offspring of such unions, though it has been argued that the structure of v. 4 deliberately affirms the existence of the Nephilim *before* the unions of v. 2.[7] We may leave aside, however, the problem of the origin of the Nephilim, and note that the majority of scholarly opinion supports the identification of the 'sons of God' as heavenly beings.[8] The principal objection to this identification is that it is far from clear in the present context why humanity as a whole should be subjected to the divine threat of v. 3 for the sin of such non-human beings; the 'daughters of humans' can hardly have been regarded as culpable (though their beauty

4.   The origins of this view, supported by many Fathers and Reformers, are adequately dealt with by P.S. Alexander, 'The Targumim and Early Exegesis of the "Sons of God" in Genesis 6', *JJS* 23 (1972), pp. 60-71; and L.R. Wickham, 'The Sons of God and the Daughters of Men: Genesis 6.2 in Early Christian Exegesis', *OTS* 19 (1974), pp. 135-47.

5.   For the view that this is not an overwhelming objection, see M.G. Kline, 'Divine Kingship and Genesis 6.1-4', *WTJ* 24 (1963), pp. 189-90.

6.   Frequently understood as 'angels' (cf. J. Holman, *Bib* 49 [1968], pp. 293-94); but see C. Westermann, *Genesis* (BKAT, 1.7; Neukirchen–Vluyn; Neukirchener Verlag, 1972), pp. 493-94, pp. 501ff.

7.   E.g. G. von Rad, *Genesis* (revised ET; London: SCM Press, 1963), p. 115.

8.   For example, H. Gunkel, *Genesis, übersetzt und erklärt* (repr.; Göttingen: Vandenhoeck & Ruprecht, 3rd edn, 1964 [1910]), pp. 55-56; J. Skinner, *A Critical and Exegetical Commentary on Genesis* (ICC; Edinburgh: T. & T. Clark, 1930), pp. 141-42; von Rad, *Genesis*, p. 110; G. Cooke, 'The Sons of (the) God(s)', *ZAW* 76 (1964), pp. 22-47 (pp. 23-24).

[v. 2] was the antecedent condition[9]), since they were taken by force.

(iii) The 'sons of God' are dynastic rulers who, as oriental despots, established royal harems by force[10] or practised indiscriminate rape. This view has the merit of taking seriously the phrase 'they took for themselves wives from all whom they chose' (ויקחו להם נשים מכל אשר בחרו). It also makes intelligible the divine punishment upon humanity as a whole because of the sin of these despots; for in oriental ideology it is not uncommon to find the fate of the people at large bound up with the fate of the king. Nevertheless, the identification of the 'sons of God' simply as human rulers has the weakness that it is rarely if ever attested in the ancient Near East as a term for kings in general. Although kings in Egypt, Mesopotamia, Canaan and Israel were frequently spoken to as 'son of God', such language seems to have been reserved in the main for courtly rhetoric and poetic adulation, and is not to be met with, in the Old Testament at least, in straightforward narrative style with such a signification.[11]

Westermann appears to feel no difficulty at this point. Although he seems not to know of the paper of M.G. Kline, he regards the term 'Sons of God' (בני אלהים) as the only one available to the narrator (J) of Gen. 6.1-4 to designate a class of beings superior to humans; for in the 'Primaeval History' humanity is otherwise undifferentiated and undivided socially and politically. Since the pericope concerns essentially the power of one group over another, only the polarity of 'sons of God' and '(daughters of) humans' is open to him .[12]

9. Cf. Westermann, *Genesis*, pp. 495-96, pp. 503-504.

10. So Kline, 'Genesis 6.1-4', pp. 187-204; followed by A.R. Millard, 'A New Babylonian "Genesis" Story (Epic of Atrahasis)', *TynBul* 18 (1967), p. 12. Similarly also F. Dexinger, *Sturz der Göttersöhne oder Engel vor der Sintflut? Versuch eines Neuverständnisses von Genesis 6,2-4 unter Berücksichtigung der religions-vergleichenden und exegesegeschichtlichen Methode* (Wiener Beiträge zur Theologie, 13; Vienna: Herder, 1966). This view was adumbrated by some Jewish interpreters who saw in the 'sons of God' rulers and in the 'daughters of humans' women of lower rank (see Dexinger, *Gottersöhne*, pp. 122ff., 129-30; Alexander, 'Targumim and Early Exegesis', pp. 61, 64ff.).

11. Both Dexinger, *Göttersöhne*, pp. 37ff., and Kline, 'Genesis 6.1-4', p. 192, lay weight upon the description of King Krt in the Ugaritic tale as *bn il* 'son of God'. The criticisms of R. de Vaux, *RB* 74 (1967) , pp. 114-15 and J. Holman, *Bib* 49 (1968), pp. 292-95, should be taken into account.

12. Westermann, *Genesis*, p. 496: 'Der Erzähler meint mit den בני אלהים die den Menschen schlechthin überlegene Klasse: Männer, die so mächtig sind, dass es für

It is perhaps no contradiction of Westermann's position, but rather a development of it, to make the new suggestion that the author of Gen. 6.1-4 in its present form did not work with a system of closed categories in which 'sons of God' must be *either* human *or* non-human.[13] Are the 'Sons of God' here then *both* divine beings *and* antediluvian rulers? The use of the term may indeed be inherited from earlier formulations of the pericope in which the 'sons of God' may have been divine beings *tout court*, but it is not improbable that the author of this text in its final form should have understood it in reference to rulers of the primaeval period who had belonged in part to the divine world. In this connection we may observe the appearance of divine names in the Babylonian lists of antediluvian kings, notably the identification of several rulers with the god Dumu-zi or Tammuz.[14] Strictly speaking, of course, Gen. 6.1-4 represents the 'sons of God' as the generation prior to the Nephilim and Gibborim,[15] so that a simple identification of 'sons of God' with the other terms is inappropriate.[16] But the intercourse of 'sons of God' with 'daughters of humans' is not envisaged as occurring at only one definite period—the imperfect verb in v. 4 should probably be translated as a frequentative, viz. 'Whenever the sons of God went in unto the daughters of men'[17]—so that it is perhaps unnecessary to distinguish too sharply between kings who were 'sons of God' in the strict sense, and

ihr Begehren der Schönheit einer Frau die Grenzen, die hier für gewöhnliche Sterbliche bestehen, nicht gibt'.

13. Cf. P.D. Miller, *Genesis 1–11: Studies in Structure and Theme* (JSOTSup, 8; Sheffield: Journal for the Study of the Old Testament, 1978), pp. 25-26:

> In the stories of the origin and beginnings of 'man' or the human creature it is not surprising that there is some attempt to define the relation of *'ādām* beings to *'ᵉlōhîm* beings and wrestle with the extent and limitation of that relationship. At one point in the story [Gen. 3.22] the relationship is seen to be very close and the human creatures are like the divine ones. But the story goes on to say that these two worlds are nevertheless distinct and that it is possible to overstep the bounds and seek to blend the two into one.

14. Millard, 'Babylonian "Genesis"', p. 12 n. 28, cites the Akkadian god-list in *Cuneiform Texts* XXIV, pl. 19, K4338b; XXV, pl. 7, K7663+11035.

15. Construing the complex sentence thus: 'There were in those days the Nephilim, whom whenever the sons of God went in unto the daughters of humans they (the latter) bore to them (the former)'.

16. So Dexinger, *Göttersöhne*, pp. 44ff.

17. So LXX ὡς ἂν εἰσεπορεύοντο; cf. Skinner, *Genesis*, p. 146.

kings who were only sons of the 'sons of God', part-human and part-divine.

Such a 'son of God' has his portrait sketched in Akkadian literature, the hero Gilgamesh:

> Two-thirds of him is god, [one-third of him is human]...
> The nobles of Uruk are gloomy in their chambers:
> 'Gilgamesh leaves not the son to his father;
> Day and night is unbridled his arrogance...
> Gilgamesh leaves not the maid to her mother,
> The warrior's daughter, the noble's spouse...
> The onslaught of his weapons verily has no equal'.[18]

That Gilgamesh was regarded in the epic as a historical human personage is beyond question; the belief in his divine or semi-divine origins explains his significance and the survival of the story of his deeds from ancient times, as well as his titles and entitlements; it does not mean that the epic poet conceives of him as any more than a man, and a mortal man at that.

The same outlook is credible in the biblical pericope: that the 'sons of God' were both regarded as rulers of ancient times, and traditionally ascribed divine or semi-divine origins. On this interpretation, the 'sons of God' pericope is no alien intrusion into the story of primaeval humanity, since it concerns—from first to last—humans; but neither is it simply an episode in the catalogue of human sinfulness, since it also concerns the relationship between the divine and the human world that is displayed in the actions of these 'sons of God'. Connections with the surrounding material will become apparent in the ensuing motif analysis.

2. *Motif Analysis*

(a) The motif of 'breaking the bounds', which recurs in every major episode of the 'Primaeval History', appears here in two forms, if the foregoing solution to the question of the identity of the 'sons of God' is accepted.

First, there is in the union of 'sons of God' with 'daughters of

18. *Gilgamesh* I.ii.I, 11ff., 16-17, 21 (*ANET*, pp. 73b-74a). It is perhaps also significant that like the 'sons of God' who find their life expectancy greatly reduced, Gilgamesh, since 'he too is flesh' (cf. Gen. 6.3), even though only one-third human, is oppressed by the thought of death and he searches for immortality, only to find it eludes him at the end.

humans' a breach of the primal boundary between the divine and the human worlds. The attempt of humanity in Genesis 3 at self-diviniza-tion—and at least partially successful attempt (cf. 3.22) to merge the spheres of the human and the divine—is here taken up afresh from the other direction in the attempt of divine beings to join the world of humanity. Their attempt also is only partially successful, in that the 'Sons of God' (בני אלהים), or at least their offspring, inasmuch as they have breached the bounds between the divine and the human, have forfeited the immortality that is a token of their divinity and have become (like Gilgamesh) subject to death (v. 3).

Secondly, there is clearly another form of 'breaking the bounds' present in the violent and polygamous lust of the 'sons of God'. Westermann[19] has pointed to the formal similarity between this story and those of Gen. 12.10-20 (and parallels) and 2 Sam. 11–12, where the beauty of a woman is the alleged reason why a man breaks the bounds of accepted morality. We may observe further backward links within the 'Primaeval History' that highlight the significance of the sons of God 'taking wives of all whom they chose'. The monogamous order estab-lished by God (2.24)—in which, incidentally, it is not the man but God who chooses the wife for the man—has in the course of human decline been casually abandoned by the tyrant Lamech of whom it is first noted (? in emphatic position) that he 'took two wives'.[20] The glimpse in Gen. 6.2 of 'titan promiscuity'[21] reveals the ultimate stage in the development of a society that has produced a Lamech. The 'sons of God' are intelligible therefore in the present context as the royal successors of Lamech, taking for themselves (להם) wives of as many women as they chose.[22] Bonhoeffer was not far from the mark when he spoke of the unrestrained sexuality here depicted as

> avid, impotent will for unity in the divided world [note the link with Gen.
> 11]; it desires the destruction of the other person as creature; it robs him

19. Westermann, *Genesis*, pp. 494-97.

20. It is hard to agree with Skinner that 'no judgement is passed on Lamech's bigamy, and probably none was intended. The notice may be due simply to the fact that the names of the wives happened to be preserved in the song afterwards quoted' (*Genesis*, p. 118). If the latter is the case, it is all the more probable that by drawing attention to the fact the narrator is implying a judgment.

21. J. Blenkinsopp, *The Pentateuch* (1971), p. 40.

22. Kline, 'Genesis 6.1-4', pp 195-96; E.G. Kraeling, 'The Origin and Significance of Gen. 6.1-4', *JNES* 6 (1947), pp. 193-208 (p. 197).

of his creatureliness, violates him as well as his limit… [It] … is therefore destruction *par excellence*. Thus it is an insane acceleration of the
Fall; it is self-affirmation to the point of destruction.[23]

(b) In the 'Primaeval History' the relation of the divine to the human
comes to expression not only in the concept of a boundary between the
two spheres, but also in the concept of communication, or communion,
between the two spheres. Thus, in Genesis 2, though God is creator and
the man is a creature, the man is infused with the divine breath (2.7),
and God walks in the garden that the man tends (3.8). To the same
effect is the concept of humanity's creation in the image of God (1.26),
whatever precisely that may mean; in some sense, at least, the boundary
between the divine and the human is not absolute, and humankind can
represent God on earth (1.28). In 6.1-4, on the contrary, we find a
satanic parody of the idea of the image of God in humankind. Far from
God being present on earth in the person of humankind as his kingly
representative exercising benign dominion over the lower orders of
creation,[24] we now have the presence of the divine on earth in a form
that utterly misrepresents God through its exercise of royal violence and
despotic authority over other humans.

(c) A further link between 6.1-4 and the surrounding material lies in
the concept of the possession of 'name'. The Nephilim, here identified, it
appears,[25] with the 'mighty men who were of old' (הגברים אשר מעולם),
were the men of renown, literally 'men of name' (אנשי השם), of ancient
times. The striving for a 'name', a permanent memorial in one's descendants, belongs to the dynastic ambitions of these antediluvian rulers.
Earlier in the 'Primaeval History', Cain, in a sense the spiritual though
not the physical ancestor of the heroes of 6.4 (here the old patristic
identification of the 'sons of God' is not entirely beside the mark), is
represented as having the same dynastic ambition: he strives to

23. D. Bonhoeffer, *Creation and Fall: A Theological Interpretation of Genesis
1–3* (trans. J.C. Fletcher; London: SCM Press, 1959), p. 80.

24. See further, D.J.A. Clines, 'The Image of God in Man', *TynBul* 19 (1968),
pp. 53-103; J. Barr, 'Man and Nature—The Ecological Controversy and the Old
Testament', *BJRL* 55 (1972), pp. 9-32 (pp. 21ff.)

25. I assume that the phrase וגם אחרי־כן, whether a later interpolation (Holzinger,
Genesis, p. 66; Childs, *Myth and Reality*, p. 55) or not, does not distinguish between
the Nephilim and the Gibborim by suggesting that the Nephilim were already in
existence before the 'sons of God' cohabited with the daughters of men, but is
intended as a note of the continued existence of the Nephilim far beyond primaeval
times, and into the period represented, for example, by Num. 13.33.

perpetuate a family name, calling the name of his city by the name of his son Enoch (4.17).[26] Similarly the self-sufficient builders of Babel set about building their city and tower with the explicit purpose of making a 'name' for themselves. This desire to make a name for oneself is more than arrogance; just as their tower whose top reaches to the sky may be seen as an assault on heaven, so their ambition for 'name' is an attack on the prerogative of God, who himself makes his own name great or glorious (2 Sam. 7.23; Jer. 32.20; Isa. 63.12, 14) and who is the true source of 'name' (cf. Zeph. 3.19-20). While it is ironically true that the builders of Babel succeeded in making a name for themselves, it was only a name of derogatory significance, Babel, 'confusion'.[27]

While the line of 'name'-seekers is scattered, there has already come into being a man of 'name', Shem (שֵׁם, Gen. 9.18), ancestor of the 'Semitic' nations, whose name is 'probably intended to be deliberately allusive, providing a contrast to the illegitimate attempt by men to achieve a name for themselves (11.4; cf. 6.4), and anticipating the great name to be accorded to Abraham... (12.1-3)':[28] וַאֲגַדְּלָה שְׁמֶךָ, 12.2; cf. also the prophetic word to David, 'I will make for you a great name, like the name of the great ones (הַגְּדֹלִים) of the earth' (2 Sam. 7.9).[29]

(d) A final motif with interesting connections in the preceding and following chapters is that of the multiplication of humankind. Its appearance in the 'sons of God' episode is interesting not so much for the fact of its presence, but more for the sake of its irrelevance. Throughout the 'Primaeval History' the multiplication of humankind is enjoined, furthered, and blessed by God. The first command to humanity in Genesis 1 is: 'Be fruitful and multiply, and fill the earth' (1.28). In Genesis 4 Eve bears Cain 'with the help of Yahweh' (אֶת־יְהוָה, 4.1), and God 'appoints' (שָׁת, 4.25) another child, Seth, instead of Abel. After the Flood, the first divine command to surviving humanity is a repetition of 1.28: 'Be fruitful and multiply, and fill the earth'. I have argued elsewhere[30] that the position of the Table of Nations (Gen. 10) *before* the Babel episode

---

26. That is, if Enoch himself is not the builder of the city and himself the perpetuator of his own name (cf. U. Cassuto, *Commentary on Genesis* [ET; Jerusalem: Magnes Press, 1961], I, p. 230).

27. Cassuto, *Genesis*, II, p. 242.

28. A.K. Jenkins, 'A Great Name: Genesis 12.2 and the Editing of the Pentateuch', *JSOT* 10 (1978), pp. 41-57 (p. 45).

29. On the connection between Gen. 12.2 and 2 Sam. 7.9 see H.W. Wolff, 'The Kerygma of the Yahwist', *Int* 20 (1966), pp. 131-58 (pp. 141-42).

30. Clines, *Theme of the Pentateuch*, pp. 68-69.

(Gen. 11) compels us to regard the dispersal of the nations not only as a mark of judgment following upon Babel, but also as a fulfilment of the divine injunctions to multiply the race.

Against that background, it is remarkable that the multiplication of humanity in 6.1 is viewed entirely neutrally, and has no real relevance to the narrative that proceeds from it. C. Westermann, it is true, argues that the increase of humanity, which is indeed an appropriate consequence of the creator's blessing, begins to create negative possibilities; the sheer size of humanity creates dangerpoints for the relation between humans and God (or the gods).[31] From the point of view of the form of the pericope, which is Westermann's startingpoint, it does indeed appear that the introductory clause will be of great moment for the development of the narrative. That is not in fact the case, for the narrative would have the same significance if the phrase 'when humans began to multiply on the face of the ground' were absent. To be sure, some multiplication of the human race from the primaeval pair of Genesis 2 must have occurred for the events of 6.1-4 to be possible, but such a multiplication has already been adequately attested by the genealogies of the Cainites (4.17-22) and the Sethites (Gen. 5).

The reference in 6.1, then, to the multiplication of humankind has narrative significance only if the tale is told differently, with the multiplication of humankind a reason or cause for the ensuing events. For the second time in this study, therefore, we are compelled to designate an item 'traditional'. (I should stress that I do not regard an over-riding concern for the 'final form' of the text as precluding acceptance of the possibility that some, if not much, of the material, has been incorporated into the final form largely because it has become traditional. We do not have to suppose final authors of our texts being actively engaged in the precise wording or arrangement of every part of their material; 'final form' criticism—if it may be so designated—makes only the assumption of authorial intention in the end redactors, and authors obviously have many different styles of handling their material. In the present case, I would argue that it makes effectively no difference whether the clause is present or not, so that its presence falls beneath the level of the author's intention.)

Have we then any evidence that the tale may have been told differently, especially in relation to the multiplication motif? Yes, in the Atrahasis epic, the story of the Deluge is prefaced by the lines:

31. Westermann, *Genesis*, p. 500.

Twelve hundred years had not yet passed
When the land extended and the peoples multiplied.
The land was bellowing like a bull.[32]

Here the growth of humankind results in such clamour that it disturbs
the sleep of the high god, Enlil:

'The noise of mankind has become too intense for me,
With their uproar I am deprived of sleep'.[33]

The Flood is sent as the final, and successful, attempt, to halt the unlimited growth of humankind. And following the drastic reduction in the size of the human race brought about by the Flood, measures are taken to ensure that henceforth the size of the human population will be controlled: there are to be sterile women as well as fertile women, various orders of religious women who will not marry, and a demon of infant mortality to 'snatch the baby from the lap of her who bore it'.[34]

The story of the Flood, therefore, with the near extinction of humankind, may be told as a story about the problem of 'over-population', while the multiplication motif presents the reason for the problem and thus effectively accounts for the origin of death. This explanation for the institution of death figures in many myths.[35] 'Earth becomes overcrowded, some check has to be put on mankind increasing to an alarming extent. Thus the only solution is Death.'[36]

Two aspects of the biblical pericope are particularly instructive against this background. First, the multiplication of humankind, though still forming the backdrop of the 'Sons of God' pericope, is not the cause of the introduction of death. Even though in the pericope a limitation of the human lifespan (or, the onset of the death-dealing Flood, 7.21-22) after only a brief period of respite—if that is what the 120 years of v. 3 points to) is decreed, the grounds for it are certainly not the over-population but the purely ethical grounds of the sin of the 'sons of God', however that sin is understood precisely. The origin of death in the 'Primaeval History' has of course already occurred, even more evidently as a result

---

32. *Atrahasis* II.i.2-3 (W.G. Lambert and A.R. Millard, *Atrahasis: The Babylonian Story of the Flood* [Oxford: Clarendon Press, 1969], pp. 72-73).

33. *Atrahasis* II.i.7-8 (Lambert and Millard, *Atrahasis*, pp. 72-73).

34. *Atrahasis* III.vii.1-8 (Lambert and Millard, *Atrahasis*, pp. 102-103); cf. W.L. Moran, *Bib* 52 (1971), p. 56.

35. See H. Schwarzbaum, 'The Overcrowded Earth', *Numen* 4 (1957), pp. 59-74.

36. Schwarzbaum, 'The Overcrowded Earth', p. 60.

of human wrongdoing. The mere multiplication of humankind, therefore, is no cause for catastrophe in Genesis 1–11 as it is in Atrahasis;[37] sheer numbers and the clamour of teeming life are no threat to the cosmos of divine order; but sin is.

Secondly—and this must be tentative—it is possible that the Hebrew text of v. 3 contains a relic of the old idea of the clamour of humankind being the immediate cause of the Flood. The unparalleled conjunction בשׁגם, usually translated 'because' or 'in that' is a notorious difficulty.[38] Not only is -שׁ not attested in the Pentateuch as an abbreviation for אשׁר, and not only is the גם difficult to make sense of, but the logic of the divine sentence is hard to decipher. We would expect, as Westermann observes, that the decree should be based on an act rather than on a state of affairs. Is it too far-fetched an explanation to suggest that בשׁגם was earlier the preposition ב with a noun cognate with the Assyrian root *šagāmu* 'to bellow, howl'?[39] The text would then have read: 'My spirit will not abide in humanity forever because of the clamour of flesh'.[40] If that was the case, it is clearly no longer the case, and the sentence, though not crystal clear, is generally intelligible. It would be strangely appropriate if the 'clamour' of the Mesopotamian myth should have faded in the biblical text into a mere conjunction in a divine speech.

The multiplication motif, along with that of the clamour of humankind, could have provided a rationale for the sending of the Flood. Although the former motif survives, and the latter is possibly present in disguise, neither of them functions significantly in the pericope. And that is what is significant about these motifs in the context of the 'Primaeval History': the fundamental sin–punishment pattern[41] has been stamped upon this doubtless ancient and variously recounted tale of the 'sons of God'.

37. Moran, *Bib* 52 (1971), p. 61, goes so far as to say, 'Gen.9,1ff. (be fruitful and multiply) looks like a conscious rejection of the Atrahasis Epic'.

38. See, e.g., Westermann, *Genesis*, p. 507.

39. W. von Soden and B. Meissner, *Akkadisches Handwörterbuch* (Wiesbaden: Otto Harrassowitz, 1965–1981), pp. 112-13. I am grateful to A.R. Millard for pointing out to me this possible connection.

40. הוא, 'he', in the present text is admittedly unintelligible on this interpretation.

41. Whether seen as a developing 'spread of sin' (as von Rad, *Genesis*, pp. 152-53) or as simply a portrayal of the variety of sinfulness (so Westermann, *Genesis*, p. 498).

3. Relation to the Flood Narrative

Enough has been said to show that the 'Sons of God' pericope is well anchored in its present position in the 'Primaeval History' by motif connections with preceding and following material.[42] One specific point, however, needs to be dealt with separately in order to clarify the connection between the pericope and the succeeding narrative of the Flood. The question is whether the 120 years of 6.3 has a specific reference to the coming of the Flood. In other words, is the 120-year period intended as the normal lifespan, or as a period of respite before the Flood descends?

In favour of the view that 120 years represents the maximum span of life, it may be argued first, negatively, that the figure 120 has no necessary or symbolic connection with a period of grace or respite,[43] whereas, positively, there is some evidence that 120 years was considered the ideal lifetime. Moses lives the full 120 years (Deut. 31.2; 34.7), while Herodotus reports that the Ethiopians habitually lived to the age of 120.[44] In Egypt, 110 years was apparently regarded as the ideal span of life;[45] Joseph and Joshua, significantly, each live to 110 (Gen. 50.22; Josh. 24.29). Elsewhere in the Old Testament, it is true, 80 years is regarded as a normal maximum lifetime (Ps. 90.10; cf. 2 Sam. 19.34-35). It is true, moreover, that the ages of the postdiluvians are not immediately reduced to 120 years;[46] but that could be accounted for as

42. As against, for example, Gunkel, *Genesis*, p. 59 (it had nothing to do with the Flood originally, but was used by J to depict the antediluvian state of humanity); A. Dillmann, *Genesis Critically and Exegetically Expounded* (trans. W.B. Stevenson; Edinburgh: T. & T. Clark, 1897), I, pp. 230-31; S.R. Driver, *Genesis* (London: Methuen, 12th edn, 1926), p. 82; Skinner, *Genesis*, p. 141; Cassuto, *Genesis*, pp. 290-301.

43. I have not had access to the article of Roscher, 'Die Zahl 40 im Glauben, Brauch u. Schrifttum der Semiten', *Abhandlungen der königlichen Sachsischen Gesellschaft der Wissenschaften* (1909), mentioned by Kraeling, 'Gen. 6.1-4', p. 201 n. 32 as containing evidence for the use of 40, which is 120 when trebled, as a period of respite in Hebrew and other Semitic literatures.

44. Herodotus, *Hist.* 3.23; in *Hist.* 1.163 he mentions a ruler of Tartessus who lived to 120.

45. Cf. J. Vergote, *Joseph en Egypte: Genèse chap. 37–50 à la lumière des études égyptologiques récentes* (Orientalia et biblica lovaniensia, 3; Louvain: Publications Universitaires, 1959), pp. 200-201.

46. Given by P, while 6.1-4 is (possibly) J; though cf. M. Noth, *A History of*

a mitigation of the penalty, just as the sentence 'in the day you eat of it you shall surely die' (2.17) only slowly begins to take effect. Some have indeed warned against imposing the Priestly system of decreasing ages arbitrarily on the Yahwist account,[47] while others have claimed to find here polemic against the Babylonian tradition (and, one might have thought, the Hebrew Priestly tradition) of primaeval kings who are said to have lived extraordinarily long lives.[48] In either case, we should ask how the redactor of J and P reconciled to himself the J figure of 120 years with the P data of the lifespans of the postdiluvians—unless perhaps the redactor no longer saw the 120 years as a lifespan. No insuperable problem remains against the view that the 120 years is the limitation or bounding of lifespan as punishment in kind (so to speak) of the bound-breaking by the sons of God.[49]

Nevertheless, it seems more probable that in the present setting the threat of the withdrawal of the divine spirit refers to some event that is about to occur. Since, if we assume that the 'spirit' (רוח) of Yahweh is equivalent to his 'breath' (נשׁמה) breathed into the man at his creation (2.7),[50] the Flood brings about the destruction of everything in whose nostrils is 'the breath of the spirit of life' (נשׁמת־רוח חיים, 7.22), the relation of the decree of 6.3 to the destruction of 7.22 appears to be that of cause and effect. Of course, it may be argued that humankind is not in fact entirely destroyed and that the spirit of Yahweh remains in humanity even after the Flood; but it is an adequate rejoinder that 6.3 is in the nature of a threat, and it is just as appropriate to speak of the Flood as the destruction of humankind as to describe it as the salvation by God of the human race from total annihilation.[51]

Some further support for the view of the 120 years as a period of respite comes again from the Atrahasis epic, where periods of 1200 years intervene between the catastrophes that are climaxed by the

Pentateuchal Traditions (trans. B.W. Anderson; Englewood Cliffs, NJ: Prentice–Hall, 1972), p. 28 n. 83; Dexinger, *Göttersöhne*, pp. 56-57, reckons it to P.

47. So Childs, *Myth and Reality*, p. 54.

48. Kraeling, 'Origin and Significance', p. 201.

49. So Westermann, *Genesis*, p. 508.

50. So already Dillman, *Genesis*, I, p. 236. For parallels between רוח and נשׁמה cf. Job 32.8; 33.4.

51. The 'all' of 7.4, 21-22 is to be taken as seriously as the exceptions to the 'all' in 7.1-2, 23b.

Flood.[52] The figures 120 and 1200 clearly originate from the Babylonian sexagesimal system,[53] and it is therefore possible that the pre-history of this item in the biblical pericope points to its significance from the beginning as a period of respite. The clinching argument seems to me to be the existence of the Atrahasis epic as a unified sequence of creation, multiplication of humankind, and Flood. Since the biblical 'Primaeval History' is built on the same pattern, it is plausible to regard the 120 years as always having had the same kind of function as the 1200 years of the Atrahasis epic, viz. a period of remission or respite.[54] If this admittedly somewhat distant parallel is not cogent enough, I would fall back on the position of B.S. Childs: 'Regardless of what the original meaning of the one hundred and twenty years was, in its present position one cannot help seeing some connexion with a period of grace before the coming catastrophe'.[55]

---

52. 'Twelve hundred years had not passed when...' (*Atrahasis*, I.352; II.i.1; Lambert and Millard, *Atrahasis*, pp. 66-67, pp. 72-73).

53. Cf. Millard, 'Babylonian "Genesis"', p. 13.

54. Millard, 'Babylonian "Genesis"', p. 12; W.G. Lambert, 'New Light on the Babylonian Flood', *JSS* 5 (1960), pp. 113-23. Similarly Kraeling argued that the pericope was designed from the beginning as the introduction to a flood story ('Genesis 6.1-4', p. 195).

55. Childs, *Myth and Reality*, p. 58.

JSOT 25 (1983), pp. 3-16

NARRATIVE STRUCTURE AND CANONICAL PERSPECTIVE IN GENESIS

Robert L. Cohn

Only a teacher of undergraduates would have the audacity to think that he could say something significant about the entire book of Genesis in a single essay. Happily, though, some recent trends in biblical scholarship point to a growing interest in holistic approaches to scripture, feeding my boldness. In particular, critics such as Robert Alter have demonstrated the composite artistry of biblical narrative by exposing the various techniques and structuring devices employed in the creation of character, motif and theme.[1] Related, but more provocative in its theological assumptions, is the canonical approach of Brevard Childs who argues that historical-critical methods, while uncovering much of value about earlier forms of the text and the community which produced it, have not taken seriously enough the canonical process in shaping the text into its normative form *as scripture*.[2] Only the received text 'bears witness to the full history of revelation' and alone can guide the interpreter by pointing to what has been highlighted and what subordinated in the traditioning process.[3] Both approaches thus focus on the final form of the text rather than its putative antecedent. The first stresses its literary integrity, the second its theological definitiveness.

Combining these two approaches, I shall examine how the literary shaping of Genesis conditions its theological meaning. In other words, I want to see the way in which its broad structural patterns contribute to a

---

1. R. Alter, *The Art of Biblical Narrative* (New York: Basic Books, 1981), esp. pp. 3-22, 131-54.

2. B.S. Childs, *Introduction to the Old Testament as Scripture* (Philadelphia: Fortress Press, 1979), pp. 71-83.

3. Childs, *Introduction*, p. 76.

particular vision of how God's presence is manifested in the human world. I will show that the narrative units which comprise Genesis exhibit increasingly tighter structures which correlate with increasingly more sophisticated depictions of the divine–human relationship.

First, we must determine those literary units. Classical source criticism, of course, divides the book into J, E and P documents which modern critics have further subdivided and refined. But from a canonical perspective such an analysis, whatever its historical validity, ignores the new structures to which antecedent literary sources have been subordinated. For Childs, the key to the structure of Genesis is the ten times repeated formula, These are the generations of (*tōledōt*).' followed by either a narrative or a genealogy.[4] Five times the formula is used to introduce narrative sequences: Adam and Eve and their children (2.4); Noah (6.9); Abraham (11.27); Jacob (25.19); and Joseph and his brothers (37.2). The genealogies, which the five other appearances of the formula introduce, follow those narrative sequences. They are either 'vertical' genealogies tracing the family line (from Adam to Noah [5.1ff], and from Shem to Terah [11.10ff]) or 'horizontal', indicating the offspring of the non-chosen line (the sons of Noah [10.1ff.], Ishmael [25.12ff] and Esau (36.1]). Thus the formula heads five major divisions of narrative and and five genealogies which connect them to each other. With the five major units marked out, I can proceed to analyze their literary character.

The similarity in narrative composition of the Adam and Noah sequences (2.4–6.8; 6.9–11.26) suggests that they be treated together. The scenes that are featured in each of these units are completely independent of each other. There is no continuity of place, action or character. Each generation spotlighted is allotted just one episode, and then time marches on to the next generation. Although the Noah story is much longer than the Cain and Abel scene, it is essentially but one episode resolving one problem. Furthermore, the links between episodes in the Adam and Noah sequences are quite loose. Either a scene about children follows one about parents, as in the case of Cain and Abel, or a genealogy suddenly stops and the writer focuses on the last character named, as in the case of Noah. In fact, the episode of the Tower of Babel is simply sandwiched between two genealogies. The episodes in these two narrative units are like flashes of light illuminating the dark passage of time marked by the recitation of genealogies.

4.   Childs, *Introduction*, p. 145.

Although the episodes are independent of each other, they share a common pattern. Each of them features a human sin and a divine punishment. Moreover, before the punishment is exacted God speaks, proclaiming his judgment and announcing that despite the gravity of the sin, the punishment will be mitigated. The resulting pattern of sin–speech–mitigation–punishment is represented more or less fully in the episodes of the garden, Cain, the sons of God, the flood, and the Tower.[5]

More interesting from a canonical perspective are the roughly parallel structures of the Adam and Noah sequences.[6] Each begins with two major scenes focusing on the first two generations, continues with genealogical information, and concludes with a scene depicting the sin of the distant descendants. Thus, the story of Adam and Eve in the garden (2.4–3.24) is followed by that of their son's fratricide (4.1-16). Then an etiological genealogy (4.17-26) and a formulaic genealogy (5.1-32) record the generations until the copulation of the sons of God and the daughters of men (6.1-4) calls God's attention to the wickedness of mankind (6.5-8). Similarly, in the Noah sequence, the story of Noah and the flood (7.11–9.17) is followed by the tale of Noah's son's sexual depravity. Noah curses Canaan (Ham) as God had cursed Cain; both Adam and Noah spawn three sons, one of whom is wicked. Then an etiological genealogy (10.1-32) leads in to the sin of the Tower genera-tion (11.1-9) which is followed by another genealogy concluding with Abraham (11.10-26). The parallel structures thus underscore the roles of Adam and Noah as uniquely first men commanded to 'be fruitful and multiply and fill the earth' (1.28; 9.1). However, Adam's descendants in the tenth generation are washed away except for Noah, and Noah's descendants are 'scattered abroad' when they fail to fill the earth. A new focus for humanity emerges only in the tenth generation after Noah with the promise to Abraham of a land.

Throughout the Adam and Noah narratives God is the main character as well as the director, property man, and stage and lighting manager. He creates the man, the woman, and their environment, and he instructs Noah in the building of the ark. He does not, however, determine human behaviour but allows people to act freely. Yet when they displease him—

---

5. See D.J.A. Clines's discussion of this pattern in which he incorporates the insights of C. Westermann and G. von Rad (*The Theme of the Pentateuch* [JSOTSup, 10; Sheffield: JSOT Press, 1978], pp. 61-64).

6. This balance is also suggested by Clines's discussion of the 'creation–uncreation–recreation' theme (*Theme*, pp. 73-76).

and, with the exception of Noah, they always do—he intervenes directly and personally to punish the guilty. He appears to operate by trial and error, creating his human subjects with the maximum amount of freedom and watching their actions until their abuse of that freedom forces him to step in. The source of tension in every episode is God's fragile relationship with the human actors whose errors bring about swift and dramatic divine reactions. There is nothing subtle about this God; he is firmly and visibly in control. Depicted in highly anthropomorphic terms, he 'walks' in the garden, he 'shuts' Noah in the ark, he 'smells' the sweet aroma of Noah's sacrifice, and he 'comes down' to scatter the Tower generation.

With God so much in the forefront, human character relationships do not develop. Because no character appears in more than one episode, all are one-dimensional figures associated with a particular sin or relationship: Cain is murderer; Noah is 'righteous before me in this generation' (7.1). Adam and Eve are only slightly deeper as characters. Adam is the hapless chump who refuses to take responsibility for his actions, while Eve is the beguiled female eager to share her sin with her husband. The only productivity to emerge from human relationships is progeny; otherwise human solidarity, as in the garden and in the city, results in sin.

The Abraham cycle, beginning with the formula in 11.27, represents a considerable advance in narrative structure and in theological sophistication, Here a single human character, Abraham, appears in every episode. The author shows him in a variety of circumstances, building a personality through multiple exposures. Although the cycle is episodic, the episodes are subordinated to a common theme stated many times: God's promise to Abraham of a son, a great nation, and a land. Even episodes that would not seem to have been originally connected with this theme contribute to its development by their placement in the cycle. For instance, the separation of Lot removes from the scene Abraham's most likely heir and creates new anxiety about how God will fulfill his promise.[7]

Through his reiterated promise God controls the action here in a more productive manner than in the primeval stories. He does not simply recoil in anger at human initiative. Instead he issues to Abraham a command—'Go from your land...'—and the promise of a reward. The futurity of the reward presses the story forward and supplies its basic

---

7.   E.M. Good, *Irony in the Old Testament* (Philadelphia: Westminster Press, 1965), p. 96.

tension. Gradually the promise to Abraham of an heir is realized as Lot, Eliezer and Ishmael are rejected and, against all human calculations, Isaac is born. Of course the fulfillment of the promise of the land remains in the future as Abraham's need to purchase a tomb for Sarah from a local Hittite baron makes only too clear.[8] God leads Abraham; he gradually makes the promise more specific and he encourages Abraham when Abraham loses hope. The relationship of God to the human actors has changed in this cycle: he does not punish but rewards the protagonist.

Furthermore, God is presented far less anthropomorphically. Although he often speaks to Abraham directly, his presence is mediated by three men when he announces the birth of Isaac and by an angel when he stops the sacrifice of the boy. He also speaks through an angel to Hagar and in a dream to Abimelekh. He continues to intervene directly in human affairs but does so more locally than in the primeval tales. Thus he closes and opens the wombs of the Egyptian women, destroys Sodom and Gomorrah with fire, and makes aged, barren Sarah conceive. All of God's actions are directed toward the fulfillment of his promise to Abraham; they are small scale miracles, not the universal creation and destruction of the first two narrative units of Genesis. Here God works *through*, not against, the obstacles which humans and nature throw up.[9] When Abraham relinquishes the future mother of Israel in order to protect his own life, God rescues her and enriches Abraham. When Sarah casts out Hagar and her son into the wilderness, God provides a spring for them to drink from. God does not compel Abraham and Sarah. They make their own decisions and he redeems their situations. God speaks personally to Abraham, like a father to a son, yet he is not present continually. He comes and goes, leaving the characters to live their own lives. Except when he tells of his intention to visit Sodom, we never see the divine mind at work as we do everywhere in the primeval stories. Those tales are told from a divine perspective; we were with God in heaven as he made his plans and decisions. Here the narrator, although revealing God's actions, is not privy to his every deliberation. Why God tests Abraham with the binding; of Isaac for instance, is never said. The omniscient narrator has moved farther from heaven and closer to earth in the Abraham cycle.

8. Good, *Irony*, p. 97.
9. N.M. Sarna, *Understanding Genesis* (New York: Schocken Books, 1970), p. 104.

Whereas in the Adam and Noah sequences the major conflicts were between God and humans, either individually or in groups, in the Abraham cycle conflicts are between persons. Abraham and Lot divide over territory, Abraham and Abimelekh quarrel over Sarah, and Sarah and Hagar become bitter rivals over their sons' inheritance. God is above these human arguments and, in fact, helps to resolve them in favor of the chosen line while, at the same time, compensating the losers. Thus God permits Sarah to expel Hagar, but assures Hagar that her son too will shall be a great nation. Similarly, Abraham retrieves Sarah unblemished from Abimelekh whose wife and female slaves then conceive as a result of Abraham's a intercession with God. God, is present not as an antagonist, as he finds himself in the primeval world, but as helpmate.

The more nuanced human interaction in the Abraham cycle is reflected in the moral realm. In the primeval history human actions were either sinful or righteous and, except for Noah, basically sinful characters, limited to appearances in single scenes, entered, sinned and were punished. Adam and Eve broke their one commandment, Cain murdered, the Tower generation failed to fill the earth and instead built a city to shut God out. In each case God pronounced judgment and punished the guilty. In the Abraham cycle, in contrast, the moral status of human actions is far more ambiguous. When Abraham tells Sarah to lie to protect his life and, furthermore, hands her over to the Pharaoh, our moral outrage is tempered by our sympathy for his all too human weakness. Indeed, he is not condemned either by God or the narrator and instead is enriched after his wife is restored. Sarah's resentment of Hagar and Ishmael is again understandable and, though Abraham is outraged, God counsels capitulation to her wishes, taking the moral sting out of her anger. Then too, the aged couple's laughter at the thought of giving birth to a son does not bring upon them the divine wrath; it is rather memorialized in the child's name. The multiple views of the leading personalities which the author provides allow for the development of characters with some moral depth. Although any one act might be viewed negatively, in context we see it as part of a larger personality pattern. Despite his lapses, Abraham emerges as a 'knight of faith'. To be sure, in the Abraham cycle we are still at a fairly rudimentary level of character development, yet the advance over the first two narrative sequences is marked.

With the Jacob cycle we reach a higher stage of both narrative and theological finesse. While the Abraham episodes were short and basically independent of each other, the Jacob stories are longer and well connected. Many of the Abraham stories could be excised without damage to our understanding of the major themes; they are self-contained vignettes. On the other hand, most of the Jacob material is necessary to the plot. Jacob's reunion with Esau, for instance, makes no sense unless we realize the circumstances in which the brothers parted company. The Jacob cycle consists of three large blocks of narrative centering on the conflicts between Jacob and Esau (Gen. 27–28; 32–33) and Jacob and Laban (29–31). These long narratives enable the author to probe deeply into the character of Jacob and his relationships with his brother and father-in-law as well as with his mother, his father and his wives. They allow for a more complex treatment of theme than did the Abraham episodes. There the reiterated divine promise kept resounding through the narrative which plodded doggedly toward its fulfillment. Here there is no such linear movement toward a resolution. Although a divine oracle at the outset of the cycle (25.23) predicts Jacob's ascendancy over Esau, subsequent events zigzag wildly, keeping tension high and the conclusion unpredictable.

The divine appearances in the Jacob cycle are less frequent than in the Abraham cycle. Although God did not enter every episode, he appeared often to Abraham and to others as well. With the exception of an oracle sought by Rebekah, God, in the Jacob cycle, speaks to Jacob alone and only at narratively strategic times and places. Jacob first encounters God on the way out of the promised land; as he flees from Esau, God promises to bring him back (28.15). Then, when Jacob returns and prepares to face Esau once more, he wrestles with a divine being and declares, 'I have seen God face to face' (32.30). These divine incursions thus act as hinges connecting the Jacob–Esau stories with the Jacob–Laban story. God appears on the border of the land blessing Jacob's exit and entrance.[10] In addition to these two connective epiphanies, God enters the story at three other important junctures. At the outset God announces to Rebekah, through an oracle, the birth of the twins. In the very center of the narrative (31.3) God initiates Jacob's return to his land with a brief imperative, reported by Jacob as a dream (31.10-13). Finally, the narrative concludes when God changes Jacob's name to Israel and affirms to him the blessing made to Abraham (35.9-12).

10. M. Fishbane, *Text and Texture: Close Readings of Selected Biblical Texts* (New York; Schocken Books, 1979), p. 54.

Not only is the divine presence more rare; it bears a more numinous quality than in the Abraham cycle. To Abraham God spoke 'naturally', without accompanying numinous phenomena. Abraham seemed neither surprised or afraid before the divine presence. To Jacob, on the other hand, God's eruptions are more eerie, more exceptional. His initial contact with God, the dream at Bethel of angels ascending and descending a ladder to the sky, surprises him with the divine *tremendum*: 'How awesome is this place! This is none other than the house of God, and this is the gate of heaven' (28.17). Similarly, the wrestling incident occurs when Jacob is alone. He is left both wounded and blessed and astonished that he has 'seen God face to face' and yet lives (32.30). No longer here is God treated as just another character in the story. Rather, he enters at crucial moments to direct the action or to affirm that events are under his control.

The lowering of the divine profile is matched by a correspondingly higher level of human responsibility for the course of events. Here it is not simply a matter of waiting, passively, for God to fulfill a promise. Rather humans intervene to alter the course of events to their own advantage.[11] So Rebekah orders Jacob to masquerade as his brother; Esau, in order to overturn Isaac's plan to give Esau his blessing; and, complementarily, Laban blocks Jacob's marriage to Rachel by substituting his older daughter Leah. Moreover, Jacob's success at selective breeding outwits Laban's efforts to prevent him from leaving Paddan-Aram. In each case, human cunning derails what seems to be certain destiny, overthrowing our expectations and putting the final outcome in doubt. Although Esau, the older son and his father's favorite, should have received the blessing, Jacob gets it. Yet he is outsmarted by Laban and then outsmarts him in turn just as there seems to be no way out of his exile in Paddan-Aram.

What is at stake in all these machinations is the fate of the blessing, the disposition of the promise to Abraham in the third generation.[12] Whereas God declared that Isaac and not Ishmael would be the chosen heir, there is no such clarity in the next generation. Not only are Esau and Jacob sons of the same mother, but they are twins. True, Rebekah hears a prenatal oracle which predicts that the elder Esau shall serve the younger Jacob (2.23), but the mode of its realization is unclear. The

11. C. Westermann, *The Promises to the Fathers: Studies on the Patriarchal Narratives* (trans. D.A. Green; Philadelphia: Fortress Press, 1980), pp. 77-78.

12. Westermann, *Promises*, p. 91.

blessing appears to be at the mercy of human wiles rather than under strict divine control. After Jacob coaxes the birthright (*bekōrāh*) out of Esau and the blessing (*berākāh*) out of Isaac, he finds himself nonetheless in mortal danger.[13] It is he, not Esau, who is forced into service: the blessing seems to bring him only trouble. Moreover, having served Laban for the younger daughter, he receives instead the older Leah (*bekōrāh*) and a reproach from Laban that stands ironically in judgment on his earlier deceit: 'It is not so done in our country, to give the younger before the first born (*bekōrāh*)' (29.26). After Jacob's blessing manifests itself in the multiplication of his flocks, he is again in peril as he prepares to meet Esau. But he wrests a blessing from the man at the Jabbok who changes his name to Israel, signalling a new beginning for the master of escapes. Indeed, he then faces Esau and gives him a 'gift' (*berākāh*, 33.11); finally reconciled with the 'blessing' and his brother though not above one last ruse: he sends Esau off to Seir without him. At the end God blesses Jacob (35.9-12) at Bethel. The blessing has travelled a circuitous human route, but at last receives divine confirmation.

Not only human action but also human character is more richly developed in the Jacob cycle. The retreat of the divine presence and the more extended narrative segments afford the author an opportunity to probe character with greater depth than in the Abraham cycle which presented short flashes of human personality. Here we see the real growth of Jacob from a 'mamma's boy', subject to Rebekah's manipulation, to a trickster in his own right against Laban, and finally to a cautious strategist in his reconciliation with Esau. Jacob becomes more independent and more shrewd but also more humble. At Bethel, first, he bargains with God, promising his fealty only if the Lord protects him (28.20-21). But at Mahanaim as he prepares to reenter the land, he prays to God, declaring himself unworthy of God's love and faithfulness (32.10-13 [Heb]). Longer dialogues and multiple appearances allow for the development of other characters as well. The pathetic Esau weeping for his father's blessing engages our sympathy, and his magnanimous treatment of Jacob at their reunion wins him respect if not admiration. The wily Laban meets his match in Jacob: their dialogues are a study in one-upmanship. And through the naming of their sons, the minor characters Rachel and Leah reveal the emotional depth of their rivalry.

If, in the Abraham cycle, individual actions were morally questionable,

---

13. See Fishbane's excellent discussion of the *berākāh-bekōrāh* motif: *Text and Texture*, pp. 50-51, 55.

Jacob's entire role as protagonist rests on deceit. At first it seems that the author condones Jacob's and Rebekah's ruse on Isaac, yet that immoral act dogs Jacob for the rest of his life. First, Laban's trick punishes Jacob with poetic justice. Then Jacob narrowly escapes Laban's wrath only to be maimed for life by the man at the river, and finally he is forced to flee from Shechem by his sons' mass murder of the inhabitants of that city. Yet, although Jacob 'pays' for his stealing of the blessing, it remains true that the promise is transmitted by immoral means. Jacob receives God's blessing despite his deceit. Conventional morality and custom cannot hold back God's chosen. Again primogeniture is overturned, by a ruse if need be, so that God's promise is realized in Jacob-Israel.

The last part of Genesis, usually called the Joseph story, is more accurately called by the name indicated in the formula which heads it: 'These are the generations (*tōledōt*) of Jacob.' This title specifies not only Joseph but the entire family of Jacob as the subject of the narrative.[14] Unlike Ishmael and Esau, who are disposed of with a genealogy, all of the sons of Jacob are part of the chosen line, and so all are included in the narrative. To be sure, Joseph is the protagonist—he is the eldest son of the favored wife, but Judah is also the subject of his own story (Gen. 38), and he and Reuben are differentiated from the other brothers in both the plot against Joseph and the later negotiations with him. Both Judah and Reuben also plead with Jacob to release Benjamin, Judah succeeding where Reuben fails (Gen. 43): Primogeniture seems to determine Judah's importance in the narrative, for the three older sons all commit crimes. Reuben, Jacob's first-born, sins by sleeping with Bilhah, Jacob's concubine, while the next two sons, Simeon and Levi, are condemned by their father for perpetrating the slaughter of the Shechemites.[15] That leaves Judah, fourth-born, as the next in line to receive his father's blessing. Indeed, in Jacob's deathbed blessing of his sons, Judah and Joseph receive the longest and most favorable blessings. So all of the sons of Jacob are accounted for in the narrative.

The narrative of Joseph and his brothers, often termed a novella, is the most tightly woven part of Genesis. It is not a cycle of stories but one continuous tale. Although certain inconsistencies, such as the identity of the people who brought Joseph to Egypt, point even here to composite authorship, the seams have been nearly erased, and the tale reads

---

14. Childs, *Introduction*, pp. 156-57.
15. Noted by J. Ackerman (personal communication).

smoothly. Every episode leads directly into its sequel in a causative chain: Jacob's favoritism leads to Joseph's pride manifested in his dreams; Joseph's dreams cause his brothers' jealousy; their jealousy prompts their plot to dispose of him; left to die he is captured and taken to Egypt; in Egypt he rises in the house of Potiphar; and so on. Each episode is thus vital to the forward movement of the plot. Even the story of Judah and Tamar, at first glance unrelated to its context, has clear verbal and thematic links to it.[16] Judah is deceived with a piece of attire even as he took the lead in deceiving his father with Joseph's tunic (Gen. 37), while his lust contrasts with Joseph's chastity (Gen. 39). The closely integrated narrative also enables the author to develop long-range suspense and thus heighten the drama of his tale. Whereas the masquerades of Jacob before Isaac and of Leah before Jacob are exposed as soon as they have accomplished their aim, in the case of Joseph's bloody robe, the brothers never disabuse Jacob of his conclusion that Joseph is dead (37.33). The 'cover-up' stands until they are forced to bring Jacob to Egypt (45.26). Similarly, Joseph conceals his identity from his brothers during several meetings with them, while the author plays upon the dramatic irony of the situation, breaking the tension only after Judah's climactic confession.

In this narrative we reach the most sophisticated treatment of God's role in human events. Here God not only does not direct the action, he never appears at all or speaks to the protagonist. Only once does God speak and then it is not to Joseph but to Jacob, sanctioning the move to Egypt and renewing the promise (46.2-4). Otherwise God is silent. However, God figures centrally in Joseph's affirmations. To God Joseph attributes his ability to interpret dreams and his providential capacity to save his family from famine (45.5-11). If God is not a visible presence, he is nonetheless credited with the invisible movement of events. He is the subtle power behind the scenes whose providence is seen in retrospect. In his final speech to his brothers Joseph affirms God's role in the entire chain of events leading up to the saving of the house of Jacob from famine; 'As for you, you meant evil against me, but God meant it for good' (50.20). Not above but within human actions God works, even if the actors are unaware of it.

In the dream motif, which serves as a fulcrum for the development of the plot, this benign power manifests itself. In the first pair of dreams (37.5-11) God is not mentioned. Joseph simply relates his dreams, and

16. Alter, *Art*, pp. 3-10.

his brother and his father declare that the dreams indicate Joseph's desire to lord it over them. Joseph might have been dismissed as an arrogant brat, but the dreams provoke the brothers enough to want to do away with him (v. 20), while Jacob 'kept the saying in mind' (v. 11). The author thus hints at the deeper significance of these dreams. In the second pair of dreams, those of the butler and the baker, Joseph acts as interpreter, declaring at the outset, 'Do not interpretations belong to God?' (40.8). Here the similarity of the two dreams belies the opposite fates awaiting the two courtiers. Joseph's accurate predictions eventually catapult him out of the dungeon and into Pharaoh's court where God's role in dream interpretation is further underscored. To Pharaoh's request that he interpret his dreams, Joseph modestly replies, 'It is not in me; God will give Pharaoh a favorable answer' (41.16). Moreover he specifically affirms that Pharaoh's two dreams have the same meaning, a signal that 'God will shortly bring it to pass' (v. 32). Even Pharaoh acknowledges that the spirit of God resides in Joseph (v. 38). So the dreams chart a steadily rising providential role in Joseph's fate. Only Joseph's own dreams remain unfulfilled. Yet, the author suggests, because Joseph's dream, like the Pharaoh's, was doubled, it will also be realized. Indeed, no sooner does Joseph in his new capacity as Pharaoh's chief aide declare that God has made him 'forget' the past (41.51) than his brothers appear and 'Joseph remembered the dreams' (42.9). His destiny now becomes clear to him, for it was written in the stars of his childhood dream. God does not actually appear to Joseph in dreams, as he did to Jacob; rather dreams serve as signals of fortune in which God's will is manifest.

Directly correlated to the diminished direct divine role in events is the augmented role of human wisdom. While Jacob is cunning, Joseph is wise. Jacob seizes the moment and acts to protect himself. Joseph is deeper, always planning for the future and biding his time. He rises to become the chief of Potiphar's house and, afterwards, to become head of the prisoners. His advice to Pharaoh involves long range strategy which wins him respect and power. And Joseph battles his own impulse to reveal himself to his brothers until they have demonstrated their trustworthiness by refusing to surrender Benjamin, as they had once left Joseph to die. Joseph's wisdom thus overarches the whole tale, from his childhood dreams to his engineering of their fulfillment

The development of Genesis characters reaches its climax in Joseph. The author depicts an even more dramatic transformation than we saw in Jacob. Joseph begins as a pompous child and, despite a series of reverses, becomes the most important man in Egypt. Unlike Jacob, who also made his fortune in a foreign country, Joseph remains there permanently and draws his family to him. The character of Joseph is built through increasingly penetrating views of his interior. At first he appears one-dimensional: he tells his dreams, but the narrator does not disclose what he thinks about them. In Potiphar's house he speaks only to refuse the wife's advances while the narrator stresses that 'the Lord was with Joseph'. But in his dealings with his brothers the author not only supplies Joseph with lengthy speeches, but reveals his behind-the-scenes behavior, calculated to show his hard-headed strategy in testing his brothers combined with his soft-hearted compassion for them. His loyalty to Pharaoh does not prevent him from using his position to protect his family. Forgiving his brothers despite their effort to kill him, Joseph rises above the fraternal rivalry that characterized his brothers and his ancestors.

Our study has charted a correlation between the successively more tightly constructed canonical units of Genesis and the progressively more subtle development of divine presence and depth of human action and character. The one episode stories cast into a sea of genealogies give way to a cycle of episodes about Abraham. The Jacob narrative features longer and better connected tales, while the story of Joseph and his brothers is a nearly seamless fabric. Over the course of these narratives God's presence in the world becomes ever more refined. The anthropomorphic God of the primeval stories who acts primarily by way of response to human initiatives becomes the promising and leading God who speaks frequently to Abraham. To Jacob he speaks only at critical junctures of his life and then in highly numinous ways, while to Joseph he does not speak at all, revealing himself instead through the ironically providential course of events. At the same time, human action becomes more independent of divine control, more autonomous. The actions of the primeval characters in the first two narrative units are followed by swift divine reactions. Abraham's activities are also rather tightly monitored by God, yet his mistakes cannot vitiate God's promise. Jacob bears the consequences of the fraud he perpetrates on his father (even as he fulfills the divine will) and matures significantly in the process. Joseph relies on his wisdom to elevate himself to Pharaoh's court and to save his family. Only in retrospect does he acknowledge God's guiding hand.

This canonical progression of structure and divine–human relationships bespeaks an effort to give clear theological shape to the ancient traditions which have been so arranged and presented. It is not a matter of the Adam and Noah materials being 'early' and primitive and the Joseph materials being 'late' and reflecting a more sophisticated theology. A late author or compiler, after all, could have reworked early material to bring it 'up to date.' But he did not. Instead Genesis appears in its final form as a four (or five) stage development of divine presence and human character. As such it presents a vision of origins which, however subliminally, has functioned normatively for those for whom this book is scripture.

Put simply, Genesis depicts the evolution of the divine–human relationship from the never-never land of Eden to the real world of exile. In the last narrative God is present in the same manner in which he is most often present in the final author's world, not hurling floods, inducing conception in geriatrics, or communicating directly in dreams, but rather present silently within the events and so acclaimed by believers. But also, human character has developed almost analogously to biological development. At first like infants, the primeval figures need to be watched closely, slapped down immediately. Then, like a growing child, Abraham is led and guided with the vision of the future always before him. Jacob, like a man who has reached majority, takes charge of his life and responsibility for his actions. Finally Joseph, like a person wise in years, acts determinedly, with faith in God, and thereby preserves his family.

In the view of Genesis, then, the operating relationship between God and humankind did not emerge full-blown. God's choice of Abraham and his descendants to be the progenitors of the chosen people gave the human drama protagonists who gradually exercise greater human freedom in consonance with the divine will. The rebellious abuse of freedom in Eden gives way to the faith of Abraham, the boldness of Jacob, and the wisdom of Joseph. In stages, the divine director retreats from the scene permitting his actors to shape their own world. Finally, equilibrium is achieved as Joseph and his brothers, acting on their own initiative, unwittingly and ironically become the agents of providence.

JSOT 30 (1984), pp. 25-50

THE CEREMONIAL AND THE JUDICIAL:
BIBLICAL LAW AS SIGN AND SYMBOL*

Bernard S. Jackson

Introduction

When my thesis was published by the Clarendon Press some 10 years ago, one reviewer kindly wrote that this book shows that biblical law can only be studied as law. At the time, I was puzzled; the reviewer was the chaplain of a Cambridge college, and had himself written a book on biblical law. It was only some years later that I learned that this chaplain had himself trained as a solicitor before turning to the ministry. Anthony Phillips has since become a very good friend, despite our long-standing and continuing controversies regarding biblical criminal law. Today, I wish to resist even the claims of disciplinary privilege; I would like to suggest that biblical law is too important to be left to the lawyers.

Some may rejoice in this apparent—and I do stress, apparent—self-denial. But I fear that the alternative for which I shall argue may prove no more palatable. For any who think that biblical law may represent a safe haven for those who would resist the inroads of structuralism and semiotics into biblical studies, I have an unwelcome message. The semiotics of biblical law can no longer be ignored.

* Much of the analysis which is applied in this lecture was developed as part of a project on the relationship between structuralism and law, generously supported by a Personal Research Award of the Social Science Research Council. The present paper was delivered at the Department of Religious Studies, Yale University, December 9th, 1982.

Aquinas

Of course, the issue is not a new one, despite the huge advances in theory and methodology made in the current generation. I would like to draw your attention to the famous Thomist classification of biblical law, into the categories of the 'moral', 'ceremonial' and 'judicial' (*Summa* 1a 2a e, Qu. 101.2). Aquinas presents the 'ceremonial' precepts, which regulate the worship of God, as 'figurative', since humans cannot directly perceive divine truth in itself; he distinguishes the 'judicial' precepts, which represent the *ius divinum positivum* governing relations between people (Qu. 104.1) as being figurative only in a secondary sense. He goes on (104.2):

> There are two ways in which a precept may be figurative. First, primarily and in itself, in that it was enacted principally to be a figure of something. The ceremonial precepts were figurative in this way; for they were instituted in order to be figurative of something connected with the worship of God and the mystery of Christ. Some precepts, on the other hand, are figurative not primarily and in themselves, but as a consequence; and this is how the judicial precepts were figurative. These were not enacted in order to be figurative of anything, but to regulate the state of the people in accordance with justice and equity. Yet they were figurative as a consequence; inasmuch as the entire state of that people, which was regulated by these precepts, were figurative, according as it was written, *All things happen to them in figure (Hebrews* 9.9).

In assessing this passage, we must distinguish the content of the interpretation which Aquinas places upon these various types of biblical laws, and the claims which he makes regarding the manner of their signification. The content of the interpretation is christological: the ceremonial laws not only prescribe the present form of worship of God, but also pre-figure the sacrifice of Jesus. From this, it follows that continued adherence to the ceremonial precepts is regarded by Aquinas as mortal sin, as involving a denial that the prophecy of the ceremonial laws had been fulfilled. But for present purposes, it is the semiotic theory of Aquinas which is of greater interest. We may rephrase his argument in the form of the following general claims: (1) within biblical law, there exist different forms of signification; (2) the same biblical law may be endowed with different levels of signification—as where the 'judicial' laws bear distinct primary and secondary semiotic functions; (3) the differences between these groups of laws, and the respective semiotic functions attached to them, are to be regarded within the context of a communications model: laws are ceremonial or judicial, they prefigure primarily or secondarily, because they have been instituted *for that purpose*. In other words, we have here an author who intended not merely that a certain message be communicated, but that it be communicated in certain ways.

It is on this last point that a modern semiotic theory would depart from the formulations of Aquinas. For it is clear that the attribution of a secondary semiotic function to the judicial laws is regarded by Aquinas as peculiar to biblical law, and that it reflects a conscious decision on the part of the—here divine—author. He tells us that the Jewish people were chosen by God as that from which Christ was to be born, and that it is for this reason that the entire state of the Jewish people—including its judicial arrangements—must have been 'prophetical and figurative'. He explicitly distinguishes the judicial precepts given to the Jewish people from those given to other peoples: 'its wars and acts are explained mystically, but not those of the Assyrians or Romans, which were far more eminent in a human view' (104.2). The editor of the Blackfriars edition gives as an example the rules under which Israel was to muster for a holy war, and the measures of sanctification prescribed for those participating in it. These rules of Deuteronomy 20 are taken to foreshadow the measures of sanctification to be adopted by the members of the Church in their war against Satan. I would suggest that we do not have to adopt any such particularist theological viewpoint in order to accept the idea that even 'judicial' laws may have a secondary semiotic function. But this function may very well not be associated with the conscious purposes of the author, the emitter of the message, but may very well be inherent in the language which is chosen, taken in the context of the social setting within which it is used.

In other respects, too, the Thomist view has to be regarded in a broader context. If we categorize the 'primary' semiotic function attributed to the judicial laws as either 'literal' or 'instrumental', it does not follow that the only type of secondary semiotic function will be 'prefiguration' in the historical or chronological sense of the Thomist argument. Today, we may be more inclined to identify such secondary semiotic functions with connotations regarding the present state of society, values and so on. Yet on reflection, even this difference partially dissolves. We have to take account of the difference between our conception of time and that of the Bible. Wacholder has well argued for what I might call an 'integral' conception of the past and the future as exemplified by the Mishnah, within the context of which the present is regarded as a temporary aberration pending the restoration of first commonwealth institutions. This is the converse of the Matthaean claim that Jesus comes to 'fulfil' (*pleroun*) the old law—which must be counted as an important source of the Thomist argument which we have here been considering.

We could spend much time reconstructing the semiotic theory of Aquinas, and its historical sources. Assuredly, we would have to take into account the distinction between the *ḥukkim* and *mishpatim* of Maimonides—to whom Aquinas refers on several occasions as Rabbi Moyses. Maimonides too adopts a communicational model, in the sense that the laws all have an author who has a purpose not only in respect of the content of the law, but also in respect of their form. The divine author makes choices regarding the manner in which different types of law signify. Some are self-evidently beneficial—the *mishpatim*; others are not self-evidently beneficial, even though in fact they are beneficial—the *ḥukkim*. In the case of the latter, Maimonides tells us that God deliberately hid their reasons in order that they should not be held in little esteem (*Guide* III.26); and it is these which largely correspond to the Thomist category of ceremonial laws. Again, there is a modern ring to this argument: witness the interest in the manner and degree to which semiotic systems conceal as well as reveal. In his classification of biblical law, Maimonides is more concerned with the rational status of the different categories than with the manner of their signification. Nevertheless, his legal philosophy contributes to legal semiotics by stressing the range of objectives of the biblical law. The intention of the law is the welfare of both the body and the soul, the latter being conceived in terms of the acquisition of true beliefs. The 613 commandments can thus be related to the three goals of the establishment of civilized society, the development of the ethical personality and intellectual perfection.[1] But ultimately the welfare of the body is itself conceived as a means towards the welfare of the soul. It follows, therefore, that the *mishpatim*—even in so far as they seek the welfare of the body—have a secondary, longer term aim. Maimonides thus anticipates Aquinas in denying any exclusively instrumental role to the judicial laws. For Aquinas they have an ultimate signification; for Maimonides an ultimate purpose.

1.   I. Twersky, *The Code of Maimonides* (Judaica Series, 22; New Haven: Yale University Press, 1980), p. 388.

Semiotics and the Philosophy of Language

Modern philosophy and linguistics have gone much further in analysing the semiotics of language in general and linguistically expressed cultural systems in particular. In Europe and Latin America, attempts are getting under way to apply the insights of these traditions to legal texts and to examine their implications for legal philosophy. Legal semiotics may still be in their infancy—certainly, when compared with the growth industry of literary structuralism. But legal semiotics will assuredly come to contribute to the study of biblical law, and I hope presently to indicate in general terms some of the areas where such contributions may be expected. But first, we must review some of the relevant claims made by philosophers and semioticians. Few of them, of course, are uncontroversial.

I start with the work of a Swedish philosopher: Bo Hanson, whose book *Application of Rules in New Situations* is significantly subtitled *A Hermeneutical Study*. Hanson suggests that rules may be used in six different ways: they may be 'archivative', storing up past values for the future, as in a data bank; they may be used in argumentation, to provide reasons for actions; they may be designed to initiate action; they may be used to awake emotions, or pose perspectives on relationships; they may be used to express ideals.[2] Positivist legal philosophy conceives of legal rules primarily in terms of the act-initiating function, with perhaps subsidiary attention to the use of legal rules in argumentation and in setting up ideals, but with very little regard to the archivative, emotion-awakening, or perspective-posing functions. Modern discussion of biblical law has concentrated upon two only of these functions, and even then has often applied a differential evaluation to them. Thus there is an increasingly common recognition that many of the norms formally stated as laws in the Bible are to be regarded as 'ideal', so that a distinction might have to be made between 'biblical law' and the 'law of biblical society'. Side by side with this distinction one frequently finds a degree of apology: the biblical law is 'only' ideal; through it we have little access to the 'real' law. But this kind of judgment takes us nowhere unless we ask a further question. If the function of a rule is ideal rather than norm-initiation, is this because of some failure in the logistics of the

---

2. B. Hanson, *Application of Rules: New Situations: A Hermeneutical Study* (Lund: Gleerup, 1977), pp. 138-140.

legal system of biblical society—which makes it impossible sufficiently to make the law known or enforce it, or does this represent the intention of the author of the law, that it should serve primarily as an ideal? To my mind, this question has not yet been sufficiently addressed by students of biblical law, with the result that the emergent consensus on the 'ideal' nature of much biblical law may prove rather shallow. The semioticians may, perhaps, be able to contribute to the answer, in so far as they can establish differentiating characteristics of utterances designed to initiate action and utterances designed to set up ideals.

I use the term 'utterances' advisedly. For here we encounter some important issues raised by the philosophy of language. Every norm proposition, such that x ought to do y, might be said to have a value, a meaning. That meaning is a matter of semantics. Contrary to the views of some philosophers of language, such as Grice, who identify 'meaning' with the utterer's intention.[3] I would argue that the meaning of a proposition (as opposed to an utterance) should be regarded as the sense which would be attributed to it, at the time of its utterance, by the linguistic community concerned, on the assumption that no contextual factors are regarded as salient. But meaning cannot be found in practice in isolation. Pure semantics are found only in the imagination of linguists, as John Lyons has acknowledged.[4] What we find in practice—at the level of *parole* rather than *langue*—is the *utterance* (whether spoken or in writing) of a norm-proposition, and any such utterance (unless made by an automaton) requires consideration of the pragmatics of language, and not merely its semantics. The use made of a rule-proposition does involve consideration of the intentions of the user of that rule. But who is the user, and what do we mean by the user's intention? Both terms are potentially ambiguous. The user, I would argue, includes the person who seeks to 'apply' the rule, just as much as the person who utters the rule with a particular purpose in mind. Every application of a rule is therefore a matter of pragmatics, not pure semantics. There is a conceptual distinction between interpretation on the one hand and meaning on the other. At the same time, the intentions of the user may be multiple, and they may not be consciously articulated. The more conventional the purposes for which rules are used, the more they may

3.   See P. Grice, 'Meaning', *Philosophical Review* 66 (1957), pp. 377-88; *idem*, 'Utterer's Meaning and Intentions', *Philosophical Review* 78 (1969), pp. 147-77.
4.   J. Lyons, *Language and Linguistics: An Introduction* (Cambridge: Cambridge University Press, 1981), p. 168.

recede into the semi-conscious realms of purposive action.

To these concerns the semiotician brings an additional element: the analysis of different types of signifying system. A commonly drawn distinction, although the terminology is apt to vary, is that between 'sign' and 'symbol'. Signs operate as part of a code, with a high level of immediate and manifest intelligibility amongst the community of sign-users. Saussure[5] taught that the effectiveness of the linguistic sign resulted from its arbitrary nature: there is normally no natural or rational connection between the sound-image (the signifier) and the mental-image or concept (the signified) in the linguistic sign. By contrast, symbols (in the sense of Barthes rather than Peirce) are relatively motivated, in that they depend upon some real connection between signifier and signified. This real connection, of course, is mediated through the human mind, and therefore requires interpretation. Thus, to polarize these distinctions, the linguistic sign belongs to the semantic sphere of signification, while the symbol belongs to the motivated, pragmatic sphere of communication.

We may now attempt to apply these conceptions to law, conceived as a system of cultural semiotics. Law is expressed largely, though by no means exclusively, through language. To the extent that its linguistic manifestation can be regarded as norm statements, isolated from their utterance, they depend upon signs which operate in an arbitrary, code like fashion. But once taken in the context of pragmatics, as norm statements which are uttered, we are confronted by the need to determine the use or uses to which they are put. One such use is 'interpretation'. Here, the norm statement, though expressed in signs, becomes a symbol, in that we are no longer concerned merely with the sense-relations presented by the linguistic manifestation, but rather with a rational reconstruction of the connection between that meaning on the one hand and the situation in which application is to be made on the other. The French linguist Georges Mounin has argued strongly that law operates with symbols, not signs.[6] It has a significance, which falls to be interpreted, like the analysis required in a science or the understanding

5. F. de Saussure, *Course in General Linguistics* (trans. W. Baskin; London: Peter Owen [from 1916 French edition]), pp. 67-70.

6. G. Mounin, 'La linguistique comme science auxiliaire dans les disciplines juridiques', *Archives de Philosophie du Droit* 19 (1974), pp. 7-16. See also B.S. Jackson, 'Structuralisme et "sources du droit"', *Archives de Philosophie du Droit* 27 (1982), pp. 147-60, pp. 148-49.

required of a work of art or piece of architecture. On this view, expressed most radically by Dan Sperber, symbolism—albeit structured—is wrongly conceived as a form of semiology: signs are instruments in communication; symbols are means towards the construction of knowledge.[7]

There are, however, some necessary qualifications to attach to this radical polarization between sign and symbol. The model of the code exemplified by the linguistic sign is that of face-to-face communication. Decoding is meant to be immediate, in temporal as well as epistemological terms. As soon as the message is written down, thus presupposing its preservation for non-immediate as well as immediate communication, we get a form of cultural semiotics where the code must take account of a wider range of receivers. The message must be expressed in a way which assumes an even lesser degree of contextual salience. In law, this results in what has been described as the 'open texture' of legal rules, according to which the presence of a fixed linguistic expression entails the presence of a 'penumbra of uncertainty' surrounding a 'central core of undisputed meaning'.[8] This may be regarded as an inevitable by-product of the departure from the face-to-face model of oral communication, and already constitutes a movement from sign towards symbol. But in addition to such unmotivated indeterminacy of language, we also encounter in law forms of 'motivated indeterminacy', where the emitter of the message deliberately uses words which can have no immediate reference without further semantic input on the part of the receiver. This is the case when general standards are used in legal rules, such as the standard of reasonableness, the notion of a 'fair rate of pay', or a 'safe place of work'. Here, the objective may be to present to the receiver an instrument which can be used as the basis of construction of further knowledge, a delegation of meaning, a symbol to be interpreted. The theory of Jewish law, we may note, recognizes the function of the biblical text as symbols requiring interpretation, but at the same time seeks uniquely to identify this constructive activity with the emitter of the original message. It does so through the theory of the oral law—a message taken to be emitted from the same source as the written law, but to be essentially rational and multivocal, in contradistinction to the arbitrary and univocal use of linguistic signs in the original message:

7.   D. Sperber, *Rethinking Symbolism* (Cambridge: Cambridge University Press, 1975).

8.   H.L.A. Hart, *The Concept of Law* (Oxford: Clarendon Press), pp. 12, 121.

'These and these are the words of the living God' (*Erubin* 13b).

In other ways too, the distinction between sign and symbol requires qualification. The Saussurian notion of the arbitrariness of the linguistic sign was formulated with reference to semantic denotation. Later, emphasis has come to be placed upon the connotative functions of language. The same linguistic sign may operate arbitrarily with reference to denotation, but non-arbitrarily with respect to connotation. And as regards connotation, however structured we may take it to be, it becomes even more difficult to isolate the semantic from the pragmatic aspects; thus language use, and the communicational purposes of the users, however unconscious, come into play. Further, we may observe the possibilities of movement between the two categories: signs may become symbols, and vice versa.

This is particularly important when we consider the different semiotic systems involved in written law. On the one hand, we have the use of linguistic signs (in their written form) which signify the content—and indeed some of the connotations—of the norm statement. But this is not the only type of signification involved; it is not, for example, the concern of Aquinas in his discussion of the figurative character of biblical law. The second level of signification is that in which the content of the norm-proposition is taken as the signifier, and where the need arises to identify the signified. If, however, the distinction between sign and symbol is applied, we might conclude that talk of 'signifier' and 'signified' is inappropriate at this level, in that we are here dealing with symbols and not signs. We assume there to be some rational, non-arbitrary connection between the content of the norm-propositions and what we might call their further significance. That further significance is a matter of interpretation, and may or may not be part of the message which the emitter of the norm-proposition intended to convey. Yet we must be alive to the possibility that the nature of this signifying relationship can change from symbol to sign. The cultural significance of a norm, going beyond the meaning of the words used to express it, may become so internalized in a society that the norm evokes a particular feeling of significance without reflection or interpretation; the significance becomes—in that cultural community—wholly conventional. Even if that further significance was not part of the message originally intended to be communicated by the original emitter, every subsequent user of the norm-proposition becomes a secondary emitter, for whom the further significance of the norm is necessarily part of its message. The symbol has become a sign.

Present Approaches to Biblical Law

Let us now survey some current approaches to biblical law, in the light of these theoretical perspectives. The study of biblical law currently exhibits a healthy range of methodological approaches, but all too many of them—including some with which I have been associated—pay insufficient attention to semiotic issues, and therefore present at best an incomplete and at worst a misleading picture. I should like to comment briefly upon six currently employed approaches, and then go on to sketch some of the implications of the semiotic orientation for which I have been arguing.

The *first* is the kind of legal approach which my friend Anthony Phillips so generously commended. It seems straightforward, natural and obvious. We are studying 'biblical law', so who better than a lawyer to interpret it. But commonsensical arguments like this can be deceptive. First we should note that really this 'legal' approach involves the use of a comparative legal methodology. The biblical text is assumed to be 'law', and is being compared, often tacitly, with the kind of expectations regarding the phenomenon 'law' which the interpreter has derived from *other* sources. One advantage of a familiarity with other systems of ancient law, such as Roman law, Greek law and ancient Near Eastern law, is that the legal analyst can seek to make his interpretations not on the basis of modern law, but in terms of something geographically and chronologically closer to the biblical law material. All the same, the analysis is comparative. But before comparison can be made, we have to establish the comparability of the data. We cannot simply assume it. More often than not, the 'legal' approach to biblical law assumes that the biblical texts can be interpreted in the light of some universal system of legal signs, to which a lawyer has privileged access. But this assumption makes three different types of claim, all of which call for scrutiny (though not on this occasion): first, that the biblical norms belong to some larger cross-cultural class—a claim, incidentally, that we have seen denied by Aquinas; secondly, that this class can be properly designated 'legal'—a further implied subsumption within an analytical concept derived from the experience of our own culture; and thirdly, that the lawyer does indeed have a privileged access. It is this last claim that most directly raises the semiotic questions posed in this lecture. Does legal training provide privileged access because the text employs the signs of some special and presumably cross-cultural legal code? Or is this privileged access the result of special facility in the interpretation of a special type of symbol? If the latter, is it indeed the symbol which is special, or the conventions—termed 'legal'—of interpreting it? Let me simply state, without arguing, my preference for this last view.

The *second* approach is that which we may call the 'literary-historical' approach. Often, this goes in combination with a legal approach, on the assumption that the lawyer has privileged access not merely to legal codes or symbols, but also to typical progressions within legal history. But the comment I wish to make on this approach does not depend on that combination. Allow me to exemplify what I mean by reference to my article on the *lex talionis* as it appears in Exodus 21.[9] I argued that the difficulties of the present text are best understood in terms of a process of literary accretion. Originally, I suggested, verses 21 and 22, which refer to the pregnant woman caught up in a brawl, stood alone, and provided rules for *Frühgeburt* on the one hand and miscarriage on the other. Later, the talionic formula was added in verse 23, with consequential effects upon the meaning of verses 21 and 22. Despite the responses which my suggestion evoked, I still consider it the best available solution to a highly intractable set of problems. But I am increasingly worried by the following general consideration. When we consider the traditional text, we have a document which can be studied from both semantic and pragmatic viewpoints. The content of the norm-propositions can be studied, not in the abstract sense in which a linguist does 'semantics', but in addition with the resources available to study the act of enunciation of those norms. This is, in principle, available to us—even though hitherto it has perhaps been insufficiently utilized. But once we seek to reconstruct earlier stages of the text, we are in the realms of norm-propositions isolated from any context of their enunciation—unless we seek to reconstruct or assume the latter. We are, in short, assuming that our postulated *Urtext* bore the meaning which would have been attributed to it by the conventions of the linguistic community in which it was uttered, on the assumption of minimal contextual salience—and this very often without any attempt whatsoever to identify what that linguistic community will have been, and how it

9. B.S. Jackson, 'The Problem of Exodus xxi 22-25 ("Ius Talionis")', *VT* 23 (1973), pp. 273-304

may have differed from the linguistic community of the text we have before us. Despite this, I would not wish to forsake literary-historical approaches, notwithstanding some strong current trends in that direction in biblical scholarship. Rather, I would urge that the literary-historical approach demands far more of us than had hitherto been assumed, in that the semiotic questions must be addressed to each successive postulated stage of the text.

A *third* approach is that which seeks to relate the norms of biblical law to their underlying principles, and further seeks to distinguish those principles from their counterparts in the ancient Near Eastern documents. This is the approach of Moshe Greenberg[10] in his famous article in the 1960 Kaufmann Festschrift, which has been followed by Shalom Paul,[11] Anthony Phillips[12] and others. It is an approach whose methodological weaknesses I sought to expose on conventional historical grounds, in an article entitled 'Reflections on Biblical Criminal Law'.[13] Today, I would formulate some of the theoretical objections to this approach in semiotic terms. I would ask the adherents of this approach whether they regard the specific norms of biblical law as signs or as symbols of the alleged principles. I would ask whether the relationship of these norms to the alleged principles are to be regarded as the primary function of the norms which their emitters seek to communicate, or whether this relationship represents but a secondary communicational intent, or even no communicational intent at all? The answer to this question would have to take account of the audience to which the norms were directed. For example, Greenberg would have to tell us what kind of audience would be expected to know about the vicarious punishment of children in the Code of Hammurabi, when he claims that Exod. 21.31, which applies to the killing of free children the same rules as are stated for the killing of adults by a goring ox, reflects the principle of rejection of such vicarious punishment in biblical law. Moreover, I think that the proponents of the 'principles' approach have a further question to answer: if stress upon the moral distinctiveness of biblical ethics is the

10. M. Greenberg, 'Some Postulates of Biblical Criminal Law', *Yehezkel Kaufmann Jubilee Volume* (Jerusalem: Magnes Press, 1960).

11. S. Paul, *Studies in the Book of the Covenant in the Light of Biblical and Cuneiform Law* (Leiden: Brill, 1970).

12. A. Phillips, *Ancient Israel's Criminal Law* (Oxford: Basil Blackwell, 1970).

13. B.S. Jackson, 'Reflections on Biblical Criminal Law', *JJS* 24 (1973), pp. 8-38.

primary message of these norms, then why are specific norms—rather than more conventional wisdom forms—employed for this purpose? The answer, of course, might very well be that this stress was not the primary communicational intent, but rather a secondary message. But then, I suspect, one would have even more difficulties in reconstructing the audience within which such a message would be meaningful. My conclusion is that the 'principles' approach does not reflect a semiotic model at all, but rather is a particular use of biblical law as 'symbols'. The fact that the form which this 'symbolic interpretation' takes is a rational reconstruction of the law in terms of some relatively familiar values does not detract from the fact that the norms are being viewed as 'symbols' in the sense, for example, of Sperber. In other words, Greenberg and the others, like the Rabbis, are engaged in hermeneutics.

I pass now to a *fourth*, and highly distinctive, approach to biblical law—the 'narrative' approach of Calum Carmichael. Carmichael increasingly argues that the norms of biblical law were not written for instrumental purposes at all—not even in the sense of 'practical wisdom'—but rather constitute a particular form of reflection upon earlier biblical narratives. Carmichael's work has attracted a good deal of bewilderment, indeed bemusement. But I don't think it can be dismissed out of hand. Carmichael has at least refused to take for granted the identification of these norms as 'laws' which has come to appear—from the moment when the Greek term *nomos* was first used to translate *torah*—as natural if not self-evident. Indeed, there are occasions when Carmichael's approach seems to me to work at least as well as any other form of interpretation. I think, for example, of his analysis of the difficult divorce norms in Deuteronomy 24.[14] When we approach the matter in more general theoretical terms, it becomes evident that the categories of 'law' and 'narrative' have a good deal in common. The French structuralist Greimas has, in fact, sought to apply his 'grammaire narrative' to a French statute on company law, and what I think emerges is the fact that his narrative grammar works even better for law than it does for narrative. The underlying points of contact are the facts that both law and narrative concern goal-oriented human action, and that both have relatively non-reversible temporal dimensions. The literary structure of the Pentateuch is itself a mixture of these two forms of discourse, and it may well be that the semiotician can provide a more satisfactory

14. C.M. Carmichael, *The Laws of Deuteronomy* (Ithaca: Cornell University Press, 1974), pp. 203-207.

account of this mixture than has hitherto been available. Some particular narratives clearly have a legal type message—notably, that of the daughters of Zelophehad—and when we reach the story of Susanna we find a whole tale which, it has been plausibly argued,[15] was written to propagandize a particular reform in legal procedure. If, then, the narrative form can be used to transmit a legal message, we should not exclude the possibility that the legal form can be used to transmit a narrative message.

Nevertheless, Carmichael too must answer the kind of semiotic questions which I posed a moment ago in respect of the 'principles' approach of Greenberg. Are the norms to be regarded as 'signs' of the narrative revisions which Carmichael proposes, or are they rather symbols? If they are signs, does the narrative message reflect the primary communicational goal of the writers, or only a secondary goal? All the indications are that Carmichael believes that these norms did serve as signs of the narrative messages, and that this message is not to be regarded as any secondary figuration but rather the primary communicational intent. Again, we must ask what kind of cultural or linguistic community must be presupposed by such a view? Presumably it must have been a highly select and sophisticated secret society, since this message has remained concealed from biblical times until Carmichael. Again, we have to ask: Why choose this particular form in order to express this type of message? Clearly, there were alternative forms available. We only have to look at the ways in which narratives are recycled within the Bible, while remaining within the narrative mode. The relationship of Chronicles to Kings is not the only example.

A *fifth* approach may be termed 'philosophical'. I am thinking primarily of the 'cosmological' approach of Jacob J. Finkelstein in his partly posthumous study of the goring ox provisions.[16] It was Finkelstein himself who termed his approach 'cosmological', in that it sought to interpret the norms against the views held in that society of the relationship of humanity to the natural world. Finkelstein discerned a

15. See D. Daube, 'Texts and Interpretations in Roman and Jewish Law', *JJS* 3 (1961), pp. 3-28, 12-14. See also B.S. Jackson, 'Susanna and the Singular History of Singular Witnesses', *Acta Juridica* (1977), pp. 37-54.

16. J.J. Finkelstein, 'The Goring Ox. Some Historical Perspectives on Deodands, Forfeitures, Wrongful Death and the Western Notion of Sovereignty', *Temple Law Quarterly* 46.2 (1973), pp. 169-290; *idem*, 'The Ox That Gored', *Transactions of the American Philosophical Society* 71.2 (1981), pp. 1-89.

major divide between the Bible and ancient Near Eastern literature in this regard in that the Bible alone regarded humans as a category apart, and gave them dominion over a hierarchical natural order. In Mesopotamia, by contrast, humanity was simply part of the continua of the natural world, so that no special value was attached to it. The norms of the respective civilizations, regarding the ox that killed a human being, reflected this difference in cosmological orientation. Finkelstein appears to make no semiotic claims in respect of this interpretation. The respective cosmological orientations might well be part of the tacit philosophical assumptions of the authors of the laws and no part of the message which they seek, even by connotation to convey. Some may think that the approach I adopted in a previous article on the concept of religious law in Judaism should be similarly viewed.[17] There I argued that a 'structural principle'—the difference between the human and the divine—is reflected, albeit in different ways, in biblical and rabbinic law, particularly with respect to the limits of human cognition. In this sense, aspects of biblical law taken together could constitute a reflection upon human nature. But since there was little semiotic connection between the different examples I offered, one might conclude that any such principle again represents a tacit philosophical assumption of the authors, rather than the message which—even secondarily—they seek to communicate.

What I would distinguish as the *sixth*—and last—approach to biblical law is more genuinely 'structural', in that its analyses are applied to a more discrete literary unit, such as a chapter of biblical text. Of Mary Douglas, I shall have a word to say very shortly. I prefer for the moment to exemplify this approach by reference to Calum Carmichael's discussion of the prohibition of seething a kid in its mother's milk. Carmichael suggests that the author was concerned to forbid what were viewed as unnatural mixtures, and in particular to keep apart the spheres of life—the life-giving milk on which the very animal was weaned—and death—that same milk being used as the instrument of the animal's death. In Deuteronomy, Carmichael is able to argue that the otherwise disparate material in whole chapters is united by this kind of theme.[18] This kind of approach might be thought to be in line with the views of

17. B.S. Jackson, 'The Concept of Religious Law in Judaism', *Aufstieg und Niedergang der römischen Welt* (Berlin: de Gruyter, 1979), pp. 33-52.

18. Carmichael, *The Laws of Deuteronomy*, pp. 152-53; see also *idem*, 'On Separating Life and Death: An Explanation of Some Biblical Laws', *HTR* 69 (1976), pp. 1-7.

Mary Douglas, who has attempted to explain the whole range of
permitted and forbidden foods in terms of the maintenance of basic
classificatory categories. But she has since come to regard the analysis in
Purity and Danger as inadequate, in that it provided merely 'an
interlocking system of categories of thought which has no demonstrable
relation to the social life of the people who think in these terms'.[19] In
other words, one might say that this type of explanation only accounts
for the semantic level of the discourse, not its pragmatics. One still has to
ask for what purpose the enunciators of the norm sought to use it, and
why they used this particular norm-proposition in order to exemplify
their abhorrence of unnatural mixtures, rather than others. When these
questions are asked, the traditional historical types of explanation are
seen not to be incompatible with the structural approach. We may,
indeed, go back to Maimonides (*Guide* III.48), who suggested that this
law may reflect a reaction against Canaanite ritual—a view which some
have thought to be confirmed in modern times by a Ugaritic text.[20]
Here, I would suggest, we are approaching an integral view of the
different semiotic levels of the text. The primary goal may very well
have been the prohibition of a known Canaanite ritual, but this does not
necessarily reduce the message regarding unnatural mixtures to that of a
background philosophical assumption, such as was suggested in some of
the other approaches here surveyed. One could very well envisage a
semi-conscious awareness of the tabu against unnatural mixtures as the
reason for the prohibition. The lawyer, incidentally, is quite familiar with
the kind of distinction I have here drawn between a 'semi-conscious
awareness' and a background philosophical assumption. In the law of
contract, a term is said to be 'implied' (and therefore part of the contract)
if, when put to the parties, they would immediately and spontaneously
affirm that it was part of their intentions. If, on the other hand, they
would be puzzled by it, or would have to take time to consider, then the
term, though compatible with their intentions—is no part of the contract.
In this way, one can distinguish between the 'implied' and the 'implicit'.
In the case of biblical law, one would usually look for some explicit

   19. M. Douglas, *Implicit Meanings* (London: Routledge & Kegan Paul, 1975),
p. 144.
   20. See B.S. Jackson, 'History, Dogmatics and Halakah', in *idem* (ed.), *Jewish
Law in Legal History and the Modern World* (The Jewish Law Annual Supplementary
Series, 2; Leiden: Brill, 1980), pp. 1-26; especially n. 35 on M. Haran, 'Seething a
Kid in its Mother's Milk', *JJS* 30 (1978), pp. 23-35.

mention elsewhere of the underlying rationale, in order to regard it as an 'implied' rather than merely 'implicit' part of the message of a particular norm.

Methodological Implications of a Semiotic Approach

How are we to implement the semiotic approach which I have outlined in this lecture? Some of the means are traditional, although the semiotic perspectives gives them a new significance. Let me proffer one general remark, and four more specific suggestions.

The general remark relates to the expectations which we may attach to our methodology. Our expectations must be linked to our objectives, and it has been part of the argument of this lecture that the semiotic objective must be distinguished from that of interpretation or hermeneutics. This has particular relevance as to the power of the explanation with reference to details of the biblical text. The historical approach to the Bible has rightly stressed the need for explanation to account as powerfully as possible for detail, this in line with the historical orientation towards the explanation of particularity. But this is not the semiotic approach, and the semiotic methodology should not therefore be expected to produce explanations which are maximally powerful with regard to detail. This view, incidentally, has a long ancestry in the rationalist philosophy of law: Aristotle argued that some norms were morally indifferent—one had to have a rule, but its content was a matter of indifference. And Maimonides even suggested that the search for *ta'ame hamitsvot*, when applied to all the *details* of the laws, became a form of madness. Again, we have to distinguish the levels of the text. Pragmatic considerations may account for many aspects of the surface manifestation, but not all of these aspects will turn out to be salient to the real message which is sought to be conveyed. Narrative again provides an interesting parallel. Most people can recognize the structure of the plot, and structuralist critics will seek to formalize this recognition. In so doing, they do not—or should not—claim to be providing a full account of the *surface* level of the narrative. Thus, those who condemn structuralist accounts as trivial or formal reductionism confuse the levels of analysis.

And now, some methodological suggestions. First, I urge that we pay full attention to what the texts tell us about the nature of the message. Often, there is more information than one might suppose in apparently

standard introductory formulae. Take the single verse introduction to the
mishpatim: ואלה המשפטים אשר תשים לפניהם (Exod. 21.1). This is hardly
what one would expect as the introduction to a law code; it is very
different indeed from the prologues to either Hammurabi or Justinian. In
fact, we get a very clear idea of what the author or editor—for even the
latter in semiotic terms must be counted as a sender of the message—
intends us to believe regarding the nature of the norms. The form is
exactly comparable to that of the instruction given by God to Moses in
ch. 19, to transmit the offer of the Covenant to Israel: אלה הדברים אשר
תדבת אל בני ישראל (19.6). And if this were not enough, the terminology
of placing the offer of the Covenant before the people is also repeated:
תשים לפניהם in 21.1 echoes the action of Moses on descending from
Sinai and calling together the Elders of the people: וישם לפניהם את בל
הדברים האלה (19.7). The understanding of the editor that these rules
were part of the Covenant must, at the very least, be taken into account
when we consider the use that was to be made of them. In short, the
introductory formula to the *mishpatim* provides us with an act of enunciation; we are not therefore reduced to studying the *mishpatim* as pure
semantics, supposedly legal statements with minimal contextual salience.
We have some access to the pragmatics as well as the semantics of
biblical law.

   Some may think that such an approach takes us back to fairly
traditional biblical theology. I beg to differ. The concept of covenant
itself cries out for a semiotic interpretation. What kind of communication
is it? What does it imply regarding the manner of use of the norms
which it contains? What assumptions of mediacy or immediacy are
made? How far does the audience extend? Does it imply any intentions
on the part of the author with regard to the manner of interpretation or
use? The agenda is tantalizingly long. And all this comes from a single
verse of Exodus. What are we to say of the presentation of the norms in
Deuteronomy? A sermon? A repetition? Biblical law probably provides
us with a richer range of acts of enunciation of norms than the legal
literature of any other people of antiquity. Even the legislator appears in
the text. He does not claim to be anonymous, impersonal or above the
law. He chooses entirely different forms of legitimation from modern
law. Contrast the Greimasian analysis of the semiotic structure of the
legislator in the French company law statute of 1966.[21]

   21. A.J. Greimas and E. Landowski, 'Analyse sémiotique d'un discours

A second suggestion. We must look more systematically at the evidence the Bible provides of the manner of use of biblical norms, and in so doing we should pose the kind of semiotic questions I have suggested in this lecture. For example, the very fact that the provisions of Exodus on the theft of animals can be used in Nathan's parable tells us that their use as symbols was acceptable. At the very least, that means that the range of uses of the rules—which we can assess, for example, against the list provided by Hanson—was wider than that with which we are familiar in modern law. In post-biblical sources, some rules of biblical law are used as proof texts. Their use as such implies a linguistic community which regards the message thereby conveyed as more demonstrable than the proposition which it is adduced to prove. A proof-text is what it says: one does not use a more questionable proposition in order to prove a less questionable proposition. Therefore, it seems that this use of biblical laws is more akin to the sign than the symbol. That conclusion becomes all the more striking when one considers the range of propositions which laws are used as proof-texts to support. Very often, they have little 'legal' import. In the New Testament, for example, the biblical witness law is used to prove the apostolic status of Paul.[22] In this context, there are interesting semiotic questions to be posed of the passage in Deuteronomy 6 which has become the first paragraph of the *shema* in the Jewish liturgy. There, the *debarim* which God commands are to count as an *ot*, a sign. Does the author there consider that they can count as a sign only through the apparently visual means of binding on your hands and as 'frontlets' between your eyes (the origins of our *tephilin*, whatever it may originally have meant) and by inscription on the doorposts of the house?

Thirdly, we should pay particular attention to all semiotic *choices* made by the text. The analysis of what is present in the text can only proceed by reference to what is absent, but what is absent has to be defined in terms of what could have been substituted in the context of that speech community. Terminology is one such area of semiotic choice. Exodus 21.21-22 uses the unusual term *aswn*, which in the present context seems to refer to the death of a human being. But the *mishpatim* in many places refer to the death of a human being, while using the

juridique', in *Semiotique et Sciences Sociales* (Paris: Editions du Seuil, 1976), pp. 79-128.

22. B.S. Jackson, *Essays in Jewish and Comparative Legal History* (Leiden: Brill, 1975), pp. 193-96 on 2 Cor. 13.1-2.

normal verb. A choice has been made. Why? I have offered a particular explanation.[23] It may or not be correct. But all too many commentators have preferred to ignore the problem. Another area of semiotic choice is the arrangement of rules—an area where increasingly interesting work is being done. Why, for example, do we find slave laws at the beginning of the *mishpatim*, when on several occasions the *mishpatim* returns to the theme of slaves? Is the arrangement here designed to reinforce the message that this is a Covenant being offered to a group of people only recently released from slavery in Egypt? And again, there is the whole area of form criticism. This would deserve a lecture in itself, but I confine myself to one general remark. Form criticism may have exhausted itself in the quasi-historical search for *Sitzen im Leben*. But in so doing, it has provided a wealth of material for the semiotic analysis of biblical law. With its help, we can construct a typology of acts of enunciation. With the help of semiotic analysis, we may be able to relate this typology to that form of pragmatics which is called speech act analysis, and in particular to the claims currently made—by Habermas[24] and others—to the existence of a universal pragmatics. The different kinds of speech act represented by the different forms of biblical law may not take us back to identifiable historical contexts, but they may cast light upon the type of utterance being used, and the semiotic implications which it carries. Let me suggest that the type of form criticism of biblical law practised by my teacher, David Daube,[25] adumbrates precisely this approach.

Fourthly and last, let me suggest that more attention be paid to the nature of the communities within which biblical law was designed to be communicated—what Greimas terms 'groupes sémiotiques'. But how can we identify them? Partly, I suggest, through comparative cultural semiotics—the study of the typical characteristics of cultural communication in different types of groups; and partly on internal evidence. Such internal evidence can include the presence of the kind of general standards which Hart has argued represent deliberate delegations of judgment. In biblical law, for example, we have *ve'asata et hayashar*

23. Jackson, *Essays*, pp. 76-78, 95-98.

24. J. Habermas, *Communication and the Evolution of Society* (London: Heinemann, 1979), especially ch. 1.

25. D. Daube, 'Some Forms of Old Testament Legislation', *Proceedings of the Oxford Society of Historical Theology* (1944), pp. 36-46; *idem*, *Studies in Biblical Law* (Cambridge: Cambridge University Press, 1947); *idem*, *The New Testament and Rabbinic Judaism* (London: The Athlone Press, 1956).

vehatov (Deut. 6.18)—a delegation which the rabbis certainly picked up and fully exploited. Again, we have indications of methodology provided by modern socio-linguistics. I think particularly of the distinction made by Basil Bernstein between 'restricted' and 'elaborated' codes. Methods such as these may even contribute to the basic question of the nature of the norms before us. If lawyers have typical modes of communication, and these are not the typical modes of communication of biblical law, then perhaps the labelling of the material as 'law'—with all that that entails—is shown to be misleading. You will note the assumption upon which this argument is based: the designation of rules as 'legal' is a matter of pragmatics not semantics—a question of the manner in which the messages are used. Labelling the material as 'law' does not relieve us of the obligation of subjecting the material to a proper reading. And we must 'read' it in the very full sense upon which modern semiotics insists.

The Ceremonial and the Judicial

Let me return, in conclusion, to the ceremonial and the judicial. Does modern thought support the kind of semiotic distinction made by Aquinas? Jacob Neusner's work on the Mishnah might be thought to provide some clues.[26] For here we have a systematic work which, though not conceived in semiotic terms, asks a number of questions pertinent to the semiotic endeavour, and addresses itself to a range of material spanning both the Thomist categories. When Neusner's work on Damages (*Nezikin*) is published, we will be able to compare the two mishnaic orders which are most 'ceremonial' with the two which are most 'judicial'. For the moment, we must confine ourselves to the 22 volumes on *Purities*, the six on *Holy Things* and the five on *Women*. At first sight, Neusner's conclusions seem to support the Thomist distinction. Neusner appears to reveal differences in the levels and perhaps modes of communication as between the Orders. Thus *Purities* communicated an underlying system of metaphysical beliefs, not excluding matters as indirectly related to the surface subject matter of the Order as conceptions of time and space. The mode of signification comprised a

26. J. Neusner, *A History of the Mishnaic Law of Purities* (22 vols.; Leiden: Brill, 1974–); *idem, A History of the Mishnaic Law of Holy Things* (6 vols.; Leiden: Brill, 1978–); *idem, A History of the Mishnaic Law of Women* (5 vols.; Leiden: Brill, 1980).

combination of logical relationships between the detailed rules of the
system (implied analogies and contrasts), with the choices made as to
themes to be covered, forms to be used, and overall arrangement. The
system was seen as reflecting a basic metaphysic, in which 'the world is
made up of balance and order'; its development reflects, *inter alia*, the
opposition between nature and human will. With *Holy Things* (the Order
devoted to the Temple cult), the level of communication becomes more
tied down to the particular historical situation: the reaction of the authors
to the destruction of the Temple and to their gradual perception of the
non-imminence of its restoration. Although everything has changed,
history is defied with the pretence that nothing has changed, except (!)
the mode of mediation between the human and the divine:

> Cosmic order is not to be replicated. But it can at least be studied in sages'
> words. The Temple cannot be regained. It can at least be remembered in
> vivid detail supplied by the sages. If there is no access to the holy place,
> there is at least engagement with the master of the rules of the holy
> place.[27]

A classic example, one might think, of the Weberian theory of religious
law as a reaction to 'disenchantment'. Thus the mode of communication
of this deeper level of signification is, in this Order, reiteration: the fact
that Mishnah here simply works over biblical themes, without introducing its own concerns. The third Order completed by Neusner is that
entitled *Women*. Here a distinction is drawn which seems to go contrary
to the method adopted in *Purities*, and to an extent also in *Holy Things*.
The details of the law are regarded as purely practical; its systemic
(deeper) features are to be gathered not by an analysis of the underlying
logical relations between its specific rules, but by consideration of its
major theme. It is here the themes chosen (as compared with those
which could have been chosen in a different treatment of the law
relating to women) which convey the message. That message is that
women are 'abnormal and excluded, something out of the ordinary'.[28]
Thus the focus of the Order is not on the nature or rights and
obligations of women (that is, women conceived as a legal subject), but
rather on the restoration of women to normality by the regulation of
their transfer from husband to father. Like Lévi-Stauss, to whom
incidentally no reference is made, Neusner is a patriarchalist.

---

27. Neusner, *Holy Things*, VI, p. 289.
28. Neusner, *Women*, V, p. 268.

It is not entirely easy to discern the semiotic model assumed by Neusner in his analyses. On the one hand, some of his work evokes structuralist approaches to the text, which seek to view the text as autonomous from any authorial intention. But in his more explicit statements, Neusner does still stress authorial intention, and the historical circumstances of the enunciation.[29] But in that case, it becomes difficult to specify the mental state of the authors with regard to the messages which Neusner discerns. Are the messages intended to be primarily figurative, in the Thomist sense, or are these messages intended as secondary figurations? Clearly, they belong to some non-surface, non-explicit level of the text. But are we to regard them as 'implicit' or rather merely 'implied'? Again, Neusner's work appears to claim a declining distance between the signifiers and the signifieds as one progresses from *Purities* through *Holy Things* into *Women*. The manner of communication also seems to change. It would be interesting to know how Neusner would regard these different communicational processes, in terms of the distinction between 'sign' and 'symbol'. Regrettably, one must suspect that some of the differences reflect Neusner's own increasing disenchantment with the enterprise. *Purities* generated 22 volumes, *Women* only five—and this difference is not fully accounted for by the exclusion in the latter study of some of the literary questions raised in the former. Perhaps Neusner tacitly accepted the Thomist distinction as his starting point, and was thus predisposed to the view that ceremonial law requires more explanation than does judicial, in that the latter is primarily instrumental and self-evidently rational. That is, in fact, a very common assumption. But it is one of which the semiotician will be wary. The self-evidence of such rational or instrumental interpretations is regarded as a concealment of the process of choice. Culture has been made to appear as nature, and the semiotician wants to know how.

If there is a difference between the ceremonial and the judicial, its nature is far from self-evident. Clifford Geertz describes the Weberian notion of the 'disenchantment' of religion as a progression from a mode of apprehension of the divine in terms of 'numberless concrete, almost reflexive ritual gestures interspersed throughout the general round of life' by 'the construction of a consciously systematized, formal, legal-

29. See J. Neusner, *Beyond Historicism, After Structuralism: Story as History in Ancient Judaism* (The 1980 Harry Spindel Memorial Lecture; Brunswick, Maine: Bowdoin College, 1980).

moral code'.[30] But such a development can certainly not be restricted to
the ceremonial. Savigny proposed a similar development for secular law.
He was interested in 'the form...in which law lives in the common consciousness of the people'. He claimed that 'that form reveals itself in the
symbolical acts which display in visible shape the essence of the jural
relation and in which the primitive laws express themselves more
intelligibly and thoroughly than in written laws'.[31] Only later did any
necessity arise for law to be conceived in the form of logical, abstract
laws. Again, we are familiar with the theories of Mary Douglas who
interprets ritual laws in terms of social psychology. But it is this same
social psychology (unless we suppose a schizophrenic society) which
generates judicial laws, and on examination some of the same concerns
are reflected in it. George Fletcher has recently written a penetrating
analysis of the modern history of the Common Law rules of larceny,
stressing the role in it of the 'collective image of acting like a thief', with
its concern for boundaries, and so on.[32] I myself have been working on
the rules of civil liability for injury and damage caused by animals, and
find there a recurrent underlying concern with standards of appropriateness of animal behaviour—another 'boundary' case which communicates
the borderline between nature and culture.

Yet the semioticians cannot ignore the fact that a difference between
the ceremonial and the judicial *is* communicated, however much they
might seek to reduce the difference between them by pointing out their
essential commonality. The paradox is all the greater when one considers
a document like the Mishnah, which removes the kind of difference
between the groups which form criticism is capable of revealing in the
biblical texts. How is it that this difference is communicated? I suspect
that it is a function of differences in the semiotic groups to which the
laws are addressed, and the respective codes which are appropriate for
those groups. I suggest that ceremonial law originates in a narrower
semiotic group, for which a 'restrictive' code is feasible. Within that
restricted group, the shared knowledge of the community enables the

30. C. Geertz, *The Interpretation of Cultures* (New York: Basic Books, 1973),
p. 174.

31. F.K. von Savigny, 'System of Modern Roman Law', in D. Lloyd (ed.),
Jurisprudence (trans. W. Holloway; London: Stevens, 4th edn, 1979), p. 654.

32. G. Fletcher, *Rethinking Criminal Law* (Boston: Little, Brown & Co., 1978);
see also B.J. Jackson, 'Towards an Integrated Approach to Criminal Law: Fletcher's
Rethinking Criminal Law', *The Criminal Law Review* (1979), pp. 621-29.

signals to operate as signs. They can be 'primarily figurative', without being 'symbolic'. Judicial law, on the other hand, presupposes a wider group, often accompanied by delegation of the message to be conveyed to a secondary sender. In such circumstances, a more 'elaborated code' is necessary. Such an elaborated code by definition makes a greater proportion of its message explicit. More of the immediate reference of the message needs to be carried by the code, and this—together with the absence of a comparable degree of social understanding in the ultimate receivers of the message—means that the more general message is concealed at a deeper level of the text. If that hypothesis is plausible, we may note that a further aspect of medieval Christian theology receives a modern, semiotic interpretation. The ceremonial laws were for the Jews alone; the moral for humankind in general; and the judicial, though conceived for the Jews, were optional for the Gentiles. Ceremonial laws, we might say, have a restricted code peculiar to a particular linguistic community; moral laws have an elaborated code which is taken to be universally accessible; and the judicial laws fall somewhere in between.

JSOT 32 (1985), pp. 23-44

THE LAWS OF WARFARE IN THE BOOK OF DEUTERONOMY: THEIR ORIGINS, INTENT AND POSITIVITY

Alexander Rofé

The present article is one chapter in an extensive introduction to the Book of Deuteronomy which I have been writing in Hebrew during the last decade.[1] The aim, as usual in works of this kind, is to elucidate the contents and meaning of the book and to shed light on its origins and formation. With this intention, the various portions of Deuteronomy, especially its diverse groups of laws, are examined one by one. Differences of style, ideational discrepancies and contradictions in content serve as starting points for detecting various layers of composition, these layers in turn offer a clue to identifying the subsequent circles of scribes active in the formation of the book. Thus, step by step, a history of Deuteronomy and of the Deuteronomic movement is taking shape.

Introductory studies today are greatly facilitated by the work of former generations of critics who in the last two centuries paved the way for historic-literary research into the Hebrew Bible. My own research is no exception. At the same time, I have been greatly assisted from a different, unexpected quarter. The study of Rabbinic interpretation, as contained in the Mishna, Halakhic Midrashim, the Talmuds and medieval commentaries, has often made clear to me both the plain meaning of scripture and the critical problems contained therein. To be sure, usually it is not the traditional interpretation, but the critical reading of it that helps modern scholars: every time they find their pious predecessors deviating from the plain meaning of the text, they are made aware that a real problem, not an invented one, lies there waiting for solution. Thus

1. *Introduction to Deuteronomy* (Jerusalem: Akademon, 1975; repr. 1977, 1981). Subsequent chapters were gathered together in *Introduction to Deuteronomy— Further Chapters* (Jerusalem: Akademon, 1982).

traditional interpretation functions both as an incentive and as a control to modern historical criticism.

It seems to me that the laws of warfare in Deuteronomy can be taken as a good instance of a critical use of traditional Jewish interpretation drawn upon in order to supplement the achievements of former research. Therefore I present here an introductory study of these laws as a sample of my critical method which up to now has been accessible only to the few scholars who master Modern Hebrew.

I

A good number of military concepts and practices from pre-monarchic and early monarchic times appear in the historical and prophetical books of the Hebrew Bible. At times a war is called a 'war of the Lord' (1 Sam. 18.17; 25.28; cf. Exod. 17.16 and Num. 21.14); God is perceived as a 'man of war' (Exod. 15.3; cf. Ps. 24.8) who 'descends with the warriors' (Judg. 5.13), actively participating in combat (Exod. 14.25; Josh. 10.14). God's presence in battle is expressed by the presence of the ark (Num. 10.35-46; 1 Sam. 4.3-11), this practice prevailing up to the rise of the monarchy (2 Sam. 11.11; 15.25). The unseen God was imagined as 'sitting on the cherubim', the figures atop the ark cover (1 Sam. 4.4; 2 Sam. 6.2; 2 Kgs 19.15; Ps. 80.2). Inasmuch as war was perceived as an activity and a revelation of God, it was considered holy, even though some expeditions were defined as a 'profane journey' (1 Sam. 21.6); hence the term 'to consecrate battle' (Jer. 6.4; Joel 4.9; Mic. 3.5) and the warriors' state of being 'consecrated' (Isa. 13.3; Jer. 22.7; 51.27-28).[2] This sacral state entitled the 'young men' to partake of the 'consecrated bread' but at the same time obligated them to 'keep away from women' (1 Sam. 21.5), for sexual contact engendered ritual impurity (Lev. 15.18). On occasion, those who came 'to the aid of the Lord among the warriors' (Judg. 5.23) *pārᵉ'û pᵉrā'ôt* (5.2)—which is to say, let their locks go untrimmed, when they 'dedicated themselves' to the Lord. There were yet more rigorous modes of oath-taking and dedication (Num. 6.5, 8)—those of the Nazirites, who divorced themselves from all products of the vine (Num. 6.2, 4). The original task of

---

2. Cf. 1 Sam. 21.5; 'The garments of the young men [*kᵉlê hannᵉ'ārîm*] were consecrated'. The Septuagint, however, as well as 4QSam^b, render *kol-hannᵉ'ārîm*, 'all the young men'. See F.M. Cross, 'The Oldest Manuscripts from Qumran', *JBL* 74 (1955), p. 167.

the 'Nazirite of God' was 'to deliver Israel' (Judg. 13.5).[3] Other vows, too, were taken.[4] Jephthah promised to sacrifice to the Lord whatever would emerge from the door of his house to greet him (Judg. 11.30-31). The Israelites vowed to proscribe the Canaanite towns and populations of the Negev—which is to say, to destroy them utterly, leaving no spoil except what was to be deposited in the sanctuary (Num. 21.1-3). A like proscription, or ban, is mentioned in the inscription of Mesha, king of Moab (lines 14-15). Saul laid an oath upon the Israelites not to taste bread on the day of battle (1 Sam. 14.24-45). Prior to going out to war 'enquiry was made of the Lord' (*š'l byhwh*), an expression referring exclusively to the action of the priest—who wore the ephod, a garment containing the divining *urim* and *thummim* (Judg. 1.1; 20.18, 23, 27; 1 Sam. 10.22; 14.18 LXX, 37, 41 LXX; 22.10, 13, 15; 23.2-12; 28.6; 30.7-8; 2 Sam. 2.1; 5.19, 23). The leader of the people would put the question with the priest attending him, presenting the ephod and 'enquiring of God thereby'.[5]

It is highly doubtful that these varied procedures, drawn from diverse sources, can allow us to reconstruct a uniform institution, the Israelite 'holy war'.[6] Some·practices, such as enquiring of the Lord through the priestly ephod, obtained even in intra-Israelite conflicts (1 Sam. 23.9-12); and, doubtless, practices exclusive to wars of the Lord changed in accordance with time and circumstance. However, all sources agree on these

---

3.   M. Weber, *Gesammelte Aufsätze zur Religionssoziologie*. III. *Das Antike Judentum* (Tübingen: Neukirchener Verlag, 2nd edn, 1923), pp. 102-10. For a recent discussion of the subject see Z. Weisman, 'The Biblical Nazarite: Its Types and Roots' (Hebrew), *Tarbiz* 36 (1966–67), pp. 207-20, especially pp. 218-19.

4.   Cf. the oath of King Kartu in the Ugaritic Epic: Krt, 1.200: C.H. Gordon, *Ugaritic Manual* (AnOr, 35; Rome, 1955), p. 186.

5.   Cf. the *Baraita* in *b. Yoma* 73a-b. The Priestly Document blurs the terminology: instead of employing *liš'ôl bYhwh*, 'to enquire by the Lord', it has *wᵉša'al lô bᵉmišpaṭ hā'ûrîm lipnê Yhwh* (Num. 27.21). Besides, it reverses the scale and describes the military commander as subordinate to the priest ('*ômēd lipnê…hakkōhēn*). These are clear indications of the late date of P.

6.   *Pace* G. von Rad, *Deuteronomium-Studien* (Göttingen: Vandenhoeck & Ruprecht, 1974), pp. 30-41; *idem, Der Heilige Krieg in Alten Israel* (Zürich, 1951). Cf. the critique of M. Weippert, '"Heiliger Krieg" in Israel und Assyrien', *ZAW* 84 (1972), pp. 460-93; F. Stolz, *Jahwes und Israels Kriege* (ATANT, 60; Zürich, 1972); G.H. Jones, '"Holy War" or "Yahweh War"?', *VT* 25 (1975), pp. 642-58. The *status quaestionis* has been reviewed by A. de Pury, 'La guerre sainte israelite', *Etudes théologiques et religieuses* 56 (1981), pp. 5-38; also cf. the contributions of J.G. Heintz, Ph. de Robert, D. Ellul in that volume, pp. 39-71.

practices preceding the monarchic period; from David's reign on, many of them fall into disuse and are forgotten.

Now when we examine the D document and its laws of warfare, we simply do not find most of the above mentioned concepts and practices. Indeed, the little commonality obtaining gives strong evidence of the gap separating ancient military institutions from the laws of D.[7] Even if D emphasizes God's presence and involvement in battle alongside the Israelites (Deut. 7.21; 20.1, 4; 23.15), this participation is not substantiated by the presence of the ark. In D the ark does not go into battle,[8] as is shown by the account of the expedition following the spies' report.[9] Moreover, the ark in D has neither cover nor cherubim, and it is not considered the seat of the Lord; rather it is solely the depository of the divine tablets of the law (Deut. 10.3-5; cf. 1 Kgs 8.9, 21 [Dtr.]). D, too, insists that 'your camp be holy' because of God's presence (Deut. 23.15) and that anyone 'rendered unclean by a nocturnal emission' be distanced from the camp due to impurity (23.11-12).[10] However, D puts this law under the same rubric as that commanding both defecation and the covering of excrement outside the camp—'be on your guard against anything untoward' (23.10). Now hygienic procedures such as these were never comprehended under the original concept of purity and impurity. Actually, D defines all as *'erwat dābār*, 'unseemly' phenomena (23.15), anything that ought not be seen. D does not command fighters to refrain from relations with women, according to the ancient practice (1 Sam. 21.5). Aware of the vow, but not as a recommended practice and in no way related to war (Deut. 23.22-24), D applies the ban also, but not as a spontaneous vow or promise. It is rather an obligatory law dictating behaviour toward the nations of Canaan and idol worshippers

7. Contra F. Schwally, *Semitische Kriegsaltertümer. I. Der Heilige Krieg im Alten Israel* (Leipzig, 1901), pp. 74-99. In my opinion, even Deut. 20.5-8 does not reflect ancient demonological conceptions; cf. *infra*.

8. S.D. Luzzatto, *Il Pentateuco: volgarizzato e commentato. V. Deuteronomio* (Padua, 1876), in his comments on Deut. 20.4 and 23.15. This is a nice instance of Luzzatto's quest for the plain meaning as against the exegesis of the Mishna: see *Soṭah* 8.1 (end).

9. While the ancient source (Num. 14.44) emphasizes that the Ark of the Covenant of the Lord 'did not stir from the camp' in that battle, D phrased the matter differently: 'Do not go up and do not fight, since I am not in your midst' (Deut. 1.44). On this and on what follows, cf. M. Weinfeld, 'The Change in the Conception of Religion in Deuteronomy' (Hebrew), *Tarbiz* 31 (1961–62), pp. 15-16.

10. Cf. Lev. 15.16.

among the Israelites (Deut. 7.1-2; 20.15-18; 13.13-19). The ban in D does not entail dedication to the Lord, but is a punitive act of destruction.[11] While in D the priest comes before the people prior to their going out to war, he wears no ephod. Indeed the duties of the priest in D do not include enquiring of the Lord at all (Deut. 10.8; 18.1-6; 19.17; 21.5; 24.89):[12] God's will is conveyed through the prophet (18.14ff.). The priest of D delivers a set exhortation that has nothing to do with spontaneous, primal enquiry of the Lord.

God's presence *sans* ark, ritual commands given an aesthetic–hygienic reinterpretation, a ban become standing law, a priest addressing the people but without ephod and not enquiring of the Lord—all point to anything but chance omission. D could easily have mentioned all the customs that we have listed: its silence indicates an ideational and temporal distance from them all. Clearly D's world, with its laws of warfare, is a different one, centuries removed from the onset of the monarchy. Even if D's military laws were a sediment of inherited materials preceding the book's composition, they could not be very much older; and that we shall substantiate in the ensuing discussion.

II

I include the following in the laws of war: ch. 20 in its entirety, and 21.10-14, 23.9-15 and 24.5, laws appearing in four disparate loci. One may question at once their forming a unified corpus; perhaps what we term 'military law' would have been included by the author under a different heading. For example, the law of 24.5, 'when a man has taken a bride, he shall not go out with the army', follows a law about divorce and remarriage of a former wife. Have we not here a brief unit concerned with personal status? Nonetheless, to my mind, the marked similarity of D's scattered laws of war, both in form and content, demonstrates that they were initially conceived of as one group. Deut. 21.10-14, dealing with the female war captive, is a continuation of 20.10-20, dealing with siege and conquest, these being divided by the law of the

---

11. Note that D does not employ the term *haḥᵃrēm lyhwh* 'proscribe for the Lord' (Lev. 27.28; Mic. 4.13) or *ḥērem lyhwh* (Josh. 6.17), both expressing, as in the Mesha stele (line 17), the original notion of consecration. In D, *ḥērem*, the ban, is an autonomous concept denoting utter destruction by command.

12. The witness of Deut. 33.8 is not relevant here: Moses' blessing does not belong to D; rather, it is an ancient poem handed down to the authors of the book.

expiatory heifer. However, the law of the heifer to be slain in expiation for a murder whose perpetrator is unknown (21.1-9) continues the laws of homicide in ch. 19. We can deduce that, due to an editorial mishap, the law of the expiatory heifer was shifted from its original locus to its present place between war laws.[13]

Furthermore, the introduction to the law of the female captive, 'when you take the field against your enemies' (21.10), parallels the opening of Deut. 20.1. The regulations of Deut. 23.10-15, comprehending laws of the army camp, do not lend themselves to any other categorization; both in form and content they are closely wed to the other laws of the compendium. They start with an opening similar to ones discussed above, 'when you go out as a troop against your enemies', and they contain the same notion of God's accompanying the Israelite camp found in 20.1, 4, and also resemble the notion of God's delivering the enemy into the Israelites' hand, found in 20.13 and 21.10. Finally, Deut. 24.5 is indeed an unusual case, being phrased in the third person, whereas the others address the individual Israelite in the second person singular (21.10-14). Nonetheless, this dictum bears clear affinity, in terms of content, with the laws of release from the obligations of military service (20.5-7); and in its tenor, too, it is one with most of the other laws, as will be shown below.

The various laws were arranged in the present order both topically and by external association—at times purely verbal.[14] The first principle holds true for the laws of the block 20.1–21.14, as we have seen; the second principle is evident in the last two sections. Chapter 23.10-15 begins with law concerning the unclean person, declaring that 'he must not re-enter (*lō' yābō'*) the camp'; he must wash before evening, 'at sundown he may enter (*yābō'*) the camp'. This law was attached to a brief compendium of laws declaring who 'shall not be admitted (*lō' yābō'*) into the congregation of the Lord' (23.2, 3 [twice], 4 [twice]) and with

13. A number of modern Bible commentators have called attention to this. Cf, e.g., S.R. Driver, *Commentary on Deuteronomy* (ICC; Edinburgh: T. & T. Clark, 1902), p. 236.

14. Cf. U. Cassuto, 'The Sequence and Arrangement of Biblical Sections', in his *Biblical and Oriental Studies*. I. *Bible* (trans. I. Abrahams; Jerusalem, 1973), pp. 1-6; N.M. Sarna, 'Psalm 89: A Study in Inner Biblical Exegesis', *Biblical and Other Studies* (ed. A. Altmann; Cambridge, MA, 1963), pp. 29-46, p. 30 and n. 7, with rich references. H.M. Wiener, 'The Arrangement of Deuteronomy 12–26', *JPOS* 6 (1926), pp. 185-95. Wiener attempts to explain the order on the principle of ideational association; to my mind Cassuto's method is to be preferred.

another category of persons whose third generation 'shall be admitted (*yābō'*) into the congregation of the Lord' (23.9). The association came about through the idiom (*lō'*) *yābō'*, 'he shall (not) come/enter'—'the congregation of the Lord' and 'the camp'.[15] A like association links *tšb ḥwṣ* of 23.14-15 with vv. 16 and 17. Verse 14 speaks about *bᵉšibtekā ḥûṣ* (in this context); squatting to attend to physical needs; while in the instance of a fugitive slave the text (vv. 16-17) reads *'immᵉkā yēšēb, bᵉqirbᵉkā*, 'dwell with you in your midst'. Associative thought bound two phrases together—*yšb ḥwṣ*, '"dwelling" outside', with *yšb bqrb*, 'dwelling inside'! Deut. 24.5 was attached to 24.1-4 due to the shared opening, 'when a man takes a wife'. As for 24.6, 'a handmill or upper millstone shall not be taken in pawn, for that would be taking someone's life in pawn', it was attached to 24.5, 'let him be merry with the wife that he has taken', due to an association of meaning: words depicting the process of grinding were often vulgarly used to refer to sexual congress. Early Amoraim were aware of such a meaning and commented, 'He did grind in the prison house' (Judg. 16.21). Rabbi Yohanan declared: 'Grinding connotes impregnation, as we read, "Then let my wife grind unto another" (Job 31.10). Hence we learn that each and every one had his wife brought to him in prison in order to impregnate her'.[16] Such association underlies the adjacency of the two verses, the one speaking of a grinding tool and the other calling for the bridegroom to be merry with his wife.

In my opinion, all the laws of warfare were arranged by theme and content; only at a secondary stage in the books' development were a few of them relocated along associative lines. Such was the case with the laws of 16.21–17.7, as I have demonstrated elsewhere.[17] In what follows we shall show that 24.5 and 23.10-14(15) at first stood at the beginning of the collection but were pushed further back—not due to any error in text transmission, but because one of the last editors of the collection chose to begin with different material, which we find at the beginning of Deuteronomy 20 today.

---

15. This point was called to my attention by my student, Mr Eli Ashraf, in a paper presented in a seminar at the Ben-Gurion University of the Negev, Beersheva, in 1972.

16. *Soṭah* 10a. See also the midrashic interpretations given for Deut. 24.6 in Pseudo-Jonathan and the Fragment Targum and by the 'deniers' cited in the commentary of Abraham ibn Ezra.

17. Rofé, *Introduction*, pp. 66-67.

III

The compendium of military laws is not of a piece, but comprises discrete strata. One way to discriminate between them readily is to examine closely the laws in Deut. 20.10-18. Verses 10-11 call upon attackers, prior to laying siege, to offer the residents of the enemy city the option of surrender and being reduced to corvée labor.[18] Verses 12-14 deal with the refusal of such terms of surrender: in that case, upon conquest, all the city's males—which is to say, all its fighting men—are to be executed; whereas the women and children become the conquerors' spoil along with livestock and property. Verse 15 limits the applicability of the laws of vv. 10-14 to 'all towns that lie very far from you' and vv. 16-18 determine that 'in the towns of the latter people which the Lord your God is giving you as a heritage' a different procedure obtains: 'You shall not let a soul remain alive. You must proscribe them!' We have here an unnatural sequence, as the consideration of distant cities precedes that of cities nearby. Until we arrive at v. 15 it is not at all clear that it is precisely distant cities that are intended. Quite properly, scholars concluded that the original law is that of vv. 10-14, whereas vv. 15-18 constitutes a later accretion, designed to accommodate an old law stipulating relatively lenient terms of surrender, to D, which calls for extermination of the country's inhabitants.[19] We have here restrictive judicial exegesis along the lines of the rabbinic dictum *bāmeh dᵉbārîm 'amûrîm*, 'to what (solely) does this apply?'[20] This internal biblical legal exegesis employs its own clearly defined phraseology. The phrase *kēn ta'ăśeh*, 'thus shall you deal' (v. 15), is an exegetic phrase here delimiting the law's application; in other contexts it implies rule by analogy.[21]

18. See I. Mendelsohn and A.F. Rainey, '*Mas, Missim—Mas 'Obēd*', '*Enṣiqlôpēdiâ Miqrā'ît*, pp. 51-56 (Hebrew).

19. C.H. Cornill, *Einleitung in das Alte Testament* (Leipzig, 3rd/4th edn, 1896), p. 26; and in greater detail: A. Biram, '*Mas 'Obēd*' (Hebrew), *Tarbiz* 23 (1952), p. 138.

20. A. Toeg, 'Exodus XXII,4: The Text and the Law in the Light of the Ancient Sources' (Hebrew), *Tarbiz* 39 (1969–70), pp. 223-31, 419, pp. 228-30.

21. Cf. Deut. 22.3: 'You shall do the same with his ass; you shall do the same with his garment; and so too shall you do with anything that your fellow loses...'; Exod. 22.29: 'You shall do the same with your cattle and your flocks: seven days it shall remain with its mother; on the eighth day you shall give it to Me'; Exod. 23.11, 'You shall do the same with your vineyards and your olive groves'. Perhaps we

This exegetic tendency is attested by the very differentiation between 'the cities that are distant from you' and 'the cities of the latter peoples'. On the grounds of this distinction the legal exegete links his adaptation of the law to changed geography. In similar fashion profane slaughter (Deut. 12.20-28) as well as the deconsecration of the tithe (14.24-26) were permitted on the grounds that a new geographic situation obtained: 'If the place where the Lord has chosen to establish His Name be distant from you' (12.21; 14.24).[22] Here the claim is couched in similar language: *he'ārîm har^eḥōqōt*, 'the towns that are distant from you,' and *kî yirḥaq mimm^ekā hammāqôm*, 'if the place be distant from you'.

What emerges then is that the law of vv. 10-14 is inherited material, a literary stratum antecedent to the composition of D. By modern standards a cruel ruling, it is yet far more lenient than the war practices of the monarchic period:[23] it limits the slaughter to the fighting population and generally calls for negotiation prior to combat. This is a far cry from the law of total ban. The difference is also reflected in the laws' perspective. The inherited material includes a law governing the conquest of any city. It does not speak of Canaan or its conquest, nor is it rooted at all in Israelite history. Such is not the case with vv. 15-18. Here the law of proscription is emphasized as well as its rationale—the danger that the Israelites might imitate the natives' abominations. From this we may deduce that the author of the secondary material was the same as the author of the laws prohibiting both Amorite practices (12.29–13.1; 16.21–17.1) and idolatry (17.2-7; 13.2-19)—or was a member of his or her circle. The author is markedly intolerant of such acts, decreeing the death penalty for anyone committing the same, be they Israelites or foreigners. The author links these promulgations to a critical moment in Jewish history, the eve of the conquest of Canaan (cf. 11.31; 12.29), and in so doing endows these laws with the authority of Mosaic legislation. We have elsewhere identified this author as D², the writer responsible for the second stratum of Deuteronomic legislation, and we

have the same phraseology in Deut. 15.17, 'Do the same with your female slave'. On the other hand, the statements commencing with *kēn ta'^aśeh* in Exod. 26.17 and Ezek. 45.20 do not look secondary.

22. Cf. Y. Zakovitch, 'To Cause His Name to Dwell There—To Put His Name There' (Hebrew), *Tarbiz* 41 (1971–72), p. 339.

23. As, for example, what we know from 2 Kgs 15.16 and Hos. 10.14.

have fixed the writer's era at the close of the seventh century, the years following the cultic reform of Josiah.[24]

Inherited materials antedating D include, as well, 21.10-14. This law prohibits the rape of a female captive of war:[25] the desirous captor is obliged to marry her[26] and, more than that, must allow her thirty days prior to marriage to properly mourn her relatives who perished in war.[27] If the man subsequently decides to divorce her, she is to be considered a free person in every respect. This humane ruling reflects a universal concern with limiting soldiers' unbridled brutality and demonstrates consideration for the feelings of captives. Conversely, it shows no awareness of Israel's comprising a holy people set apart (Deut. 7.6); of the prohibition against marrying resident natives (7.3; cf. Exod. 34.15-16);[28] and of the call for the extermination of every living soul (Deut. 7.2; 20.16-17). Here, too, we have a law wholly divorced from Israelite history and hence akin to the dictum of 20.10-14. The two laws bear formal similarity as well: both begin by stating a condition, 'when you approach a city', 'when you go out to battle'; and both continue by dealing with different possibilities, the briefer beginning with the words $w^e h\bar{a}y\bar{a}$ *'im*, 'it shall be' (20.11; 21.14). The two laws also seem to follow one from the other: the first concerns negotiations prior to combat siege and conquest; the second continues the first, treating of captives. It would seem, then, that 20.10-14 and 21.10-14 derive from a single legal corpus.

24. Rofé, *Introduction*, pp. 76-77, 80.

25. Cf. *Midrash Tannaim to Deuteronomy* (D.Z. Hoffman edition) on the phrase, 'You shall bring her into your house' (Deut. 21.12): 'He may not press her in war'. See, as well, *b. Qidd.* 22a.

26. The apodosis begins with $w^e l\bar{a}qaht\bar{a}$ $l^e k\bar{a}$ $l^e i\check{s}\check{s}\hat{a}$ = 'you shall marry her'; see A.B. Ehrlich, *Mikra ki-Pheschuto*, I (Berlin, 1899; repr., New York: Ktav, 1969). Clearly the text is not concerned with the instance of a man lusting after a female captive and overcoming his desire.

27. See the detailed claims of Nalimanides, who explicitly challenges rabbinic exegesis here, and of Bertholet (A. Bertholet, *Deuteronomium erklärt* [Freiburg im Berm, 1899]). The only behaviour prescribed for the female captive that is not clearly a sign of mourning is the trimming of fingernails.

28. Rabbinic homilies express fierce opposition to a man marrying a female captive (see, for example, *Sifre* 213-214), going so far as to call her a devil—*śāṭān* (*Midrash Tannaim* to Deut. 21.22). These homilies clearly show us the wide gap between the spirit of the law of the female captive and D's particularistic laws which became normative in the Second Commonwealth.

This having been demonstrated, we can now review the remaining military laws and identify therein the inherited material, even when it does not contradict D. First, we can so define Deut. 20.19-20, the law prohibiting the destruction of trees in enemy territory when preparing for siege of a city.[29] According to v. 19 it would seem that this prohibition refers to all the trees; hence the rhetorical question, 'Are trees of the field human, to withdraw before you under siege?'[30] It is only v. 20 that delimits the prohibition to fruit trees; and the delimiting phrase beginning v. 20 is much like that beginning v. 16. It is therefore possible that v. 20, as well as 'you may eat of them but you must not cut them down' in v. 19, is an interpretative enlargement of this law. In any event, the law bears a clear resemblance to the two laws discussed above. As there, here we have a conditional phrase with the people being addressed in the second person singular: *kî tāṣûr...*, 'when in your war against a city you have to besiege it a long time'. This law, too, is divorced from Israelite history in general and from the situation obtaining on the plains of Moab in particular; it exudes, as well, humaneness and a universal concern, its sympathy extending here even to vegetative life. In contrast to the laws of D[2] this prohibition exhibits no concern or fear over foreign cultic practices 'under any luxuriant tree' (Deut. 12.1), or over the sacred trees that D[2] commanded be cut down (Deut. 7.5; 12.3 LXX) lest the Israelites be led astray by them.

We must include five additional verses in the inherited material—23.10-14, a string of regulations governing behaviour in the camp in time of war: the exclusion from the camp of anyone who has had a nocturnal emission until evening after he has washed (vv. 11-12), the necessity of setting aside a place outside the camp for hygienic needs (v. 13); and the obligation to carry, in addition to weaponry,[31] a shovel with which to dig and cover excrement (v. 14). Here, too, we have a conditional protasis: 'when you go out as a troop against your enemies', with direct address to the entire people in the second person singular. Exceptional cases, however, are mentioned in the third person singular: 'If

29. This custom was widespread. In addition to the examples cited in the commentaries, as in Driver, *Deuteronomy*; see also Thucydides, *The Peloponnesian Wars*, I, par. 107.

30. I have no doubt that the article of *hā'ādām* is an interrogative article. See GKB, §100, for a condensed list of similar instances of false vocalization.

31. This explanation has been put forward by Rashi. For detailed substantiation, see Driver, *Deuteronomy*.

anyone among you has been rendered unclean' (vv. 11-12). As we have said above, these regulations are not grounded in laws of ritual purity and impurity, but are rules of cleanliness deriving from an aesthetic sensibility and here too, the laws are not connected in any way with the national history of Israel. On the other hand v. 15 has been added by a Deuteronomic author. He describes God as 'moving about in your camp to protect you and to deliver your enemies to you', precisely in accordance with Deuteronomic concepts (Deut. 7.21-24; cf. 1.42); similarly, the demand is justified on the grounds of the need to keep the camp holy (Deut. 7.6; 14.2). Finally, we arrive at 24.5, the law freeing a newlywed man from all military service whatsoever[32] for one year so that he might use that time to be with his new wife.[33] Here, too, there is a conditional formulation; and since the law is not concerned here with the people as a whole but rather with an exceptional circumstance, it is appropriately couched in the third person singular as was the case with 23.11-12. That same element of universal compassion that we have seen in 20.19-20 and 21.10-14 is evident here, in a law that takes into account the desires and needs of young newlyweds.[34] This law also then is to be regarded as inherited material.

We emerge with a series of laws concerned with different stages of military activity: recruitment (24.5); setting out as a military camp (23.10-14); negotiations with the enemy prior to waging war, and treatment of the conquered foe (20.10-14); laying siege to an enemy city (20.19-20); and comportment toward a female captive (21.10-14). The unity of the series is doubly manifest in the initial phraseology of each law:

1. 'When a man has taken a bride, he shall not go out with the army...' (24.5).
2. 'When you go out as a troop against your enemies, be on guard against anything untoward...' (23.10-14).

---

32. $w^e l\bar{o}$' $ya^{ca}b\bar{o}r$ '$\bar{a}l\bar{a}yw$ $l^e kol$ $d\bar{a}b\bar{a}r$. The NJPS translation 'He shall not be assigned to it for any purpose', rightly follows Ehrlich's interpretation (*Mikra ki-Pheschuto*, I).

33. Here we must read $w^e \acute{s}\bar{a}mah$ 'et '$ist\hat{o}$, 'let him make merry with his wife', as does Pseudo-Jonathan.

34. Cf. W. Herrmann, 'Das Aufgebot aller Kräfte, *ZAW* 70 (1958), pp. 215-20. Herrmann recognized a humanitarian element in Deut. 24.5. At the same time, relying on Ugaritic epic material (1 Krt 2.96-103), he traced in this Deuteronomic law ancient religious practices.

3. 'When you approach a town to attack it, you shall call on it to surrender...' (20.10-14).
4. 'When in your war against a city you have to besiege it a long time in order to capture it, you shall not destroy its trees...' (20.19-20).
5. 'When you take the field against your enemies...and you take some of them captive and you see among the captives a beautiful woman and you desire her, you shall take her[35] to wife...' (21.10-14).

Each of these laws addresses the Israelites in the second person singular—corporately and individually;[36] exceptional cases—men not taken to war or those who must leave the camp, being unclean—are spoken of in the third person. The first element of every law, an adverbial clause, explains what stage of military activity is addressed by the author. The second element lays out instructions for this specific set of circumstances. Another commonality in this series is that of a shared focus. All proscribe negative behaviour characteristic of military life: rampant destruction of nature (20.19-20); private and public negligence in the camp (23.10-14); lack of regard for individual circumstances (24.5); and cruelty toward a civilian population (20.11, 14), especially women (21.10-14). All these laws are decidedly humane, calling for compassion, restraint and self-respect.[37] At root they have no relation whatever to the special religious status of the Israelites or to their military history.[38]

We may now ask whether this series includes the verse that begins the compendium of military laws (20.1): 'When you take the field against your enemies, and see horses and chariots, forces larger than yours—have no fear of them...'. Formally, the statement is of a piece with the series of laws that we have identified. Still, I submit that the question must be answered in the negative. This admonition differs from the other laws of the series on several counts. The laws of the series

35. Read *wlqhth* (with 3rd pers. fem. pronominal suffix) according to some ancient translations, the Temple Scroll and Samaritan MSS.

36. The form has been properly discussed in H.W. Gilmer, *The If-You Form in Israelite Law* (SBLDS, 15; Missoula, MT: Scholars Press, 1975).

37. A. Dillmann, *Numeri, Deuteronomium und Josua* (KEHAT, 2; Leipzig, 1886), p. 334.

38. The contents of the laws are not affected by such phrases as 'and when the Lord your God delivers it into your hand' (20.13) and, similarly, 20.14 and 21.10. Perhaps they are not even components of the original phrasing.

comprise specific regulations for specific situations, whereas here we have a command pertaining to a state of mind.[39] The laws of the series are universal in spirit; here we have a particularly Israelite historic consciousness, 'the Lord your God who brought you from the land of Egypt'. This declaration, 'the Lord your God...is with you', expresses the typically Deuteronomic ideology of God's participation in the wars of the Israelites (Deut. 7.21, 9.3; 31.3, 6, 8; and Josh. 10.14, 42 and 23.3, 10). The opening verse, in sum, must be an imitation appended to the original series of military laws when these were absorbed into the Deuteronomic corpus.[40]

We have yet to determine the nature of the remaining material in Deut. 20.1-9 and how it relates to the series of laws that we have reconstituted. Let us begin with the declarations of the *šōṭ^erîm*, 'officials', in vv. 5-9. These officials have no military function, but are civilian appointees of the various cities.[41] As such they are responsible for enlistment and it is they who turn over *hā'ām*, the conscripts, to the *śarê ṣ^ebā'ôt*, the military commanders. The declarations of the officials, then, are made at the time of troop enlistment in the officials' respective cities. Now the institution of the *šōṭ^erîm* was an administrative innovation in the kingdom of Judah in the seventh century BCE, one that tied in smoothly with Josiah's cultic unification; hence this verse, speaking of a function of these officials, belongs to Deuteronomic writing rather than to the series of military laws that we have identified as inherited material within D.

The comparison of the officials' declarations with the law of exemption from service in 24.5 leads us to the same conclusion. In 24.5 a man who has taken a new wife is freed from military service; here in 20.5-7, such exemption is given one who has become engaged to a bride but has not yet married (*'^ašer 'ēraś 'iššâ w^elō' l^eqāḥâ*), who has planted a

---

39. This was sensed by Merendino (R.P. Merendino, *Das deuteronomische Gesetz* [BBB, 31; Bonn: Peter Hanstein, 1969], pp. 220-33); consequently he wished to read vv. 1-2 as follows: 'When you take the field against your enemies, the priest shall come forward and address the troops, "Hear, O Israel, etc."' In my opinion, this kind of analysis is too mechanical to befit literary texts.

40. Blatant examples of such imitation are to be found in Amos 2.4-5 and 9.4.

41. On this and on the relation of the institution of the *soterim* to the unification of the cult, see A. Rofé, 'The Law about Organization of Justice in Deuteronomy' (Hebrew), *Bet Miqra'* 21 (1976), pp. 199-210.

vineyard but has not harvested it,[42] or who has built a house but has not inaugurated it.[43] What relation do these two laws have to each other? The rabbis (*Soṭ.* 8.2-4) maintained that the two are quite different. The man who did not complete the act (20.5-7) is shifted from action at the front (service with '*ōrᵉkê milḥāmâ*, 'wagers of war' in their terminology) to supply-and-ordinance units ('they supply food and water and repair roads'); but he who has completed the act (24.5), which includes building a house and dedicating it and planting a vineyard and harvesting it, does not set foot from his home until one year has elapsed from the date of his marriage or the dedication of his house or the harvesting of his vineyard. This interpretation presupposes the existence of two categories of exemption from service—that of 20.5-7 and that of 24.5. However, this explication is not consistent with the plain meaning of the text inasmuch as 20.5-7 also states (three times) 'let him go back to his home'.

In my opinion, the relationship between these laws is to be elucidated within the context of the history of biblical law, or to be more specific, intra-biblical legal exegesis. First of all, we have in 20.5-7 an attempt to expand the law of 24.5 by analogy, the kind of expansion that falls within the category of halakhic midrash. The rabbis carried this line of thought further by detailing more categories of men exempted from duty (*Soṭ.* 8.2-4). Such expansion of a law through analogy is to be found in a few more loci in Deuteronomy.[44] Secondly, and most importantly, we have in 20.5-7 a reinterpretation of a law's meaning. In 24.5 the rationale for the law is humanitarian: the legislator, having taken into consideration the feelings of bride and groom, allowed them to remain together. The rationale of 20.5-7 is of another order, one that will become apparent when we identify a recurring pattern of curses whereby a man is not able to reap the fruits of his labours,[45] and another, and worse, kind of paradigm whereby a man labours, only to have another

42. Literally: has not deconsecrated it, since the first harvest was sacred; cf. Jer. 31.4.

43. On *hnk* indicating initial action, as Rashi interpreted, see, recently, S.C. Reif, 'Dedicated to *chnk*', *VT* 22 (1972), pp. 495-501.

44. See above, n. 21, and add thereto Deut. 23.20: 'You shall not deduct interest from loans to your countryman, whether in money or food or anything else that can be deducted as interest', in contrast to Exod. 22.24 and Lev. 25.36-37. Cf. also S.E. Loewenstamm, '*Nešek* and *M/Tarbît*', *JBL* 88 (1969), pp. 78-80.

45. Amos 5.11; Mic. 6.15; Zeph. 1.13.

reap the benefits of his efforts.[46] This latter paradigm is manifest in the malediction of Deut. 28.30: 'If you become engaged to a woman, another man shall enjoy her. If you build a house, you shall not live in it. If you plant a vineyard, you shall never harvest it.' Leaving aside the question of the relationship between these curses and Deut. 20.5-7, it would seem that the underlying intent of the officials' declaration of exemption was precisely to prevent a curse from falling upon Israel.[47] This was the author's understanding of the rationale for exemption from military duty: consequently he changed the categories of the persons exempted, expanding upon them.

Having said that 20.5-7 comprises a secondary and exegetic accretion to 24.5, we posit yet a further addendum, 20.8, with its fresh opening, 'And the officials shall speak further unto the people and say', and its broadening of the category of exemptees to include 'the fearful and fainthearted'. This unit is based, apparently, upon the author's acquaintance with the tale of Gideon.[48]

The address of the priest in 20.2-4 stands alone; it bears no relation to what precedes and to what follows. It seems a repetition of v. 1, conveying the same idea only in more detail and in priestly declaration. Indeed, it is not clear why in v. 2 we have a shift from the singular to plural form.[49] The continuation exhibits a tension between the complete confidence of the priest and the fears expressed in the recurring refrain 'lest he die in battle', as well as the declaration addressed to all who are 'fearful and fainthearted'.[50] Most unclear, however, is the question of

46. Job 27.16-17; 31.8. As against them, a blessing formula obtains in Isa. 62.8 and 65.22. The former are not 'futility curses' as has been posited by D.R. Hillers, *Treaty Curses and the Old Testament Prophets* (Rome: Pontificio Istituto Biblico, 1964), pp. 28-29. A futility curse is extant in Lev. 26.26.

47. A. Knobel, *Die Bücher Numeri, Deuteronomium und Josua erklärt* (KEHAT; Leipzig, 1861); and Ehrlich *Mikra ki-Pheschuto*.

48. G. von Rad, *Deuteronomy: A Commentary* (London, 1966), p. 132. As opposed to Deut. 20.8, phrased as an addendum, Judg. 7.3 is well integrated in its context, and insofar as this section of the Book of Judges shows no trace of Deuteronomistic editing, Gideon's declaration must be seen as preceding D.

49. K. Marti, 'Deuteronomium', in E. Kautzsch und A. Bertholet (eds.), *Die Heilige Schrift des AT* (Tübingen: Mohr, 4th edn, 1922); C. Steuernagel, *Das Deuteronomium übersetzt und erklärt* (Göttingen: 2nd edn, 1923).

50. D.I. Abravanel, *Commentary on the Pentateuch* (Hebrew) (repr., Jerusalem, 1964), 'The Twenty-Second Doubt', of his introduction to the pericope of '*šōpᵉṭîm*'.

timing, a problem already noted by the rabbis.[51] The officials' remarks are made during conscription; the priest's, prior to making contact with the enemy. Had vv. 1-9 been the product of one pen, the priestly address would have followed upon the appointment of the army commanders. Thus we are justified in deducing that the priest's address was added by another hand, the same editor whom we have elsewhere defined as D^P and whose traces are evident in Deut. 17. 9*-12*, 21.5, and 26.3-4.[52] He took pains to bring in the priest, emphasizing his role in the cultic ritual, the judicial process, ceremonies of confession and (here) the war ceremonial as well. As we have noted above, the editor is unaware of any mantic function of the priest on the eve of battle; rather, he has him deliver an exhortatory address of Deuteronomic theology.

The opening section of the compendium of military laws (Deut. 20.1-9) contains, therefore, a number of strata from the Deuteronomic school. The original material, from the series of military laws that we have identified, comes only later, from v. 10 and thereafter. This is a common practice in biblical literature—that the later literary stratum, rather than being appended to the close of the original corpus, is placed before it. In the book of Deuteronomy this practice is evidenced in the laws of the centralization of the cult: 12.8-12 comprises the ancient law while 11.31–12.7 is the later stratum.[53] In the compendium before us it would seem that the later material pushed back the original series. Surely, in terms of content, 24.5 and 23.10-14 ought to have come first! The fact that these laws now appear in fragmented fashion outside the compendium does not seem to be the result of mere accident. Whoever appended to the collection the present formal opening (20.1) that speaks of actual warfare must have found it awkward to go back to treating conscription—the more so since he put forward his own version of exemption from military service (20.5-7)! Consequently, this editor went on to treat laws of war and siege (20.10-20), deferring to the end of the compendium of

51. *Sifre* 191: '"w^chāyâ k^cqārobkem 'el hammilḥāma$''$ (v. 2); could this refer to the very day of drawing nigh to battle? When Scripture states "He shall say to them, 'Hear, O Israel! You are about to join battle with your enemy'" (v. 3), Scripture speaks of the very day of their drawing nigh to battle. What then is the intent of the phrase (v. 2) w^chāyâ k^cqārobkem 'el hammilḥāma? It means, when the troops reach the border, the priest lays down all these conditions before them'. Cf. also *t. Soṭa* 7.18, and the *Baraita* in *b. Soṭa* 42 a- b.

52. Cf. my *Introduction*, pp. 58-60, 77-78.

53. A. Rofé, 'The Strata of the Law about the Centralization of Worship, etc.', VTSup, 22 (Congress Volume: Uppsala, 1971; Leiden: Brill, 1972), pp. 221-26.

war laws the regulations concerning conscription and the camp, or, alternately, introducing them into a catch-all of laws on various topics, laws that were in his possession and which he meant to include later.

IV

I believe that we can now put forward the history of the military law compendium. The oldest stratum in this collection comprises the series of laws described above: 24.5; 23.10-14; 20.10-14, 19-29; and 21.10-14. We have already noted that this series shows no trace whatever of ancient war practices dating back to the pre-monarchic Israelite period. Had the compendium been composed in the period of the judges or even at the outset of the monarchic period, such customs would have left their imprint upon the work. The realia reflected in these laws, however, present us with an entirely different picture. The demand for diplomatic negotiations, for the status of corvée for the subjected populations and especially the mention of construction during siege warfare—all presuppose the existence of political, administrative and military structures that had not come into being prior to the Israelite monarchy. Such realia are indeed cited in the sources describing the reigns of David and Solomon.[54] This does not mean, however, that the laws governing these acts were promulgated concomitantly with the acts themselves. Law neither precedes circumstance nor is it created simultaneously therewith; rather, law responds to reality *post factum*, only then attempting to govern it. We may posit that the original series was composed quite a few generations later than David and Solomon—from the middle of the monarchic period onward.

No less important is the question whether or not the series was promulgated as positive law. Since nothing of consequence is said about conscription procedures, organization and maintenance of the army, chain of command and military discipline, the original series cannot be considered a code, or even novellae, of military law, collated by

54. G.A. Smith, *Deuteronomy* (Cambridge: Cambridge University Press, 1918), p. 249. A diplomatic mission from Tyre and a regular siege work first appear during David's reign (2 Sam. 10.2-4; 20.15) and the setting up of a corvée during the reign of Solomon (1 Kgs 9.15-22). On the latter see: J.A. Soggin, 'Compulsory Labor under David and Solomon', *Studies in the Period of David and Solomon* (ed. T. Ishida; Winona Lake, IN: Eisenbrauns, 1982), pp. 259-67.

employees of the state or military commanders.[55] Indeed, these laws seem anything but practicable. This was realized by the rabbis even in their capacity as scholars removed from affairs of state. In effect, the rabbis abrogated two of the laws: they allowed the cutting down of fruit trees for purposes of laying siege,[56] and some of them permitted initial sexual relations with an attractive female captive in the course of warfare.[57] We have already noted that these laws bespoke a humanitarian idealism that sought to hold in check military abandon, bestiality, destructiveness and cruelty; in addition, they do not emphasize the distinctive peoplehood of the Israelites. Such indicators suggest wisdom circles as the laws' point of origin, for wisdom literature always commended compassion, restraint and self-respect. Indeed, it is a wisdom saying that gives the underpinning of the law of 20.29: 'Are trees of the field human to withdraw before you under siege?' Formally this question resembles Job 7.12: 'Am I the sea or a sea monster that you set a watch over me?'; and the comparison of human to tree appears in expanded form in Job 14.7-10. All this leads us to believe that the original series of laws was written by a sage conversant with conscription procedures and with military life generally, but not directly involved therewith. He set down rules and norms of behaviour—but for whom? And how did he know military life? It is reasonable to assume that he was close to the royal court and acquainted with state affairs.[58] We cannot, however, assume that his scroll, with its lofty goals, gained the status of positive law during his lifetime.

This little scroll was passed down to one of the writers of the Deuteronomic school, the author who recommended the unification of the judiciary, the appointment of officials (= *šōṭᵉrîm*, scribes) to render judgment in the gates and one judge 'in the place that the Lord shall choose'. Elsewhere we have labelled this person as D^S(opeṭim) and identified him as the one who introduced secular judicial elements into

55. Cf. Dillmann, *Numeri*, p. 335.

56. *Baba' Qama'* 91b; *Sifre*, par. 204.

57. Cf. *y. Mak.* 2.6, about the divergence between Rabbi Johanan and the rabbis of Babylonia. A similar difference of opinion holds between Rab and Samuel in *b. Qiddušîn* 21b.

58. In this regard, Weinfeld is correct in his remarks on the affinity of the Book of Deuteronomy to wisdom literature; see *Yehezkel Kaufmann Jubilee Volume* (Jerusalem: Magnes Press, 1960), pp. 89-108 (Hebrew). However, we again emphasize that not all D demonstrates affinity to wisdom literature, but only certain specific strata therein.

Deuteronomic legislation. [59] Here this author's hand is recognizable in his allotting to the officials the critical function of exempting persons from military duty (20.5-7). He may well be the author of the compendium's opening (20.1) also. This opening, by the way, employs the idiom, 'the Lord...who brought you from the land of Egypt', a phrase not commonly used by most Deuteronomic authors. [60]

During the next stage of redaction the scroll was broadened by two Deuteronomic addenda. The one comprises exegetic expansions, adapting the scroll to the law of the ban (20.15-18). This is the work of D^2: it bears the hallmark of religious zeal and extremism. To a large degree this author nullified the tolerant and humane spirit that imbued the original series. The second expansion involves the priest in the exhortatory address to the warriors going to battle. This expansion, the work of $D^{P(riest)}$, reflects the strength and demands of the Jerusalem priesthood following upon the Josianic reform.

It emerges then, that the three Deuteronomic strata that we have mentioned—$D^{\check{S}}$, D^2 and D^P—were composed shortly before and after Josiah's unification of the cult. At this juncture literary activity was intense, inasmuch as the topics under consideration were anything but theoretical. The Deuteronomic movement had come to power and had made its scrolls binding law. From this there follows the strenuous efforts of certain elements within the movement to update the laws, to assign specific functions to the officials and to the priests and to make the laws conform to the laws of the ban.

Notwithstanding the diverse origins and tendencies differentiating the various strata of the corpus, a consistent picture of the army emerges: here is no professional mercenary force, Israelite or foreign, but a citizen

---

59. Rofé, *Organization of Justice*.

60. In the Priestly and Deuteronomic schools it was customary to say that God took Israel out (*hōṣî' 'et yiśra'ēl*) of the land of Egypt. The phrase, 'the Lord brought Israel up' (*he''lâ 'et yiśra'ēl*) from the land of Egypt characterizes the Elohistic editing of the books of the Former Prophets. See C.F. Burney, *The Book of Judges* (London: 2nd edn, 1920; repr. New York: Ktav, 1970), pp. xli-l. A useful listing of instances can be found in J. Wijngaards, '*Hōṣî'* and *He''lâ*, a Twofold Approach to the Exodus', *VT* 15 (1965), pp. 91-102. However, I take exception to his categorization of documents as well as to his ideational conclusions. On the meaning of 'taking out from Egypt' in Deuteronomic literature, see B.S. Childs, 'Deuteronomic Formulae of the Exodus Traditions', *Festschrift W. Baumgartner* (VTSup, 19; Leiden: Brill, 1967), pp. 30-39. The idomatic singularity of Deut. 20.1 might point to that locution's deriving from a special stratum of D, namely $D^{\check{S}}$.

army rallying to the battle at the hour of need.[61] The original series of laws makes this clear: the man exempted from military duty because he has taken a new wife (24.5) is not a professional soldier; he is, rather, an ordinary citizen called from his home and daily regimen for an extraneous and distant duty. The officials' speeches in the $D^\check{s}$ stratum (20.5-8) are doubtless directed as well to this kind of soldier: it would be unthinkable to exempt from duty a professional fighter salaried all his life for the express purpose of preparing for war—because of family needs or because of sudden faintheartedness![62] Also, the encouraging exhortation beginning this compendium (20.1), echoed by D^P (20.2-4), reflects faith in a God of deliverance, and national historic consciousness—both appropriate to the people as a whole rather than to a caste of professional soldiers. The fear of horses and chariots, too, is natural to a fighting force untrained in rare weaponry such as this or in appropriate counter measures. It emerges then that a popular footsoldiery drafted from the citizenry—mostly farmers and shepherds—comprised the backbone of the Judean army during most of the monarchic period.[63] It is this army that is spoken of in the laws before us. Of course this does not rule out the existence of crack units of charioteers—see, for example, Micah 1.13—or of mercenaries, including the *kittîm*.[64] Such costly units were constituted to the degree that the Judean kings could afford them.

In Josiah's generation this compendium of military laws became binding in the kingdom of Judah. However, not only did the laws become binding: the ideology of those persons who had transmitted them to that generation became binding as well. This ideology was written at the compendium's outset: 'When you take the field against your enemies, and see horses and chariots—forces larger than yours—have no fear of them, for the Lord your God, who brought you from the land of Egypt, is with you' (20.1; cf. vv. 3-4). Josiah, the pious king,

---

61. Y. Yadin (*The Art of Warfare in Biblical Lands* [New York: McGraw-Hill, 1963], pp. 275-84), paints a detailed picture of an army built up of discrete reserve units. However, it is difficult to depend upon so late a source as 1 Chronicles 27 for reliable witness to the organization of David's reign.

62. I owe this explanation to Professor H.L. Ginsberg.

63. *Contra* the opinion of E. Junge, *Der Wiederaufrau des Heerwesens des Reiches Juda unter Josia* (BWANT, 75; Stuttgart: Kohlhammer, 1937). See also Y. Yadin, 'The Reorganization of the Army of Judah under Josiah' (Hebrew), *BJPES* 15 (1950), pp. 86-98.

64. See Y. Aharoni, *Arad Inscriptions* (trans. J. Ben-Or; Jerusalem: Israel Exploration Society, 1981).

whole in his faith, who walked 'in all the ways of his father David' (2 Kgs 22.2) and 'returned to the Lord with all his heart and soul and might' (23.25) accepted this ideology unreservedly. By its light he entered upon a campaign that had no precedent in the international relations of the small suzerainties of Syria and the land of Israel: alone with no allies he challenged a mighty empire, blocking at his own initiative the passage of the *via maris* to the Egyptian army.[65] The result was extremely grim: Josiah's death at Megiddo in 609 BCE marked the end of Judean independence. Subjugation to foreign rule—Egyptian, Babylonian, Persian and Macedonian—lasted almost 'seventy weeks' (Dan. 9.24-25), down to 142 BCE, totalling 467 years. For most of this period the Jews no longer had an army of their own: the laws of war were defunct.

65. Cf. H. Gressmann, 'Josia und das Deuteronomium', *ZAW* 42 (1924), pp. 313-37, esp. p. 336. One may not infer, however, that Josiah lacked any sense of reality. He surely must have waited for a propitious time to march out against Egypt. Cf. A. Malamat, 'Josiah's Bid for Armageddon', *JANESCU* 5 (1973) = *The Gaster Festschrift*, pp. 267-79. Malamat holds that Josiah was encouraged in his military strategy by the fact of the Egyptian army's having been roundly defeated at the Euphrates at the close of the summer of the preceding year, 610 BCE.

JSOT 37 (1987), pp. 3-14

DREAM FORM IN GENESIS 2.4B-3.24:
ASLEEP IN THE GARDEN

Dan E. Burns

The story of Adam and Eve as told in Gen. 2.4b–3.24 contains a number of apparent inconsistencies that challenge intepreters, and that draw the careful reader in for a closer look. The garden in Eden contains not one but two talismanic trees, the tree of knowledge and the tree of life, yet the central part of the narrative knows nothing of the tree of life. Additionally, God warned Adam not to eat from the tree of knowledge, 'for in the day that you eat of it, you will surely die'; nevertheless, Adam goes on to live nearly a thousand years. Gerhard von Rad, Jerome Walsh, John McKenzie, and more recently Crossan, Jobling and Boomershine have attempted to resolve the apparent inconsistencies with varying degrees of success.[1] There are, as Robert Alter has observed, 'aspects of the composite nature of biblical narrative texts that we cannot confidently encompass in our own explanatory system', a fact which leads to the nagging suspicion that 'the Hebrew writer may have known what he was doing but we do not'.[2]

Yet previous criticism points the way. Erich Auerbach's *Mimesis* contrasts two styles of narrative: the Homeric and the biblical. The Homeric style, says Auerbach, 'leaves nothing it mentions in half

---

1. G. von Rad, *Genesis: A Commentary* (trans. J.H. Marks; Philadelphia: Westminster Press, 1972); J.T. Walsh, 'Genesis 2.4b–3.24: A Synchronic Approach', *JBL* 96 (1977), pp. 161-77; J.L. McKenzie, 'The Literary Characteristics of Genesis 2–3', *TS* 15 (1954), pp. 541-72; J.D. Crossan, 'Response to White: Felix Culpa and Foenix Culprit', *Semeia* 18 (1980), pp. 107-13; D. Jobling, 'The Myth Semantics of Genesis 2.4b–3.24', *Semeia* 18 (1980), pp. 31-51; T.E. Boomershine, 'The Structure of Narrative Rhetoric in Genesis 2–3', *Semeia* 18 (1980), pp. 113-31.

2. R. Alter, *The Art of Biblical Narrative* (New York: Basic Books, 1981), p. 136.

darkness and unexternalized'; the biblical technique, on the other hand, with its much sparser narration, creates both a foreground and a background, 'resulting in the present lying open to the depths of the past'.[3] The result, as in Hawthorne, is that the narrative is multilayered: the biblical authors 'are able to express the simultaneous existence of various layers of consciousness and the conflict between them'.[4]

It seems to me that what Auerbach calls the hallmarks of the biblical tale—recurrence, parallels, analogy and 'backgrounding'—are similar to narrative devices characteristic of romance as well as modern fiction, particularly the modern short story: recursion, multivalence, nesting, isomorphism, self-reference, mirroring and use of intrareferential motifs characteristic of Gogol, Chekhov, Joyce, Hawthorne, Barth, Barthelme, Borges, Kafka, Nabokov. These techniques result in formal structures capable of symbolizing multiple and even contradictory levels of meaning. Whatever else it may be, Gen. 2.4b–3.24 is clearly a literary construct; its inconsistencies are problematic only if we expect the narrative to conform to logical standards, rather than literary ones. My approach is to use the tools, techniques and critical vocabulary that have evolved to deal with fiction, especially modern and contemporary literature, applying those tools to an analysis and interpretation of Gen. 2.4b–3.24. I compare the story with later fictions that resemble it in structure, asking what Gen. 2.4b–3.24 might be saying when read through the conventions associated with what I have come to think of as dream form.

Gen. 2.4b–3.24 is similar to an ancient prototype of literature whose structure is invested in the fairy tale. The fairy tale, which has its roots in the Breton lay and in Germanic folklore, is triptych in form, consisting of panels that correspond to 'before', 'during' and 'after'. Typically, the central part of the narrative—the central panel of the triptych, if you will—is numinous, and has the characteristics of dream, including transformation, sudden juxtaposition, paradox, riddle and masking.[5] Motifs

---

3. E. Auerbach, *Mimesis: The Representation of Reality in Western Literature* (trans. W.L. Trask; Princeton, NJ: Princeton University Press, 1953), p. 7.

4. Auerbach, *Mimesis*, p. 13.

5. 'Images from the phenomenal world', as Burns and Rohrberger have suggested, 'are transposed to the numinous realm, where they are free to operate in the reader's mind metaphorically, as in dream'. See D.E. Burns and M. Rohrberger, 'Short Fiction and the Numinous Realm', *Modern Fiction Studies* 28 (1982), pp. 5-12 (6).

from the framing sections appear in the dream section transformed or disguised, just as, in *The Wizard of Oz*, the farm hands from the opening section appear to Dorothy in her dream as the tin woodsman, the straw man and the lion (Cinderella, Jack and the Beanstalk, and Little Red Ridinghood fit this pattern). We see a similar structure in James Joyce's short story *An Encounter*: motifs from the mundane setting of the school and neighborhood—the green eyes, the whipping, the Priest, the chase—reappear, transformed, in the marvelous dream-like section at the center.

Gen. 2.4b–3.24 partakes of this numinous structure. The text locates Eden at the hub of four rivers. Together, they encompass the Indo-European civilizations of the ancient world. Two of them, the Tigris and Euphrates, are identified with the rivers we know by those names, and commentators have linked the remaining two rivers with the Nile and the Indus, which in reality are nowhere closer than thousands of miles apart. Geographically speaking, then, as McKenzie has pointed out, Eden is nowhere. Rather, it is a never-never land located in a mythological landscape which, like the imaginary continents portrayed on an ancient cartographer's map, begins where the known world leaves off. Textual evidence suggests, furthermore, that Eden is located at the very center of that mythological world: the description of the garden as guarded by a cherub with sword 'pointing in every direction' implies that the angel is standing at the earth's pole.

Furthermore, the paradise story is triptych in form. The opening panel (2.4b-20) sets the stage. Then Adam is put to sleep (2.21). Events in the center of the narrative (2.22–3.6), which may be read as if it were Adam's dream, are characterized by numinous qualities, including transformation, juxtaposition, paradox and disguise. Finally, after Adam and Eve eat from the forbidden tree, their eyes are opened (3.7), and the narrative concludes with an emergence of motifs from the opening section. Three of the major motifs in the story—Eve, the tree and the serpent—may be traced throughout the triptych, where they evolve through the dream form. Reading Gen. 2.4b–3.24 in terms of its dream structure resolves the inconsistencies in the text, and leads to a new and revealing interpretation of this marvelous story—an interpretation that broadens and deepens the tradition and has important implications for us in the nuclear age, with our recently heightened awareness of good and evil.

Eve

Phyllis Trible has pointed out that grammatical gender (*'ādām* is a masculine word) is not sexual identification, and has argued that 'the earth creature', as she calls Adam, is in the opening section of the text sexually undifferentiated.[6] Though Trible's efforts to dispel notions of sex roles based on the myth seem to me to raise even more formidable questions, her close and skillful analysis of the text reveals some interesting patterns. She notes, for example, that the unit *'îs* and *'iššâ* (man and woman) functionally parallels *hā-'ādām* and *hā-'ªdāmâ*, highlighting the fact that dream woman is formed from Adam just as Adam was formed from earth.[7] Trible's analysis provides evidence which suggests that Eve appears in Adam's dream as a projection of his unconscious, that she acts out his prohibitions, and that she is externalized when his eyes are opened, at which point procreation can begin.

Analytical psychologists will recognize the process described here as a crucial step in what Jung called individuation: a transformation in which the center of the personality shifts from the conscious ego to a balancing point between the ego and a subconscious 'shadow', releasing, in the process, an inner figure. Individuation occurs in stages marked by dreams. If the dreamer is a man he will project the inner figure as a female personification of his unconscious (if the dreamer is a woman, the sex roles are reversed). The Jungian term for this dream woman is the *anima*—the woman within.

The dream figure and the dreamer, who are 'bone of bone and flesh of flesh', function here as if they were in fact united in one person: the serpent addresses the woman in plural verb forms (3.4); the woman knows the prohibition, though in the story no one tells her (3.3); Adam is silent and invisible during the dream section, yet we are told in 3.6 that he is *'immāh*, 'with her'.[8] All in all, the textual evidence is consistent with the view that the woman is, in Jungian terms, a projection of Adam's inner self.

At the climax, however, the dream and the dreamer are both

6.   P. Trible, 'A Love Story Gone Awry', in *idem*, *God and the Rhetoric of Sexuality* (Philadelphia: Fortress Press, 1978), pp. 72-142.

7.   The word for Adam's 'rib' may he accurately translated as 'side', suggesting that the creation of *'iššâ* occurs as the result of a process closer to meiosis or cell fission than to plastic surgery.

8.   Trible, 'Love Story', p. 113.

externalized. At that point, which corresponds to the birth of self-consciousness, individuation occurs. As evidence of the change, God addresses the man and the woman as separate persons, using singular verb forms. For the first time, the man and the woman use the pronoun 'I'. Four times, Adam speaks of himself: 'I heard'; 'I was afraid'; 'I was naked'; 'I hid' (*'iššâ*'s response parallels Adam's; self-centeredness prevails). As further evidence of the change, Adam renames the woman, using a verbal formula which, as Trible observes, 'chillingly echoes the vocabulary of dominion of the animals'. He calls her name Eve, a Hebrew word which resembles in sound the word *life*, 'because she was the mother of all living' (3.20). Eve reflects the womb like fertility of Eden itself, which in a sense gives birth to everything else. Thus we have a series of analogous plot segments whose ends touch, forming a circle: the earth, inspired by God, gives birth to Adam, who through his dream gives birth to Eve, who then as a result of verbal intercourse with the serpent becomes the mother of all living, while Adam goes forth to till (or bring fertility to) the barren earth.

The encompassing theme of the narrative, as von Rad has pointed out, is *'ādām/'ªdām*: man/earth. It is a theme which begins and ends the narrative: first in the creation of man (from the earth), then in his return to it (dust to dust). Additionally, the narrative is circular in form. Man was formed of the ground outside the garden, was placed in the garden, and ended his life outside of it. The circular form raises the expectation of a return. Jobling has suggested that the program of the story, in structuralist terms, is to establish a race of human beings to till the soil, which at the beginning of the narrative is barren: 'no bush of the field was yet on earth, no plant of the field had yet sprung up...' (2.5). '"Inside"', says Jobling, 'there was one male, born autochthonously. "Outside", there is a multiplicity of people, born sexually. The creation of the woman is both the cause of the transition and the ground of its possibility'.[9] What Jobling is suggesting, it seems to me, is that Eve is a personification of the archetypal earth mother. Eliade has noted that the ancient Greeks and the Romans associated tilling the soil with the act of generation, and that, throughout Mediterranean folklore, the soil is identified with the uterus: 'the earth produces living forms; it is a womb which never wearies of procreating'.[10] Pushed far enough, the image of

9.   Jobling, 'Myth Semantics', p. 45.

10.   M. Eliade, *Patterns in Comparative Religion* (trans. R. Sheed; New York: Sheed & Ward, 1958), p. 261.

Eve as 'mother earth' gives us a picture of a cosmic marriage between God the Sky Father and Eve the Earth Mother, with Adam both as surrogate father and as son—a relationship which adumbrates the image of God the Father; the Virgin Mary, mother of God; and Christ, the divine son. (Jung's analytical psychology suggests that the Trinity—Father, Son and Holy Spirit—implies a fourth figure, projected as Mary, who in some medieval representations contains all three.) Pushed even further, perhaps too far for orthodox Christianity, the image would yield a vision of the Godhead endlessly giving birth to itself through sexual reproduction, with the sexes containing each other.

Trees

In the opening section of the triptych, there are apparently two trees, for we are told that God caused to grow 'the tree of life in the midst of the garden, and the tree of the knowledge of good and evil' (2.9). The numinous section, however, says nothing of the tree of life, speaking only of the tree of knowledge. In the final framing section, the missing tree reappears: God fears that Adam will 'take also from the tree of life and eat, and live forever' (3.22).

The discrepancy is one of the 'seams' that trouble critics; it is evidence, some conclude, that the narrative is crafted imperfectly. Von Rad confesses that he can scarcely suppress the suspicion that the duality of trees is 'the result of a subsequent combination of two traditions'.[11] The dream form, I think, explains the discrepancy: the two trees simply fuse in the numimous section to create what Clark has called 'the tree of command'. The underlying question posed by the text, then, is not how many magic trees grow in Eden; it is, rather, how knowledge and immortality are related. 'Is there an organic and necessary rapport between the theme of knowledge and that of immortality?' asks Humbert. 'The entire meaning of the myth hangs on that question'.[12]

Serpent

One detects in the pious criticism of Gen. 2.4b–3.24 a barely concealed nervousness about the role of the serpent. Brueggemann, for example,

11. Von Rad, *Genesis*, p. 78.
12. P. Humbert, *Etudes sur le récit du paradis et de la chute dans la Genèse* (Mémoires de l'Universite de Neuchâtel, 14, 1940), pp. 1-193 (21).

protests that the serpent has been excessively interpreted. 'Whatever the serpent may have meant in earlier versions of the story', he instructs us, 'in the present narrative it has no independent significance. It is a technique to move the plot along'.[13] But Brueggemann protests too much. The serpent is more than mere stage machinery; it is an indispensable member of the cast. Its job is to urge the woman to opt for knowledge (and implicitly for immortality), and to prophesy the result.

The serpent is admirably suited to its role. In folklore, as Gaster notes, the serpent is associated with wisdom: since it creeps into the earth and frequents tombstones, it is believed to embody the sapient dead. Moreover, because it sloughs its skin, the serpent is continually rejuvenated and therefore, like the gods, believed to be immortal. According to the beliefs of ancient Greeks and other Mediterranean people, the serpent is mantic. 'Serpents were kept in Greek temples', reports Gaster, 'so that oracles might be sought from them'.[14] Finally, if there are any doubts about the suitability of the serpent for its role as delator, Eliade's exhaustive study of Mesopotamian iconography and folklore should lay those doubts to rest. Eliade identifies the underlying archetype: the serpent, throughout the Near East, is frequently imaged as guardian of the sacred trees of spring, and is supposed to bestow fecundity, knowledge and immortality.[15]

With these supernatural qualities in mind, it is interesting to note that the Hebrew word that names the serpent, *nāhāš*, is presumably related to the word meaning bewitchment or magic curse.[16] The root affinity between the words is evidently the source of the nervousness displayed by such critics as Brueggemann. It has, as von Rad notes, 'led to the supposition that at the basis of the narrative there is a very different older form, in which only two acting partners appear: a man and a serpent-deity'. ('Nothing of the kind', he hastens to add, 'is evident now'.) What is evident now, I think, is much more interesting. In the numinous section of the narrative, *Yahweh-Elohim* does not appear; in

13. W. Brueggemann, *Genesis: A Bible Commentary for Teaching and Preaching* (Atlanta: John Knox Press, 1982), p. 47.

14. T.H. Gaster, *Myth, Legend, and Custom in the Old Testament: A Comparative Study with Chapters from Sir James G. Frazer's Folklore in the Old Testament* (New York: Harper & Row, 1969), p. 36.

15. Eliade, *Patterns*, p. 164.

16. W.L. Holladay (ed.), *A Concise Hebrew and Aramaic Lexicon of the Old Testament* (Grand Rapids: Eerdmans, 1971), p. 235.

his place, we have the *nāḥāš*. The conventions of the dream genre, in which motifs from the waking section appear transformed in the numinous section, suggest that the serpent 'is' God, 'in disguise'. John Crossan approaches a similar conclusion by very different means. Noting that the serpent does not speak to God, he reasons as follows:

> When I speak within my own consciousness I can say to myself '*I* think that *You* are wrong'. But if I wish to answer back and contradict myself I can only do so by saying '*I* think that *You* are not wrong'. That is: there can be no mutual and reciprocal *I–You* spoken within the same consciousness'.

Thus, when we consider the narrative as a whole, 'The omnipresence of the Divine *I* and the complete absence of the Serpent *I* bespeak a common consciousness'.[17]

The central panel of the triptych has as its focus the temptation scene, and in the middle of that scene the serpent makes a statement that is central thematically as well. 'Die, you will not die!', it says, speaking of the consequences of eating from the forbidden tree, 'Rather, God knows that on the day that you eat from it, your eyes will be opened, and you will become like gods, knowing good and evil' (3.4-5).

The structural outlines of the plot are thrown into relief when we recognize that the serpent's statement is an oracle—appropriately couched, as Walsh observes, in Delphic ambiguity. Eating from the tree is declared to be a capital offense, and the consequences are clear and immediate: 'For on the day that you eat from it, you must die, yes, die'. But it is worth remembering, as nearly everyone notes, that no one dies in this text. From one point of view, then, the serpent is telling the truth: Adam and Eve do not die, their eyes are indeed opened (3.7) and they do become like gods, knowing good and evil (3.22). The apparent contradiction is resolved when we recognize that Gen. 2.4b–3.24 is the type of tale informed by an oracular pronouncement that is in fact an encryption of the plot (examples of this kind of narrative include *Oedipus Rex*, *Tristan and Iseult*, Chaucer's 'Pardoner's Tale', and *Macbeth*). In stories that share the dream form structure, the true and usually sinister meaning of the oracle, which typically takes the form of a riddle or enigmatic divination concerning the fate of the protagonist, is hidden during the exposition and development, to be revealed in an ironic epiphany at the climax.

17. Crossan, *Response*, pp. 108-109.

The serpent's oracle, in its ambiguity, appears in various permutations in all three panels of the triptych: as prohibition ('on the day that you eat of it, you will die'), divination ('Die, you will not die!'), and curse ('dust thou art, and to dust thou shalt return'). More importantly, it implies the key questions that echo beyond the narrative: What does it mean to have one's eyes opened? to 'know good and evil'? to be 'like God'?

To answer these questions, we must assume that the story is both paradoxical and multivalent, saying apparently contradictory things at different levels.[18] Yet if we attempt to disengage the elements which may originally have been independent, the narrative falls apart. Perhaps the paradoxical nature of the story is a function of its duality: the fact that it is a potentially explosive package of myths wrapped together in the awesome and terrible cloak of God. If so, a new reading of the narrative based on an understanding of its structural principles could well transform our understanding of the story.

Consider the matter of being 'like *Elohim*'. What is God like? His chief attribute, as revealed by example in the first two chapters of Genesis, is neither immortality nor omniscience, but *creativity*. In the text he plants a garden, causes trees to produce fruit, and brings forth living creatures. Similarly, after eating from the forbidden tree, Adam and Eve take up horticulture and childbearing (God's commandment to 'be fruitful and multiply' is expressed negatively in Gen. 3.16 as a curse). They are not as good at creation as God is—they are not quite like God—but that was not predicted in the oracle.

Consider also the question of knowing good and evil. The meaning of the phrase 'good and evil' is the subject of a vast literature, which has failed to lay the question to rest. Bonhoeffer, however, strikes out in the right direction. He suggests that '*tob* and *ra* have a much wider meaning than "good and evil" in our terminology... The essential thing

18. One way to look at the story is as a fusion of sources, with a Sumerian paradise story tucked into the central or numinous section. Thomas Boomershine has observed that 'the underlying semantic code has been definitively shaped by the antinomies between Yahwism and the Canaanite fertility cult' (*Genesis 2–3*, p. 127). As McKenzie has pointed out, speaking of cultic practices which may have generated the central part of this tale, 'The fertility rite was a mystic communion of the worshiper with his gods; by intercourse under the auspices of the rites he shared the divine prerogative of procreation; he became, in a sense, the master of the force of life' (*Genesis 2–3*, pp. 570-71). McKenzie goes on to say that 'This mastery, this communion with Elohim, is what the serpent promises'.

about them is that they belong inseparably together'.[19] It is possible, then, to read the words 'good and evil' as a pair meaning, in essence, 'everything'. However, to focus attention exclusively on the meaning of 'good and evil' is to miss the mark. It is also important to consider the word 'know'. The Hebrew verb *yd'*, von Rad points out, never signifies purely intellectual knowing, but carries the much broader meaning of 'to become acquainted with' or 'to experience'.[20] To know good and evil, then, does not imply a new moral capacity but a new program for life. Freedom, like power, is something that cannot be given; it can only be taken. What Adam and Eve took was the one thing God could not build into his creatures: control, however imperfect, of their destinies. It seems at least arguable that Adam and Eve did not fail the tree test, but passed it—a possibility which suggests, to borrow the words of John Crossan, that Gen. 2.4b–3.24 'is in both senses of the word the first plot'.

Is there, then, in Humbert's terms, an organic rapport between the tree of knowledge and the tree of life? I believe so. Mythologically speaking, if Eden is at the center of the world, and the forbidden tree is at the center of Eden, it becomes, as Northrop Frye has suggested, an *axis mundi*, 'the vertical perspective of the mythological universe'.[21] The tree of knowledge in Gen. 2.4b-3.24 is, then, a manifestation of the tree in the German medieval conundrum which speaks of a tree whose roots are in hell, and whose summit is at the throne of God, and whose branches contain the whole world.[22] Its function in the present context becomes clear when one considers the iconography of the tree in western culture: the cross, the Christmas tree, the burning bush. Christianity, the Son of God dying on the tree of life certainly one of its central images, could be categorized as a tree cult by a being innocent of our culture. Like the oracle, the tree has a double meaning: through the crucifixion Christ (the new Adam), the tree of life and the tree of death merge in the cross. Thus, the link between the tree of knowledge and the tree of life becomes explicit when we recognize that the Eden story is the germinal episode in an encyclopedic narrative that begins in Genesis and ends in Revelation. For the Eden story seems to be saying

19. D. Bonhoeffer, *Creation and Fall: A Theological Intepretation of Genesis 1-3* (trans. J.C. Fletcher; London: SCM Press, 1962), p. 53.

20. Von Rad, *Genesis*, p. 81.

21. N. Frye, *The Great Code: The Bible and Literature* (New York: Harcourt Brace Jovanovich, 1983), p. 149.

22. Eliade, *Patterns*, p. 294.

that humans must have knowledge, with its attendant conditions sorrow and death, before they can achieve immortality: that humans must die to be like God. Thus, Gen. 2.4b–3.24 tells the story of a liberating event in the guise of a restrictive or imprisoning one. It is as if, in Adam's fall (if that term is indeed appropriate) we fell not just into the world of imprisonment, but *through* it to a new dimension of freedom, like Virgil passing through Dante's hell to the world of grace beyond.

Schneidau notes that

> When Shakespeare promises us that the 'Great Globe itself', the theater, the audience, and the world, will fade away and leave not a rack behind, he voices the fundamental Yahwist insight into the constructedness of created things. Not only the fictions but we ourselves are made, and something made is not real in its own right, but that of its maker; so that the easy distinction between real and fictional breaks down.[23]

Gen. 2.4b–3.24 seems to be heading toward some such revelation. Form, content and meaning are related in the sense that the dreamer is contained in his own dream. Furthermore the dream is nested inside a frame—the triptych—which expands when Adam's and Eve's eyes open, and the dreamers awaken. God creates the earth; the earth gives birth to Adam; Adam gives birth to Eve who, breaking out of his dream, becomes the mother of all living. Each possibility is nested within the previous level of creation; each level is isomorphic to the next. But where does the process end?

As it stands, the Eden story is a systematic reversal of Eliade's 'quest for the center'. Rather than winding inward toward a never-never land, humanity winds outward toward a broader world. We have, at the end, an image which suggests that Adam and Eve, literally disenchanted, leave the garden and go forth to experience the worst that life has to offer, and the best. The image suggests among other things, that interpreters have got their directions reversed. One 'falls' asleep, but one wakes 'up', and Gen. 2.4b–3.24 appears to be better understood not as a fall, but as an awakening. The future, and the imaginative experience of life which we call literature, lie before them.

23. H.N. Schneidau, *Sacred Discontent: The Bible and Western Tradition* (Berkeley: University of California Press, 1977), p. 277.

JSOT 47 (1990), pp. 3-14

PEASANTS IN REVOLT: POLITICAL ALLEGORY IN GENESIS 2–3

James M. Kennedy

1. *Ideological Analysis and Political Allegory*

Meir Sternberg asserts that the creation of narrative is part of the historical process and as such is inextricably tied to the social realities of the historical process. Sternberg believes that the question is not whether the literary coexists with the social, but rather how it does. He states that 'all narratives imply or advocate some ideology-bound model of reality'.[1] The object of this article is to explore one possible way that Genesis 2–3 functioned as such an 'ideology-bound model of reality'. In other words the paper intends to offer a reading of Genesis 2–3 in terms of its function as political allegory.

In Fredric Jameson's opinion, ideological analysis of narrative designates the task of unmasking a narrative's social and political substance; it is to rewrite a text in terms of the historical and political context which informs its creation.[2] Yet, the phrase 'ideological analysis' begs a definition of the word 'ideology'. Following John B. Thompson, for whom ideology designates the process by which meaning or signification serves

---

1.   M. Sternberg, *The Poetics of Biblical Narrative: Ideological Literature and the Drama of Reading* (Bloomington, IN: Indiana University Press, 1987), pp. 35-37.

2.   F. Jameson, *The Political Unconscious: Narrative as Socially Symbolic Act* (Ithaca, NY: Cornell University Press, 1981), p. 81. Elsewhere ('Symbolic Inference', in *The Ideologies of Theory, Essays 1971–1986*. II. *Situations of Theory* [Minneapolis: University of Minnesota Press, 1988], pp. 140-41) Jameson expands on this concept by describing ideological analysis as 'the rewriting of a particular narrative trait, or seme, as a function of its social, historical, and political context'.

to sustain or legitimate social relations of domination,[3] the present article aims to study Genesis 2–3 as ideology in order to analyze how it functioned as a legitimation of power and domination in ancient Israel.

I believe that the contents of the story are themselves allegorical literary embodiments of the social values of the Israelite monarchy.[4] By way of procedure, therefore, the article builds upon a notion of allegory by which the social and economic values of the Israelite monarchy find social symbolic equation with the contents of the narrative.[5] I am not offering a reading of Genesis 2–3 against any specific historical context, but as a political literary expression of the wider monarchic social system that held sway until at least 587/586 BCE.[6]

3. J.B. Thompson, *Studies in the Theory of Ideology* (Los Angeles: University of California Press, 1984), pp. 130, 131.

4. The recognition that literature is allegorical is re-emerging in biblical studies. Scholars of literature such as Northrop Frye ('Allegory', in *Princeton Encyclopedia of Poetry and Poetics* [rev. edn.; Princeton, NJ: Princeton University Press, 1974], pp. 12-15) reminds his readers that allegory is a structural element in literature. Literature is allegorical in so far as it always relates to a wider world of ideas in order to find explanation. For example, Frye asserts that although Hamlet is not an allegory, it does relate to an extra-narrative world of values and idea. 'To say that Hamlet is a tragedy of indecision', he writes, 'is to start setting up beside Hamlet the kind of moral counterpart to its events that an allegory has as part of its structure'. Joel Rosenberg's discussion of allegory in *King and Kin: Political Allegory in the Hebrew Bible* (Bloomington, IN: Indiana University Press, 1986) is a helpful step toward the rehabilitation of allegory as a useful tool in biblical literary analysis.

5. This article builds on a pre-exilic date for the narrative in Genesis 2–3, which is traditionally assigned by biblical scholars to the Yahwist of the tenth century BCE. Recent studies have cast doubt on this dating and on whether there even was such a thing as the 'Yahwist'. For a discussion of the problem of the Yahwist and bibliography see D.A. Knight, 'The Pentateuch', in *The Hebrew Bible and Its Modern Interpreters* (Philadelphia: Fortress Press; Decatur, GA; Scholars Press, 1985), pp. 277-82. One of the most recent works on the so-called Yahwist is that of R.B. Coote and D.R. Ord (*The Bible's First History* [Philadelphia: Fortress Press, 1989]), who interpret the Yahwist's history as emerging in the reign of David (pp. 28-30).

6. Relevant to this way of reading Genesis 2 and 3, the Chaucerian scholar, D. Aers (*Chaucer* [Atlantic Highlands, NJ: Humanities Press, 1986], pp. 1-2), suggests that narratives be read not in the light of certain historical contexts, but as extensions or as part of a certain social setting. For Aers, the socio-political and economic facts of an author's environment are not mere background for interpretation, but 'are inscribed in the minute particulars of texts; they permeate them, enable them, shape them'.

If allegory and ideology beg for definition, so does the term political.[7] In this article, 'political' relates to issues of social power and who shall wield it. One may assume that there were certain social and political interests at stake for the author and the contemporary audience. This is justified on the basis that cosmogonies in the ancient Near East were never politically disinterested stories about the creation of the universe. They were expressions of power that legitimated the social and political agenda of the culture that produced them. For example, politically and ideologically the *Enuma Elish* does not portray the creation of the universe so much as it gives a reason for its adherents' right to dominate the world. For the framers of the *Enuma Elish* the narrative portrays creation in such a way as to serve the political agenda of the Mesopotamian royal elite.[8]

Similarly, the Eden story of Genesis 2–3 is not a dispassionate rendering of how the world came to be, but a narrative describing creation in terms conducive to the Israelite elite's preservation of political power and privilege. More specifically, the narrator presents the story of creation with a view toward offering a solution to the problem posed by tendencies of revolt among the peasantry. Genesis 2–3 solves this social problem in favor of the royal elite by portraying the first human couple as peasants who must submit to the royal centralized authority of the state represented in the character of Yahweh Elohim. The couple's revolt against Yahweh is the literary and theological equivalent to the social threat of peasant unrest and rebellion. As a cosmogony, the narrative portrays peasant unrest as natural and endemic to the rural setting. Because peasants are constant threats to elitist

7. In his recent discussion of the political nature of Genesis 2 and 3, Rosenberg suggests that the Garden story can be read generally as a metaphor of the human lifecycle. According to his reading, the mythic first man's life in the fabulous garden represents the individual at the height of maturity. Rosenberg describes this as the human being's most political period (*King and Kin*, p. 57). More specifically, he views the narrative as encoding the rise of the Davidic dynasty and its subsequent grappling with the problems and responsibilities of power (pp. 189-99). In my opinion Rosenberg reads Genesis 2 and 3 not as a political narrative but as a biography set in mythological terms.

8. The divine hero's work of creation of the universe conceals in mythological terms, to quote T. Jacobsen, 'a state, a well-run paternalistic monarchy with permanent king, capital, parliament, and royal palace in Babylon' (*The Treasures of Darkness: A History of Mesopotamian Religion* [New Haven: Yale University Press, 1976], p. 191).

interests, the narrative thus implies the need for strong measures of elitist control.

2. *Yahweh's Realm*

Gen. 2.4b-6 depicts a world in its raw uncultivated state. The world is that of a Judah-like wilderness with only a spring to provide water. The narrative dwells at length on the fact of the world's barrenness and then states two reasons for it. First, Yahweh Elohim has not yet sent rain to the land, and secondly, there is no man to till the ground. The notice of a spring rising from the earth to water the land hints at the potential for fertility and productivity. Although the narrative refrains from stating that Yahweh caused the stream to emerge from the ground, it nevertheless implies that the deity has here provided for productivity. After all, the reader already knows that 'Yahweh Elohim made the earth and heavens'. The emphasis on fertility and the fact that the narrative dwells extensively on the reason for its lack suggests that its chief concern is the garden Yahweh will eventually establish.

The narrative next moves into a description of how Yahweh Elohim works to establish a productive garden. To provide a source of labor, the deity shapes a man out of clay and then bestows upon him the breath of life.[9] This act reflects the ideological perspective that the king's subjects find their life in the monarch.[10] After making the man, Yahweh Elohim

---

9.　P. Trible (*God and the Rhetoric of Sexuality* [Philadelphia: Fortress Press, 1978], pp. 79-82) suggests that the term *hā'ādām* be interpreted asexually as 'earth creature'. S.S. Lanser ('[Feminist] Criticism in the Garden: Inferring Genesis 2–3', *Semeia* 41 [1988], pp. 67-84) applies the principles of speech act theory to Trible's proposal and sets out a case for understanding *hā'ādām* as a male human. Lanser suggests that when a being is introduced into a narrative, that being is assumed to have a sexual gender. The text, she observes, offers 'no marking, no context, to lead readers to make a new inference about the meaning of *hā'ādām*'.

10.　W. Wifall ('The Breath of His Nostrils: Gen. 2.7b', *CBQ* 36 [1974], pp. 237-40) suggests that the divine breath in the first man indicates that he symbolizes the king. He observes that in Egyptian texts, the king receives the breath of life from a god. The parallel with Genesis is certainly present but elsewhere it is the conquered subjects of the human king who long for the king's breath so that they may receive life from him (*ANET*, p. 249). Note also Lam. 4.20 where the poet laments that the king, 'the breath of our nostrils', is no longer. Although, as Wifall observes, kings do receive the divine breath, ancient texts also portray the divine breath as moving from the king to the king's subjects.

plants a garden and places the man therein to tend it.[11]

Two aspects of the narrative provide further parallelism with the ancient Near Eastern ideal of the king as the provider of life and sustenance. First, Yahweh Elohim gives the trees of the garden to the man as food. Secondly, the deity creates a source of water for the garden. Regarding the first aspect, the image of the deity providing food to Adam reflects a patronage system of peasant organization. A patronage system involves an institutionalized relationship between two parties who differ in degree concerning which one has the most power to control the distribution of goods and services.[12] The relationship involves personal agreement between parties and builds on the understanding that the one with the most influence will use it in favor of the other party, the client, providing the client is loyal and performs various services in turn. The patronage system embraces several specific ways by which patron and client relate, one of which is the latifundium, a large manor or estate that employs peasant labor. As Jacobsen has shown, the bureaucracy of the Mesopotamian gods reflects human bureaucracy. Although Jacobsen does not use the term 'latifundium', it nevertheless clarifies the role of the gods in their moments of relaxation. Jacobsen points out that the important gods while at home are 'manorial lords' who administer their temple estates. They make sure that plowing, sowing and reaping are done at the right time and that the towns and villages belonging to the manor are in good repair.[13] In the Genesis story, Eden is the fertile

11. M. Hutter ('Adam als Gärtner und König (Gen. 2,8.15)', *BZ* 30 [1986], pp. 258-62) points out that part of the ideological role of the monarch in the ancient Near East was to build gardens to symbolize the fertility of the realm. Because Adam is placed in the garden to care for it, Hutter views him as bearing royal symbolism. Yet, Adam is not the garden's maker, a role which is reserved for Yahweh Elohim. In my opinion, Yahweh, as maker of the garden, fills the symbolic role of the king. The characterization of Adam draws upon the social role of peasant (N.K. Gottwald, *The Hebrew Bible: A Socio-Literary Introduction* [Philadelphia: Fortress Press, 1985], p. 329). Although D.C. Hopkins ('Life on the Land: The Subsistence Struggles of Early Israel', *BA* 50 [1987], pp. 178-91) does not draw any kind of social symbolic equation between Adam and Eve and the social world of the narrator, he observes that the view of labor in these chapters makes good sense in a context of rural subsistence labor. Hopkins does not use the term 'peasant' but the social and material world he describes is that of the ancient Israelite peasant.

12. B.F. Geljart, *Peasant Mobilization and Solidarity* (Assen: van Gorcum, 1976), p. 26; B. Lang, 'Social Organization of Peasant Poverty in Biblical Israel', *JSOT* 24 (1982), pp. 47-63.

13. Jacobsen, *Treasures of Darkness*, p. 81.

garden of Yahweh's latifiundium or his manorial estate. Indeed, he is noted as strolling through his garden like a manorial lord surveying and enjoying his surroundings (Gen. 3.8).

Regarding the second aspect, the description of the four rivers in Gen. 2.10-14 codifies in narrative form the ideological role of the monarch as superintendent of irrigation. In the ancient Near East, an important aspect of the king's role was to build and maintain irrigation systems. Although the narrative does not explicitly state that Yahweh Elohim created the river that flowed from Eden, that the deity is the ultimate source of the river must be understood.[14]

3. *The Politics of Life and Knowledge*

The tree of the knowledge of good and evil has provoked much discussion among scholars.[15] Although the image draws upon the conceptual world of ancient Near Eastern mythology, the social referent here has to do with the intellectual distance between the social elite and the peasant class. At an ideological level, the tree of knowledge can be viewed as the symbolic embodiment of royal privilege pertaining to knowledge.

According to G. Lenski and J. Lenski, in agrarian societies peasant culture included nothing but the most basic information.[16] Civilization, philosophy, history, science, administrative techniques and art are all the domain of the social elite. The social elite maintain power by keeping as large a gulf as possible between such humanistic knowledge and the peasant class. Enforced ignorance is a technique of control. In accord with this ideology the Genesis garden story portrays peasant ignorance as natural, that is, as part of the created order. Theoretically, education can increase the peasantry's awareness of a world beyond the confines

14. The narrator's reference to gold and precious stones in relation to the rivers perhaps suggests that wealth is to be obtained from them and so speaks to an imperial agenda hidden in the story. Coote and Ord (*Bible's First History*, p. 53) interpret the reference to precious stones as confirming that the first human is a royal personage since a peasant would have no experience of precious metals and stones. Indeed, one might respond that the man, like a peasant, *does not* have anything to do with the precious metals.

15. For a summary see C. Westermann, *Genesis 1–11: A Commentary* (Minneapolis: Augsburg–Fortress, 1984), pp. 242-45; H.W. Wallace, *The Eden Narrative* (HSM, 32; Atlanta: Scholars Press, 1985), pp. 101-103.

16. G. Lenski and J. Lenski, *Human Societies: An Introduction to Macrosociology* (New York: McGraw Hill, 1982), pp. 177-78.

of their immediate environs and so open up behavioral options and alternative styles of living.[17] Peasant education, therefore, undermines the landowner's control. Thus, it is in the interests of the landowner-patron to convince the peasant that the *status quo* is acceptable and even desirable.[18] For the man and the woman in the garden, this convincing takes the form of an ultimatum: if the man and woman eat from the tree of the knowledge of good and evil they will die. The absence of a reason for Yahweh Elohim's command not to eat of the fruit is a literary gap that underscores the deity's sovereignty. Read politically, it undergirds the king's authority. The monarch need not justify policy; obedience is simply expected. For the narrator, peasantry are not to be rationally convinced but commanded. The knowledge which is to be kept from the peasants is, as Westermann concludes, not 'good' and 'evil' as discrete objects, but knowledge in general. It is functional knowledge: knowledge directed toward mastering the human situation. Such knowledge would not be an individual's personal possession but would belong to the community; it would be concerned most of all for the life of the group.[19] This is the kind of knowledge most dangerous to any elitist maintenance of control. It admits into the peasant's world awareness of a greater reality than is experienced on a daily basis and so opens up greater opportunities. A political reading suggests that Yahweh Elohim's forbidding of the man to eat from the tree of the knowledge of good and evil is the theological reification of the monarch's control of knowledge.[20]

The tree of life provides the narrator a mythological symbol with which to underscore the monarch's unique position as giver of life. Here life does not refer only to biological functions but to all that makes physical vigor possible. This means that the king, as guarantor of life, is therefore the guarantor of justice and social righteousness (Pss. 45.4; 72.12-14). From the perspective of the monarch, the poor and needy are not able to save themselves but must depend on the king to meet their needs.

---

17. Geljart, *Peasant Mobilization*, p. 36.

18. E. Feder, *The Rape of the Peasant: Latin America's Landholding System* (Garden City, NY: Doubleday, 1971), p. 268.

19. Westermann, *Genesis 1–11*, pp. 241-42.

20. S. Mowinckel (*He that Cometh* [Nashville: Abingdon Press, 1951], p. 66) points out that by virtue of 'his anointing and endowment with the divine spirit, the king...receives superhuman wisdom'.

Although Yahweh Elohim gave orders to abstain from the tree of the knowledge of good and evil, no such injunction was given against eating from the tree of life. Yet in spite of this, the man and the woman do not eat from the tree of life. A twofold ideological concern suggests itself: first, the king is not portrayed as jealous of his lifegiving power. To the obedient peasant, the monarch is a source of life, which embraces the qualities of justice and righteousness. Secondly, the narrative underscores the ideology that peasants are by nature ignorant of what truly benefits them. If they are to eat from the tree of life, they must be led to it like children. If the fact that the text does not portray Yahweh Elohim as specifically leading the couple to the tree casts doubt on the benevolence of the king, it nevertheless emphasizes that the deity made the tree available (Gen. 2.16).

4. *Peasant Revolt*

Yahweh Elohim's recognition that 'it is not good for the man to be alone' takes its interpretative clue from the narrator's primary concern, which is the maintenance of the garden. In a political reading the point of the deity's musing is that man cannot be as productive alone as he can be with a family. The description of Yahweh Elohim forming the animals from the earth and then bringing them to the man for names perhaps gives mythic expression to the elitist idea that peasant and animal life cohere in a mutually supportive manner. Although a helper like the man is not found among the animals, an inference can reasonably be made that the narrative portrays the man in the process of domesticating the animals that he will need for the cultivation of Yahweh's manorial estate. The arrival of the woman signals to the man that his task of productivity will now be shared.

There is nothing in the text to indicate that the woman is considered as equal in value and worth to the man. The narrator established a 'natural' hierarchy. Readings that view the woman as the man's equal and indeed as the crown of creation arise more from a constructive theological concern than a purely literary descriptive one. The female figure here is plainly to be interpreted in terms of peasant society under the patriarchal control of the Israelite monarchy. The social values encoded in the narrative are anything but egalitarian.[21] Overarching the

21. The question of interpretative context is important to keep in mind. Readings such as are represented by Trible's (*God and the Rhetoric of Sexuality*) which

subordination of the woman to the man is the subordination of the peasant couple to the royal elite.

In social terms, the snake's convincing of the woman to eat from the tree of knowledge entails letting her know what she is missing. The snake's activity reflects the attempts of certain strata in society to educate the peasantry and perhaps to lead them to rebellion.[22] M. Beqiraj views the peasant class as difficult to persuade; thinking in terms of probabilities is not to be trusted. He points out that the mobilization of peasant energies toward revolution must be based on enabling the peasant to see a link between new social possibilities and what the peasant himself wants.[23] The snake asks Eve, 'Did God say, "You shall not eat of any tree of the garden?"' This shrewdest of beasts leaves it up to the woman to add the datum that there is one tree that cannot even be touched. The snake thus leads Eve into an awareness of what she wants, namely, knowledge to master life's situations. In a narrative encoded with monarchic values, Eve—and later her husband—are portrayed as being deceived. The social referent for the snake is ambiguous. Perhaps all that can be said is that the snake embodies dissatisfied elements of society that pose a danger to the state by educating and encouraging peasants to independent action. This social symbolic equation of the snake with dissatisfied groups takes advantage of mythological serpent symbolism in the narrator's ancient Near Eastern environment. The narrator draws upon a rich tradition of snake lore to

emphasize sexual equality engage a constructive theological program. Lanser ('[Feminist] Criticism in the Garden') observes that Trible has not stated her context, which is an interpretative and confessional community. Regarding the present article, the context embraces a twofold dimension. First, there is the narrative's own historical and cultural context which views the peasant woman as not being as valuable as the man. D.L Carmody (*Biblical Woman: Contemporary Reflections on Scriptural Texts* [New York: Crossroad, 1988], p. 11) makes a valid point by observing the 'fairly obvious patriarchalism or male supremacism' of the Genesis narrative. Secondly, there is my own interpretative context in which I seek to show that one of the ancient strands of tradition that has been taken up into canonical scripture served at one time to oppress instead of liberate.

22. N.K. Gottwald (*The Tribes of Yahweh: A Sociology of Liberated Israel 1250-1050 BCE* [Maryknoll, NY: Orbis Books, 1979], p. 490) suggests that the Levites played a similar role in a pre-monarchic peasant revolt out of which, in his opinion, Israel emerged as a tribal confederation.

23. M. Beqiraj, *Peasants in Revolution* (Ithaca, NY: Cornell University Press, 1966), p. 93.

portray the snake in Eden as a creature embodying wisdom, evil and chaos.[24] The very ambiguity of the snake's social referent suggests a sense of foreboding and danger. The fomenters of peasant unrest are amorphous entities that live in the nooks and crannies of life. The narrative thus voices the fear that the monarch's enemies are not so much foreign invaders as those who undermine control from within.

The snake's comment that the human pair can become like *'elōhîm* (Gen. 3.5) provides a clue concerning the narrator's strange practice of referring to the deity as *yhwh 'elōhîm* and not merely as *yhwh*. According to Westermann, the narrator's use of *yhwh 'elōhîm* underscores Yahweh's role as creator.[25] After all, only in the creation account of Genesis 2 and 3 does the phrase occur unambiguously. Another interpretation is possible. The point may not be to emphasize Yahweh as creator but to accent the gulf that exists between the deity and humanity. Only Yahweh and his heavenly court are *'elōhîm*. The recurring juxtaposition of the term *'elōhîm* with the name Yahweh forces upon the reader the recognition that the world of human reality and divine reality are not the same and must be kept distinct. By telling the woman that eating from the tree of the knowledge of good and evil will make her and her husband like gods the snake is suggesting that the gap between the human and the divine can be closed. At a political level this translates into a threat to the unique role of the king as guarantor of knowledge, and by extension, power. The narrator warns therefore about the necessity of maintaining distance between the royal elite and the peasant class. The creation account of Genesis 2 and 3 thus anchors the gulf between royalty and peasantry in creation itself and so reifies it. The phrase *yhwh 'elōhîm* serves the narrative's social function of providing theological legitimation for Israelite class distinctions.

Why does the narrator portray the woman as being lured by the snake? The narrator cannot but shape the story in terms of a society controlled by men, that is, patriarchy. From the perspective of Sheila Ruth, patriarchy nurtures a profound fear of women; a fear associated with the fear of non-being and death.[26] Ruth refers to a 'masculist association' of body, nature and the birthing–dying process which sets woman 'clearly on the side of death'. She points to Genesis 3 as an

---

24. K.R. Joines, 'The Serpent in Gen. 3', *ZAW* 87 (1975), pp. 1-11.

25. Westermann, *Genesis 1–11*, p. 198.

26. S. Ruth, 'Bodies and Souls/Sex, Sin and the Sense in Patriarchy: A Study in Applied Dualism', *Hypatia* 2 (1987), pp. 149-63.

example of the institutionalization of this fear. Eve, who is created not only after the man but after the animals represents the weak one who is susceptible to seduction. She yields and drags down the man with her. Ruth interprets the Genesis narrative as a tale told over and over to each new generation of men in order to warn them that they are in danger. Instead of portraying women as liberators, the monarchist narrator portrays them as able to be fooled and manipulated, and therefore, as dangerous. An educated peasant male is one thing, but an educated peasant female is another!

Upon hearing the confession of the rebellious couple, Yahweh Elohim does not execute them as one might have expected. Instead, he condemns them to a life of hardship. The curses of Gen. 3.14-19 reflect the harsh realities of peasant existence. The man must constantly battle the forces of nature for a living. He is subject to the venom of the snake in the field where he must work. He must wrest productivity from a land which resists his labor. His wife is his servant. She herself contributes to the peasant economy by bearing children and this task now involves pain. The narrator thus traces the harsh realities of rural life and the socio-economic distance between king and peasant to the rebellion of the primeval peasant couple.

Just as the king banishes the wicked (Ps. 101.8), so Yahweh Elohim next exiles the man and woman from the garden. Although Yahweh Elohim had told the couple that eating from the tree of the knowledge of good and evil would mean death, they do not in fact die. If Yahweh Elohim is the literary equivalent of a king who must deal with rebellious peasants, then why does he not execute them? Could it be that the narrator is intimating something regarding the monarch's reputed relation to peasantry? The proposal advanced here is that the expulsion from the garden—instead of execution—underscores the ideological concern to portray the monarch as both powerful *and* merciful.

Like a shepherd, the deity in Genesis sets out to provide even for his rebellious peasants while simultaneously rendering a harsh judgment; he clothes them with animal skins (Gen. 3.21). Westermann observes that this act of divine kindness stands in marked contrast with the weak attempt of the couple to cover themselves with fig leaves in 3.7.[27] Again, an ideological translation suggests itself; namely, that even after having eaten from the tree of knowledge, the couple do not exhibit the knowledge to master life's situations. The monarchic control of

27. Westermann, *Genesis 1–11*, pp. 269-70.

knowledge is intact; the peasantry still find themselves outside the cultural and administrative knowledge for which only the royal elite are fit.

Having remained in control of knowledge, Yahweh Elohim blocks the
path to the tree of life, so preserving for the deity the power of vigor
and wellbeing. The deity sets a cherub to guard the tree of life so that
the rebellious couple cannot eat from the it and live forever. The mythic
statement of the expulsion from the garden does more than underline
the physical distance between monarch and peasant. It brings the
episode to a conclusion with the understanding that the social struggle
between royal elite and peasant is destined to continue but that the
outcome will always be in the favor of the elite.

JSOT 49 (1991), pp. 31-45

LEVITICUS 15.18 RECONSIDERED:
CHIASM, SPATIAL STRUCTURE AND THE BODY*

Richard Whitekettle

Wenham's Approach and its Difficulties

In 1983 Gordon Wenham examined Lev. 15.18, one of the more
'puzzling' laws in the Old Testament.[1] As he points out, this law is
puzzling, given the overwhelming evidence that children and marriage
were highly prized by the Israelites. It is puzzling, then, that the consum-
mating act of marriage and the physiological prerequisite for children
should be deemed to produce impurity. In arriving at an explanation for
the law, Wenham utilizes a symbolic structuralist methodology. The
work of Mary Douglas in particular figures prominently in the shape of
Wenham's thinking.

In her analysis of the dietary laws of Leviticus 11,[2] Douglas saw that
these laws were tied closely to a sense of physical perfection and wholeness within the created order. An animal was classified as either normal
or abnormal, depending on how closely it conformed anatomically and

---

* I would like to thank Dr T. Longman III and Dr M.S. Smith, as well as
D. Green and J. Boutilier, for their suggestions. I would also like to thank Mr J.A.
Groves and the Westminster Theological Seminary Hebrew Computer Project for
the generous use of their facilities. Since this article first appeared I have written two
other articles applying the same conceptual framework to related texts or issues in
Lev. 12 and 15: 'Levitical Thought and the Female Reproductive Cycle: Wombs,
Wellsprings and the Primeval World', VI 46 (1986), pp. 376-81, and 'Lev 12 and
the Israelite Woman: Ritual Process, Liminality, and the Womb', ZAW 107 (1995),
pp. 393-408.

1. G.J. Wenham, 'Why Does Sexual Intercourse Defile (Lev. 15.18)?', *ZAW*
95 (1983), pp. 432-34.

2. M. Douglas, *Purity and Danger* (Boston: Routledge & Kegan Paul, 1978
[1966]), pp. 41-57.

physiologically to an ideal type of creature for that realm of the creation. For Douglas, this implied a concern for the maintenance of boundaries, which ultimately reflected a larger societal concern that distance from the surrounding Canaanite culture be maintained.

In analyzing Leviticus 15, however, Wenham found Douglas's schema incapable of handling the whole of the chapter, especially v. 18. In Wenham's words, Douglas's schema 'breaks down as an explanation of the uncleanness associated with childbirth, menstruation and sexual inter-course, all conditions which the Israelites must have regarded as natural and normal'.[3] Considering this a flaw which made the schema incapable of explaining the processes of Leviticus 15, Wenham instead worked from the polarity of life and death. In this polarity he saw a general organizing principle behind cultic purity, one capable of providing an explanation for the cultic laws of the chapter.

The laws of Leviticus 15, for Wenham, describe a condition involving the loss of 'life liquids'. Bodily discharges, because they involve the loss of 'life liquids', are movements by the organism away from life and towards death. Defilement occurs not because death will necessarily result, but because the organism has about it the 'aura' of death. Since these various physiological processes have about them this 'aura' of death, legislation about them becomes necessary because of the nation's holy character. As Wenham says, 'God who is perfect life and perfect holiness, can only be approached by clean men who enjoy fulness of life themselves'.[4] When a body has no discharge coming from it, its 'fulness of life' is intact. It evidences perfect life. A discharge, however, indicates that the body's 'fulness of life' has been compromised. Wenham's attempt to explain Lev. 15.18 encounters some difficulty here. Surely what he has said about perfection is true. The idea of perfect life is a refrain running throughout Leviticus (1.3; 3.1; 5.18; 21.16ff.; 22.17ff.). But can this sense of perfect life really be thought of as compromised in an individual when he or she engages in sexual intercourse?

The problem here is multifaceted. First, although the bloody discharge of Lev. 15.19ff. might plausibly reflect the opposition of life and death, the place of semen in such a schema is not as clear. Elsewhere Leviticus draws a very direct connection between blood and life (17.11, 14). It is obvious that blood is necessary for the maintenance of life (Gen. 4.10; Num. 35.15-34). It is, however, nowhere apparent in the biblical record

---

3.   Wenham, 'Sexual Intercourse', p. 433.
4.   Wenham, 'Sexual Intercourse', p. 434.

that the loss of semen causes the body to die (Gen. 38.8ff.; Deut. 23.10). To associate the emission of semen with an 'aura of death' is therefore to state an unreality.[5]

Secondly, Lev. 15.18 associates impurity with the emission of something called 'seed'. The association which this most readily generates is that of life being created. The focus is therefore not on maintaining the man's life (such that its loss would suggest an 'aura' of death), but on the nascent life in the 'seed'. In addition, the child that is created through the emission of semen in intercourse is spoken of only as a sign of the father's strength, never as having sapped his strength (Gen. 49.3; Deut. 21.17).

Thirdly, because the sexual union between husband and wife is understood in terms of their being 'one flesh', it does not seem appropriate to classify ejaculation as the loss by one human body of a 'life liquid'. Instead, it would seem to be a movement within a unitary whole (physical and emotional) from one part to another part. The seed moves from an environment of origin to an environment of growth, but entirely within the confines of 'one flesh'. Defilement, therefore, does not come in v. 18 from a violation of the body's boundaries, a schema which Neyrey sees as a symbolic matrix able to explain the defilement of other bodily discharges.[6] Because the movement is within the confines of 'one flesh', the 'body's' boundaries remain intact.

In summary then, Wenham does not take proper account of the distinctives of the physiological event occurring in Lev. 15.18. Although the polarity of life and death yields some understanding of the impurity resulting from the menstrual and pathological discharges of Leviticus 15, it encounters difficulty in explaining why the physiology of v. 18 should result in impurity.

---

5.   Wenham ('Sexual Intercourse', p. 434) embeds this discrepancy in the asymmetric development of his argument: 'Bleeding may eventually lead to death. So the discharging woman is regarded as unclean...indeed unchecked her condition could end in her death. Similarly too we *presume* that male semen was viewed as a "life liquid". Hence its loss...was viewed as polluting.' As seen by my emphasis, nowhere does he draw a direct correlation between death and ejaculation.

6.   J.H. Neyrey, 'The Idea of Purity in Mark's Gospel', *Semeia* 21 (1986), pp. 91-128.

The Structure of Leviticus 15

Wenham has developed his understanding of Lev. 15.18 from his understanding of cultic purity in general. This for him entails the polarity of life and death. But, without careful regard for the structure of the chapter, he applies this encompassing principle directly to its contents, first to discharges in general, and then to each distinct discharge in the chapter. The problem here is not the question of his schema's applicability to Israel's cult and its regulations. Rather, it is the fact that its application to this chapter is effected without attention to context. The consequence of this method is that shades of meaning within the chapter are potentially overlooked.

In particular, Wenham's inattention to syntactic detail limits the possible significance of its chiastic structuring. His basic structure is as follows:[7]

A	vv. 2b-15	long term	male discharges
B	vv. 16-18	transient	male discharges
B´	vv. 19-24	transient	female discharges
A´	vv. 25-30	long term	female discharges

For Wenham, this chiastic structure points towards 'the unity of mankind in two sexes...[this] finds its most profound expression in the act of sexual intercourse...[which is] the midpoint of the literary structure'.[8] The problem here is that although he sees v. 18 as the literary midpoint of the chapter, he still considers it to be structurally a subdivision of the second unit, transient male discharges. He therefore resolutely generates its meaning based on his general understanding of Israel's cult.

The chapter's syntactic structure however does not bear out the inclusion of v. 18 in the section of vv. 16ff. The independence of v. 18 within the chapter is apparent from its conditional syntax, a structuring device used throughout the chapter. Each distinct legal unit begins with a conditional clause formation:

A	2b	*'îš 'îš kî*
B	16	*weʾîš kî*
B´	19	*weʾiššâ kî*
A´	25	*weʾiššâ kî*

---

7.   G.J. Wenham, *The Book of Leviticus* (Grand Rapids: Eerdmans, 1979), p. 216.

8.   Wenham, *Leviticus*, p. 217.

Verse 18 begins with *wᵉ'iššâ 'ᵃšer*. The word *'ᵃšer* is of course most commonly read as a relative pronoun. This reading, however, would indicate that the subject of the verse is the woman, a reading ruled out by the plural subject of the verse's apodosis. An alternative is to read *'ᵃšer* as a conditional particle, admittedly a fairly rare function, but one which does occur.[9] This reading would be more in keeping with the legal nature of the chapter and in fact is the sense with which Wenham reads the verse ('If a woman'). Verse 18, therefore, is written with its own conditional construction comparable to the conditional constructions used throughout the chapter to demarcate distinct legal units.

In addition, v. 18 is entirely unique within the chapter in that its subject is plural. Elsewhere within the chapter, individuals other than the person with the discharge do become entangled in the impurity of the discharge (vv. 7, 21ff., 27). But because this always involves contagious impurity, the subject remains singular, the individual with the discharge becoming an actual or implied object within the syntax of the regulation. These settings of impurity contagiously acquired are therefore subsets within a larger unit. Verses 23 and 24, for example, even though written with a conditional *'im* construction, show themselves not to warrant an independent reading for this very reason. The subject there is singular and the impurity is menstrual impurity contagiously acquired.

If the setting of v. 18 was to be classed similarly as contagious impurity, we would expect the wording to be different. First, we would expect a singular subject. Secondly, we would expect a clause analogous to v. 24ab, 'and her monthly flow touches him'. This would then constitute the impurity as that of vv. 16 and 17, for which v. 18 would present a subset of the larger unit's concern (as vv. 23 and 24 are to vv. 19ff.). In addition, if this were the case there would be no need to mention the man in v. 18, because he would be unclean by the definition provided in vv. 16 and 17 (even as the woman is understood to be impure in v. 24 by the definition provided in v. 19).

The impurity of v. 18 is therefore not simply that of the emission of semen. It is also not simply intercourse because (1) the phrase *šikbat-zāra'* would then be unnecessary, and (2) the summary statement of vv. 32 and 33 does not mention sexual intercourse as a category, only the emission of semen. Rather, the impurity stems from some aspect of the whole event, the emission of semen in sexual intercourse.

9. P. Joüon, *Grammaire de l'hébreu biblique* (Rome: Institut Biblique Pontifical, 1923), p. 515.

Because of its thematic and structural independence, it seems advisable to distinguish v. 18 structurally within the whole of the chapter. This yields the following structure for the chapter:

A	vv. 2b-15	long term	male discharges
B	vv. 16-17	transient	male discharges
C	vv. 18	intercourse	male/female
B´	vv. 19-24	transient	female discharges
A´	vv. 25-30	long term	female discharges

Verse 18 serves as the very clear fulcrum of the chapter. Accentuating the pivotal role of v. 18 is the way in which components of the verse interlock with sections B and B´. The interlocking components can be pictured as the following:

B	v. 16	And a man...a laying of seed
C	v. 18	And a woman...a laying of seed
B´	v. 19	And a woman...a flow of blood

This interlocking pivotal structure heightens the independence of the verse within the chapter and further suggests its nature as a fulcrum towards which the chapter draws the reader.

With the chiastic outline of the chapter now clear in its intention to draw the reader towards its fulcrum verse, we can begin to assess more accurately the chapter's symbolic significance, and especially that of v. 18.

Structure and Meaning

One of the most obvious characteristics of Leviticus 15 is that it addresses itself only to the issue of sexual discharges. It does not handle any other type of discharge, such as waste excretion or the flow of blood from a cut or wound. This indicates that the chapter is concerned with only sexual physiology and not physiology in general. Secondly, only the setting of v. 18 is akin to the ideal sexual relationship described in Gen. 2.20-25. Since the chapter's structure is intent to draw the reader towards this fulcrum, the chapter is apparently concerned with not simply regulating diverse sexual processes. It is designed to develop within the reader some deeper understanding about ideal sexual physiology. A general statement regarding the meaning of Leviticus 15 could therefore be that it is concerned with the ideal physiological functioning of the reproductive system.[10]

The nature of physiological functioning is composed of two distinct but closely interrelated concerns. First, a purely physiological level: Is there physiological deviation from processes which are regarded as 'normal'? Given the centrality of v. 18 in this chapter, we can further refine the question to: 'Is there physiological deviation from sexual processes regarded as normal in relation to the ideal setting of sexual intercourse?' Secondly, considering the reproductive system as a system, 'Is the "system" functioning toward fulfilling the purpose of the system?' Very simply, 'Is the reproductive system functioning so as to bring about reproduction?'

Taking into account these two questions, the structure of the chapter can be pictured in the following way:

		Physiological Integrity	*Systemic Function*
A	vv. 2b-15	Abnormal	Abnormal
B	vv. 16-17	Typical	Dysfunctional
C	v. 18	Normal	Normal
B´	vv. 19-24	Typical	Dysfunctional
A´	vv. 25-30	Abnormal	Abnormal

Sections A and A´ describe physiological settings which are clearly pathological. The reproductive system is unsound. Wenham's schema is helpful here: the body is not whole as it manifests signs of deterioration. Each discharge is also systemically abnormal because neither can lead to the creation of life.

Sections B and B´ are not pathological conditions: that is, they are not life threatening or degenerative. They cannot, therefore, be called physiologically 'abnormal'. On the other hand, the setting is not the chapter's ideal of sexual intercourse. The term 'normal' cannot therefore be applied in its fullest sense. But, inasmuch as they are the typical physiological processes experienced by an individual and a particular sex, the label 'typical' seems appropriate. Despite this physiological pseudo-normality, however, section B is systemically dysfunctional because the discharge, though typical, cannot bring about reproduction.

Section C, as the fulcrum of the chapter, portrays sexual physiology in

10. The sociological functioning of the reproductive system is dealt with elsewhere (Lev. 18.6-23; 20.10-21).

its fully functional setting. The reproductive system of neither individual is showing signs of a life-threatening or degenerating condition. But also, each evidences physiology which is appropriate for the ideal sexual physiological setting of intercourse: ejaculation in the male and the absence of menstrual discharge in the female.

The chiastic structure of contagion and cultic resolution within the chapter similarly complements the structure just described:

	Contagion	*Resolution for Animate Objects*
A	animate/inanimate/tabernacle he sacrifices	others wash/he washes
B	inanimate/tabernacle	he washes
C	tabernacle	both wash
B´	animate/inanimate/tabernacle	others wash
A´	animate/inanimate/tabernacle	others wash/she sacrifices

Given this nuance of the chapter's structure, in conjunction with the structure described above, there can be no question that the degree of impurity decreases as the reader moves through the various physiological settings towards the center. Note, however, that impurity only decreases towards the center. It does not disappear.

It cannot be said, therefore, that the chiastic structure of Leviticus 15 is built solely around purely descriptive differences (male–female, long term–transient). With varying degrees of impurity and reproductive integrity, it seems apparent that the chiasm is more than simply a rhetorical device which intends to show the reader 'the unity of mankind in two sexes'. Without denying this layer of significance, it seems clear that some deeper qualitative significance is at work. I quote at length Welch's thoughts on the issues involved here:

> The more interesting and challenging observations regarding chiasmus are in respect to complex structural applications of the form. Here the form becomes more than a mere literary device, and more than a skeleton upon which thoughts and words are attached. When chiasmus achieves the level of ordering the flow of thoughts...the character of the form itself merges with the message and meaning of the passage. Indeed what is said is often no more than how it is said.[11]

11. J.W. Welch (ed.), *Chiasmus in Antiquity: Structures, Analyses, Exegesis* (Hildesheim: Gerstenberg, 1981), p. 11.

Toward a Solution

Lev. 15.31 is the chapter's motive statement. As such, it must figure in any explanation given to v. 18. Verse 31 states that if the body is not cleansed from the discharges in the prescribed way, then the tabernacle is defiled. This contagion, however, is different from the contagion described in the laws themselves, because it is not conveyed through actual contact.

The mechanism which might explain this association is that of homology. A homology is the resemblance between two objects based on similarities in structural and functional aspects. In biology, homologous relationships are integral to evolutionary reconstruction and systematics. In cultural systems, homologies link different aspects or levels of reality, not simply as a means of organization, but also for purposes of interpretation. If a homologous link exists, what one 'understands' about the one object shapes the 'understanding' one has of the other object, and vice versa.

The body figures prominently in homologous relationships, with its long and extensive history of being seen as a microcosm.[12] Mircea Eliade has described the presence in certain cultures of a 'house–body–cosmos' homology.[13] According to Eliade, 'The "house"...is at once an *imago mundi* and a replica of the human body...'.[14] The presence of a homology between body and tabernacle in Leviticus 15 is therefore not peculiar. It is possible, then, that the defilement of intercourse might be understood in light of some aspect of the correspondence between the body and the tabernacle.

One of the principal aspects of the tabernacle as an object in everyday life was its function as the center of spatial perception within the wilderness encampment. At the center was the presence of God in the 'Most Holy Place' of the tabernacle. The divine presence transformed that structure into sacred space. Organized around this center was a continuum composed of varying degrees of consecration to the sacredness of the center (Num. 1–4). In defining the quality needed to approach

12. L. Barkan, *Nature's Work of Art: The Human Body as Image of the World* (New Haven: Yale University Press, 1975).

13. M. Eliade, *The Sacred and the Profane* (trans. W.R. Trask; New York: Harper & Row, 1961), p. 172.

14. Eliade, *Sacred and the Profane*, p. 179.

the center, a plethora of words could be used, all capturing something of the center's character. Words like 'purity', 'wholeness', 'perfection' and 'unblemished' come readily to mind. These can perhaps best be summed up in Wenham's use of the word 'life'. If anything is to approach the center of the community, it must be full of life and fully given over to life.

Anything having a center by definition must also have a periphery. In the spatial organization of the wilderness encampment, the periphery was the wilderness which encircled the community. The periphery must necessarily have reflected the obverse of the center's character, a quality encompassed in the words 'death' and 'non-life'. Thus a corpse, being empty of life, was capable of contaminating the priest, whose allegiance was overtly towards the center (Lev. 21.1-4). Sacrificial animals, because they were labelled as full of life (unblemished, perfect), were brought to the center. However, once their resemblance to life was erased through their destruction in the sacrificial rite, they were taken to a place of death and non-life outside the wilderness encampment (Lev. 4.11-12).

Other things which were removed to this realm of death and non-life in the periphery were waste products[15] and those whose bodies were deteriorated by disease (Deut. 23.12-14; Lev. 13–14). In terms of sexuality, the firstborn was brought towards the center, but someone in the war encampment who emitted dysfunctional semen had to go outside the camp (Deut. 23.10-11). Someone who emitted dysfunctional semen in the non-military encampment was separated from the center (Lev. 15.16).

It is obvious, then, that Levitical spatial perception was built on a continuum, which had as its poles a center (the tabernacle) and a periphery (the wilderness). Within the camp itself, social organization was devised so that there was increasing consecration/purity with movement towards the center. With this in mind, the structure of the encampment can be pictured as the following:

increasing purity ————————————————————————→
wilderness   encampment   tabernacle
←———————————————————————— increasing impurity

15. Excreta were technically not pollutants, as T. Frymer-Kensky points out ('Pollution, Purification, and Purgation in Biblical Israel', in C.L. Meyers and M. O'Connor [eds.], *The Word of the Lord Shall Go Forth* [Winona Lake, IN: Eisenbrauns, 1983], p. 401). However, Deut. 23.15, while not stating technical impurity, does suggest an antithesis to holiness.

The individuals would have perceived their relation to the center based on their positioning within this grid. They would have understood their 'location' in juxtaposition to individuals on one side who were farther away from the center and those to the other side who were nearer to the center.

Restrictions were placed upon actual approach to the center. Only the High Priest could approach, only after undergoing purification rituals, and only on one day of the year (Lev. 16). And although the center was constituted as sacred space by the presence of Yahweh, it was not immune from the impurity of the community, since a sacrifice was needed for it to be cleansed (Lev. 16.16). The writer of the book of Hebrews has quite accurately described the problem (10.1-4). If it were possible to attain absolute and abiding purity commensurate with the purity of Yahweh, through cleansing and sacrifice, sacrifice would cease and approach to the center would be unrestricted. Such was not the case, however; cleansing was a continuous process because absolute and lasting purity was impossible to bring about in the fallen world. Thus, although there was increasing purity with movement towards the center, it was impossible to generate the absolute and abiding purity needed to allow one to remain there.

What light do these aspects of the tabernacle shed on the 'puzzling' law of Lev. 15.18? It is apparent that the structure of Leviticus 15 places sexual intercourse at its center. In the structures outlined above, we can also see varying levels of impurity in the physiological settings described. Impurity decreases as the setting becomes more and more 'correct', with movement towards the chapter's center. Sexual physiology is organized by the chapter on a continuum between poles of most impure (A/A´) and least impure (C). This too is similar to the situation of the wilderness encampment, in which the tabernacle is the site of fullest purity and the periphery is the obverse.

In Leviticus 15, the idea of the periphery is presented in two ways. First, the textual shape suggests settings which are nearer the center and those nearer, or in, the periphery. And secondly, some of the discharges suggest waste and non-life, something which is more appropriate to the peripheral wilderness of the encampment. Thus pathological discharges are non-life/waste; semen apart from intercourse is non-life/waste because the setting is not a life-giving emission in intercourse. Similarly, the bloody discharges of the female are non-life/waste, because within the functioning of the reproductive system they are not life-giving. If the parallel with the tabernacle holds, the only explanation to be given for the impurity of Lev. 15.18 is that something compromises the integrity of the reproductive system in that setting. In other words, there is something which is alien to the fulness of life, in its many dimensions, in that setting.

In connection with her analysis of Leviticus 11, Douglas states that 'Holiness requires that individuals shall conform to the class to which they belong. And holiness requires that different classes of things shall not be confused... Holiness means keeping distinct the categories of creation'.[16] In relation to the animals of Leviticus 11, Douglas sees this principle operating to classify animals based on anatomical/functional boundaries. Thus, for example, crustaceans are unclean because their anatomy provides them with a means of locomotion inappropriate to their realm of creation. This can also apply to the structure of the encampment. Non-life/waste can have nothing to do with life and is therefore spatially separated.

In the emission of semen, the penis is fulfilling the appropriate function for the setting. But, according to Douglas's schema of anatomical functional boundaries, the penis is not fully given over to this function. It is also used for urination. And urine is non-life/waste. Urine is something of the periphery.[17] The Deuteronomist sets urine over against a characteristic image of abundance and life in 2 Kgs 18.27 and 31-32, at a time when the peripheral chaos is encroaching upon the covenant community. As non-life/waste, urine also shares in the qualities of the textual periphery of Leviticus 15. It is unable to bring about the creation of life, and urination is physiologically incompatible with intercourse.

The penis is therefore not completely given over to the reproductive nature of the setting. As an anatomical structure it is functionally ambiguous, confusing features of both the production of life and the production of waste, features of the center and of the periphery. The reason why the emission of semen is central to the creation of the impurity is because it is only with the emission of semen that the functional ambiguity of the penis becomes actual. At that moment its 'unholy' character (see Douglas's definition of holiness above) is factored into the event. Thus sexual intercourse, when there is the emission

16.   Douglas, *Purity and Danger*, p. 53.

17.   It should be noted that it is never specified in the Hebrew Bible that urine was to be removed outside the encampment to the periphery. This does not, however, diminish the fact that urine is non-life/waste.

of semen, defiles because with the emission of semen, that which structurally unites husband and wife as one flesh, crosses functional boundaries. At that moment, an element from the periphery of both the chapter and the encampment, through association, intrudes upon the event.

Conclusion

In summary the following points can be made:

1. The chiastic structure of Leviticus 15 is significant for the interpretation of its content.
2. The reproductive system, as perceived through the filter of these laws, is in a homologous relationship with the tabernacle.
3. Both the tabernacle and the setting of sexual intercourse are at one end of a continuum, which has at its other end the characteristics wilderness/non-life/waste.
4. The penis combines features of the production of life and the production of waste; with the emission of semen it exhibits functional ambiguity and is therefore not 'whole' or 'pure', qualities necessary in approaching the 'center'.

JSOT 52 (1991), pp. 43-60

FREEDOM OR KNOWLEDGE?
PERSPECTIVE AND PURPOSE IN THE EXODUS NARRATIVE
(EXODUS 1–15)

Lyle Eslinger

To have read much of the Bible is to have read something about the exodus. Where it isn't lying on the surface, as in the argument for establishing the law (Exod. 20.2), the exodus is often an assumption without knowledge of which a reader will go astray.[1] It becomes a leitmotif whose theological-political significance echoes through the pages of the Bible. Joshua leads Israel through the parted waters of the Jordan into the promised land (Josh. 4) in a mirror image of the crossing of the Red Sea. Prophets have visions of a return from captivity: the new exodus, a mirror image of the old (Isa. 43.14-21; Ezek. 20.32-44). And finally, even Jesus takes up the Mosaic mantle with new signs and wonders for a new generation wandering in yet another wilderness.[2]

This process of reappropriating the exodus story does not stop with biblical literature. Again and again Christian and Jew have understood that this story fits times and places far removed from those miserable slaves in ancient Egypt. The rabbis saw the story as an archetypical model of human redemption. For a Jew, they said, when you read the story it is as if you were standing at Mount Sinai, ready again to hear the commandments of God.[3] The philosopher Ernst Bloch may have gone

---

1.   E.g. Hos. 7.11-16; cf. W. Eichrodt, *Theology of the Old Testament* (trans. J.A. Baker; Philadelphia: Westminster Press, 1961), I, pp. 36-37.

2.   E.g. Acts 2.19, 22; cf. D.P. Moessner, 'Luke 9.1-50: Luke's Preview of the Journey of the Prophet like Moses of Deuteronomy', *JBL* 102 (1983), pp. 575-605.

3.   M.M. Kasher, *Encyclopedia of Biblical Interpretation*. VII. *Exodus* (trans. and ed. H. Freedman; New York: American Biblical Encyclopedia Society, 1967), p. 1.

too far for modernist tastes when he spoke of an 'exodus principle' in the biblical story, which he then transformed even further into a general 'principle of hope'.[4] But his attempt to remake the story into a metaphoric metaphysical principle testifies to its impact on readers right up to the modern age; it exemplifies this continual effort to make the inspiring and hopeful story ours. Even more recently, liberation theology has found its own manifesto boldly anticipated by God's own action to emancipate the Hebrew slaves from Egyptian tyranny. The liberationists' reading is, of course, hotly debated. That debate is itself testimony to the importance that the Bible's religious reading communities place on the story and its correct interpretation.

More important than the abiding significance of the exodus story, and perhaps responsible for that durability, is the long-standing belief that the story bears a message of hope. Bloch's derivation of a 'principle of hope' from the story is but a recent link in a long chain of similar emotional responses stretching back into the Bible itself. To supply examples of positive attitudes towards the exodus story from within the Bible might seem superfluous, given the ancient and modern accord about the heartening theological optimism of the story. Since it is my intention to question the validity of such a reading, however, two or three examples might be useful to illustrate the positive inner-biblical attitude. The book of Deuteronomy may have been written, as its Greek title 'Deuteronomy' suggests, as a commentary on the law contained in the four books of the law that precede it.[5] In Deuteronomy Moses continually reminds the children of Israel that Yahweh staged the exodus to deliver them from slavery into the privileged state of being God's own possession (4.20, 32-37; 5.15; 6.12, 21-23; 7.8, 18-19; 8.14-16; 9.26; 10.19; 11.2-7; etc.). Those miraculous events are venerated and displayed as a summons to thankful obedience. Joshua, Moses' successor, continues the positive presentation of the exodus in his summons to covenant renewal near the end of the conquest (Josh. 24.6-7, 17). Not long afterwards Samuel does the same at the inauguration of the monarchy

4. E. Bloch, *Das Prinzip der Hoffnung* (Gesamtausgabe, V; Frankfurt: Suhrkamp, 1959); cf. W. Zimmerli, *Der Mensch und seine Hoffnung im Alten Testament* (Göttingen: Vandenhoeck & Ruprecht, 1968), pp. 163-78.

5. Cf. C.M. Carmichael, *The Laws of Deuteronomy* (Ithaca, NY: Cornell University Press, 1974); J. Milgrom, 'Profane Slaughter and a Formulaic Key to the Composition of Deuteronomy', *HUCA* 47 (1976), pp. 1-17; J. Weingreen, *From Bible to Mishna* (Manchester: Manchester University Press, 1976).

(1 Sam. 12.8). Somewhat later, Isaiah and Ezekiel add a second liberating exodus to renew the first: surely they approve of what God had done and would do. Lastly, in the third division of the Hebrew Bible, the Ketubim, one finds a wealth of references and allusions to the exodus story, all positive in tone (e.g. Pss. 66.6; 68.7-9; 77.14-15, 20; 78.12-53; 80.8; 81.6, 10; 99.6; 105.25-45; 106.6-12; 114; 136.10-16).

We shall probably never decide whether these biblical evaluations of the exodus are based on the narrative now found in Exodus 1–15, on some antecedent narrative or tradition(s), or perhaps even on their authors' personal knowledge of historical events in Israel's past. Though someone might be able to demonstrate specific instances of literary dependence, it seems impossible to affirm that all subsequent inner-biblical reflection on the exodus depends on chs. 1–15 of the book of Exodus. If, therefore, it could be shown that the narrative in Exodus 1–15 is of a markedly different opinion about the significance of the exodus from Egypt, there would be no call to criticize these other biblical evaluations as misreadings or intentional perversions of that narrative. Obversely, given the tenuous nature of our knowledge about the literary and traditional connections between other biblical reflections on the exodus and those in the book of Exodus, there is insufficient reason to reject my untraditional reading of the first fifteen chapters in the book of Exodus, simply because it does not agree with these other biblical reflections.

The case with existing scholarly commentary on the exodus narrative in Exodus 1–15 is quite different. Here there is no question that evaluative responses are supposed to be based on the narrative in Exodus 1–15. With few exceptions, modern readers find these chapters expressing the same triumphalist sentiments voiced in the other biblical reflections on the exodus. A few examples will illustrate this uncontroversial assertion. In a source-critical dissection of the account of the plaguing of Egypt, Elias Auerbach says that the number of plagues was originally much smaller. In support of his case he says, 'Popular imagination reveled in this victory over powerful Egypt, and the number of plagues was never too great'.[6] The Mennonite scholar Millar Lind, in spite of writing from a pacifist Christian perspective for which biblical warfare is a theological and moral problem, nevertheless sees the conflict filled narrative as an agreeably positive assessment of the exodus events:

---

6.   E. Auerbach, *Moses* (trans. and ed. R.A. Barclay and I.O. Lehman; Detroit: Wayne State University Press, 1975), p. 51.

> Exodus 1–15 is a story of conflict, the conflict of an enslaved people with the most powerful empire of the day. The resolution of this conflict, through the nature plagues climaxed with the victory at the sea, was seen by Israel as Yahweh's central act of salvation for his people.[7]

And Gerhard von Rad, in his *Old Testament Theology*, says that, in Exodus 1 and the following chapters, the theme of the deliverance from Egypt has been

> theologically worked up into a sublime chorale. In the deliverance from Egypt Israel saw the guarantee for all the future, the absolute surety for Yahweh's will to save, something like a warrant to which faith could appeal in times of travail.[8]

The triumphalist reading of Exodus 1–15 finds additional support in the religious convictions of biblical scholars, Christian and Jewish. D.M.G. Stalker's work on the book of Exodus in *Peake's Commentary on the Bible* is but one example from a standard handbook of biblical commentary. Speaking of the exodus event described in Exodus, he says it is

> the great constitutive action of God by which he not only brought the nation of Israel into being, but also gave his plan for the salvation of mankind its final shape... The Exodus is for the OT and Judaism what the life, death and resurrection of Christ are for the NT and Christianity. And for Christians, what Jesus brought to fulfilment was the purpose of the Exodus.[9]

Finally, scholars working within the area of liberation theology have seen the exodus as a paradigm of God's will for the oppressed of the earth:

> This God YHWH, as the God who frees humans to a dignified life wherever this might be threatened, becomes the foundation of biblical Israel...[so that] it is told how the God YHWH had delivered his worshippers from the state slavery of Pharaoh. This was, indeed, the fundamental experience to which all in the new society were party and which they were supposed to preserve, no matter whether they had experienced the liberation from Egypt or from the Canaanite city-states (or from the mortal dangers of the journey through the wilderness).[10]

---

7. M. Lind, *Yahweh is a Warrior* (Kitchener, Ont.: Herald Press, 1980), p. 46 (cf. p. 49).

8. G. von Rad, *Old Testament Theology* (trans. D.M.G. Stalker; New York: Harper & Row, 1962), I, p. 176.

9. D.M.G. Stalker, 'Exodus', in *Peake's Commentary on the Bible* (ed. M. Black and H.H. Rowley; Don Mills, Ont.: Nelson, 1962), p. 208.

10. E. Zenger, 'Der Gott des Exodus', *BK* 42 (1987), pp. 98-103 (101).

This reading of the exodus events fits the theologian's purpose and supplies the biblical-theological underpinning that some think liberation theology needs. But does it fit the exodus story? Is Exodus 1–15 really a triumphal celebration of the 'great work' (*ma'ᵃśēh yhwh haggādôl 'ᵃšer 'āśâ*, Deut. 11.7) that Yahweh did for Israel or not? If it is, there is much in this narrative that might be said to contradict its author's purpose; if it is not, then it is time for the religious communities that use the story to reassess their claims on it. Only a close reading of the text can decide the issue.

The most likely place to find an answer to the question of what kind of light the narrative casts on the events is in the narrative itself, in its own explicit narratorial comments and evaluations. The narrative mode of writing, in which the majority of biblical narrative was composed, depends on the literary convention of two separate ontological levels from which evaluations may be voiced.[11] There is a hierarchy of ontology and epistemology from the level of the narrator, who is external to the story world, untouched and unconditioned by it, down to the level of the characters, including God, who are stuck fast and firm within the limitations of their respective positions in their story environment. Evaluation of events from the subordinate level of the characters is relative to the conditions of their existence within the story, whereas assessment from the external, unconditioned narrator is relative only to the situation from which the narrator speaks. Usually in the Bible, and certainly in Exodus 1–15, the narrator's own existential context is undetermined; it is not revealed in anything the narrator says, and it is not described by the author or authors who have created this narrator, who has been invested with full and unconditioned authority to tell the story. Hence evaluation from the narrator is equivalent to the evaluative meaning of the narrative. Taking this conventional literary ontology of narratives such as Exodus 1–15 for granted—and the failure to do so is the cornerstone of a triumphalist reading—let us look at the evaluations in the narrative.

The most important example of praise for the actions of God in the exodus appears in the poem known as the 'Song of Moses' in Exodus 15, and in Miriam's antiphonal response (Exod. 15.20-21). Following

---

11. Discussion of the kinds of narrative situations found in the Bible, their relative frequency, and more detailed description of the majority narrative situation may be found in L. Eslinger, *Into the Hands of the Living God* (Bible and Literature Series, 24; Sheffield: Almond Press, 1989), pp. 10-21.

hard on the heels of Yahweh's final triumph over Pharaoh and the Egyptian army at the Red Sea, the song is usually regarded as a fitting conclusion that summarizes the tone and significance of the entire story up to ch. 15. Brevard Childs, for example, states that 'the poem in its present setting offers an important interpretation of the event itself, and thereby affects the reading of the prose tradition which preceded it'.[12] Childs is correct about the rhetoric of the song of praise, but his neglect of the narrative's voice structure inverts the actual context of authority. We readers are addressed directly by the author only through the external, unconditioned narrator who is relating the story, the author's own creation.[13] To understand what we are being told, we must take care to evaluate all statements made within the story in the light of their relationship to the overall authorial/narratorial statement, which is made both by explicit commentary and by less apparent implications in the narrative's structure.[14] When Childs assumes that Miriam's point of

12. B.S. Childs, *The Book of Exodus: A Critical Theological Commentary* (OTL; Philadelphia: Westminster Press, 1974), p. 249.

13. M. Bakhtin (*Problems of Dostoevsky's Poetics* [Minneapolis: University of Minnesota Press, 1984]) has argued that this rule must not be presumed to apply to all narrative. In Dostoevsky's novels, Bakhtin recognizes what he calls 'polyphonic' narrative, in which character voices are not subordinate to the narrator's. In such a case, says Bakhtin, the narrative has no single, unified message such as is heard in the 'classic' narrative mode of narration with an external, unconditioned narrator. Perhaps it is more accurate to say of the polyphonic narrative that its meaning is not so easily discernible as in the 'classic' mode of narration, which dominates biblical narrative. Instead, the meaning of a polyphonic narrative is constituted by a combination of the voices of characters and narrator. If what remains is an irresolvable number of differences of perception, then perhaps those differences between individual perceptions of life are 'the meaning'.

In any case, the narrative in Exod. 1–15 is not polyphonic. It is narrated by a narrator external to the story, unconditioned by it, and having an access to information that is unsurpassed by any character in the story, including God. The narrator is able, for example, to look in on God even in his most private moments with Moses (Exod. 3.4–4.16) and into God's most private, unspoken thoughts (2.24-25). But God gives no indication of any knowledge of the narrator, his whereabouts, or his prying reportage. Of course, it is only the conventions of this mode of narration that are responsible for God's fictional subordination.

14. In her study of the narrator's voice in *Paradise Lost*, A. Ferry also underlined the need to subordinate characters' statements to the 'omniscient' narrator's author-given authority (*Milton's Epic Voice: The Narrator in Paradise Lost* [Chicago: University of Chicago Press, 1963], p. 15):

view is that of the narrative, all that his reading reveals is his own preference for the theological mindset expressed by Miriam. Unless some
narrative feature suggests otherwise, the narrative conventions within
which Exodus 1–15 is written say that we must, rather, seek to understand character utterances within the context of their situation in the
story world as presented in the narrative.

With respect to the 'Song of Moses', the narrator has provided an
explicit expositional introduction (the locale and circumstance of the
song) and conclusion for the poem (why they sang the song):

Introduction	Then sang Moses and the children at Israel this song to Yahweh. They said…(v. 1).
Body of poem	vv. 2-18
Concluding Comment	because Pharaoh's horse, chariot, and cavalry went into the sea and Yahweh brought back the waters of the sea upon them. But the children of Israel walked on dry land in the midst of the sea (v. 19).

The narratorial statements bracket the poem, providing a perspectival
frame within which the poem is to be read and understood. The existential and temporal distancing of the reader from the sentiments
expressed in the poem is intentional and complete: going in and coming
out of the reading the reader is reminded that 'that was then', and is
also reminded about the particulars of the situation that provoked the
song.

The introduction points to a specific point—'Then (*'āz*) sang
Moses…'—in the chain of events that evoked the song.[15] The situation

> By ignoring the role of Milton's narrator in *Paradise Lost* and concentrating instead
> on the speeches and actions of characters, we have in some ways allowed our
> critical presuppositions to mislead us. We have assumed that the meaning of the
> poem was to be found in our response to the characters in it as to figures in a piece
> of dramatic literature… We cannot simply respond to them directly because in the
> poem without the aid of the inspired narrator we could neither see nor hear them; it
> is his vision which determines ours and we listen only to what he recites for us.

Ferry goes on to point out that where there is a conflict between the characters'
statements and the narrator's, the latter must be given precedence. With respect to the
narrative in Exod. 1–15, the problem has been, rather, that interpreters have not even
recognized the existence of a distinct narratorial voice, let alone the possibility that it
might contradict the sentiments expressed in the song of Exod. 15.

15. The narrator emphasizes the causal connection between the song and the situation of its evocation by using the strong adverb *'āz* with the imperfect, rather than
simple parataxis, cf. GKB §107b, c; F.E. König, *Historisch-kritisches Lehrgebäude*

was, of course, the crossing of the Red Sea, and the narrator reiterates the causal connection in his concluding note on the song, 'because (*kî*) Pharaoh's horse...' (v. 19). So we have a specific context within the story world that explains the sentiment of the song. But the narrator goes even further to pinpoint the source of the song. In v. 19, he explains that the Israelites extolled Yahweh's merits because, in contrast to the Egyptians, whom Yahweh drowned, the Israelites were preserved from death. This is a song sung by a group of people who have just escaped an awesome, weird death; they sing in response to the Being who, as they have just seen, holds their lives in its hand. Given their state of mind at that point (*'āz*), not to mention the fact that Yahweh's servant, Moses, was choirmaster, what else but the praises of Yahweh could they sing?[16]

As a response to the Red Sea crossing, the song parallels the reaction described in Exod. 14.31: 'And the people feared Yahweh and they believed in Yahweh and in Moses, his servant'. The fact that the narrator has emphasized the reaction and its context by repeating it (repetition being the most common tool for foregrounding in the Bible) shows

---

der hebräischen Sprache. Zweite Hälfte. II. *(Schluss-)Theil. Syntax der hebräischen Sprache* [Leipzig: Hinrichs, 1897], §§137, 138). Isaac Rabinowitz's study of *'āz* followed by an imperfect verb supports this reading of Exod. 15.1:

> referring to the foregoing context of narrated past events, *'āz* + imperfect indicates this context as approximately the time when, the time or circumstances in the course of which, or the occasion upon which the action designated by the imperfect verb form went forward: this was when [then?]...so-and-so did (imperfect) such-and-such ('"*āz* Followed by Imperfect Verb-Form in Preterite Contexts: A Redactional Device in Biblical Hebrew', *VT* 34 [1984], p. 59).

16. The narrator's unusual grammatical choice of a singular verb with a plural subject in 15.1 has been understood to imply that Moses had a guiding hand in the singing of this song (cf. M.M. Kasher, *Encyclopedia of Biblical Interpretation.* VIII. *Exodus* [trans. and ed. H. Freedman; New York: American Biblical Encyclopedia Society, 1970], pp. 162-63, 165). The grammar and syntax of the introductory sentence make 'the Israelites' appear as subordinates in the singing; the singular verb, '[Then] sang' (*yāšîr*), has its necessary singular subject filled by the subsequent Moses, a connection highlighted by the intervening *maqqeph*; the addition of 'the Israelites' with the conjunction 'and' requires the reader to reopen the doors of a completed thought to allow these stragglers to join in with Moses (cf. M. Sternberg, *Expositional Modes and Temporal Ordering in Fiction* [Baltimore: Johns Hopkins University Press, 1978], index *s.v.* 'Primacy Effect'). The sentence should, therefore, be translated: 'Then sang Moses—and the children of Israel—this song' (cf. KJV).

concern that the reader understand the psychological impact of the event on the characters in the story. At the same time that the narrator brackets the song with his own statements about its context, he displays his separation from that time, place and state of mind. Only if the narrator had already affiliated himself with such a viewpoint would the reader be justified in reading the song as an interpretative key to the preceding narrative, as Childs suggests we do.

A careful study of Exodus 1–14 reveals no trace of triumphalism or congratulatory comment in the narrator's exposition. Given the long history of triumphalist interpretation of this narrative, the absence of laudatory narratorial comment is surprising. How can we explain the discrepancy between narration and interpretation? Two factors have led readers to misconstrue the exodus narrative, both literary matters of voice and perspective. First, though the narrator has the largest share of words, and though the narrator's is the only voice expressly addressing the reader, the narrator does not provide explicit evaluation of the events. All narratorial commentary is implicit, and must be deduced from the narrator's ordering of material, allusions to other passages, and contextualizations of the characters' utterances in the story. Though the narratorial voice in the book of Exodus is strong, it is mostly silent. It is strong in its implicit evaluation of events and characters' verbal reactions, contextualizing them with a variety of literary devices; but it is silent when it comes to explicit evaluation. Secondly, such expositional silence might well be taken for narratorial agreement with the evaluative perspective of a protagonist, especially a supposedly heroic one, like Yahweh or Moses, in the story. Or, it could go unnoticed by a careless reader, who simply assumes that authors voice their opinions through principal characters, especially through the ones who express the 'established truths' of the Bible. No one has suggested, to my knowledge, that the overarching perspective of the exodus narrative is neutral. Both assumptions depend on the absence of explicit evaluation, and both look to the most prominent character—frequently God in biblical narrative—for interpretative guidance.

It is difficult to decide what, if any, narratological theory underpins a given triumphalist reading of Exodus 1–15, owing to the common critical disregard for voice structure in narrative. But a quick review of God's utterances leaves no doubt about the primary source of confirmation for triumphalist readings. God speaks in three veins in Exodus 1–15: first, he identifies himself to Moses and the enslaved Israelites;[17] secondly, he instructs Moses about various tasks and duties;[18] and thirdly, he speaks triumphantly about his showing in Egypt.[19] In support of God's resounding exultation is the revered voice of Moses, who is pointedly characterized by the narrator as 'the servant of the Lord' (14.31).[20] At least two factors support readers' endorsement of Moses as a leading authority in this story. There is the illusion of the narrator's reticence, which can only be dispelled by a careful study of the implicit expositional strategies.[21] And there is the encouraging support of inner-biblical

17. Exod. 3.4-6, 12, 14-16; 6.2-4.

18. Exod. 4.2, 5-9, 11-12, 14-17, 19, 27; 6.11, 29; 7.1-2, 9, 15-16, 17b-18, 19; 8.1, 5, 16, 20; 9.1, 8-9, 13, 22; 10.12, 21; 11.1-2; 12.1-11, 15-20, 43-49; 13.2; 14.2, 15-16, 26.

19. Exod. 3.7-10, 17-22; 4.21-23; 6.1, 5-8; 7.3-5, 17a; 8.2-4, 21-23; 9.2-4, 14-19; 10.1-2; 11.9; 12.12-14; 14.3-4, 17-18.

20. Moses' triumphalism is visible in 10.3-6 (with Aaron); 11.4-8; 13.8-9, 14-16; 14.13-14; and above all in 15.1-18.

21. To give but one example, nowhere does the narrator state, in so many words, that God was responsible in any way for Israel's misfortunes in Egypt. But in ch. 1, at the very outset of the story, the narrator implies by allusions to the narratives of Genesis that God has at least a finger in Israel's fate. In 1.9 the king of Egypt explains that it is necessary to deal (wisely) with the Israelites because they had become a people 'greater' (*rab*) and 'mightier' (*'āṣûm*) than Egypt. The king's words reiterate words used by the narrator just two verses before, in the narrator's objective description of Israel's overwhelming growth.

The emphatic repetition of synonymic descriptions of Israel's growth in 1.7 alludes, of course, to God's previous blessings on humankind (*pᵉrû ûrᵉbû ûmil'û hā'āreṣ*, Gen. 1.28); to his blessing on Noah and his sons (*pᵉrû ûrᵉbû ûmil'û hā'āreṣ*, Gen. 9.1; *pᵉrû ûrᵉbû širṣû bā'āreṣ ûrᵉbû-bāh*, Gen. 9.7); to his promises to bless Abraham with burgeoning descendants (Gen. 13.16; 15.5; *wᵉʾarbeh 'ôtᵉkā bim'ōd mᵉʾōd*, Gen. 17.2; *wᵉhiprētî 'ōtᵉkā bim'ōd mᵉʾ ōd*, Gen. 17.6; *wᵉharbâ 'arbeh 'et-zarʿᵃkā*, Gen. 22.17); to his promises to Isaac (*wᵉhirbêtî 'et-zarʿᵃkā*, Gen. 26.4, 24); and to his command to Jacob (*pᵉrēh ûrᵉbēh*, Gen. 35.11). In Exod. 1.7 the narrator pounds the allusion into the readers' minds so that they will not fail to see that it is exactly the fulfilment of the blessings and promises that leads to the Israelites' enslavement in Egypt. By placing the key allusive words and the state they represent immediately before the Egyptian king's use of the same words to explain the need to subdue the Israelites, the narrator implies an ultimate explanation for the enslavement. The Egyptian king and his reasoning are only cogs in the machine engineered and run by God.

In support of the implicit exposition of the ultimate cause of Israel's misfortune are two other bits of information given in the book of Genesis. In Gen. 15.13 God

evaluations of the exodus. Psalm 105, for example, begins:

> v. 1   O give thanks to the Lord, call upon his name; make known his deeds among the peoples.
>
> v. 2   Sing to him, sing praises to him; speak of all his wonders.

Included among the list of deeds to be praised is the following item, which mirrors the causal analysis of Exod. 1.7, 9, but not its overt neutrality:

> v. 24   He made his people very fruitful (*wayyeper 'et-'ammô m^e'ōd*), he made them mightier (*wayya'^aṣimēhû*) than their adversaries.
>
> v. 25   He turned their heart to hate his people, to deal shrewdly with his servants.

The vocabulary of v. 24 suggests that the psalmist might have been interpreting the text (or tradition, or fixed formulas) of Exod. 1.7. But his inclusion of these deeds in a psalm of triumphant praise can only be regarded as a contradiction of the overt neutrality of the narrator in Exodus 1, which holds no trace of the bias expressed in the psalm.

Finally, there is the matter of readers' religious presuppositions. Is it at all possible for a reader who believes that the God he or she worships is the same one who speaks and acts in Exodus 1–15 to read this story without also accepting as normative the view promulgated by the divine character to the human participants in the story? Likewise, is it possible

---

predicts the bondage in Egypt; his foreknowledge in combination with his self-professed ability to manipulate the Egyptian oppressors (Gen. 15.14) indicates that he intends Israel to be enslaved. Secondly, the reader has already seen an example, in the case of Isaac, of God having made his chosen people 'mighty' (*'ṣm*, cf. Gen. 26.16) with the result that the king in whose land Isaac dwelt banished Isaac because of the obvious disparity in the fortunes of the blessed foreigner and the citizens of the land (Gen. 26.12-14, 16). The allusion (by way of the word *'ṣm* in Exod. 1.7, 9) to the analogous situation in the life of Isaac suggests, paradoxically, that it is the divine blessing that brings bondage to Israel, just as it brought expulsion to Isaac.

This cursory treatment of the narrator's implicit exposition in Exod. 1.7, 9 should suffice to show how the narrator can say much without seeming to say anything. If the reader approaches such a narrative without an ear attuned to such allusions, and without an eye trained for the expositional manipulations within the narrative, it is inevitable that his or her reading of the narrative will have its vacuum of exposition filled by the voice of the divine character, which appears to be the closest and most obvious thing within the story to an authoritative explanation of events within the story. The dominance of triumphalist readings of Exod. 1–15 proves the rule that nature abhors a vacuum even, or rather especially, in a reader's mind.

for such a reader to entertain the notion that the pious authors and faithful transmitters of Israel's sacred literature might have voiced opinions that contradict or, worse, subvert statements made by God in the stories they tell? The history of interpretation shows that, long before such doubts might be raised by the narration in Exodus 1–15, the reader has filled the evaluative meaning of the narrative with triumphant exultations promulgated by the divine character. This triumphalist skewing of the delicately balanced presentation of the exodus in the book of Exodus is due in part to the religious beliefs of interpreters whose conceptual categories are determined by the soteriological framework more or less common[22] to contemporary Judaism and Christianity: God acts within history to save humanity. As Walter Brueggemann has suggested, the triumphalist tendency in exegesis has led to a misconstruction of the overall biblical message, which is conveyed only by the total canonical context of scripture. According to Brueggemann, 'we also have not acknowledged how much the selection of Scripture, sometimes knowingly but frequently unknowingly, has helped to shape and determine the self-perception of the Church, its understanding of faith and ministry'.[23]

Brueggemann's argument that theological presuppositions have led to an unbalanced reading of the scriptural canon is confirmed and strengthened when one observes how the same tendency in exegesis has even misconstrued existing textual bases, such as Exodus 1–15, of salvation history theology. Triumphalist readings of scripture proceed by ignoring the context of statements within scripture. Just as certain books or passages are selected from the canon for isolated interpretation and theological meditation, so the statements of God (and Moses) are plucked out of their narrative context. Isolated and distilled, the triumphal theological derivatives are swallowed by the interpreter who then sees the text through the euphoric fog induced by this theological tonic.

Suppose, for the moment, that the narrative in Exodus 1–15 is not triumphalistic, and that it does embody some critical evaluative point of view. Are there any obvious clues, any less silent implications of the narration that indicate the general tendency of narratorial evaluation? To begin at the beginning, with Exodus 1, it is a pace-setting irony that the

---

22. Cf. C. Westermann, *Elements of Old Testament Theology* (trans. D.W. Stott; Atlanta: John Knox, 1982), p. 40.

23. W. Brueggemann, 'The Triumphalist Tendency in Exegetical History', *JAAR* 38 (1970), pp. 367-80 (368).

fulfilment of God's promise of vast numbers of progeny to Abraham should get the Israelites into a fix in the first place (Exod. 1.7-10). Next, having 'blessed' the Israelites with fecundity, God leaves them to suffer the consequences at Egypt's hand. Not until one Egyptian king has lived out his life, and 'many days' have passed (2.23), does God take notice of Israel's plight.[24] Describing God's tardy renewal of concern with—not yet explicitly *for*—the Israelites, the narrator points out that it is the sound of Israel's groaning rising up to God that stirs his recollection of the covenant he made with Abraham, Isaac and Jacob (2.23-24). This description highlights Israel's great sufferings and God's small concern. Neither is the irony of the narrator's description of what God remembers when he hears Israel's groans complimentary to the divine character, though it is certainly not overtly critical either. Dispassionate and neutral, one might say, an objectifying description. The groans remind God of his covenantal promises of numerous descendants to Abraham, Isaac and Jacob, exactly those promises whose fulfilment has brought Israel to slavery and groaning. Yet God seems to remember the same covenant only when he hears the groaning that it has led to. The exposé is implicit and ironic, and it involves the reader in its perception because successful irony always requires and creates reader complicity.[25]

God's ultimate responsibility for Israel's woes is revealed again in the privileged views afforded by the narrator's manipulation of the recurring motif of Pharaoh's hardened heart.[26] Before any attempt is made to

24. Cf. C. Isbell, 'Exodus 1–2 in the Context of Exodus 1–14: Story Lines and Key Words', in D.J.A. Clines, D.M. Gunn and A.J. Hauser (eds.), *Art and Meaning: Rhetoric in Biblical Narrative* (JSOTSup, 19; Sheffield: JSOT Press, 1982), pp. 37-61 (52).

25. Cf. D.S. Kaufer, 'Irony, Interpretive Form and the Theory of Meaning', *Poetics Today* 4 (1983), pp. 452-53.

26. The most careful and detailed study of this motif to date is that of D.M. Gunn. Gunn shows how the narrator's manipulation of the sequential presentation of information is combined with small modifications of the hardened heart motif. The surprising result is an uncomplimentary characterization of God, not Pharaoh.

> Superficially the story provides a glorious tableau of deliverance with great signs and wonders, from slavery into freedom. The more one looks into it, however, the more muted that picture appears. The signs and wonders conceal destruction and suffering, deserved and undeserved—an excess of havoc we might be tempted to argue ('The "Hardening of Pharaoh's Heart": Plot, Character and Theology in Exodus 1–14', in D.J.A. Clines, D.M. Gunn and A.J. Hauser [eds.], *Art and Meaning*, p. 89).

obtain Israel's release from Egypt, the narrator twice lets the reader overhear God telling Moses that Pharaoh will not let Israel go except under duress (Exod. 3.19; 4.21-23). The reason for God's certainty is revealed in the second disclosure: God intends to harden Pharaoh's heart precisely so that he will not release Israel too soon. With this glimpse into the divine character's intention and motivation for hardening the heart of Pharaoh, the narrator has discarded the possibility of telling a tale of real triumphs over the Egyptian king. After this, any conflict or victory can only be seen as a sham.

Depicting the plagues, the narrator grants the reader four more privileged auditions of conversations between the God and his agent, Moses. With these insights into the divine character and his uncanny plan for Israel's rescue, the narrator bars the way to any readerly exultation over God's sham fight with Pharaoh. In 7.3 God explains that he will harden Pharaoh's heart so that he can multiply his signs and wonders; in the same chapter, he uses Pharaoh's continuing intransigence to justify the next devastation of turning the Nile to blood (7.14). Two things are clear: the staged conflict represented by the plagues is a divine production used by God to display his power, and any consequent rescue effort is as much subordinate to God's self-glorification[27] as is Pharaoh's inspired stubbornness.

In the final two privileged auditions, the narrator reveals exactly how both Israel's and Pharaoh's fates are subordinate to the single purpose for which the entire episode was staged. In 10.1-2, God tells Moses that Pharaoh's heart was hardened so that God could perform his multiple miracles, and so that Moses and presumably the other Israelites would tell their descendants about the events. All Israel is to hear about God's mighty acts so that they will know that he is Yahweh. Similarly, in 14.4, 17-18 God gives the same explanation for the exodus, only there it is the Egyptians who are to be educated by these acts of divine self-glorification. Israel and Egypt are pawns in the hands of the divine player

---

On account of historical criticism's basic literary strategy of 'divide and conquer', historical critics have not been able to see the literary dynamics that Gunn describes. Instead, they have taken the various modulations of the motif as the marks of separate sources, and so have divided and destroyed one of the narrator's most important tools for providing implicit commentary (e.g. J.P. Hyatt, *Exodus* [NCB; Grand Rapids: Eerdmans; London: Marshall, Morgan & Scott, 1971], pp. 102-103.

27.   Self-glorification is not a negative characterization of God here or in the Exodus narrative.

who plays both sides of the board.[28] The Israelites suffer as slaves in Egypt because God so miraculously multiplies them that they threaten Egypt's wellbeing.[29] And then their sufferings are multiplied (5.4-23) and drawn out (5.1–12.30) because God wants to present an extensive demonstration of his powers. Similarly, Egypt's sufferings under the plagues are prolonged[30] for the greater glory of God. In reward for the part they play in this divine comedy, both Israel and Egypt are rewarded with the knowledge, 'I am Yahweh'.

In fact the knowledge of God's nature as such is linked to the name Yahweh, whatever the name means, and the human characters' acquisition of this knowledge is the only real accomplishment of the entire episode. No less than eight times God says that his actions are calculated to make Israel and Egypt know that he is Yahweh.[31] The idea is that the nature of the divine action reveals something of the meaning of the name Yahweh and thus of the being who bears that name.[32]

For the reader whose knowledge is, rather, of God's educative intent, and of the contrivances he uses to teach his lessons in historical

28. C. Isbell repeats the common misconception about a power struggle in Exodus 1–14 when he says that the Israelites 'are consistently portrayed as helpless pawns being moved back and forth by the two larger-than-life chess masters' ('Exodus 1–2', p. 45). Both slaves and taskmasters, would-be escapees and would-be masters, are fated by the crucial manipulations of Yahweh. Only Yahweh's actions and plans have any real bearing on the course that events take, as he so clearly says in Exod. 9.15-16.

29. That the hand of God lies behind Israel's multiplication is made clear in two different pieces of narration in ch. 1. In v. 12 the narrator points to the unnatural consequence of affliction—a yet greater population explosion (cf. M. Greenberg, *Understanding Exodus* [New York: Behrman House, 1969], pp. 32-36). And, in v. 20, after we have already seen Egypt react to Israel's unnatural multiplication (*wayyirbû*, v. 7; *pen-yirbeh*, v. 10), we see God rewarding the midwives for supporting the divine programme to make Israel multiply (*wayyireb*).

30. Cf. Exod. 8.8, 15; 9.27-28, 34-35; 10.16-17, 20; and 10.24, 27.

31. Cf. Exod. 6.7; 10.2, with reference to Israel; 7.17; 8.18; 9.14, with reference to Israel; 7.17; 8.18; 9.14, with reference to Pharaoh; 7.5; 14.4, 18 with reference to the Egyptians; cf. Moses, 8.6; 9.29. See also L. Eslinger, 'Knowing Yahweh: Exodus 6.3 in the Context of Genesis 1–Exodus 6.3', in *Literary Structure and Rhetorical Strategies in the Hebrew Bible* (ed. L.J. de Regt, J. de Waard and J.P. Fokkelman; Assen: Van Gorcum; Winona Lake, IN: Eisenbrauns, 1996), pp. 188-98.

32. Cf. W. Zimmerli, 'Knowledge of God according to the Book of Ezekiel', in *I am Yahweh* (trans. D.W. Stott; Atlanta: John Knox, 1982), p. 47.

theology, it becomes difficult to applaud the divine pedagogy of the exodus. The reader does learn a lesson about who Yahweh is from the exodus events, but the knowledge leads anywhere but to a spot in Moses' choir in Exodus 15. The apostle Paul was aware that this narrative raises questions about the morality of such teaching techniques (Rom. 9.16-23). His remarks and his answers to the problem—humans ought not to question the justice of their creator's actions (Rom. 9.20-21), and the creator has glorious ends to justify these means (vv. 22-24)—provide us with an early example of a reader grappling with the difficult implications of Exodus 1–15. But it is left to other biblical contexts, most particularly the book of Genesis and its 'prehistory' (Gen. 1–11), to suggest whether God's end justifies these means. Only within that larger frame can the disturbing implications of Exodus 1–15 be sublimated.

Throughout, the narrator relies on the cognitive disparities between the three epistemological layers in the narrative to create and sustain the structural and dramatic irony that makes the narrative implicitly anti-triumphalist. The three layers of knowledge in the narrative are, of course, (a) the predominant level of the narrator and the reader, (b) the dominant level of God and Moses, and (c) the subdominant level of the human characters. The narrator's unlimited access allows him to reveal the secrets of God, which are kept from the human characters. Simply by exposing the divine intentions to the light of the predominant level, the narrator sets all triumphalism in the story (the dominant level), and indeed all character reaction (the subdominant level) to the events, in an ironic light; they react to appearance, we perceive the reality.

A rhetorical reason for the absence of explicit narratorial commentary now becomes clear, for to support this overarching irony with explicit evaluation would be to destroy it. Instead of telling the reader that the exodus was not what it seemed to most human participants in the drama (Moses being the only obvious exception), the narrator allows God himself to play out the truth.[33] To supply the reader with negative evaluations or excuses for God's conduct—as the latter goes about the business of acting out his historical deceit—would unnecessarily define the reader's response, and ruin the narrator's aura of impartial objectivity. Unlike God, whose involvement and personal stake in the exodus

---

33. Cf. R. Polzin's discussion of the power of implicit exposition in the deuteronomistic narratives (*Samuel and the Deuteronomist: A Literary Study of the Deuteronomic History*. II. *1 Samuel* [New York: Harper & Row, 1989]), p. 149.

events is exposed more than once, this narrator appears concerned only to reveal the truth of the matter. Whatever the truth of the matter is, and whether or not this impartial objectivity is also a disguise for a hidden polemic, it is time to stop reading Exodus 1–15 through the eyes of its unwitting Israelites. We can understand why they celebrated God's mighty acts in song (Exod. 15); we should also understand and allow that the narrator and the narrative do not.

JSOT 57 (1993), pp. 3-22

TOWN AND RURAL COUNTRYSIDE IN ANCIENT ISRAELITE LAW: RECEPTION AND REDACTION IN CUNEIFORM AND ISRAELITE LAW[*]

Eckart Otto

Introduction

Since A. Jepsen's form-critical monograph on the Book of the Covenant,[1] which was the basis for A. Alt's famous article about the origins of Israelite law,[2] it has become a commonplace of Old Testament scholarship that the ancient Israelite casuistic laws of the Covenant Book had their origins in Mesopotamian cuneiform law. Critical voices remained, but with little influence. In 1931 M. San Nicolò[3] argued that from the perspective of legal history the Israelite law of the Book of the Covenant was more archaic than the Old Babylonian law of the Codex Hammurabi. In 1939 M. David[4] stated that the Old Babylonian law was incomparable with the Israelite law of the Book of Covenant because of the incompatibility of Mesopotamian and Israelite society. The discussion became even more complicated when the tablets of Alalakh and Ugarit showed Syria

---

[*]   This paper was delivered at the SBL International Meeting in Copenhagen, August 1989. I thank my colleague Dr L.L. Grabbe (University of Hull) for improving the English text.

1.   A. Jepsen, *Untersuchungen zum Bundesbuch* (BWANT, 41; Stuttgart: Kohlhammer, 1927).

2.   A. Alt, 'Die Ursprünge des israelitischen Rechts' (1934), in *idem, Kleine Schriften*, I (Munich: C.H. Beck, 1953), pp. 278-332.

3.   M. San Nicolò, *Beiträge zur Rechtsgeschichte im Bereiche der keilschriftlichen Rechtsquellen* (Oslo: H. Aschehoug, 1931), p. 77.

4.   M. David, 'De codex Hammoerabi en zijn verhouding tot de wetsbepalingen in Exodus', *Tijdschrift voor Rechtsgeschiedenis* 17 (1939), pp. 1-26; *idem*, 'The Codex Hammurabi and its Relation to the Provisions of Law in Exodus', *OTS* 7 (1950), pp. 149-78.

and Palestine as a legal province of its own[5] and when the 1980 dissertation of G.I. Miller[6] showed the legal differences between Alalakh and Ugarit. It was no longer possible to claim a dependence of Israelite law on cuneiform law just by comparison, without answering the question of how the legal transfer of cuneiform law into Israelite law took place. What were the connecting links between Old Babylonian laws of the first centuries of the second millennium and of Israelite laws of the first millennium?[7] A new problem for the thesis of a dependence of Israelite law on cuneiform law arose when it was recognized that sentences of Israelite casuistic law had their traditio-historical roots in Israelite trial records[8] (e.g. Exod. 21.18-19) and were of indigenous Israelite origin. Finally, there is a methodological problem in distinguishing legal borrowings from independently parallel legal developments. For R. Yaron[9], the sentences must be 'truly peculiar and extraordinary', that is, there must not be any parallel in any third legal system (for example, in early Roman law) to think of borrowing. But B.S. Jackson[10] objected that, 'if truly "peculiar and extraordinary" means that no other example must be found outside the culture area in question, then one doubts whether influence can ever be proved'. So what P. Koschaker[11] wrote in 1929 remains true:

5.   A. Alt, 'Eine neue Provinz des Keilschriftrechts' (1947), in *idem*, *Kleine Schriften*, III (Munich: C.H. Beck, 1959), pp. 141-57.

6.   G.I. Miller, 'Studies in the Juridical Texts from Ugarit' (PhD Dissertation, Johns Hopkins University, Baltimore, 1980), pp. 219-316, 348-52.

7.   The hypothesis of the 'Hyksos' as such a historical link (so G. Liedke, *Gestalt und Bezeichnung alttestamentlicher Rechtssätze: Eine formgeschichtlich-terminologische Studie* [WMANT, 39; Neukirchen–Vluyn: Neukirchener Verlag, 1971], pp. 53-59) must be abandoned.

8.   Liedke, *Rechtssätze*, pp. 39-42; C. Locher, *Die Ehre einer Frau in Israel: Exegetische und rechtsvergleichende Studien zu Deuteronomium 22, 13–21* (OBO, 70; Freiburg [Schweiz]: Universitätsverlag; Göttingen: Vandenhoeck & Ruprecht, 1986), pp. 83-110. For cuneiform law, cf. already P. Koschaker, *Quellenkritische Untersuchungen zu den 'altassyrischen Gesetzen'* (MVAG, 26/3; Leipzig: J.C. Hinrichs, 1921), pp. 17-22, 68.79-80, 83.

9.   R. Yaron, 'The Goring Ox in Near Eastern Law', in H.H. Cohn (ed.), *Jewish Law in Ancient and Modern Israel* (Jerusalem: Ktav, 1971), pp. 53-54.

10.   B.S. Jackson, 'The Goring Ox', in *idem*, *Essays in Jewish and Comparative Legal History* (SJLA, 10; Leiden: Brill, 1975), pp. 137-38.

11.   P. Koschaker, 'Forschungen und Ergebnisse in den keilschriftlichen Rechtsquellen', *Zeitschrift der Savigny-Stiftung für Rechtsgeschichte (Rom. Abt.)* 49 (1929), pp. 194-95; for the methodological problems of legal transfer, cf. F. Wieacker, 'Zum heutigen Stand der Rezeptionsforschung', in E. Fries (ed.),

> In my opinion nothing is more difficult to prove than the reception of law.
> The comparison of different laws has taught us that a conformity of legal
> sentences of different legal provinces even in details proves nothing about
> borrowing and that parallel developments are much more important than
> we formerly thought.

The discussion of these problems focused on the laws of the goring ox in
Codex Ešnunna [CE] §§53-55, Codex Hammurabi [CH] §§250-52 and
the Book of the Covenant, Exod. 21.28-32, 35-36. Whereas A. van
Selms,[12] following M. David,[13] was of the opinion that there was no
traditio-historical connection between the cuneiform and Hebrew legal
sentences, R. Westbrook[14] maintains that Codex Ešnunna was part of
the school curriculum of Israelite legal education and Exod. 21.38 a
Hebrew translation of CE §53. R. Yaron[15] tries a kind of mediation
between these extreme positions. Against Westbrook he objects that so
far no remnant of the Codex Ešnunna has been found outside the
borders of Ešnunna and that its emergence, many centuries after the
destruction of the city, in the Israelite cultural sphere is less than plausible.
On the other side, against David and van Selms he states:

> Anyone looking at the two texts without preconceived notions will see at
> once how closely similar they are, not only in the actual solution proposed
> but even in the mode of formulation. The identity of the very peculiar
> ruling laid down in both the sources makes it virtually certain that they are
> connected with each other, probably since both borrowed from a common
> fount, Oriental legal practice.[16]

For Yaron, the 'proper laws' (in his first edition he spoke of 'positive
law'[17]) were independent but rooted in a common ancient Oriental legal

Philosophie und ihre Geschichte: Festschrift für J. Klein (Göttingen: Vandenhoeck
& Ruprecht, 1967), pp. 181-201; A. Watson, *Legal Transplants: An Approach to
Comparative Law* (Edinburgh: T. & T. Clark, 1974); M. Alliot, 'Uber die Arten des
"Rechts-Transfers"', in W. Fikentscher *et al.* (eds.), *Entstehung und Wandel
rechtlicher Traditionen* (Veröffentl. des Instituts für Historische Anthropologie, 2;
Munich: Karl Alber, 1980), pp. 161-231.

12. A. von Selms, 'The Goring Ox in Babylonian and Biblical Law', *ArOr* 18
(1950), pp. 321-30.

13. David, 'Codex Hammurabi', pp. 149-50.

14. R. Westbrook, 'Biblical and Cuneiform Law Codes', *RB* 92 (1985), p. 257.

15. R. Yaron, *The Laws of Eshnunna* (Leiden: Brill, 2nd edn, 1988 [1969]), pp.
291-92.

16. Yaron, *Laws of Eshnunna*, p. 293.

17. Yaron, *The Laws of Eshnunna* (1st edn), p. 11. J.J. Finkelstein ('The Ox that

practice of 'customary law'. But how can we distinguish between 'proper law' and 'customary law', if we have 'customary law' only as 'proper law'?[18] If we assume a traditio-historical connection between Old Babylonian laws and Israelite laws, we have to reconstruct the processes of transfer of cuneiform law into Israelite law.[19] Especially, we have to answer the question of how cuneiform laws found their way to the early Israelite rural countryside of the Judaean and Ephraimite highlands. Only town centres in Palestine could be loci of transfer of cuneiform law because this transfer needed a scribal education. If we reckon with a mediated reception of cuneiform law in Israelite law, there must have been a town-centred legal organization of the early Israelite countryside. If we come to the conclusion that Israelite casuistic legal sentences were of indigenous Israelite origin, then we must think of a movement of laws from the rural countryside to town centres, where these laws were collected in law codes that were part of a school curriculum.

Another paradigm for discussing the problems of a traditio-historical connection beween cuneiform law and Israelite law is the law of bodily injury to a pregnant woman, that is, the laws YOS I 28 §§1, 2, UM 55-21-71 §§4-6(7) written in a late Sumerian idiom, the Old Babylonian laws CH §§209-14, the Middle Assyrian laws M.Ass. C. tabl. A §§21, 50-52, the Hittite laws Hitt.C §§17, 18, XVI, XVII and Exod. 21.22-23. For J.J. Finkelstein, these laws were of a 'paradigmatic school-exercise type'.[20] The miscarriage by bodily injury of a pregnant woman was so rare an occurrence, with no treatment in legal records elsewhere (and, from a medical point of view, statistically highly improbable), that the only explanation of the fact that we find this law in nearly all the ancient

Gored', *Transactions of the American Philosophical Society* 71 [1981], p. 18 n. 10) was opposed to this term.

18. Cf. E. Otto, review (in German) of *The Laws of Eshnunna* (2nd edn, 1988), by R. Yaron, *VT* 40 (1990), pp. 361-69.

19. J.J. Finkelstein ('Ox', pp. 19-20) renounced this kind of solution:

> Moreover, the form which the goring-ox laws take in the Covenant Code is so close to its cuneiform analogues that it bespeaks the presence in Palestine of an almost canonical knowledge of the precise phraseology of the earlier Akkadian formulations. There is, in short, no certain way at present of explaining the verbal identity between sources that are perhaps as much as five hundred years and as many miles apart. But the fact of this identity is uncontrovertible and compels us to postulate an organic linkage between them even if this linkage cannot be reconstructed.

20. Finkelstein, 'Ox', p. 18.

Oriental law codes must be the assumption that this case is a literary phenomenon rather than a legal one, chosen for illustrative purposes in a school tradition.[21] This would underscore the thesis that town institutions of scribal education were the places for transmission of cuneiform law into Israelite law. But one can only agree to this solution if it is proved that Exod. 21.22-23 is dependent on cuneiform law and no indigenous origin of this Israelite law can be found.

Bodily Injuries of a Pregnant Woman in Cuneiform Law[22]

The earliest provisions we have are in YOS I 28[23] and UM 55-21-71.[24]

Text

YOS I 28 [RS] iv 1-10

tukum-bi dumu-mí lú zagan-ús níg-šà-ga-ni a-im-šub-šub 10 gín kù-babbar ì-lá-e
tukum-bi dumu<-mí> lú ba-an-sìg níg-šà-ga-ni a-im-šub-šub 1/3 ma-na kù-babbar
    ì-lá-e

Translation

§1
If (…)[a] strikes[b] the daughter of a freeman (involuntarily), kills[c] the foetus, he will pay 10 shekels of silver.
§2
If (…) strikes the daughter of a freeman (intentionally), kills the foetus, he will pay 1/3 mina of silver.

---

21. Finkelstein, 'Ox', p. 19 n. 11.

22. Cf. E. Otto, *Körperverletzungen in den Keilschriftrechten und im Alten Testament: Studien zum Rechtstransfer im Alten Orient* (AOAT, 226, Neukirchen–Vluyn: Neukirchener Verlag; Kevelaer: Butzon & Bercker, 1991).

23. This is the conventional citation shorthand for the edition of A.T. Clay, *Miscellaneous Inscriptions of the Yale Babylonian Collection* (YOS, I/28; New Haven: Yale University Press, 1915); cf. R. Haase, *Die keilschriftlichen Rechtssammlungen in deutscher Fassung* (Wiesbaden: O. Harrassowitz, 2nd edn, 1979), p. 18; W.H.P. Römer, 'Einige Bemerkungen zum altmesopotamischen Recht, sonderlich nach Quellen in sumerischer Sprache', *ZAW* 95 (1983), p. 326 n. 65.

24. Editions: M. Civil, 'New Sumerian Law Fragments', *Assyriological Studies* 16 (1965), pp. 4-5; E. Szlechter, *Les lois sumériennes. I. Le Code d'Ur Nammu. II. Le Code de Lipit Ištar* (Pont. Inst. Utr. Juris Stud. et Doc., 6; Rome: Pontifical Biblical Institute, 1983), pp. 80-81; for translation, cf. H. Lutzmann, (Texte aus der Umwelt des Alten Testaments, I/1 [Gütersloh: Gerd Mohn, 1982]), pp. 25-26.

Notes

a. For the subject of the protasis, cf. E. Szlechter, 'Nouveaux textes législatives sumériens II', *RA* 62 (1968), pp. 147-60 (157 n. 2, 159 n. 1); U. Sick, 'Die Tötung eines Menschen und ihre Ahndung in den keilschriftlichen Rechtssammlungen unter Berücksichtigung rechtsvergleichender Aspekte' (Dissertation, Tübingen, 1984), pp. 46-47.

b. Cf. Otto, *Körperverletzungen.*

c. For the prefix -a, cf. M.-L. Thomsen, *The Sumerian Language: An Introduction to its History and Grammatical Structure* (Mesopotamia. Copenhagen Studies in Assyriology, 10; Copenhagen: Akademisk Forlag, 1984), p. 168: '/ā-/ is used in sentences where the agent is not mentioned, i.e. impersonal forms'. For the reduplication, cf. Thomsen, *Sumerian Language*, p. 126; D.O. Edzard, '*Hamṭu, marû* und freie Reduplikation beim sumerischen Verbum. I', *ZA* 61 (1971), pp. 208-32 (231): 'Betonung des hohen Wirksamkeitsgrades, der Reichweite der Handlung', in this case it is deadly.

Law §1 demands 10 shekels of silver in case of an involuntary injury as the cause of a miscarriage; Law §2 demands the *duplum* of 1/3 mina of silver[25] in case of an intentional injury.

Legal sentences of UM 55-21-71 §§4-6 are different from those of YOS I 28 §§1, 2.

Text

UM 55-21-71 iii 2'-13'
    2' [*t*]*uk*[*um-bi   x-r*]*e*
    3' *dumu-mí-*l[*ú-ka i-ni-in-*]*ra*
    4' *níg-šà-*[*ga-n*]*a*
    5' *šu mu-u*[*n-   *]
    6' *1/2 ma-na* [*kù-babbar ì-lá-*]*e*
    7' *tukum-b*[*i   b*]*a-úš*
    8' *nita-bi ì-*[*gaz*]*-e*
    9' *tukum-bi x -*[*r*]*e*
    10' *gemé-lú-ka i-níg-in-ra*
    11' *níg-šà-*[*ga-n*]*a*
    12' *šu mu-u*[*n-da-an-lá*]
    13' *5 gín kù-*[*babbar ì-lá*]*-e*[26]

25. For the redactional context of YOS I 28 §§1, 2; cf. the analysis by Otto, *Körperverletzungen*, pp. 29-30.

26. Most of Line 14' of UM-55-21-71 is destroyed. For a reconstruction according to CH §214, cf. Szlechter, 'Textes', p. 158; *idem, Lois sumériennes*, p. 81: *tuku*[*m ba-úš*] *sag-sa*[*g*(?)]*-gim ba-ab-sum-mu*(?)]. C. Saporetti (*Le leggi della Mesopotamia* [Florence: Casa Editrice Le Lettere, 1984], p. 33) accepted this reconstruction.

Translation

§4
If a (…)[a] strikes the daughter of a freeman and she has a miscarriage, he will pay 1/2 mina of silver.

§5
If she dies, the man will be killed.

§6
If a (…) strikes the slave of a freeman and she has a miscarriage, he will pay five shekel of silver.

Notes

a. The ends of lines 2' and 9' are missing. M. Civil (*Fragments*, p. 6) reads as possible [*tu*]-*re*; cf. Szlechter, *Textes*, pp. 157, 159; *idem, Lois sumériennes*, pp. 157-59; I. Cardellini, *Die biblischen 'Sklaven'—Gesetze im Lichte des keilschriftlichen Sklavenrechts: Ein Beitrag zu Tradition, Überlieferung und Redaktion der alttestamentlichen Rechtstexte* (BBB, 55; Bonn: Peter Hanstein, 1981), p. 38.

UM 55-21-71 §§4-6(7) does not differentiate with regard to the motives of intentional and unintentional injuries by the perpetrator, but with regard to the consequence for the victim and to her social status.

The Codex Hammurabi (§§209-14) makes further distinctions:

Text

CH col. xviii [RS] 23-30: CH §209
*šumma awīlum mārat awīlim imḫaṣ-ma ša libbī-ša uštaddī-ši 10 šiqil kaspam ana
   ša libbī-ša išaqqal*

CH col. xviii [RS] 31-34: CH §210
šumma šinništum šī imtūt māras-su idukkū

CH col. xviii [RS] 35-40: CH §211
šumma mārat muškēnim ina maḫāṣim ša libbī-ša uštaddī-ši 5 šiqil kaspam išaqqal

CH col. xviii [RS] 41-44: CH §212
šumma šinništum šī imtūt 1/2 mana kaspam išaqqal

CH col. xviii [RS] 45-50: CH §213
šumma amat awīlim imḫaṣ-ma ša libbī-ša uštaddī-ši 2 šiqil kaspam išaqqal

CH col. xviii [RS] 51-54: CH §214
šumma amtum šī imtūt 1/3 mana kaspam išaqqal

Translation

CH §209

If an *awīlum* strikes the daughter of an *awīlum* and causes a miscarriage to her, he will pay 10 shekels of silver for her foetus.

CH §210

If the woman dies, they will kill his daughter.

CH §211

If he causes an abortion to the daughter of a *muškēnum* by striking, he will pay five shekels of silver.

CH §212

If this woman dies, he will pay 1/2 mina of silver.

CH §213

If he strikes the slave of an *awīlum* and causes a miscarriage to her, he will pay two shekels of silver.

CH §214

If this slave dies, he will pay 1/3 mina of silver.

The redactional structure of CH §§209-14 is identical with UM 55-21-71 §§4-6(7). The injury cases of women of one social class were combined but differentiated with regard to the consequences for the victim. Contrary to YOS I 28 §§1 and 2, there is no distinction of the assailant's motives. CH §§209-14 seems to be dependent on the tradition represented by UM 55-21-71. Only the redactor of CH §§195-214 distinguishes between intentional and unintentional injuries.[27]

The laws of pl. A of the Middle Assyrian Codex[28] combine marriage law (M.Ass.C. tabl. A §§25-49) with criminal law concerning women (M.Ass.C. tabl. A §§1-24, 50-59). The special concern of this law code

27. Cf. Otto, *Körperverletzungen*, pp. 56-57.

28. Cf. O. Schroeder, *Keilschrifttexte aus Assur verschiedenen Inhalts* (Leipzig: Hinrichs, 1920); V. Scheil, *Recueil de lois assyriennes: Texte assyrien en transcription avec traduction française et index* (Paris: Paul Geuthner, 1921); C. Saporetti, *Le leggi medioassire* (Malibu: Undena, 1979); translation and commentary: G. Cardascia, *Les lois assyriennes* (Paris: Editions du Cèrf, 1969); cf. also now E. Otto, 'Die Einschränkung des Privatstrafrechts durch öffentliches Strafrecht in der Redaktion der Paragraphen 1-24, 50-59 des Mittelassyrischen Kodex der Tafel A (KAV 1), in W. Zwickel (ed.), *Biblische Welten: Festschrift für M. Metzger* (OBO, 123; Freiburg [Schweiz]: Universitätsverlag; Göttingen: Vandenhoeck & Ruprecht, 1993), pp. 131-66.

for women influenced the legal sentences of bodily injuries to a pregnant woman in M.Ass.C. tabl. A §§21, 50-52.

Text

KAV 1, col. iii 98-104: A §21

*šumma a'īlu mar'at a'īle imḫaṣ-ma ša libbi-ša ultaṣli-š ubta"erû-š ukta"inū-š 2 bilat
    30 mana annaka iddan 50 ina ḫaṭṭāte imaḫḫuṣū-š 1 uraḫ ūmāte šipar
    . šarre eppaš*

KAV 1, col. vii 63-81: A §50

*[šumma a'īlu aššat] a'īle imḫaš-ma [ša libbi-ša] ušaddi-ši [ša] aššat a'īle ša [ ]-u-
    ni ù [kī ša ēpuš]ū-ši-ni eppu[šū-šu kīmūš]a libbi-ša napšāte umalla u
    šumma sinniltu šīt mītat a'īla idukkū kīmū ša libbi-ša napšāte umalla u
    šumma ša mut sinnilte šiāti marā-šu laššu aššassu imḫuṣū-ma ša libbi-ša
    taṣli kīmū ša libbi-ša māḫiṣāna idukkū šumma ša libbi-ša ṣuḫartu našāte-
    ma umalla*

KAV 1, col. vii 82-86: A §51

*šumma a'īlu aššat a'ile lā murabbīta imḫaṣ-ma ša libbi-ša ušaṣli-ši ḫīṭu anniu 2
    bilat annaka iddan*

KAV 1, col. vii 87-90: A §52

*šumma a'īlu ḫarimta imḫaṣ-ma ša libbi-ša ušaṣli-ši miḫṣe kī miḫṣe išakkunū-š
    napšāte umalla*

Translation

§21

If an *awīlum* strikes a *mar'at a'īle*[a] and causes a miscarriage to her, they prove it and convict him, he will give 2 talents 30 mina of tin, he will be beaten 50 blows with rods, he will do labour for the king for 1 full month.

§50

If an *a'īlu* strikes an *aššat a'īle*, and causes a miscarriage to her [ ], as he [has done] to her, [they will do to him][b]. For her foetus he will pay the full price of a life. And if this woman dies, the *a'īlu* will be put to death. For her foetus he will pay the full price of a life. And if the woman's husband has no son, his wife has been thrust and has cast her foetus, the striker will be put to death. If the foetus is a girl, he will pay the full price of a life.

§51

If an *a'īlu* strikes an *aššat a'īle* who does not rear (a child) causes a miscarriage to her, this is a crime. He will pay 2 talents of silver.

§52

If an *a'īlu* strikes a harlot and causes a miscarriage to her, blow for blow shall be laid upon him. The full price of a life will he pay.

Notes

a. For a discussion of the relation between *mar'at a'īle* and *aššat a'īle*, cf. Saporetti, *Leggi medioassire*, 13.44-45; Otto, *Körperverletzungen*, pp. 82-83.

b. For a discussion of the text, cf. Otto, *Körperverletzungen*, pp. 83-84. The object of the punishment is the assailant himself; cf. already E. Ebeling, *Altorientalische Texte zum Alten Testament* (Berlin: de Gruyter, 2nd edn, 1926), p. 420.

The Middle Assyrian laws tabl. A §§21, 50-52 distinguish between the ranks of the victims and between bodily injuries with and without the consequence of death. These laws thus link up with the legal development that is represented by the Old Babylonian laws UM 55-21-71 §§4-6(7) and CH §§209-14. There are no regulations concerning slaves because the laws of M.Ass.C. tabl. A were only interested in the legal cases of free women. The distinction between *mar'at a'īle*, *aššat a'īle*, *aššat a'īle lā murabbītu* and *ḫarimtu* was rooted in the redactional intent of plate A as a 'Frauenspiegel'. The Middle Assyrian laws of §§21, 50-52 were derived from the tradition of CH and UM 55-21-71[29] but did not know the distinction between intentional and unintentional injuries in YOS I 28 §§1, 2 and the redactional structure of CH §§195-214.

The Hittite laws of Hitt.C. §§17, 18 and XVI, XVII[30] also deal with the topic of injury of a pregnant woman.

Text

Ser. I B 40-42

[*ták-ku*] SAL-*aš EL.LI šar-ḫu-wa-an-du-uš-šu-uš ku-iš-ki* p[*í-e*]*š-*[(*ši-ya-*)]-*zi*
[*ták-ku*] ITU. 10.KAM 10 GÍN KÙ.BABBAR *pa-a-i ták-ku*[[-*uš*]] ITU.-5.KAM 5
    GÍN K[Ù.BABBAR] *pa-a-i* [*pár-n*]*a-aš-š*[*e-e-a*] *šu-wa-a-i-*
    [*iz-z*]*i*

Ser. I B 43-44

ták-ku GÉME-*aš šar-ḫu-wa-an* [*du-u*]*š-šu-uš ku-iš-ki pí-e*[(*š-ši-y*)]*a-zi ták-ku*
    ITU.10.KAM 5(?) GÍN KÙ.BABBAR *pa-a-*[*i*]

29. For the traditio-history of M.Ass.C. pl. A §§21, 50-52, cf. Otto, *Körperverletzungen*, pp. 79-80.

30. For the text of Ser. I and KBo VI 4, cf. J. Friedrich, *Die hethitischen Gesetze* (Documenta et Monumenta Orientis Antiqui, 7; Leiden: Brill, 2nd edn, 1971), pp. 20-21, 52-53; F. Imparati, *Le leggi ittite* (Incunabula Graeca, 7; Rome: Edizioni dell' Ateneo, 1964), pp. 42-43, 104.

Translation

Hitt.C. §17
If somebody aborts a free woman's foetus, [if] it is the 10th month, he will give 10 shekels of silver; if it is the 5th month he will give 5 shekels [of silver]; he also looks at his house[a].

Hitt.C. §18
If somebody aborts a slave woman's foetus, if it is the 5th month he will give 5 (?) shekels of silver.

Notes

a. For the formula *parnaššeia šuwaizzi*, cf. R. Haase, *Die Fragmente der hethitischen Gesetze* (Wiesbaden: Otto Harrassowitz, 1968), pp. 157ff.; *idem*, 'Gedanken zur Formel *parnaššeia šuuaizzi* in den hethitischen Gesetzen', *WO* 11 (1980), pp. 93-98; H.G. Güterbock, 'Noch einmal die Formel *parnaššeia šuwaizzi*', *Or* NS 52 (1983), pp. 73-80; for Akkadian and Hebrew parallels, cf. E. Otto, 'Die keilschriftlichen Parallelen der Vindikationsformel in Dtn 20,10', *ZAW* 102 (1990), pp. 94-96.

Parallel to UM 55-21-71 §§4-6(7) and CH §§209-14 are the legal sentences of Hitt.C. §§17, 18 differentiating between laws concerning a free woman and a slave woman.[31] The distinction between injuries with and without fatal consequences is lacking in YOS I 28 §§1, 2 and the Hittite laws, but it is constitutive in the other laws. Does this mean that these Hittite laws are independent of the Old Babylonian tradition? As for the influence of the Old Babylonian laws on Hittite laws, there are different opinions.[32] The redactional-historical analysis of Hitt.C. §§7-18

31. The distinction concerning the months of pregnancy in version BI is a traditio-historical addition which version CI (KBo VI 5) and the later text KBo VI 4 do not know; cf. F. Imparati, *Leggi*, pp. 17-18. CI 20-22 reads: *ták-ku* SAL-*an* EL.LÁM *šar-ḫu-u-wa-an-da ku-iš-ki pí-eš-ši-ya-az-zi* 20 GÍN KÙ.BABBAR *pa-a-i pár-na-aš-še-ya šu-wa-a-iz-zi-an*. CI 23-24 reads: *ták-ku* GÉME-*an šar-ḫu-u-wa-an-da ku-iš-ki pí-eš)-ši-ya-zi* 10 GÍN KÙ.BABBAR *pa-a-i*. For the history of transmission, cf. Otto, *Körperverletzungen*, pp. 97-98.

32. For E. Neufeld (*The Hittite Laws* [London: Luzac, 1951], p. 106), there is no traceable influence, whereas V. Korošec sees a provable influence ('Das hethitische Recht in seiner Stellung zwischen Osten und Westen', *Süd-Ost-Forschungen* 15 [1956], pp. 29-30; *idem*, 'Hethitica', *Razprave* [Dissertationes, IV/7; Ljubljana, 1958], pp. 52-53; *idem*, 'Einige Probleme zur Struktur der hethitischen Gesetze', in J. Harmatta and G. Komoróczy [eds.], *Wirtschaft und Gesellschaft im Alten Vorderasien* [Budapest; Akadémiai Kiadó, 1976], p. 297; *idem*, 'Die hethitischen Gesetze in ihren Wechselbeziehungen zu den Nachbarvölkern', in H.-J. Nissen and

shows that these paragraphs form a structure of their own that is distinct from Hitt.C. §§1-6, which deal with capital delicts.[33] The fatal injury of a pregnant woman would be out of place within Hitt.C. §§7-18. That there is a distinction between fatal and non-fatal cases different from UM 55-21-71 §§4-6(7), CH §§209-14 and M.Ass.C. tabl. A §§21, 50-52 is no argument for the independence of the Hittite laws from the Old Babylonian laws. The differences can be explained by the redactional context of the Hittite laws. So the identities between Hittite and Old Babylonian laws are a strong argument for a traditio-historical connection between these laws.[34]

Bodily Injuries of a Pregnant Woman in Israelite Laws of the Book of the Covenant (Exodus 21.22-23 [24-25]).

In the Israelite laws of Exod. 21.22-23 (24-25), we find an entirely different situation. They are part of a collection of laws concerning bodily injuries with and without fatal consequences in Exod. 21.18-32.[35]

Translation

> When men fight and injure a pregnant woman so that she[a] has a miscarriage, but suffers no fatal injury[b], the responsible one will pay whatever the woman's husband demands in the presence of witnesses. But if there is fatal injury, then you must give life for life[c], (eye for eye, tooth for tooth, hand for hand, foot for foot, burn for burn, wound for wound, lash for lash)' (Exod. 21.22-24).

J. Renger [eds.], *Mesopotamien und seine Nachbarn* [Berliner Beiträge zum Vorderen Orient, 1; Berlin: Dietrich Reimer, 1982], pp. 295-310).

33. Cf. Otto, *Körperverletzungen*, pp. 103-104.

34. For the problem of reception of the Mesopotamian traditions in Hittite context, cf. W. Röllig, 'Der Mondgott und die Kuh: Ein Lehrstück zur Problematik der Textüberlieferung im Alten Orient', *Or* NS 54 (1985), pp. 260-73; G. Wilhelm, 'Neue akkadische Gilgameš-Fragmente aus Ḫattusa', *ZA* 78 (1988), pp. 99-121.

35. Cf. E. Otto, *Wandel der Rechtsbegründungen in der Gesellschaftsgeschichte des antiken Israel: Eine Rechtsgeschichte des 'Bundesbuches' Exod. XX 22–XXIII 13* (Studia Biblica, 3; Leiden: Brill, 1988), pp. 24-25; *idem*, 'Die Rechtssystematik im altbabylonischen "Codex Ešnunna" und im altisraelitischen "Bundesbuch": Eine redaktionsgeschichtliche und rechtsvergleichende Analyse von CE §§17; 18; 22-28 und Exod. 21, 18-32; 22, 6-14; 23, 1-3.6-8', *UF* 19 (1988), pp. 175-97; *idem*, 'Die Geschichte der Talion im Alten Orient und in Israel', in *Kontinuum und Proprium: Studien zur Sozialgeschichte und Rechtsgeschichte des Alten Orients und des Alten Testaments* (Orientalia Biblica et Christiana, 8; Wiesbaden: Otto Harrassowitz, 1996), pp. 224-45.

Notes

a. The plural form *w^{e}yāṣ^e'û* is used inclusively. Also in the case of abortion of twins, for example, this legal solution is valid; cf. already K. Budde, 'Bemerkungen zum Bundesbuch', *ZAW* 11 (1891), pp. 99-114 (108); L. Schwienhorst-Schönberger (*Das Bundesbuch [Ex 20, 22–23, 33]: Studien zu seiner Entstehung und Theologie* [BZAW, 188; Berlin: de Gruyter, 1990], pp. 97-98) thinks of a translation of *y^{e}lādēhâ* by 'Kindszeug'.

b. Against B.S. Jackson's translation of *'āsôn* by 'premature birth' ('The Problem of Exodus 21:22-5 [IUS TALIONIS]', in *idem, Essays in Jewish and Comparative Legal History* (SJLA, 10; Leiden: Brill, 1975), pp. 75-107 (96); cf. S.E. Loewenstamm, 'Exodus 21, 22-25', in *idem, Comparative Studies in Biblical and Ancient Oriental Literature* (AOAT, 204; Neukirchen–Vluyn: Neukirchener Verlag; Kevelaer: Butzon & Bercker, 1980), pp. 517-25 (523); against R. Westbrook's thesis ('Lex Talionis and Exodus 21, 22-25', *RB* 93 [1986], pp. 52-69], p. 57; *idem, Studies*, pp. 69-70) 'that *'swn* refers to cases where responsibility cannot be located'; cf. Otto, *Körperverletzungen*, p. 226. I am also not convinced by L. Schwienhorst-Schönberger's translation of *'āsôn* (*Bundesbuch*, p. 92) by 'jede Art von Unglück'. Gen. 42.38, 44; 44.29 deal with fatal injury; cf. C. Westermann, *Genesis* (BKAT, I/3; Neukirchen–Vluyn: Neukirchener Verlag 1982), p. 110.

c. Exod. 21.24-25 is a traditio-historical addition to Exod. 21.22-23 (cf. Otto, *Rechtsbegründungen*, pp. 28-29), but it is already an integral part of the collection Exod. 21.18-32 (cf. Exod. 21.20-21, 26-27); against H.J. Kugelmass, 'Lex Talionis in the Old Testament' (PhD Dissertation, University of Montreal, 1985), pp. 140-41, who separates Exod. 21.23-25 as a priestly addition (P) from the Book of Covenant. For an interpretation of the formula *nepeš taḥat nepeš* as a capital sentence, cf. Kugelmass, 'Lex Talionis', pp. 65-66, 128-29, 142-43, 202-203; Otto, *Körperverletzungen*, pp. 122-23.

The laws of bodily injury of a pregnant woman distinguish between cases of fatal and non-fatal consequences. In case of an injury without fatal consequence for the pregnant woman, the assailant has to pay compensation. In case of a capital delict, the assailant will be put to death *nepeš taḥat nepeš*. This distinction is also valid in UM 55-21-71 §§4, 5; CH §§209/210, 211/212 and M.Ass.C. tabl. A §50. But decisive elements of this Israelite law differ from cuneiform law. Exod. 21.22-23 explicitly demands the death penalty in case of unintentional injury with fatal consequence. Already for rabbinic interpretation (*Mek.* Exod. 21.22) the motif of men fighting had the function of characterizing the injury by an *aberratio ictus* as unintentional. This interpretation is supported by the motif in CH §206: *šumma awīlum awīlam ina risbatim imtaḥaṣ-ma...* The intention to characterize the injury as involuntary also explains the use of the odd term *'asôn*. Human life was to be protected by threat of the death penalty in all cases as capital delicts.[36]

Contrary to all the legal sentences of cuneiform law concerning the non-fatal injury of a pregnant woman, the Israelite legal sentence of Exod. 21.22 does not demand a fixed sum of compensation. The amount of compensation is a matter of negotiation between the families concerned. As the record UCBC 756 shows,[37] the fixed amounts in the cuneiform legal sentences were not binding. They have a function in legal training,[38] so that the scholar learns to differentiate between the cases. Just as the cuneiform legal sentences mirror the practice of legal education, Exod. 21.22 mirrors the legal practice of local courts in Israel.

Exod. 21.22-23 also knows of no distinction between laws concerning the free woman and those concerning the slave, although this distinction is one of the main characteristics of the cuneiform laws. In contrast to the Middle Assyrian laws, there is no reason why such a distinction should be suppressed by the redactor of the collection of injury-laws in Exod. 21.18-32. On the contrary, the redactor combined laws concerning the freeman and the slave in an alternating A–B structure (Exod. 21.18-19 | 20 | 22-25 | 26-27 | 28-31 | 32).[39]

All this hints at the independence of this law from cuneiform law. The laws of the goring ox show the same result.[40] And even the Israelite laws of deposit (Exod. 22.6-14), which regulate an economic institution of the same shape in Mesopotamia and Israel, were traditio-historically independent of cuneiform law (CE §§36, 37, CH §§122-26).[41]

36. For the problem of Exod. 21.13-14 in relation to Exod. 21.23, cf. Otto, *Rechtsbegründungen*, p. 87 n. 106; *idem, Körperverletzungen*, pp. 136-37.

37. Cf. H.F. Lutz, 'The Verdict of a Trial Judge in a Case of Assault and Battery' (University of California Publications in Semitic Philology, 9/6; Berkeley: University of California Press, 1930), pp. 379-80.

38. Cf. E. Otto, *Rechtsgeschichte der Redaktionen im Kodex Ešnunna und im 'Bundesbuch': Eine redaktionsgeschichtliche und rechtsvergleichende Studie zu altbabylonischen und altisraelitischen Rechtsüberlieferungen* (OBO, 85; Freiburg [Schweiz]: Universitätsverlag; Göttingen: Vandenhoeck & Ruprecht, 1988), pp. 181-82, *et passim*.

39. Cf. Otto, *Rechtsbegründungen*, p. 27.

40. Cf. Otto, *Körperverletzungen*, pp. 147-48.

41. Cf. E. Otto, 'Die rechtshistorische Entwicklung des Depositenrechts in

To confirm my argument I must clarify the indigenous origin of Exod. 21.22-23. The motif of the men fighting (*w^{e}kī y^{e}rîbun/yinnāṣû '^{a}nāšîm*) relates Exod. 21.22-23 to Exod. 21.18-19. The law of Exod. 21.22-23 settles a special case of bodily injury, which cannot be solved by application of Exod. 21.18-19. In case of an abortion resulting from bodily injury, there are normally no costs because of confinement to bed. All the more must the loss of a child be compensated for. Obviously other bodily injuries of women were resolved according to Exod. 21.18-19. Exod. 21.22 deals with a special case, that existing law was unable to resolve.[42] Exod. 21.22 was not far from legal practice but closed a gap in this practice. This is also true of Exod. 21.23. One may ask why fatal injuries were treated with regard to women but not in connection with Exod. 21.18-19 concerning men. Exod. 21.18-19 gives the answer. The case of fatal injury is explicitly excluded by a hint at Exod. 21.12 in Exod. 21.18, *w^{e}hikkâ-'îš 'et-rē'ēhû...w^{e}lô' yāmût...w^{e}niqqâ*.[43] Exod. 21.12 originally protected only the free Israelite man. This archaic apodictic law was reformed by the casuistic collection Exod. 21.18-32.[44] In Exod. 21.22-23, (24-25), 28.29, (30), women and, in Exod. 21.31, children were also protected from capital delicts. A case was resolved in that context where it was especially contested.[45] As for Exod. 21.12, sooner or later the question must be asked whether also the life of an Israelite woman was protected by law. As for Exod. 21.18-19 the question must also be asked whether an Israelite woman was protected from bodily injuries. Both questions are answered by Exod. 21.22, 23. These laws filled a legal gap by reforming the existing law by inclusion of the Israelite woman. The thesis that Exod. 21.22-23 was a school paradigm

altorientalischen und altisraelitischen Rechtskorpora', *Zeitschrift der Savigny-Stiftung für Rechsgeschichte (Rom. Abt.)* 105 (1988), pp. 1-31.

42. H. Petschow ('Beiträge zum Codex Ḥammurapi', *ZA* 76 [1986], pp. 17-75) made a similar observation with the laws of the Codex Hammurabi.

43. Cf. Exod. 21.12: *makkēh 'îš wāmēt môt yûmāṯ*.

44. Cf. Otto, *Rechtsbegründungen*, pp. 30-31, 61-62.

45. Cf. also, for the Codex Hammurabi, H. Petschow, 'Die §§45 und 46 des Codex Ḥammurapi: Ein Beitrag zum altbabylonischen Bodenpachtrecht und zum Problem: Was ist der Codex Ḥammurapi?', *ZA* 74 (1984), pp. 181-212. Even if this kind of abortion does not happen very often, this does not speak against the practical function of this law. Laws are often formulated for cases that are especially contested and difficult to solve, and are used inclusively for the less contested and difficult cases by analogy. The frequency of cases is not an argument to consider a law as a school exercise paradigm (*pace* Finkelstein, 'Ox', pp. 18-19).

derived from the cuneiform school curriculum of the Mesopotamian É.DUB.BA.A (*bīt tuppim*),[46] and far from Israelite legal practice, is not necessary to explain the origin of these laws. How should cuneiform legal tradition find its way to the Israelite courts in the gates of small Israelite villages and townlets[47] in the Judaean and Ephraimite countryside where this law was practised? The independence of the single Israelite law under discussion from the tradition of cuneiform law and its indigenous origin in Israel correspond to what P. Koschaker[48] has shown for cuneiform law and G. Liedke[49] and C. Locher[50] have shown for Israelite law, namely, that the sentences of casuistic law were derived from trial-protocols and legal narratives; that is, these laws had their origin in Israelite legal practice.[51] My argument concerning the redaction of Israelite law codes is entirely different. But Israelite drafting techniques were dependent on those of cuneiform law.

Cuneiform Legal Influence on the Redactions of Predeuteronomistic Law Codes in Israel

In the law codes that became part of the Book of the Covenant,[52] we already find techniques of redaction that were also used in cuneiform law codes.[53] In the collection of laws concerning bodily injuries in Exod. 21.18-32, a redactional structure of alternation in an A–B scheme of laws concerning the slave and the free Israelite was used. The same drafting technique was also used (for example) in CE §§54-57. A further drafting technique of Exod. 21.18-32 organizes the laws by placing the principal regulation (*lex generalis*) in the centre of Exod. 21.23b-25. The collection shows that talionic punishment was only applicable in cases of

---

46. Cf. A. Sjöberg, 'The Old Babylonian Eduba', in S.J. Lieberman (ed.), *Essays in Honour of T. Jacobsen* (Assyriological Studies, 20; Chicago: University Press, 1974), pp. 159-79.

47. Cf. E. Otto, ''îr', *ThWAT*, VI, pp. 56-74; *idem*, 'ša'ar', *ThWAT*, VIII, pp. 358-403.

48. Koschaker, *Untersuchungen*, pp. 68, 79-80, 83.

49. Liedke, *Rechtssätze*, pp. 39-40.

50. Locher, *Ehre*, pp. 83-84, 90-91.

51. Cf. especially Exod. 21.18-19.

52. For a delimitation of originally independent law collections in the Book of the Covenant, cf. Otto, *Rechtsbegründungen*, pp. 9-51.

53. Cf. Otto, *Rechtsgeschichte*, pp. 135-36; *idem*, 'Rechtssystematik', pp. 175-97.

capital delicts, and was inapplicable in all other cases of bodily injuries,[54] which demanded only compensation. The result of combining these drafting techniques is the following redactional structure of the originally independent law collection Exod. 21.18-32:

A:	Exod. 21.18	law concerning the freeman
B:	Exod. 21.20-21	law concerning the slave
A:	Exod. 21.22-23	law concerning the freeman
	Exod. 21.23b-25	*principal regulation*
B:	Exod. 21.26-27	law concerning the slave
A:	Exod. 21.28-31	law concerning the freeman
B:	Exod. 21.32	law concerning the slave

The same redactional techniques were used in structuring the laws of bodily injuries in the Hittite code §§7–18:

A:	§7	law concerning the freeman
B:	§8	law concerning the slave
	§§9, 10	*principal regulation*[55]
A:	§11	law concerning the freeman
B:	§12	law concerning the slave
A:	§13	law concerning the freeman
B:	§14	law concerning the slave
A:	§15	law concerning the freeman
B:	§16	law concerning the slave
A:	§17	law concerning the freeman
B:	§18	law concerning the slave

The technique of structuring legal sentences by a principal regulation (*lex generalis*) as a systematic centre (Exod. 22.8-9) is also found in the deposit laws in Exod. 22.6-14.[56]

Results

This study yields a complex result. Whereas the single Israelite legal sentence was independent of the tradition of cuneiform law, the drafting techniques of Israelite law codes were deeply rooted in cuneiform legal

54. Cf. Otto, *Rechtsbegründungen*, pp. 24-25.

55. Cf. J. Grothus, *Die Rechtsordnung der Hethiter* (Wiesbaden: Otto Harrassowitz, 1973), p. 57; Otto, *Körperverletzungen*, pp. 103-104.

56. Cf. Otto, *Rechtsbergündungen*, pp. 14-15; *idem*, 'Depositenrecht', pp. 16-17. For further relations between cuneiform and Hebrew drafting techniques, cf. Otto, *Rechtsgeschichte*, pp. 68-69, 135-36, 177-78.

tradition. Casuistic laws were derived from legal decisions of local courts
in rural communities of the Israelite countryside. The laws still show the
range of problems of these communities, such as the loss, hire and tending of cattle (Exod. 21.33–22.3, 9-14), the damage to fruit and harvest
(Exod. 22.4-5), help with animals in danger (Exod. 23.4-5[57]), and the
firstlings of fruit and animals (Exod. 22.28-30). The regulations concerning the slave (*'ebed*, Exod. 21.2-11, 20-21, 26-27, 32), day-labourer
(*śākîr*, Exod. 22.14b), stranger (*gēr*, Exod. 22.20aα), small farmer (*dāl*,
Exod. 23.3) and the impoverished (*'ebyôn*, Exod. 23.6; *'ānî*, Exod.
22.24) show the process of social differentiation in the monarchic period
of Israelite history.[58] In a rural milieu of local courts, the knowledge of
international legal tradition is rather improbable. This is also valid if the
origins of Israel are to be sought in Canaan,[59] because there is no direct
origin of the proto-Israelite herdsman[60] in the Late Bronze culture of
Canaanite towns.[61] But the drafting of laws in law codes took place in
the towns of Israel as places of higher education. The legal education

57. Cf. E. Otto, 'Sozial- und rechtshistorische Aspekte in der Ausdifferenzierung
eines altisraelitischen Ethos aus dem Recht', in *idem, Kontinuum*, pp. 94-111;
G. Barbiero, *L'asino del nemico: Rinuncia alla vendetta e amore del nemico nella
legislazione dell'Antico Testamento (Est. 23, 4-5; Deut. 22, 1-4; Lev. 19, 18)*
(AnBib, 128; Rome: Editrice Pontificio Instituto Biblico, 1991), pp. 125-30.

58. Cf. F. Crüsemann, 'Das Bundesbuch—Historischer Ort und institutioneller
Hintergrund', in J.A. Emerton (ed.), *Congress Volume, Jerusalem 1986* (VTSup,
40; Leiden: Brill, 1988), pp. 27-41; E. Otto, 'Interdependenzen zwischen Geschichte
und Rechtsgeschichte des antiken Israels', *Rechtshistorisches Journal* 7 (1988),
pp. 347-68. For Deuteronomy, cf. R.A. Butterfield, 'Deuteronomy 12–20 in Cultural
Evolutionary Perspective' (PhD dissertation, Lutheran School of Theology, Chicago,
1986), pp. 13-14, 135-36.

59. Cf. G.W. Ahlström, *Who Were the Israelites?* (Winona Lake, IN:
Eisenbrauns, 1986); R.B. Coote and K.W. Whitelam, *The Emergence of Early Israel
in Historical Perspective* (Social World of Biblical Antiquity, 5; Sheffield: Almond
Press, 1987); N.P. Lemche, *Ancient Israel: A New History of Israelite Society* (The
Biblical Seminar, 5; Sheffield: JSOT Press, 1988). For these monographs, cf. E.
Otto, 'Israels Wurzeln in Kanaan: Auf dem Wege zu einer neuen Kultur- und
Sozialgeschichte des antiken Israels', *TRev* 85 (1989), pp. 3-10.

60. Cf. I. Finkelstein, *The Archaeology of the Israelite Settlement* (Jerusalem:
Israel Exploration Society, 1988), pp. 336-37; previously E. Otto, 'Historisches
Geschehen–Überlieferung-Erklärungsmodell: Sozialhistorische Grundsatz- und
Einzelprobleme in der Geschichtsschreibung des frühen Israel', *BN* 23 (1984),
pp. 63-80.

61. Cf. Otto, ''îr', pp. 61-62.

was part of the curriculum of scribes[62] in towns as administration centres of Israel.[63] This education was possibly located at schools, where a knowledge of cuneiform legal texts could be a Canaanite tradition. Cuneiform texts of the Mesopotamian É.DUB.BA.A curriculum were known in pre-Israelite towns of Palestine.[64] So we have to distinguish between the single casuistic legal sentence, which had its indigenous origin in the rural local court institution of early Israel, and the skilled drafting techniques of law codes that were located in administration centres of monarchic Israel. Here laws were collected and became part of the legal training of scribes.

In the Assyrian period cuneiform law had a more direct influence on Israelite law, as an analysis of Deuteronomy will show.[65] But this is beyond the scope of this essay.

62. For the influence of wisdom on the law, cf. M. Weinfeld, *Deuteronomy and the Deuteronomic School* (Oxford: Clarendon Press, 1972), pp. 244-45; J. Blenkinsopp, *Wisdom and Law in the Old Testament* (Oxford: Oxford University Press, 1983). For the education of scribes in monarchic Israel, cf. E. Lipiński, 'Royal and State Scribes in Ancient Jerusalem', in Emerton (ed.), *Congress Volume*, pp. 157-64; E. Puech, 'Les écoles dans l'Israël préexilique: Données épigraphiques', in Emerton (ed.), *Congress Volume*, pp. 189-203.

63. Cf. G.W. Ahlström, 'Royal Administration and National Religion in Ancient Palestine' (Studies in the History of the Ancient Near East, 1; Leiden: Brill, 1982).

64. Cf. K. Galling, *Textbuch zur Geschichte Israels* (Tübingen: J.C.B. Mohr, 2nd edn, 1968), pp. 13-14; H. Weippert, *Palästina in vorhellenistischer Zeit* (Handbuch der Archäologie, II/1; Munich: C.H. Beck, 1988), pp. 266-67.

65. Cf. Locher, *Ehre*; A. Rofé, 'Methodological Aspects of the Study of Biblical Law', *Jewish Law Association Studies* 2 (1986), pp. 13-14; E. Otto, 'Rechtsreformen in Deuteronomium XII–XXVI und im Mittelassyrischen Kodex der Tafel A (KAV 1)', in J.A. Emerton (ed.), *Congress Volume Paris 1992* (VTSup, 61; Leiden: Brill, 1995), pp. 239-73; *idem*, 'Treueid und Gesetz: Die Ursprünge des Deuteroniums im Horizont des neuassyrischen Vertragsrechts', *Zeitschrift für Altorientalische und Biblische Rechtsgeschichte 2* (1996), pp. 1-52.

JSOT 58 (1993), pp. 13-33

ON DESCRIBING THE PURPOSE OF DEUTERONOMY*

A.D.H. Mayes

I

The problem with which this paper is concerned is not that of objectively assessing the merits of this or that description of the purpose of Deuteronomy, nor that of simply coming up with some novel account. Rather, it is in the first place a matter of determining where and how to begin: what approach is appropriate, what criteria are appropriate, on what grounds can *this* and not *that* be argued to be the purpose of Deuteronomy? This is most certainly a topic that has methodology as its central focus. No apology is necessary for this focus; the reasons for making methodological issues explicit are substantive and not simply the consequence of being in thrall to a transient fashion. At a fairly banal level, it may indeed still be the case that a statement is objectively either right or wrong, but in the face of the variety of ways in which the purpose of Deuteronomy has been described it is difficult, to say the least, to find persuasive justification for making that kind of judgment. Some other way of coping with the multiple purposes that commentators have found in this book is needed.

The exact contours of the pre-deuteronomistic book of Deuteronomy, which is to be the focus of our attention, remain in some details uncertain; but that it was characterized by the following aspects is widely assumed, and forms the basis for our present discussion. It contained the

---

* A Presidential Address to the Society for Old Testament Study at its Winter Meeting held in Sheffield, December 1991. Since this article was first published I have written further on this topic: 'De l'idéologie deutéronomiste à la théologie de l'Ancien Testament', in A. de Pury, T. Römer and J.-D. Macchi (eds.), *Israël construit son histoire: L'historiographie deutéronomiste à la lumière des recherches récentes* (Le Monde de la Bible, 34; Geneva: Labor et Fides, 1996), pp. 477-508.

bulk of the law of chs. 12–26, with an introduction, now edited in chs. 6–11, and a heading, possibly preserved in 4.45, describing it as the testimonies, the statutes and the ordinances that Moses gave to Israel when they came out of Egypt; the book probably concluded with the blessings and curses of ch. 28, which were linked to the law by the end of ch. 26, an important passage identifying the law not simply as the law of Moses but as the law that defined Yahweh's relationship with his people.[1]

II

A fairly random survey of some of the principal commentaries and studies yields this as one kind of perception of the purpose of this book:

> Deuteronomy is a manual addressed to the people and intended for popular use, which, without as a rule entering into technical details, would instruct the Israelite in the ordinary duties of life,[2]

similarly,

> The book of Deuteronomy appears indeed to have the character of an ideal national constitution representing all the official institutions of the state: the monarchy, the judiciary, the priesthood and prophecy. These institutions are successively referred to in Deut. 16.18–18.22 and are depicted not only in realistic terms but also in terms of the ideal at which this neutral circle of scribes was clearly aiming—a national regime which incorporated all the normative, spiritual, and religious circles of the period,[3]

1.   Detailed argument concerning the deuteronomistic contributions to the original Deuteronomy will be found in my commentary, *Deuteronomy* (NCB; London: Ohiphants); any modifications of the account there are in the light of N. Lohfink, 'Pluralism', in *Great Themes from the Old Testament* (Edinburgh: T. & T. Clark, 1982), pp.17-37, 24-25. Whether or not the detail concerning deuteronomistic supplementation of Deuteronomy is generally agreed does not, for our present purposes, greatly matter. The process of development of Deuteronomy through its deuteronomistic stages was a continuous one, the decisive step being the one taken in the creation of the original pre-deuteronomistic Deuteronomy. It will become clear, however, that in one significant respect I would now modify an earlier view (in A.D.H. Mayes, 'Deuteronomy: Law of Moses or Law of God?', *Proceedings of the Irish Biblical Association* 5 [1981], pp. 36-54), viz. that the original Deuteronomy was understood not simply as law of Moses but as law deriving from Yahweh.

2.   S.R. Driver, *Deuteronomy* (ICC; Edinburgh: T. & T. Clark, 1902), p. xxvi.

3.   M. Weinfeld, *Deuteronomy and the Deuteronomic School* (Oxford: Clarendon Press, 1972), p. 168.

and, again, similarly,

> [T]he overwhelming point of view which is assumed, argued for, and
> striven for, in Deuteronomy is that of a progressive, organized and pros-
> perous nation-state. Israel is considered as a nation like other nations, yet
> unique because it has Yahweh as its God who will guard, guide and pros-
> per its affairs, so long as the people respond loyally and sincerely to his
> revealed will. In this respect it can be regarded as certain that the demand
> for cult centralization was simply one aspect of a policy aimed at securing
> a unified, coherent and centrally administered state.[4]

On the other hand, we also find this: The nature of the code is clear: no
more than any other biblical code is it a constitution. It would be absolutely insufficient to organize the life of a society. It is designed to
educate and to inculcate religious convictions and attitudes.[5]

And this:

> [It] is not a juridical book, [but] a proclamation and exposition of the
> faith...there can be no doubt that the original purpose of Deuteronomy
> was not to impose a legalistic system...but rather to convey the Mosaic
> teaching or doctrine.[6]

The general contours of the particular issue for discussion are clear. Is
Deuteronomy constitutional law, more or less closely related to the
everyday life of Israel, or is it teaching? Does it aim to articulate a basis
and framework for the political existence of a nation-state, or is it a
homiletical work designed to reform individual attitudes? These may not
be mutually exclusive understandings, but that they represent real alter-
natives has been strongly argued by McBride.[7] So he suggests that
fascination with literary, tradition-historical and homiletical aspects of
Deuteronomy has blinded us to its broader social and political significance:

> Conception of *tora* as 'teaching' or 'instruction' has promoted a much too
> facile understanding of Deuteronomy itself as essentially a didactic,
> moralizing or homiletical work. More importantly, neither term conveys
> the normative, prescriptive force of *tora* in Deuteronomy. The 'words' or

---

4.   R.E. Clements, *Deuteronomy* (Sheffield: JSOT Press, 1989), p. 87.
5.   P. Buis and J. Leclerq, *Le Deutéronome* (SB; Paris: Gabalda, 1963), pp. 98-
99.
6.   G.E. Wright, 'Deuteronomy', *IB*, II, pp. 311-537, 312-13.
7.   S.D. McBride, 'Polity of the Covenant People: The Book of Deuteronomy',
Int 41 (1987), pp. 229-44.

stipulations of 'this Torah' are not simply admonitions and sage advice offered in the name of Moses to guide the faithful along a divinely charted path of life; they are set forth as sanctioned political policies, to be 'diligently observed' by Israelite king and common citizen alike (17.19; 31.12; 32.45), and on their strict observance hangs the fate of the entire nation.[8]

McBride finds a precedent for his view in Josephus, who asserted that Deuteronomy preserves the divinely authorized and comprehensive 'polity' or national 'constitution' that Moses delivered to the tribes assembled in Transjordan. This reflects Deuteronomy's own self-understanding, for it repeatedly claims to embody as its central segment (4.44–28.68) a *written* deposition of the authoritative Torah mediated through Moses to Israel.[9] So *tōrâ* in Deuteronomy is not only a theological but a decidedly jurisprudential concept, which connotes 'the totality of particular categories of legislation and judicial practice appropriate to it'; it is 'covenantal law, the divinely authorized social order that Israel must implement to secure its collective political existence as the people of God' (p. 233). Although indebted to lawcodes and treaties, Deuteronomy differs from these in form, content and purpose—it is a comprehensive social charter that seeks to realize specific political objectives, and in particular to safeguard each member of the political community as a political person possessing a sphere of genuine autonomy.

McBride's constitutional reading of Deuteronomy is not unlike that proposed by Alt,[10] who argued that Deuteronomy is a restoration programme, drawn up after the fall of the northern kingdom and designed for a time when the Assyrian yoke would be lifted. It is, however, a reading which, McBride argues, has been obscured in recent years largely as a result of the influence of Noth and von Rad. Noth argued that 'we need not strain the significance of Deuteronomy against its own obvious intention by representing it as a composition intended to be introduced as state legislation'.[11] Deuteronomy was set in force by Josiah not by an act of state but by a sacral ceremony in which a covenant was established between God and the people; this was simply a renewal or

8.   McBride, 'Polity', pp. 232-33.

9.   McBride, 'Polity', pp. 231-32.

10.   A. Alt, 'Die Heimat des Deuteronomiums', in *Kleine Schriften zur Geschichte des Volkes Israel*, II (München: C.H. Beck, 1953), pp. 250-75.

11.   M. Noth, 'The Laws in the Pentateuch: Their Assumptions and Meaning', in *The Laws in the Pentateuch and Other Essays* (Edinburgh: Oliver & Boyd, 1965), pp. 1-107 (42-43).

reconfirmation of the old Sinaitic covenant that was basically still in existence, and the frame of reference of this law was, therefore, not the state but the old sacral confederacy. The confederacy had indeed been severely weakened in the course of the monarchic history, but it still basically existed. Josiah, in making the elders of Judah and Jerusalem, that is, the spokesmen of the people of his kingdom, a party to this covenant with God, indeed treated it as state law, making it the foundation for political measures on cultic matters,[12] but this went quite against its purpose, which is in part why that reform eventually failed, for the deuteronomic lawcode was not state law, but the foundation of the covenant between God and people.

In von Rad's *Old Testament Theology* this distancing of Deuteronomy from state law is even more pronounced as a result of the strong contrast drawn between law and saving event. Commandments such as the decalogue are addressed not to any form of secular community, such as the state, but to the community of Yahweh.[13]

> Indeed, in reducing all the profusion of the commandments to the one fundamental commandment, to love God (Deut. vi. 4), and in concerning itself so earnestly with the inner, the spiritual, meaning of the commandments, Deuteronomy rather looks like a last stand against the beginning of a legislation.[14]

And further:

> Deuteronomy does not set out to be civil law—none of the legal codes in the Old Testament is to be understood in this way. Deuteronomy addresses Israel as a sacral community, the holy people, that is, the people belonging to Jahweh, and her life and her offices (priest, king, prophet, and judge) are ordered as having this character.[15]

III

Diversity of interpretation of this nature is, of course, very familiar. A recent attempt to cope with it from a methodological point of view has been made by Mark Brett in a study of varied exegetical treatments of

---

12. Noth, 'Laws in the Pentateuch', pp. 46-47.
13. G. von Rad, *Old Testament Theology*, I (Edinburgh: Oliver & Boyd, 1962), p. 195.
14. Von Rad, *Old Testament Theology*, I, p. 201.
15. Von Rad, *Old Testament Theology*, I, pp. 228-29.

Genesis 1.[16] A study by Quentin Skinner[17] has been exploited and considerably expanded by Brett in order to distinguish different levels of intentionality effectively present in a given author, each of which may give rise to a different reading and understanding of a single text produced by that author. A distinction is drawn between the communicative intention of the author, which is essentially the content of the text, the indirect communicative intention, which is concerned with the implications of the text, and the motive of the author, concerned with why the author created the text.

As far as Deuteronomy is concerned one could, perhaps, say that the communicative intention of the author is to describe the foundation of Israel by Moses in the plains of Moab as a constitutional theocracy. The implications, expressing the indirect communicative intention, would include, for example, the rejection of a treaty relationship with Assyria (it is with Yahweh alone that Israel has a covenant relationship) and perhaps also the rejection of a Davidic royal covenant theology (Yahweh's covenant is with the people as a whole and not solely with the royal house). The relationship between Deuteronomy and the extra-biblical treaty texts is clearly immediately relevant here: for Judaeans familiar with those texts, Deuteronomy would have carried a range of indirectly intended meanings.[18] The motive of the author would have incorporated a concern for the integrity and political independence of individual Israelites, and for the essential unity of Israel particularly in a situation where the foundation of its unity had been obscured through social and economic developments in the monarchic period.

There is much in this approach that is useful and open to further development. Some such treatment as this may indeed manage to comprehend something of the range of interpretations to which Deuteronomy has given rise. Many of these, if not most, may be set somewhere on the continuum that extends from the communicative intention to the motive. So, a variety of intentions/motives, in a form of hierarchy, may be present in a single text, so that the text may be held to have multiple purposes. Moreover, this is an approach that, as Brett has noted, is

16. M. Brett, 'Motives and Intentions in Genesis 1', *JTS* NS 42 (1991), pp. 1-16.

17. O. Skinner, 'Motives, Intentions and the Interpretation of Texts', *New Literary History* 3 (1972), pp. 393-408.

18. The precise formulation of both of these implications would depend on whether or not the term 'covenant' was used by the original Deuteronomy to describe Israel's relationship with Yahweh; on that there is some doubt.

perhaps particularly attractive for those who hold to the more traditional ways of doing biblical study: plenty of room is left for asking for the meaning of the original text and the circumstances of its origin, involving all the latest archaeological, historical and sociological approaches.

It is clear, however, that, particularly in the form in which the argument has been presented by Skinner, this approach leaves significant dimensions of interpretation quite inadequately covered. Even within the limits that Skinner permits[19] there is a serious narrowing of focus that excludes areas of immediate relevance to the question of the author's intention. Skinner believes that 'it must always be dangerous, and ought probably to be very unusual, for a critic to override a writer's own explicit statements about what he was doing in a given work',[20] and that 'To discount a writer's own statements...is only to make the (perhaps rather dramatic, but certainly conceivable) claim that the writer himself may have been self-deceiving about recognizing his intentions, or incompetent at stating them'. Intentions and motives are here understood as the *conscious* intentions and motives entertained by a given author, an approach to a text that Brett[21] has labelled 'synchronic emics'. It is a merit of Brett's work to have shown how the 'etic' level—that of the unconscious motives, which can be reconstructed only by the observer—may not be so easily ignored as Skinner believes, but belongs on a single continuum with the 'emic' level of conscious intention. This allows the adoption of socio-economic and psychoanalytic approaches to literary works in a way that would otherwise be irrelevant.

Perhaps the major problem with Skinner's analysis, however, lies yet one step further back. For if it is permissible to discount an author's explicit statements about his or her own intentions in describing the purpose of a work, then the implicit assumption is that the first step, the first decision, in relation to meaning is in fact taken by the interpreter. Such a step can be taken, such a decision made, only if, from the

19. Although Skinner states at the beginning of his article (p. 393) that 'We must be careful to avoid the vulgarity...of supposing that we can ever hope to arrive at "*the* correct reading" of a text, such that any rival readings can then be ruled out', he is really interested in meaning only as author's meaning; his conclusion, that the author's intentions and motives are inseparable from this, is little more than a tautology. Skinner does not discuss the relationship of the author's meaning to the meaning of the text or to the meaning for the reader, both of which he distinguishes as potentially different from the meaning intended by the author.

20. Skinner, 'Motives', p. 405.

21. Brett, 'Motives', p. 4.

beginning, the interpreter is an active participant in the production of meaning.

IV

The notion that the reader, the interpreter of a text, can by an imaginative act of empathy transpose himself or herself into the mind of the author, and take over the author's conscious intentions, has been a view more or less unconsciously assumed in much historical study, but is now widely dismissed as simplistic. It takes no account of the way in which a text, once created, becomes something independent of its author; it takes no account of the fact that interpreters generally do not just *find* meaning in the object of interpretation, but rather *put* meaning on that object. Alternative approaches, especially those dependent on Gadamer's *Truth and Method*,[22] see interpreters not as neutral observers with immediate access to the object of their interpretative activity, but as those who bring with them their own life world with all its beliefs and practices, its ideas and norms. So, understanding is not a matter simply of adopting the life world of the text; it is, rather, a matter of bringing that life world into a relationship with the life world of the interpreter. The meaning of a text, then, is the meaning articulated in the context of this dialogue. Understanding is the 'articulation in the interpreter's language of meanings constituted in another universe of discourse'.[23]

Within this dialogical framework, the actual process of interpretation is a circular one:

> we must understand the whole in terms of the detail and the detail in terms of the whole... *The anticipation of meaning in which the whole is envisaged* becomes explicit understanding in that the parts, that are determined by the whole, themselves also determine this whole.[24]

That is to say:

> [T]he interpreter makes a preliminary projection of the sense of the text as a whole. With further penetration into the details of his material, the preliminary projection is revised, alternative proposals are considered, and new projections are tested. This...process...has as its goal the achieving

22. H.-G. Gadamer, *Truth and Method* (London: Sheed & Ward, 2nd edn, 1979).

23. T. McCarthy, *The Critical Theory of Jürgen Habermas* (Cambridge: Polity Press, 1984), p. 172.

24. Gadamer, *Truth and Method*, pp. 258-59; emphasis added.

of a unity of sense: an interpretation of the whole into which our detailed knowledge of the parts can be integrated without violence.[25]

Therefore:

> The harmony of all the details with the whole is the criterion of correct understanding. The failure to achieve this harmony means that understanding has failed.[26]

Two points follow from this. The first, which has general reference to the process of interpretation as such, is that insofar as interpretation is a matter of dialogue between interpreter and text, there can be no such thing as the final and definitive interpretation; every community, every age must understand the tradition in its own way. The second point has particular relevance to the interpretation of classical and especially religious texts within the tradition in which those texts are acknowledged. This is that the 'anticipation of meaning' or the preliminary projection of the sense of the text as a whole derives not simply from the interpreter but rather from the tradition to which both text and interpreter belong. 'The anticipation of meaning that governs our understanding of a text is not an act of subjectivity, but proceeds from the communality that binds us to the tradition'.[27] In a significant way, then, interpretation is a matter of the rearticulation of the text within the tradition.

Both points are of fundamental significance for our topic: Deuteronomy is not open to a final and definitive interpretation; the articulation of its meaning and purpose is in large measure dependent on the life-world out of which the interpreter comes; in the description of its meaning and purpose the text is being rearticulated within the tradition. In a perceptive study of von Rad, John Barton has shown how his *Old Testament Theology* clearly reflects this interpretative process. Von Rad rejects all positivism in biblical scholarship, with its emphasis on recovering the facts of Israel's history; that approach creates insuperable tension between the facts of history on the one hand and Israelite understanding on the other, and also between Israelite understanding and the understanding of the present day. By shifting the focus from what really happened in Israel's history to the Old Testament understanding of that history as saving history, von Rad succeeded in distancing theological

25. McCarthy, *Critical Theory*, pp. 172-73.
26. Gadamer, *Truth and Method*, p. 259.
27. Gadamer, *Truth and Method*, p. 261.

truth claims from the changes and chances of historical research. It is Israel's faith, a faith maintained and strengthened by proclamation and teaching, that is distinctively significant about Israel and the Old Testament, and thus the proper subject for Old Testament theology. As Barton notes:

> The Israel of von Rad's *Old Testament Theology* walks by faith, not by sight, believing where she may not prove. The English reader may well suspect here that a rather particular theological axe is being ground, which goes by the name of Justification by Faith...the voice here is von Rad's voice, but the hands are hands of Luther.[28]

In other words, von Rad's *Theology* may well be a historical rather than a systematic theology, oriented to the believing community of Israel rather than to the believing community of today, but it is a historical theology that is meaningful and relevant to the particular faith context to which von Rad himself belongs.

On the other hand, as Barton notes, this is not to suggest that with von Rad

> confessional prejudice has simply *replaced* academic objectivity...the interpretation of the biblical data may owe much to a particular theological position, but it is an interpretation of data that are really there in the text. The Old Testament very plainly *is* a book of faith, expressing a conscious decision to take history as manifesting a certain divine plan, whatever the odds; and the stories in Genesis...do now serve the purpose of endorsing Israel's faith, rather than of providing objective historical information about clan-movements in the second millennium BC.[29]

In applying the idea of justification by faith to the Old Testament, 'von Rad may be reading Lutheran notions into the Bible—but where do those notions come from in the first place? Partly, at least, from the Bible itself'.[30] In other words, von Rad's *Old Testament Theology* in general, and his treatment of Deuteronomy in particular, illustrate perfectly Gadamer's description of what goes on in the interpretation of texts.

A closely parallel account can be given of the alternative approach to Deuteronomy represented by McBride. It may seem that in this case we are in a completely different field of interest, historical rather than

28. R. Morgan with J. Barton, *Biblical Interpretation* (Oxford Bible Series; Oxford: Oxford University Press, 1988).

29. Morgan and Barton, *Biblical Interpretation*, p. 103.

30. Morgan and Barton, *Biblical Interpretation*, pp. 103-104.

theological, but McBride does argue that by losing sight of the broader social and political import of Deuteronomy, which he proposes to highlight, Old Testament study has 'failed to confront directly its particular theological witness'.[31] The theological significance of Deuteronomy, for this approach, lies precisely in its direct and immediate relationship to the institutional arrangements by which Israel should order its historical, social and political life in the world. This is not to say, of course, that in this approach what Israel believed was of no particular importance; but the context within which this approach belongs is one that understands that truth is an objective phenomenon of the real world, to which texts are more or less adequately related.

The philosophical tradition within which this belongs is very different from that of von Rad, and it is characterized by the empirical and positivist viewpoints that von Rad rejected. In the context of biblical study it is the dominant tradition in American and British scholarship, perhaps particularly clear in American biblical study still strongly influenced by Albright. For the latter, 'the primary function of the historian is to collect as many facts as possible about the past'[32] and effectively to discover the pattern, and so the purpose, that is objectively present in history. At the conclusion of his study he writes as follows: 'We have endeavoured to make the facts speak for themselves, though our care to state them fairly and to provide evidence to support them, where necessary, may sometimes have made it difficult for the reader to follow the unfolding scroll of history'.[33] Having thus provided an objective, factual account of the historical process, judgment is then passed on the biblical tradition:

> The tradition of Israel represents Moses as a monotheist; the evidence of ancient Oriental religious history, combined with the most rigorous critical treatment of Israelite literary sources, points in exactly the same direction... Christian tradition represents Jesus of Nazareth as the Christ of faith; historical and literary criticism, assisted by the evidence of Near-Eastern religious history, finds that there is nothing against the tradition—except prejudice.[34]

Theological significance lies not in the ideas and beliefs in themselves,

31. McBride, 'Polity', pp. 230-31.

32. W.F. Albright, *From the Stone Age to Christianity* (Garden City, NY: Doubleday, 1957), p. 114.

33. Albright, *Stone Age to Christianity*, p. 400.

34. Albright, *Stone Age to Christianity*, p. 400.

but in their correlation with the events and institutions of the external, physical world.

Once again, however, McBride's emphasis on the historical, institutional significance of Deuteronomy is not to be taken simply as a reflection of confessional prejudice informed by a particular philosophical outlook, for as with von Rad, so here, this emphasis can be said to be rooted in the Old Testament itself and thus to represent a rearticulation of that tradition. For if it is true that 'The Old Testament very plainly *is* a book of faith, expressing a conscious decision to take history as manifesting a certain divine plan, whatever the odds',[35] it is also most certainly true that the Old Testament consistently locates the divine revelation not in the beliefs held by Israel but rather in the things that God has actually said and done in history. If von Rad's interpretation of Deuteronomy belongs in a wider interpretative practice by which the Old Testament tradition is rearticulated for von Rad's world, then McBride's interpretation likewise belongs in a wider interpretative practice by which the Old Testament tradition is reactualized for his world. In both cases the truth claims of the text for different interpretative situations are being recognized and articulated.

V

Gadamer's interpretation theory results, therefore, in a relativistic position. The interpretation of a text can never be final and definitive, but is always relative to the situation of the interpreter. The range of possible readings of a text, including Deuteronomy, is, then, more or less infinite. In reflecting on this, it is important to note, in the first place, that Gadamer was not proposing a method of text interpretation, but was rather only describing what actually took place in text interpretation. From the perspective of method, however, this has been seen as a thoroughly unsatisfactory situation requiring developments from and improvements on the practice described by Gadamer.

In particular, Gadamer's theory has been held to be relevant only to understanding within the tradition, for it is the tradition which supplies the anticipations of meaning or preliminary projections that are the foundation of the interpretative process.[36] Moreover, even within this

---

35. Morgan and Barton, *Biblical Interpretation*, p. 103.

36. Cf. W.G. Jeanrond, *Text and Interpretation as Categories of Theological Thinking* (Dublin: Gill & Macmillan, 1988), pp. 22-24.

context, it has been argued that Gadamer does not appreciate the power of reflection that is developed in the process of understanding; that is, interpretation has been identified simply with continuing and participating in the tradition, ignoring the strength of the critical reflection that allows the interpreter to reject rather than simply affirm the claims of tradition. In developing this critique of Gadamer, Habermas[37] avoids any return to the idealistic supposition that the interpreter may take up a neutral standpoint of judgment outside the tradition; rather,

> hermeneutics comes up against walls of the traditional framework from the inside, as it were. As soon as these boundaries have been experienced and recognized, cultural traditions can no longer be posed as absolute.[38]

If interpretation is not simply a necessary continuation of the tradition, but rather may be at least a quasi-objective activity, then the possibility is raised of agreed interpretations that should transcend the boundaries constituted by the tradition to which the interpreter belongs. The conditions of this possibility must be such that the pre-understandings or anticipations of meaning that govern interpretation should be agreed pre-understandings (even across different traditions) that rest on a critical self-awareness that is, so far as possible, objectively grounded.

In relation to von Rad and McBride we can say this: insofar as there is anything defective in their approach to the understanding of the purpose of Deuteronomy, this defectiveness is not to be found in a failure objectively to perceive what is present in Deuteronomy; rather, it must relate to a lack of critical awareness of the nature of the pre-understandings with which they have approached the text, a lack of critical awareness of the significance of the traditions to which they belong. Any criticism of von Rad and McBride would then in the first instance have to be a criticism directed to this area.

The purpose of Deuteronomy could be expounded from a variety of perspectives. The validity of any of these would be very much a matter

---

37. J. Habermas, *Knowledge and Human Interests* (London: Heinemann, 2nd edn, 1978), pp. 313-14.

38. McCarthy, *Critical Theory*, pp. 182-83. The full richness of Gadamer's account of interpretation cannot be discussed here. Such a discussion would have to take note of his argument that the truth of the text, even when expressed in terms of the meaning of the author, is not to be confined within the closed horizon of its circumstances of production, but emerges only after the merely contingent conditions of its origin have been left behind. For a discussion, cf. M. Brett, *Biblical Criticism in Crisis?* (Cambridge: Cambridge University Press, 1991), pp. 135-37.

of its appropriateness both to the object of study, Deuteronomy, and to the leading questions of the interpreter's own situation. For the moment, given that the contrast with which this paper began was between two consciously *historical*, and not only theological, understandings of Deuteronomy, I would like to take an approach that is as comprehensively historical as possible, in order to ask how we as historians may go beyond our particular interpretative backgrounds and contexts in order to establish that anticipation of meaning which is most appropriate to the object of our study, the book of Deuteronomy as the product of seventh- or sixth-century BCE Judah. To this end, reference must be made once more to Habermas, and specifically to his reconstruction of historical materialism, for this, I believe, does offer the methodological foundation for an objective appreciation of Deuteronomy in which the pre-understandings we bring to this task are more securely formulated.

The basic characteristic of Deuteronomy is linguistic. Language, however, is not simply a medium through which subjective intentions or feelings are brought to expression; rather, it is especially that through which communication is made possible. It is essentially social and, moreover, it represents a given that both precedes and transcends the thought of individuals. It creates and sustains the life world of individuals, comprising all the shared norms and values, beliefs and attitudes that make communication possible. Insofar as Deuteronomy is communication, it belongs to, and participates in creating, the life world of author and original hearer or reader. That original life world, with all its shared norms and values, beliefs and attitudes, is partially and indirectly accessible to us to the extent that it is possible empirically to recreate the material conditions within which it emerged and to which it responded. It is to that task that Habermas's reconstructed historical materialism contributes, and in so doing provides the foundation for the critical formulation of categories appropriate to the understanding of that text.

VI

Habermas's reconstruction of historical materialism provides an objective theory of culture and evolution that allows for historical reconstruction free of the subjective limitations of the historian. As the foundation of his reconstruction, Habermas emphasizes the mutually irreducible nature of both forces and relations of production. That is to say, human action on the environment, the forces of production, is based on technical knowledge; these forces of production do not determine the nature of social interaction and integration—that is, the relations of production, which are based on communicative knowledge. There is, in fact, no simple causal relationship between them in either direction. Rather, for Habermas, forms of social integration, although they develop in reaction to change in forces of production, do so only by their own logic, and it is then these internal developments in social integration that make possible the institutional implementation of changes in forces of production. What Habermas calls endogeneous learning processes belong to both technical knowledge (which is decisive for forms of production) and to moral practical consciousness (which is decisive for structures of integration). Developments in technical knowledge are a problem-generating mechanism in a society whose form of integration is inadequate to cope with them; but the resolution of that problem, providing a new form of social integration within which the new technical knowledge may be implemented, depends upon learning developments in communicative knowledge, in moral practical consciousness.[39] These learning developments provide a resource that can be drawn on in the formation of new forms of social integration, when the impetus to do so is provided by advances in technical knowledge. Thus, while advances in forces of production, technical instrumental knowledge, may be the necessary condition for changes in social system, these changes in social system are in fact based upon endogenous learning processes in society that are themselves not dependent on economic forces.

So, in order to account for social development, Habermas argues that three factors are necessarily involved.[40] First, the older social form must no longer have the capacity to cope with the economic problems that have arisen through developments in technical knowledge. So, for example, a society that has kinship as its principle of social organization would come under strain through advances in technical knowledge associated with water supply systems and agriculture that required a more complex form of social interaction than kinship could allow for. Secondly, the socially conditioned learning ability of individuals in society must have provided a resource of knowledge capable of being exploited by society in the development of a new form of social integration. The learning

---

39. J. Habermas, *Communication and the Evolution of Society* (London: Heinemann, 1979), pp. 97-98, 142-48; see also McCarthy, *Critical Theory*, pp. 244-71.

40. Cf. McCarthy, *Criticial Theory*, pp. 249-50.

processes of individuals, which are the basis of societal learning, may be understood in terms of cognitive developmental psychology.[41] The stages of ego development, through which the individual passes to reach the point of no longer naively accepting traditional assertions, values and norms, provide a model for the evolution of society's self-understanding, its world view. This is the resource on which a society, under strain from economic problems, can draw in order to create a new form of social integration. Thirdly, reference must be made to those 'contingent initial and boundary conditions, which stimulate or prevent, support or hinder, further or limit these processes' of learning. The learning processes of individuals that constitute the resource of societal learning are not simply personal and individualistic; they are social and historical processes to be understood in those contexts. In the case of Israel, reference would have to be made, for example, to the effect of contact between Israel and the world powers upon learning developments within Israel.

The contribution that Habermas's reconstruction of historical materialism makes to our understanding of the purpose of Deuteronomy is substantial. In the first place, the monarchic period was undoubtedly marked by technological and economic development that put considerable strain on traditional social forms. The prophetic critique of Israelite and Judaean society from the eighth century is clear enough testimony to the fact that developing technical knowledge had brought about an imbalance between forces and relations of production, between the social system demanded by economic development, on the one hand, and the traditional form of Israelite society governed by its traditional world view, on the other. Only in advanced societies has it been possible for the economic system to become dominant, with world views relegated to the private and subjective level; in the traditional type of society represented by Israel, the relationship was the reverse: the economic system had to keep 'within the limits of the legitimating efficacy of cultural traditions'.[42] Deuteronomy, therefore, stands in relationship to systems problems in Judaean society of the late monarchy period.

Secondly, cognitive psychology provides a model of individual moral development to the state where the individual breaks with the dogmatism of the given and assumes a relativistic understanding of the self from a universalistic perspective. In this development, there is a gradual

41. Habermas, *Communications*, pp. 99-102.
42. J. Habermas, *Toward a Rational Society* (Boston: Beacon Press, 1970), pp. 95-96.

marking out of the self from the environment and an increasing move away from cognitive and moral egocentrism, to the stage of being able to think reflectively, being aware of the relative standpoint of the self. A roughly analogous development of social world views leads from a mythological interweaving of natural and social phenomena through the stage where the social group is demarcated from the environment with its structures of domination legitimated by a mythological world view, to the eventual point of a break with mythological thought and its replacement by cosmological world views founded on philosophical reflection and argument.[43]

Within this framework it is possible to trace the general development of societal learning processes within Israel. It may be that the earliest stage, characterized by a mythological fusion of the social and the natural and an inability fully to demarcate society from its environment, antedates the appearance of Israel, but the mythological legitimation of social structures of domination is clearly to be found in the early monarchic period in the work of the Yahwist. Both this stage and the possible residues of earlier stages of development centred on cultic celebrations at the local high places were effectively rejected by the prophets; their preaching fundamentally questioned the egocentrism of the traditional Israelite world view and opened the way to the emergence of a more reflective universalism that had broken with mythological thought. '"Are you not like the Ethiopians to me, O people of Israel?", says the LORD. "Did I not bring up Israel from the land of Egypt, and the Philistines from Caphtor and the Syrians from Kir?"' (Amos 9.7). The deuteronomic doctrine of the election of Israel fulfilling a promise to the patriarchs is the outcome of a struggle to harmonize this emergent universalism with more traditional beliefs.[44]

43. Habermas, *Communications*, pp. 100-106.
44. This process, by which a reflective universalism comes to replace an earlier egocentrism, is a paradigmatic model for the understanding of social and religious development. Similarly, M. Douglas (*Purity and Danger* [London: Routledge & Kegan Paul, 1966], pp. 77-79) has developed Durkheim's model of social development from mechanical to organic solidarity societies in terms of a comparable movement in the realm of ideas. This movement is that of thought advancing by 'freeing itself from the shackles of its own subjective conditions'. The primitive world view is unreflectively personal and subjective, cosmic powers being understood to react with the behaviour of individual humans. Reflective self-consciousness, which breaks with this world view, belongs with the process of social differentiation by which society changes from mechanical to organic solidarity. Relevant also

Thirdly, these learning processes were stimulated by 'contingent initial and boundary conditions'. One would here refer especially to the expansion of the Israelite cultural environment that came about through its involvement with the world powers. This, and particularly Judah's long period of subjection to Assyria, exposed it to alternative and incompatible world views that had the destabilizing effect of calling into question the legitimacy of its own world views. The response to this century-long culture shock and the attempt to resolve or reduce it would have involved a process of rationalization or reinterpretation of already held beliefs in order to accommodate and cope with the new situation.

The relationship of Deuteronomy to this culture shock has been clearly recognized by Lohfink.[45] In Deuteronomy we have for the first time in Israel a theology, a reflective attempt to systematize belief. A theology emerges, however, in the context of the need to give systematic formulation to traditional belief in the face of and in reaction to threat. In the case of Deuteronomy, the nature of this threat is something more than the fact of Assyrian overlordship with its own particular world view; rather, it is that this Assyrian world view has come to constitute an alternative attraction to traditional Yahwism. Deuteronomy is theology in the face of the threat of heresy, a systematic attempt at a revitalizing statement of traditional belief in the face of alternative possibilities. Within the particular historical context of late monarchic Judah, Deuteronomy is in fact an excellent example of the operation of the endogenous learning process that Habermas has described. It was an essentially internal development, but one prompted by contingent boundary conditions, the internal development of existing potential in the creation of a new world view.

It was from Assyrian culture that Judah derived the idea of a contract relationship; this was integrated into Israelite tradition in such a way as to negate the foreign world view that it originally represented, while at

is the distinction that John Hick (*An Interpretation of Religion* [London: MacMillan, 1989], pp. 21-35), drawing on the work of Robert Bellah (*Beyond Belief: Essays on Religion in a Post-Traditional World* [New York: Harper & Row, 1970], pp. 20-50), makes between pre-axial and post-axial religion. Pre-axial religion functions to conserve the existing balance of good and evil and ward off chaos. It is marked by a sense of the continuity of human and other forms of life. In the axial age (800–200 BCE) individuals emerge into self-consciousness, their religious values lying no longer in identification with the group, but in personal openness to transcendence.

45. N. Lohfink, 'Culture Shock and Theology', *BTB* 7 (1977), pp. 12-22; *idem*, 'Pluralism'.

the same time attracting those for whom it was still a meaningful category within which to express self-understanding and perception of the world. Lohfink rightly argues[46] that the deuteronomic systematization of tradition can only be adequately grasped when it is recognized that new ideas, 'present in the tradition but not so self-evident, became operative'—that Deuteronomy represents 'a systematization which proceeds from a new conceptual viewpoint which was previously foreign to the systematized material or at most only dimly perceived in it' (p. 17), but that it was 'long present possibilities' of Israel's own culture, 'which until now had been forced into the underground', that now came to the fore (p. 19). Lohfink's view of the work of the deuteronomic theologians is then that it was a necessity in order to meet the threat posed to the Yahwistic world view by the dominant Assyrian culture; in order successfully to meet this threat deuteronomic theology had to be a systematization of tradition that integrated into Yahwism those elements of the competing culture that constituted an attractive alternative in contemporary Judah.[47]

To understand Deuteronomy in these terms, within the framework of a living process in Judah that is stimulated by both technological development and historical conditions, means that it is to be understood in the first instance as a resource, not in itself a constitution or piece of state legislation, but rather a resource to give objective grounding to such a constitution or legislation. Deuteronomy thus expresses a systematically organized world view that revitalized Israel's own tradition and so presented the Yahwistic option as a persuasive alternative within the uncertain and pluralist framework of late pre-exilic Judah.

Our access to the particular intentions and motives of the author(s) of Deuteronomy is, at the least, limited; when, however, Deuteronomy is situated within the context of language as communication, creating and sustaining the life-world of those who use it, its historical meaning may

46. Lohfink, 'Culture Shock', p. 15.

47. This view can then be understood to represent the application to the context of monarchic Judah of the general model of gradual development implied in the work of Douglas noted above. It should be noted, however, that the particular modification to the general model that Lohfink's presentation implies is to be seen not simply as arising from the particular historical conditions of monarchic Judah; rather, this represents a necessary modification to the general model itself in the light of sophisticated understanding of social and cultural evolution presented in Habermas's reconstructed historical materialism. Judah's particular conditions are but one form of the 'contingent boundary conditions' that the general model should incorporate.

be objectively reconstructed through the application of an adequately developed theory of cultural evolution such as that presented by Habermas.[48]

48. Two concluding observations are relevant. First, it is increasingly recognized that Deuteronomy may not easily be directly and immediately related to the actual implementation of law in ancient Israel. One does not have to follow C. Carmichael (*The Laws of Deuteronomy* [Ithaca, NY: Cornell University Press, 1974]; *Law and Narrative in the Bible* [Ithaca, NY: Cornell University Press, 1985]) in the sometimes tortuous arguments he constructs to show that the deuteronomic law derives from scribal activity on Israel's narrative traditions, but he is surely right to reject any immediate relationship to the practical socio-economic conditions of Israel's life. The parallel drawn between biblical law-codes and the Code of Hammurabi points in the same direction, for here too there is no indication of its implementation by the lawcourts (cf. B.S. Jackson, 'Ideas of Law and Legal Administration: A Semistic Approach', in R.E. Clements (ed.), *The World of Ancient Israel* [Cambridge: Cambridge University Press, 1989], pp. 185-202; M. Fishbane, *Biblical Interpretation: Ancient Israel* [Oxford: Clarendon Press, 1985], pp. 91-97). Secondly, the description given above is very much only a first step in understanding Deuteronomy. If Deuteronomy is to be understood in the context of social communication, it is not without relation to the structures, especially those of power and authority, within the community. The ascription of Deuteronomy to Moses and the identification of its law as law of Yahweh are, then, fundamental claims to authority that have to be seen not solely in terms of the clash of world views within Judah but in terms also of the interaction of different social groups.

JSOT 59 (1993), pp. 3-23

THE FORBIDDEN ANIMALS IN LEVITICUS*

Mary Douglas

Introduction

An anthropologist hardly needs to apologize for trying a new approach to the dietary laws in Leviticus. For one reason, the various interpretations offered so far are not agreed. For another, these rules are generally interpreted as rules of purity, whereas they are unlike any purity rules in the anthropological record. Thirdly, the explanations offered in the book itself are ignored, for lack of interest in its rhetorical structure. A general lack of interest in the priestly work may be attributed to a long-established anticlerical tradition, which puts the priests in an unfavourable light compared with the prophets. The editors of Leviticus have the reputation of being engrossed by themes of material, especially bodily, defilement. This has entered into some of the comparisons between the priestly tradition and that of the prophets, the former being regarded as desiccated bureaucrats of religion, obsessed with material definitions of impurity, and the latter concerned with nobler spiritual teachings. The priests were evidently so focused on externals that they transformed the religion from what it was in the eyes of the prophets.

Isaiah 1.10-17 is a natural point at which to divide the two allegedly opposed modes of religious thought. The prophet delivers the message that the sinful nation has forsaken the Lord, thus he (the Lord) does not want their 'vain offerings'; he rejects their burnt offerings and prayers, because their hands are full of blood (Isa. 1.15-16). Finally he tells them to make themselves clean, and by 'clean' he does not mean avoiding ritual defilement, for he lists a set of moral rules: 'cease to do evil, learn

* This paper was presented in an earlier version at the University of Sheffield on 2 March 1993. I gratefully acknowledge help from Jacob Milgrom and Robert Murray, SJ.

to do good, seek justice, correct oppression, defend the fatherless, plead for the widow' (Isa. 1.10-17). This first chapter goes on to describe Jerusalem as the place where righteousness used to lodge (1.21), and to announce the promise that once again she will be called the city of righteousness (1.26) redeemed by justice and righteousness (1.27). The Lord calls on worshippers to 'loosen the bands of wickedness, undo the heavy burdens, let the oppressed go free' (Isa. 58.7) and says, 'For I, the Lord, love justice'.

The popular opposition between the two kinds of religion is false. It is basically implausible that the Priestly editors were such narrow-minded bigots as many interpretations of Leviticus imply, or that they were insensitive to the more spiritual interior meanings of religion. It is just not plausible that the same priests who edited the five glorious books of the Pentateuch should display this niggling concern for physical cleanliness that seems to be the purpose of Leviticus chs. 11–16. They describe the Lord as manifest in fiery radiance, thundering against injustice, beseeching his people for love and trust, but how can the same God make a mighty issue over hygiene and contact with scavenging insects and carrion-eating birds and beasts?

The case for a new interpretation of ch. 11 is strengthened by the putative date for the redaction. If the Pentateuch was edited during and just after the exile in Babylon, the scribes and other learned ones of Judah would have met with sages of many civilizations and sharpened the distinctive profile of their own religion in full knowledge of the controversies current in Asia Minor and even in India. It was about the fifth century BCE that the relation between humans and animals had become a matter for serious philosophical speculation. Individual philosophers, Empedocles and Pythagoras, for instance, and their followers were vegetarian. Hinduism abandoned animal sacrifice and Buddhism preached no violence to animals. In that climate the idea of forbidding certain kinds of animals because they were dirty or otherwise offensive sounds like an extreme anachronism.

Finally, when we try to appreciate the literary and logical structure of the book, we are led to expect that the two main dietary rules (one forbidding eating blood and the other forbidding eating the listed unclean animals) would be connected. The rule for avoiding blood is based on a concept of honouring the life in the animal, while the rule for avoiding the listed unclean beasts is interpreted as based on disgust and repulsion. It is implausible that two separate modes of explanation should apply to the two kinds of dietary rules, as if diet was the main preoccupation. The explanation to be offered below will put both kinds of prohibition at the same theological level.

Ritual Purity

Leviticus and Deuteronomy forbid certain animal species as food for the people of Israel. It is generally supposed that the reasons for forbidding them are given in the same chapter that lists them, ch. 11 of Leviticus and in Deuteronomy 14; all that is said here is that they are forbidden because they are abominable and unclean, and contrary to holiness. In the absence in those chapters of any further clue as to what those words mean, the interpretations have assumed that uncleanness or defilement in these texts have the same meaning as they have in other religions and in secular conceptions of dirt. Consequently the text of Leviticus 11 has been analysed under the heading of ritual uncleanness. In reading it this way I have also worked in the same vein as other scholars.[1]

At each period there is a fashionable theory of how to interpret foreign ideas about ritual purity. In the rabbinic tradition the forbidden animals were regarded as allegories of virtues and vices. As allegories they were heuristic, named and known for teaching purposes, implying nothing inherently good or abominable in their animal state as such. So when Philo of Alexandria said that the clean animals represent the virtues of discrimination because they chew the cud of meditation and cleave the hoof of discernment, and that the unclean animals represent vices, he emphasized their symbolic function, and Maimonides later insisted on the arbitrariness of the sign.

However, nineteenth-century commentators were not content with this reference to a holy convention. Failing to make any other sense of the list, they took it to be an ancient magical block coming from very early stages of the history of Israel, which would have been included in the Bible without any understanding of the meaning, out of piety for the past. This opened the way for psychological theories, fear of snakes, dread of creepy-crawlies and things that go bump in the night, discomfort in the face of anomaly.

After Lévy-Bruhl's examination of these modes of thought and his effort to identify a form of 'primitive mentality', these speculations became old-fashioned. No theory of innate human psychological

1. M. Douglas, *Purity and Danger* (London: Routledge & Kegan Paul, 1966).

responses can be defended unless there is human regularity in the response to the same effects. The Bible list of abominated animals is just the Bible list; bits of it are found in other similar codes, but not all; and in many parts of the world what is abominated in the Bible is eaten, or loved or even revered. The universal fact is that there are no universal symbols.

Anthropologists would hesitate to accuse editors of sacred texts of mindless anthologizing. If a 'symbolic' meaning is suspected (which implies: if there is any meaning at all), it will be part of a local culture, and part of an intelligible mode of communication between editors and readers or listeners. In 1966 I tried the idea that the forbidden animals in Leviticus made sense as a cognitive ordering of the universe. They seemed to be very comparable to taboos in other parts of the world, a rational construction of nature, society and culture. The main argument of *Purity and Danger* was that taboo organizes consensus by attributing the dangers which regularly threaten to breaches of moral law. In the case of the forbidden animals in Leviticus I could not find this link with morals and social distinctions, but trusted that, as the idea was relatively new, further research by qualified biblical scholars would discover ways in which eating the animals could be used as accusations in the same way as breaking taboos.

In 1970,[2] when no wiring of the system of prohibitions to the internal structure of the life of Israel had been identified, I tried out the idea that the rules maintained the external boundary of the community. I also tried to develop the analogy between altar and table implicit in the Levitical rules. This notion has been related interestingly by Jacob Neusner to the rabbinical period when the second temple had been destroyed and the religion was being rebuilt around the domestic unit.[3] However, it does not pretend to explain the original selection of animals forbidden.

Although several Bible scholars have been generous in acknowledging some value for the anthropological approach, and now recognize the rational basis for the levitical rules[4]—so the subject has engaged some

2. M. Douglas, *Natural Symbols* (London: Routledge, 1996).

3. J. Neusner, 'History and Structure: The Case of the Mishnah', *JAAR* 45 (1977), pp. 161-92.

4. G. Wenham, *Leviticus* (NICOT; Grand Rapids: Eerdmans, 1979); B. Levine, *Leviticus* (JPS Torah Commentary; Philadelphia: Jewish Publication Society of America, 1989); J. Milgrom, *Leviticus I–XVI* (AB; Garden City, NY: Doubleday,

interest—yet no one has leveled the main and obvious objection, the lack of equivalence between taboo as understood in the rest of the world and the rules of Leviticus. Everywhere else taboo is specifically tied to behaviour in such a way as to protect valued social and moral standards. The connection with danger allows ideas to organize society by persuading, justifying, warning, mustering moral pressure. Yet the unclean animals in Leviticus do not serve these uses. No danger is attached to contact with them. The person who has had contact with a carcase does not have to make atonement, he or she only has to wash and wait until evening to be clean. This is merely a minor ritual disability. The rules make no engagement whatsoever with social life.

Contaminating Dangers

Over the last 25 years great advances have been made in understanding pollution ideas in secular contexts. The result has been to create a different puzzle about the levitical idea of impurity. The problem is that the treatment of defilement in Leviticus lends itself to an entirely cognitive interpretation. It seems to be something in the mind of the priestly editors, a feature of the cult, without anchorage in the daily experience of the people. Nowhere else do pollution concepts get elaborated intellectually without basis in practical use. To be blunt, pollution is used for defaming a category of persons, or denouncing further something that is already a public outrage. Pollution ideas enforce a community code, and their penalties restrain deviant morals; they become part of the religion and encoded as the divine sanction of discriminations which the congregation normally makes.

A short way of expressing the difference between the purity code of Leviticus and all the others is to point out that according to the Bible no one is born purer than any one else. Levitical impurity is a fact of biology, common to all persons, and also a result of specific moral offences that anyone is liable to commit, such as lying or stealing. When an individual transgressor is to be 'cut off', it is not for an unwitting dangerous contact but for wilful high-handed persistence in sin.

Biblical impurity is of no use in demarcating advantaged social classes or ranks (except for a little protection for the privileges of the priests). It does not recognize hereditary defiling categories. Leviticus does not draw social distinctions. Idolatry covers all kinds of moral as well as

1991); P. Jenson, *Graded Holiness* (JSOTSup, 106; Sheffield: JSOT Press, 1992); W. Houston, *Purity and Monotheism* (JSOTSup, 140; Sheffield: JSOT Press, 1993).

bodily imperfection, but all are capable of purification if the will to repent is there. In effect, biblical defilement is a cerebral creation, it has no philosophical uses, it does not accuse. It is part of a philosophy of being, but in that case, why does the list of forbidden animals resist incorporation into the rest of the philosophy of the book? My argument will be that they do belong with the rest, that they enrich and complete it.

A new interpretation of the forbidden animals should respond to the initial question about whether the priests were following a fundamentally different religious programme from the prophets. The argument requires us to look for an explanation of the forbidden animals in Leviticus itself, not beyond it. We should be prepared to read the book as a superlatively skilful composition in which issues are raised early on, but solutions and explanations are delivered later. Like the delayed denouement of a narrative, the retarded explanation is a conventional literary technique for unifying an elaborate composition.

Archaic Learning and Literary Elegance

Of the literary quality of Leviticus Jacob Milgrom says that 'the artistry of the structure is evidence of an advanced compositional technique'.[5] His commentary on Numbers demonstrates how the Priestly books need to be read, with an attentive eye for the parallelism which he recognizes as the main structural device of the book.[6] Short verses, whole chapters, law and narrative are combined in sustained parallels of simple or elaborate chiasm. He also shows how two chapters may be entwined together in chiastic parallel, and sometimes how the larger units made by these combinations are worked again into even more comprehensive patterns. He even draws a chiastic diagram for the whole Pentateuch, leading up to and away from Mount Sinai. Such texts are composed for a lateral reading and not to be read in straight linear sequence. Linguists and anthropologists of the last 50 years have documented parallelism in oral and written literature all over the world.[7] This is not the place to

5. Milgrom, *Leviticus*. Admittedly he gives this praise to later chapters (17–27).

6. J. Milgrom, *Numbers* (JPS Torah Commentaries; Philadelphia: Jewish Publication Society of America, 1990).

7. A magisterial review of the topic by James Fox places Roman Jakobson's analysis of Russian poetry at the beginning of modern understanding. The techniques of parallelism are found in widely scattered regions, including China, Vietnam,

describe in detail the argument for finding that Leviticus is a form of ring composition, but some general pointers to the conventions governing the structure are necessary.[8]

Among its main characteristics the ring has a tightly packed prologue which is an exposition of the programme to be developed. Secondly, a series of discrete steps introduces new material without necessarily explaining their connection to each other. They tend to follow quite jerkily and some switching signal indicates a new phase. These steps lead to a well-marked turning point that reverts to the initial theme and thus indicates the central message of the work. The turning point is usually signalled by a flanking pair of obviously parallel chapters, one on each side. After the turn a second series of steps parallels the earlier steps in reverse order until the last step, when it has reached the first, brings the composition to its ring ending. Some of the parallels are chiastic, and inside each section complex parallels and introversions are worked out. Finally, to make the closure definitive, there is an extra passage acting as a latch, which locks the whole composition into the prologue.

The structure has the advantage of making the meaning of the work apparent, but reading it *against* the structure makes it almost impossible to follow. The temptation of the linear reading is to treat each step as a discrete item, without regard for its linking signals, which seem to be so much unnecessary repetition.

The meaning is attested at several stages, first in the prologue, secondly in the turn that matches the prologue, thirdly in the conclusion that matches them both, and fourthly in the latch. The technique is to match everything that has been said in the first round by a second round which enriches, completes and explains what was left unexplained before. The ring is a comprehensive parallelism that incorporates the whole work.

The book of Leviticus is an example. Its prologue is extremely formulaic. It plunges straight into the subject of burnt offerings; it gives the priest instructions for how to prepare an animal for sacrifice; from

Burma and Thailand, Finland and North America (J. Fox, 'Roman Jakobson and the Comparative Study of Parallelism', in *Roman Jakobson: Echoes of his Scholarship* [Lisse: The Peter de Ridder Press, 1977]).

8. A description of the ring structure of Numbers is provided in M. Douglas, 'The Glorious Book of Numbers', *Jewish Studies Quarterly* 1, 3 (1993), pp. 193-216.

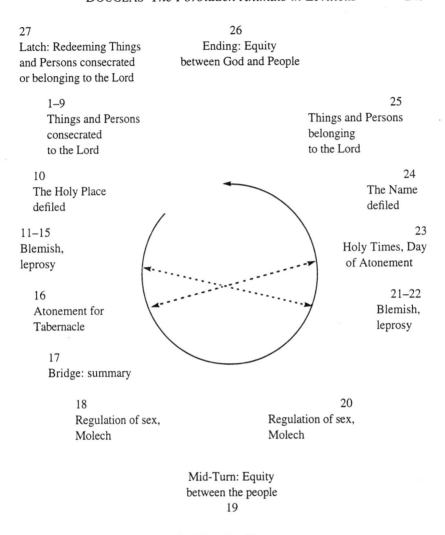

27
Latch: Redeeming Things
and Persons consecrated
or belonging to the Lord

26
Ending: Equity
between God and People

1–9
Things and Persons
consecrated
to the Lord

25
Things and Persons
belonging
to the Lord

10
The Holy Place
defiled

24
The Name
defiled

11–15
Blemish,
leprosy

23
Holy Times, Day
of Atonement

16
Atonement for
Tabernacle

21–22
Blemish,
leprosy

17
Bridge: summary

18
Regulation of sex,
Molech

20
Regulation of sex,
Molech

Mid-Turn: Equity
between the people
19

Leviticus in a Ring

this the reader must guess that the subject of the whole book is going to be things offered to the Lord; but later a contrasting pair, things belonging already to the Lord, will be uncovered in ch. 25. The last chapter gives the rules for redeeming things and persons consecrated to the Lord, but says that firstlings are the Lord's absolutely (27.26) and cannot be alienated. So the ending successfully integrates the two themes, things consecrated and things belonging to the Lord.

From its opening on the theme of things dedicated to the Lord, the book's circuit runs to the mid-point, ch. 19, which is on the concept of righteousness, largely in the sense of honesty and fair dealing, and with regard for correct recognition of status. The twice repeated lists of prohibited sexual relations (chs. 18.6-19 and 20.11-22) and the references to children offered to Molech (18.21 and 20.2-5) fulfil the convention of a flanking parallel on either side of the turn. After the turn the selections return step by step until ch. 25, which deals with things belonging to the Lord, the land (25.23) and the people (25.55). The grand peroration and conclusion is ch. 26 which matches to the mid-point, ch. 19, which has announced the meaning of righteousness in dealings from persons to persons. Now at the conclusion it is a matter of applying the same concept to the dealings of the people with their God: justice and mercy if they keep their promises and pay their dues, terrible punishments if they do not. The latch, ch. 27, locks on to the beginning by speaking both of things consecrated and things belonging to the Lord. The latter are firstlings which cannot be consecrated because they belong to him already (27.26).

This is only a rough and ready approximation of the general structure. It is enough to demonstrate that the delayed completion is part of the scheme. When the end is reached, the proportions of the theme fall into place. Just as the prologue warned, the book is about the holy things which have been consecrated or which belong to the Lord. It started with the meat of sacrifice and went on to blood, the priests, dedicated animals, and the land and the people in ch. 25. The Lord's holy things and his holy people cannot be alienated.

To say that the book divides in half at 19 goes against the scholarly consensus that ch. 17 belongs with 18–26 as part of the Holiness code. Milgrom's new commentary on Leviticus follows this tradition by ending the first volume at ch. 16. Basing his analysis on source structure, Baruch Levine sees Leviticus as a set of rules about the laws of the cult, a handbook of instructions for worship which he sees as divided into a prologue, chs. 1–16, and the rest.[9] However, there is no serious

---

9.   Baruch Levine uses source criticism to present the structure of Leviticus as follows:

    I: 1–16 Introductory
    II: 17-26 Holiness Code
            a: Prologue, 17, proper worship
            b: Legal texts, 18–26
            c: Epilogue, 26.3-46 blessings and chastisements
    III: 27 Dedicated things

conflict on this score. First, as to ch. 17, it could belong with the preceding or with the succeeding sections, according to whatever decision an experienced Bible scholar may suggest. Secondly, source structure does not prevent us from reading synoptically across the book. However, to deny the lateral construction of the finished book, for the sake of emphasizing sources or for any other reason, creates puzzles in the first 16 chapters that arise because their completion has been reserved for their counterpart halves: puzzles such as the meaning of blemish, the selection of forbidden animals and birds, the scattering of certain themes on both sides of the divide.

Delayed Completion

The meaning of ch. 11 and its relation to the main themes of the book are withheld until chs. 21–22, and all three meanings had to be withheld until the burden of ch. 19 had been delivered. Until we know that the Lord's primary command is for equitable dealings between his people and between them and himself, we cannot appreciate the teaching about forbidden and blemished animals. When the whole structure of the book is known, there need be no doubt about the meaning of the abominations. Two examples of delayed completion will show something of the rhetorical style that governs Leviticus. The first is the example of burnt offerings, the second the discussion of blemish.

Burnt offerings of animals are dealt with in the first chapter and in the third; ch. 2 interrupts with the rules for cereal offering, but the theme of burnt animal offerings is left incomplete until ch. 23.

1.1-9	10-14	15-20
Consecrate any animal, male or female;	flocks:	birds:
no blemish;	no blemish;	
at door;	on North side;	at altar;
hand on head;		

The Holiness Code itself he finds divided into its own prologue, its substance of laws, and its epilogue. Over and above this nested textual division he finds the book governed by another basic design: I: 1–16, manuals of practice addressed to the priests, instructions for their office; II: 17–27, priestly teaching to the people (B. Levine, *Leviticus* [JPS Torah Commentary; Philadelphia: Jewish Publication Society of America, 1989], p. xiv.

1.1-9	10-14	15-20
blood on altar;	blood;	drain blood;
fire on altar; cut/meat on fire;	cut/meat on fire;	feathers to East; wings;
wash innards; legs;	wash;	
burn;	burn;	burn;
pleasing odour	pleasing odour	pleasing odour

Peace offering   Holy times

3.1-5	3.6-11	3.12-17	23.1-25
from herd;		goat;	lamb;
no blemish;	no blemish;		no blemish;
at door;	at door;	at door;	unleavened
hand on head;	hand on head;	hand on head;	bread; wine;
fat;	blood;	blood;	burnt
blood;	fat;	fat;	offerings;
kidneys;	kidneys	kidneys;	first fruits;
burn;	burn;	burn;	
pleasing odour	pleasing odour	pleasing odour; perpetual statute	pleasing odour v. 23

There is no mistaking the intention to bring to completion the theme developed in the first three chapters, since ch. 23 reproduces the same formulaic ending. 'A pleasant odour' is the refrain that has the role of sig-nalling the match between start and conclusion of that part of the book.

Notice that at ch. 2 the topic of animal offerings has been interrupted by the topic of cereal offerings. When rules for burnt animal offerings are picked up again in Lev. 23.1-25, the rule that the animal be unblemished is repeated, and it ends with the words 'a pleasing odour', if a clue were needed as to the correspondence between the two halves of the book.

Notice how the list of animal burnt offerings in 1 and 3 goes in regular progression from all animals inclusive, to the largest animals, from the herds, from the flocks, to birds, and in ch. 2 through cereal offerings, fruit, oil, to frankincense. This is so orderly and systematic that we do not think at once of what has been left out, but the first double list of occasions for animal offerings is far from complete. Why have they not been dealt with all at once?

The answer, noted by Levine,[10] is that the first lists deal with the individual's duties, and the second with the public obligations of the community. Accordingly, all the required burnt offerings for the fixed holy days of the year have been left to be dealt with in ch. 23, and the offerings of cereals have been left incomplete until the continuous care for the Holy Place can be described in ch. 24.

Leviticus 2	Leviticus 24.1-9
Cereals:	Holy Place;
unleavened bread;	lamp;
burn;	oil;
pleasing odour;	showbread;
bread reserved for priests, 'Most	frankincense;
Holy Things';	offering by fire;
no leaven; no honey; salt;	shows, continually,
to be burnt;	perpetual statute.
first fruits, oil, frankincense.	
Offering by fire.	

Notice how the topic of cereal offering receives its conclusion in ch. 24, where a little section in vv. 1-9 summarizes the rules for honouring the holy place, and the rules for cereal offerings. It ends, as did the list in ch. 2, with frankincense, and with one of the significant perorations of this book: the invocation of a perpetual statute, a covenant for ever.

Offerings	Times	Places
1–3	23.1-24	24.1-9
Burnt offerings, free	Burnt offerings for	Offerings for the
will offerings,	public worship;	tabernacle;
thanksgiving, vows.	holy times, from	oil for burning in
Animals:	Sabbaths to new moons	lamp;
cattle>sheep>goats>	23.18, pleasing odour	frankincense;
birds.	23.23-21 perpetual	summary of most
Cereal>	statute.	holy portion for
frankincense.		priests to be eaten
3.17, a perpetual		in holy place;
statute.		24.9 perpetual
		statute.

10. Levine, *Leviticus.*

Burnt Offerings: Summary

When we come to Lev. 24.1-9 we become aware of a larger structure
that has been played out. Four classes of burnt offerings have been
introduced: freewill offerings, votive offerings, sin offerings and offerings
for public worship at set times; now are added the continuous offerings
for the tabernacle. And notice the solemn peroration for each block, a
perpetual statute. The completeness of the master plan begins to appear.
We now see that sacrifice has to appear on both sides of the book
because due place in the structure has to be made for the range of ritual
actions prescribed at the beginning to be situated in holy times and the
holy place. This prepares the reader to look for the meaning of blemish
beyond the chapter in which it is first described, and to look out for
verbal repetitions and formulaic flourishes which signal the matched
pair.

Unclean Animals

The chapter on unclean animals comes immediately after ch. 10 which
recounts the tragic deaths of Aaron's sons who offered unholy fire at
the altar (Lev. 10.1-3). Moses has just told Aaron that it is the duty of
the priests to teach the people of Israel the difference between the clean
and unclean (10.10-11). It has always been understood that this is the
essential lesson, to discriminate, to judge between clean and unclean.
Leviticus makes it clear that the discrimination goes beyond rules for
eating to all kinds of behaviour. The new chapter starts quite abruptly
with:

> The Lord said to Moses and Aaron, say to the people of Israel, These are
> the living things you may eat among all the beasts that are on the earth
> (11.1-2).

The list goes straight on, so we should assume that it is the first lesson in
the difference between the clean and the unclean. The dietary laws
systematically pick up the order of creation in Genesis. In Genesis 1, the
first two days of creation set up the four cardinal points and the next
four days are spent putting living denizens into the earth, sky and water
and putting the lights of the stars and planets into the sky. Genesis:

First two days: 1.1-10. Creation of Light, Earth, Firmament and Water. Compare the four elements, fire, earth, air and water in other philosophies in Asia Minor.

Third day: 1.11-13. Vegetation on the earth.

Fouth day: 1.14-19. Stars in the heavenly firmament for signs and for seasons, for days and years, creation of the sun and the moon.

Fifth day: 1.20-23. Filling the waters with moving creatures that have life.

Sixth day: 1.24-31. Populating the earth with all kinds of living creatures, and creation of humankind to have dominion over them.

Compare Leviticus's list of prohibited animal foods:

On the earth (Lev.11.2-8)

In the waters (Lev.11.9-12)

In the air (Lev.11.13-25)

In these three environments the book goes on systematically to distinguish clean and unclean creatures. On the earth, among quadrupeds, if they do not cleave the hoof like domestic herds and flocks, they cannot be eaten; even if they do not cleave the hoof but do chew the cud, or if they do cleave the hoof but do not chew the cud, they are unclean. In the waters fish with scales and fins are clean, but not the rest. In the air clean two-winged creatures are those that can walk and hop on the earth.

On land some are named as unclean (with apparently a disapproved number of limbs), if they have paws (Lev. 11.27), too many feet (v. 42), instead of four. In the air certain named birds are unclean, but the problem for posterity is to know which they are. The Talmudic tradition is that they are carnivorous birds. One class is picked out in all habitats: we can call them crawlers. Creatures that crawl on the belly are abominable and unclean, whatever their environment (11.41-43). What is meant by crawling is explored in vv. 29-30, and is illustrated by creatures translated in the KJV as the weasel, the mouse, the tortoise, the ferret, the chameleon, the lizard, the snail. Crawling also includes winged insects that go on all fours (v. 20), or have four feet (vv. 20-23) but cannot hop or leap upon the earth (like birds?). If an insect has four feet and jointed legs that are actually used to walk or hop on the ground, it is in the class of regular clean kinds (vv. 21-22).

There is a temptation to read this list as a normative account of modes of propulsion for different habitats. This is how I originally read it, taking it as an extension of Leviticus's concern for due honour and circumstance for every rank and context. However, as Bible scholars have pointed out, such an interpretation does not explain the emphasis on mode of locomotion. The following is a quite different explanation of these classifications, one that gives the capacity to hop or leap on the earth as much attention as its centrality in ch. 11 deserves. It works at two levels. The first concerns the doctrine of blood, and the second the doctrine of blemish. Remember the three habitats, earth, water, air, in each of which there are some clean and some unclean animals.

If we go back to Genesis, a reason for the rules for land animals can be derived directly from the prohibition on eating blood. At creation all living beings were expected to subsist on leaves, berries and seeds (Gen. 1.29-30). The world was going to be vegetarian, very much in line with Isaiah's vision[11] of a world in which the predatory animals would take to peaceful herbivorous habits—the lamb could hardly lie down with the lion if the lion did not change his diet. After the people had proved their wicked natures, in the new covenant after the flood God modified his law: the people were allowed to eat meat, but never blood. An extension of the rule of avoiding blood is to forbid blood-eating animals and carrion eaters, for their bodies have already ingested blood.

By specifying herbivorous animals as the proper kind of meat (after the blood has been drained off) the legislator has drawn a line around certain quadrupeds: it is safe to include all those that cleave the hoof and chew the cud, domestic or wild, for they never eat blood. The line is drawn tighter by listing borderline cases, the pig, the camel, the hare and the rock badger, all four forbidden for the declared reason that they have one but not both the criteria for inclusion in the list of edible four footed beasts. The rule against eating blood underlies the list of clean and unclean land animals. The rule once formulated in terms of hoofs and cud-chewing generates its own exceptions which are legislated against specifically.

The forbidden creatures of the air are named but not identified. The Talmudic tradition is that they are predators that seize their prey with claws and tear its flesh with their beaks. The tradition is in line with the rule for land animals, avoiding predators avoids blood at second remove.

11. R. Murray, *The Cosmic Covenant* (Heythrop Monographs; London: Sheed and Ward, 1992), ch. 6, on relations between humans and animals in the Kingdom of Peace.

When we come to the denizens of the waters without scales and to the crawlers, blood eating is not at issue. This time a negative principle is invoked: they lack something that they need. They are contrapuntally distinguished from the excluded predators. I will argue that the crawlers stand for the victims of predation.

Blemish

Chapter 11 only gives morphological principles for recognizing the animals as clean or unclean. The duty of the priests to teach the people the difference between clean and unclean has been given so much emphasis (10.10) that it would be remarkable if more was not said to instruct the faithful. We have never been told in what the uncleanness of the animals consists. The same for the rules for burnt offerings: it is frequently repeated that an animal with a blemish is not allowed to be offered for sacrifice. Again, why not? And again, no definition of 'blemish', and no reason is given in the first four chapters. The easy answer, that a spoilt gift is unworthy of the altar, is an uplifting thought but not theologically acute.

The answers begin to emerge in ch. 21. First the word 'blemish' is applied to the body of the priest, with some description of what it means:

> no one who is *blemished* shall draw near, a man blind or lame, or one who has a mutilated face or *a limb too long*, or a man who has an injured foot or an injured hand, or a hunchback, or a dwarf, or a man with a defect in his sight, or an itching disease or scabs or crushed testicles... he shall not come near the veil or approach the altar, because he has a *blemish*...(21.18-24).

So blemished means mutilated, or having some extra length or substance, a limb too long, a hump on the back.

Then in the next chapter the same words are applied to the sacrificial animal. Leviticus has already drawn the parallel between the body of the priest and the body of the sacrificial animal. In ch. 8 several of the same rubrics apply to the consecration of both priest and animal. Both are consecrated at the door of the tabernacle, both are washed with water, the animal's skin has to be removed, the priest has to put on a sacred garment and remove it afterwards. The parallel between priest and altar is also made: the altar is anointed with oil (8.9-11), and also the priest (8.12, 30); blood is sprinkled on the altar (8.15, 19) and smeared on the priest (8.22). Priest, altar and offering are made equivalent to one another in a series of detailed, pointed rites.

Then, after the halfway point, the blemished priest is made an analogy for the blemished oblation:

> it must be perfect, there shall be no *blemish* in it. Animals blind, or dis-abled, or mutilated, or having a discharge, or an itch or scabs, you shall not offer to the Lord...a bull or a lamb which *has a part too long or too short* you may present for a free will offering, but not for a votive offering...since there is a *blemish* in them, because of their mutilation, they will not be accepted for you (22.26).

Why the mutilated oblation is not acceptable becomes an interesting question when the priest is included in the same class. The King James Version has a telling translation of the 'part too long or too short'; it gives 'nothing superfluous and nothing lacking'. It is difficult for us to see the connection with justice and injustice, but it would not be difficult to anyone who had been used to reading in a ring and who looked to the mid-turn for the key to what is going to be expounded later.

The key words come in ch. 19, where it is forbidden to steal, rob, defraud, oppress, lie, slander (19.11-17), and forbidden to use false weights and measures (19.35-36). A simple principle of equity is at the basis of the laws. It is an injustice if one party to a transaction will have too little and the other too much. Later in ch. 24 there is a reference to blemish that connects it directly with injustice. It comes in the story of the blasphemer whose case was referred by Moses to the Lord. The result of the consultation was a diatribe against cursing the Name of the Lord, and the following legislation:

> When a man causes disfigurement in his neighbour, as he has done, it shall be done to him, fracture for fracture, eye for eye, tooth for tooth, as he has disfigured a man, he shall be disfigured (24.19-20).

In the KJV the phrase is:

> If a man causes a *blemish* in his neighbour, as he has done, so it shall be done to him: breach for breach, eye for eye, tooth for tooth, as he has caused a *blemish* in a man, so it shall be done to him.

So causing a blemish in a neighbour is doing him a damage according to the elementary principles of justice: taking away something that is his by right, leaving him with too little. Or by oppression, giving him a heavy load to bear. Causing a blemish is giving a labourer excessive burdens. The interesting thing is that the neighbour who has suffered outrage in the case of the blasphemer is the Lord himself, and we soon see, in ch. 26, that the Lord is included squarely in the law of talion with the rest of his creation. The statements on blemish connect it with inequitable dealings. It would now appear that the forbidden species which are not covered by the law against eating blood, either have something lacking (like joints, legs, fins or scales) or something superfluous (like a burden on their backs) and that their disfigurement has something to do with injustice.

Justice and Righteousness

Having shown the cross-references between chs. 11 and 21 and 22, we should now examine the two turning points, chs. 19 and 26. The main message of the book is given at these points, and the rest of the book has to be consistent with them. We are alerted to finding a connection between ch. 11 and ch. 19. Encouragingly, 19.2 starts with the injunction to be holy, in the same way that ch. 11 ends. We find that through ch. 19 we are being told what holiness means at every verse. You shall revere your parents (Lev. 19.3), you will not turn to idols, the harvester will respect the wants of the poor and the sojourner. Then (19.11-22) follows the list of discriminations and righteous behaviour: no hate, no vengeance, no grudge, no slander, impartiality in judgment, 'love your neighbour as yourself' (19.17), and even 'love the stranger as yourself' (19.34). Holiness will achieve the ideal of the city renowned for judgment and righteousness that Isaiah's prophecy promised. Chapter 19 ends with the simple injunction that sums it all up:

> you shall do no unrighteousness in judgment, in measures of length, in weight, or in quantity. Just balances, just weights, a just ephah, and a just hin, shall you have (19.35-36).

If righteousness means, as Robert Murray cogently argues, the complete cosmic order, these analogies of equitable dealings have to be taken to their fullest extent. It should no longer be a surprise to realize, as he has pointed out,[12] that compassion inspires the Pentateuch as much as it does the prophets.

Chapter 11 has told us of how animals that have too little or too much should not be butchered for food, and ch. 26 has told us that

---

12. Murray, *The Cosmic Covenant*, pp.110-16. His argument has called for a complete reconstruction of the world-view of the Bible (see Introduction and ch. 1).

righteousness requires not too much and not too little. Chapter 26 starts with the warning against idolatry and says that if the people will walk in his statutes the Lord will give them rains and the land will be fertile, and he will walk among them and they will be his people (26.13). Then the other side of the covenant is given: if they will not do his command-ments, a series of terrible disasters will afflict them (26.14-39). Reminding them of how he rescued them from Egypt, the covenant is presented as a debt owed to God, and the law is that debts should be honoured. Finally, the threats give way to loving kindness and renewal of the covenant (26.40-46). This is how the law of talion applies to the covenant between God and his people. He demands righteousness of them in their dealings with one another, the rightness of true weights and measures, hurt for hurt, blessing for blessing. And he exacts the same rightness from them to himself.

Two conditions stand for the results of injustice: to be despoiled, that is to be victim of theft or fraud, and to be oppressed, that is to carry a heavy load. The unfair loss on the one hand, the unfair burden on the other, these are the conditions of poverty. Think of beggars in any city, crowding the steps of public buildings, staggering on crutches, or crawling with maimed feet, hands clutching their scavenging bags, and we can recognize the prophet's description of the poor and oppressed.

In Leviticus the body is the cosmos.[13] Everything in the universe shows forth the righteousness of the Lord. Animals and humans, people and priests, animals for food, animals for the altar, their bodies are figures of righteousness and unrighteousness. The forbidden animal species exemplify the predators, on the one hand, that is those who eat blood, and on the other, the sufferers from injustice. Consider the list, especially the swarming insects, the chameleon with its lumpy face, the high humped tortoise and beetle, and the ants labouring under their huge loads. Think of the blindness of worms, and bats, the vulnerability of fish without scales. Think of their human parallels, the labourers, the beggars, the orphans and the defenceless widows. Not themselves but the behaviour that reduces them to this state is the abomination. No wonder the Lord made the crawling things and found them good (Gen. 1.31). It is not in the grand style of Leviticus to take time off from cosmic themes to teach that these pathetic creatures are to be shunned

13. The importance of the theme of the microcosm in Leviticus has been central to my analysis of the meaning of Atonement, 'Atonement in Leviticus', *Jewish Studies Quarterly* 1, 2 (1993–94), pp. 109-30.

because their bodies are disgusting, vile, bad, any more than it is consistent with its theme of justice to teach that the poor are to be shunned. Shunning is not the issue. Predation is wrong, eating is a form of predation and the poor are not to be a prey.[14]

Now we are in a position to make the connection between all three types of forbidden animal foods. First, out of honour to the blood and the life that is in the blood (Lev. 17.14), no flesh with blood in it is to be eaten. This rule identifies herbivorous land animals and birds, and excludes carnivores on the earth or in the air. Secondly, animal species that resemble in shape the sufferers from physical injury must not be eaten, that is, an equivalence is drawn between species and individuals lamed, or maimed or otherwise disfigured, and connects with the rule against offering blemished animals. Thirdly, in the waters those creatures without fins or scales must not appear on the table as food. The Mishnaic tradition has looked to water monsters for exemplars of this rule, octopus or crab. But it would be more congenial to the interpretation that we are here suggesting that young fish were intended in the prohibition. It is not their repellent monsterhood but their vulnerable youthfulness that would be symbolized by absence of scaly covering. Fishes hatch out naked, their fins and scales grow on them, so shoals of baby fishes, minnows, whitebait and larvae of insects, the orphans of the water world, would be forbidden by this rule.

Holiness is incompatible with predatory behaviour. The command to be holy is fulfilled by respecting blood, the symbol of violent predation, and respecting the symbolic victims of predation. The forbidden animals in this perspective represent the endangered categories for whom Isaiah spoke, the oppressed, the fatherless, the widow (Isa. 1.17). Respect for them is a way of remembering the difference between the clean and unclean, the holy and the unholy.

Though this interpretation makes the dietary rules symbolic for virtues and vices, the permitted animals do not stand for any virtues, they simply keep the rule of avoiding blood, and the forbidden animals do not represent vices in their own bodies, but the effects of vicious actions on the part of others.[15] It is unexpected for readers who do not take it for

14. This theme is developed in my chapter for David Grene's Festschrift forthcoming, entitled 'A Mouse, a Bird and Some Fish: For a New Reading of Leviticus 11'.

15. Although this interpretation depends on symbolizing virtue and vice, it is very different from that offered by Philo, whose free-wheeling allegories do not

granted that kindness to animals, or wit about animals, or the slightest sense of humour concerning humans and animals, would be found in Leviticus. The other rules about respecting shed animal blood, respecting the right of a mother animal to be with her new born infant for 8 days, are congenial with the dietary rules. This so-called purity code only looks superficially like purity codes in other parts of the world: it has none of the usual political uses, and it is primarily a code of justice and honour. As a philosophical exercise it multiplies allegories of justice for all. Making a general survey of the universe, its elements, its origins, and the destiny of the people of Israel, Leviticus declares that God is manifest in his righteousness, completely in accord with what the prophets said.[16]

depend on Isaiah's teachings about righteousness. *Philo with an English Translation*, VIII (trans. F.H. Colson; London: Heinemann; Cambridge, MA: Harvard University Press, 1954).

16. This theme has been developed in my 'Holy Joy: Rereading Leviticus', *Conservative Judaism* XLVI, 3 (1994).

JSOT 62 (1994), pp. 19-36

WHAT IF DINAH IS NOT RAPED? (GENESIS 34)

Lyn M. Bechtel

When the story of Dinah in Genesis 34 is interpreted from a twentieth-century, predominantly 'individual-oriented' perspective,[1] it is automatically assumed that Shechem rapes Dinah, that all the males in the story treat Dinah as an 'object', that Hamor and Shechem act deceitfully toward her family, that Jacob abandons her, and that she becomes the victim of both Shechem and her own family.[2] From the standpoint of

1. For the categories of individual-orientation and group-orientation, see M. Douglas, *Natural Symbols: Explorations in Cosmology* (New York: Pantheon, 1970).

2. Most analysis of Gen. 34 proceeds on the assumption of rape: S.R. Driver, *The Book of Genesis* (London: Methuen, 1904); J. Skinner, *A Critical and Exegetical Commentary on Genesis* (Edinburgh: T. & T. Clark, 1930); G. von Rad, *Genesis* (Philadelphia: Westminster Press, 1961); E.A. Speiser, *Genesis* (Garden City, NY: Doubleday, 1964); J.H. Otwell, *And Sarah Laughed: The Status of Women in the Old Testament* (Philadelphia: Westminster Press, 1977); C.M. Carmichael, *Women, Law, and the Genesis Tradition* (Edinburgh: Edinburgh University Press, 1979), pp. 33-48; R. Davidson, *Genesis 12–50* (London: Cambridge University Press, 1979); S.A. West, 'The Rape of Dinah and the Conquest of Shechem', *Dor le Dor* 7 (1980), pp. 144-51; W. Brueggemann, *Genesis* (Atlanta: John Knox, 1982); M.M. Caspi, 'The Story of the Rape of Dinah: The Narrator and the Reader', *Hebrew Studies* 26 (1985), pp. 25-45; M. Sternberg, *The Poetics of Biblical Narrative: Ideological Literature and the Drama of Reading* (Bloomington, IN: Indiana University Press, 1985); 'Biblical Poetics and Sexual Politics: From Reading to Counter-Reading', *JBL* 111 (1992), pp. 463-88; C. Westermann, *Genesis 12–36* (Minneapolis: Augsburg, 1985); R.B. Coote and D.R. Ord, *The Bible's First History* (Philadelphia: Fortress Press, 1989), pp. 167-71; D.N. Freedman, 'Dinah and Shechem: Tamar and Amnon', *Austin Seminary Bulletin: Faculty Edition* 105 (1990), pp. 51-63; S.P. Jeansonne, *The Women of Genesis: From Sarah to Potiphar's Wife* (Minneapolis: Fortress Press, 1990), pp. 87-97; S.A. Geller, 'The

some feminists the story becomes a paradigm of many situations of rape in modern society because the story (together with its exegetes) minimizes or ignores Dinah's suffering. Thus, it has been used to show both ancient and modern insensitivity toward women and the experience of rape. But the story stems from a group-oriented society and contains enough contradictions, ironies, paradoxes and ambiguities to raise the question, Does the story really intend to indicate that Dinah is raped? The problem lies in the fact that what modern society calls 'rape' is described in several Hebrew Bible texts, but there is no specific term for 'rape' in Hebrew. Consequently, criteria need to be established in order to determine the presence or absence of 'rape' in Genesis 34. In addition, to avoid imposing the assumptions of individual-oriented societies on the text, relevant characteristics of group-oriented societies need to be established.

Modern Definition of Rape

Rape may be defined[3] as a man's forcible, aggressive sexual intercourse with a woman who at the time does not consent and shows obvious resistance or vigorous struggle. It is a forceful, nonconsensual boundary and identity violation, a hostile sexual act that uses the penis as a weapon and can therefore cause psychological damage and/or physical injury to the woman. Although rape is a sex act, for the male the primary motive

---

Sack of Shechem: The Use of Typology in Biblical Covenant Religion', *Prooftexts: A Journal of Jewish Literary History* 10 (1990), pp. 1-15; I.M. Rashkow, 'Hebrew Bible Translation and the Fear of Judaization', *Sixteenth Century Journal* 21 (1990), pp. 217-33 and *Upon the Dark Places: Anti-Semitism and Sexism in English Renaissance Biblical Translation* (Sheffield: Almond Press, 1991); I. Sheres, *Dinah's Rebellion: A Biblical Parable for our Times* (New York: Crossroad, 1990); D.N. Fewell and D.M. Gunn, 'Tipping the Balance: Sternberg's Reader and the Rape of Dinah', *JBL* 110 (1991), pp. 193-211.

3.   My definition of rape is a composite of the work of T. Beneke, *Men on Rape* (New York: St Martins, 1982); L.B. Bouque, *Defining Rape* (Durham, NC: Duke University Press, 1989); S. Brownmiller, *Against our Will: Men, Women and Rape* (New York: Simon & Schuster, 1975); S. Griffin, 'Rape: The All-American Crime', in D. Chappell, R. Geis and G. Geis (eds.), *Forcible Rape: The Crime, the Victim and the Offender* (New York: Columbia University Press, 1977); C.V. Horos, *Rape* (New Canaan, CT: Tobey, 1974); S. Tomaselli and R. Porter (eds.), *Rape* (Oxford: Basil Blackwell, 1986); P.R. Sanday, *Female Power: Male Dominance: On the Origin of Sexual Inequality* (Cambridge: Cambridge University Press, 1981).

for rape is not intimate sexual pleasure or pure sexual release. Instead, it is an exploitative act that silences the male's feelings of vulnerability, inferiority and lack of control[4] (which in individual-oriented society are considered 'feminine' and, therefore, unacceptable for a male) by creating the illusion of power, control, dominance and superiority.

Characteristics of Group-Orientation

It is widely recognized that all people approach life from a particular perspective on reality, or 'thinking pattern', into which they have been *socialized* by their society. A thinking pattern molds the way they perceive the social, economic, cultural, political and religious dimensions of life. Ancient Israel fits generally into the category of a group-oriented society. When a society is group-oriented, most people derive their identity externally from the strongly bonded group to which they belong, that is, the society as a whole and the household groups within it. This orientation, then, influences all aspects of their thinking and lives. Group-orientation is not just simply belonging to a group, but involves the automatic allegiance, responsibility, obligation and attachment of the individual to the group. This sense of responsibility and obligation forms an important part of the bonding that holds the group together. What is generally misunderstood about group-oriented societies is that people function as individuals, but are encouraged to reach their full potential for the benefit of the group, rather than for the sole benefit of the individual. The ego needs of the individual are filled, but within the context of the needs of the entire group. Since identity stems from the group, the welfare of the group is considered identical to the welfare of the individual. To promote this relationship of the individual to the group, there is an ethic of sharing ('give' and 'take'), cooperation, a primary dependence on kin and a general assumption of mutual aid and reciprocity.

In group-orientation it is important that the closely knit group and the households within it have well-articulated and highly valued boundaries[5] as well as carefully guarded entrances and exits, because boundaries and orifices are associated with both power and danger. Boundaries are powerful because they hold the group and its identity together, and dangerous because they can be violated, threatening the existence of the

4. Bouque, *Defining Rape*, p. 15.
5. For general boundary issues see R.J. Lifton, *Boundaries: Psychological Man in Revolution* (New York: Vintage Books, 1967).

group and the identity of the members. Boundaries are related to geography, ethnicity, the correct ancestral lineage and most importantly allegiance. There is purity inside the group and impurity outside the group. Often the group projects impurity onto outsiders, in order to form a stronger boundary and justify negative attitudes toward outsiders. Entrances and exits are points of potential violation or pollution of the group, as well as loss of power from the group. Consequently, the experience of inclusion/purity, exclusion/impurity and marginality[6] are decisive in differentiating between 'us' (the insider) and 'them' (the outsiders).

Probably the most important issue in group-orientation is how people cope with death. Salvation from the finality of death comes from the biological continuation of life through children from one generation to another, which guarantees the continued existence of the household and the group as a whole. The individual and his or her identity continue as long as the group continues. In this light, the high priority that the individual places on the welfare of the group is understandable.

Marriage and the family[7] are highly valued, and women, the producers of children, are the producers of continued life, the producers of salvation. Therefore, women have significant power and value within the society. The idea of women being devalued or having no power is inconceivable. Women create salvation; there is no greater power, no greater functioning in this kind of society.

And in order to perpetuate the household and the group, fertility and sexual intercourse within the family are vital. Sexual intercourse between a man and a woman is not perceived in romantic or spiritual terms, but in terms of its perpetuation of the family/group. The idea of sex being dirty or casual is out of the question. The salvation of the individual lies in the continuation of the group, which depends on proper sexual intercourse—that is, proper use of sexual power. Sexual power leads to salvation, when correctly regulated to prevent intrusions that pollute the family/group and extrusions that represent loss of strength. But when unregulated (particularly outside the family or group) it is dangerous, diminishing the power of the group and threatening its longevity. In addition, sexual intercourse creates strong bonding, obligation and

6.   See L. Rowlett, 'Inclusion, Exclusion and Marginality in the Book of Joshua', *JSOT* 55 (1992), pp. 15-23.

7.   See N. Steinberg, 'Alliance or Descent? The Function of Marriage in Genesis', *JSOT* 51 (1991), pp. 45-55.

responsibility that establishes the male–female ties that are so essential to the bonding of group-orientation.

The Meaning of the Verb 'nh

Given the definition of rape, is rape what is described in Genesis 34? In vv. 2-3 it says that Shechem (1) sees (*r'h*) Dinah, (2) takes (*lqḥ*) her, (3) lies (*škb*) (with) her,[8] (4) does something with her that is described by *'nh* in the Piel; (5) his whole being (*nepeš*) bonds (*dbq*) with her, (6) he loves (*'hb*) her and (7) speaks 'to her heart'. The verb that points scholars to rape is *'nh*, which is in the center position of a string of verbs describing the incident and which follows the verb *škb* (to lie), often used as a euphemism for sexual intercourse. Since the incident involves sexual intercourse, most scholars assume *'nh* implies 'rape', but this assumption needs to be carefully tested.[9]

In the Qal the verb *'nh* means 'to put down' or 'to humble', and in

8.   *škb* is used here with the particle *'t*, pointed as a definite direct object marker with suffix (*'otāh*), rather than as a preposition with suffix (*'ittāh*). It is also found in 2 Sam. 13.14 pointed as an object marker with suffix (*'otāh*). In Gen. 34.2 the Greek text presupposes *'ittāh* 'with her' (Westermann, *Genesis 12–36*, p. 534, follows the Greek text) and in 2 Sam. 13.14 three manuscripts have *'immāh* and one has *'ittāh*. The significance of this variation is not clear. Freedman ('Dinah and Shechem: Tamar and Amnon', pp. 53-54) surmises that *škb* has been substituted for *šgl* 'ravish', as has been done elsewhere (cf. Isa. 13.16; Jer. 3.2; Zech. 14.2). I.N. Rashkow ('Hebrew Bible Translation', p. 226) and others feel that when *škb* is used with the preposition *'m* (with), it connotes a mutually agreed upon sexual act. But when it is used with *'t* as an object marker, it indicates rape. Caspi ('The Story of the Rape of Dinah', p. 32) argues that the use of the direct object draws 'attention to the force used in committing the crime'.

The problem with these later two suggestions is that in Deut. 22.25-27 the man overpowers (*ḥzq*) the young woman, lies (*škb*) with her (*'immāh*), and she cries out (*ṣ'q*), yet it uses *'immāh*.

9.   Those *not* assuming rape: N. Ararat, 'Reading according to the "Seder" in Biblical Narrative: To Balance the Reading of the Dinah Episode', *Hasifrut* 27 (1978), pp. 15-34; Y. Zakovitch, 'A Survey of the Literary Study of the Bible in Israel', *Newsletter of the World Association for Jewish Studies* 20 (1982), pp. 19-38. Although Fewell and Gunn ('Tipping the Balance', pp. 193-211) question the direction and implications of Sternberg's rape reading, they still conclude that Dinah is raped.

the Piel one of its meanings is 'to humiliate intensely'.[10] 'To put down', 'humble' or 'humiliate intensely' are central to the experience of shaming, which in Israelite society was both an important emotional response (feeling shame) and a social sanction of undesirable behavior (shaming).[11] Shame/shaming, which is the predominant means of social control in group-oriented societies, relates to the anxiety aroused by 'inadequacy' or 'failure' to live up to internalized, societal goals and ideals, and it impacts on 'who a person is'. An individual's healthy sense of pride is based on sustaining these goals and ideals. Failure or inadequacy violates pride, and the response to a violation of pride is shame. The fear that shame stimulates is that of contempt which leads to psychological or physical rejection, loss of social position, abandonment or expulsion. In group-oriented societies rejection or expulsion from the group means being cut off from the major source of identity, support and salvation, which spells death. The social sanction of shaming is a means of social control that attempts to inhibit aggressive or undesirable behavior. Fundamentally, shaming lowers a person in status, and in a group-oriented society where standing within the group (the predominant source of identity) is primary, status manipulation is a highly coercive means of social control.

The verb '*nh* ('to put down') reflects the process of status manipulation inherent in shaming. Given the meaning of 'shame' connoted by the verb '*nh*, I will contend that within a sexual context the verb '*nh* in the Piel indicates the 'humiliation' or 'shaming' of a woman through certain kinds of sexual intercourse including rape, through not necessarily.[12]

What makes some sexual intercourse shameful and some not shameful? In group-oriented societies like ancient Israel, sexual intercourse is shameful to a women (1) when it violates existing marital, family or community bonding and obligation or (2) when there is no prospect of its leading to marital or family bonding and obligation. In cases where these conditions are present, the verb '*nh* is used to describe the shaming, and I will translate the verb '*nh* 'to humiliate'.

---

10. W. Baumgartner, *Lexicon in Veteris Testamenti Libros* (Leiden: Brill, 1951), p. 719.

11. See L. Bechtel, 'Shame as a Sanction of Social Control in Biblical Israel: Judicial, Political, and Social Shaming', *JSOT* 49 (1991), pp. 47-76.

12. See D.N. Freedman ('Dinah and Shechem: Tamar and Amnon', pp. 51-63) who contends that '*nh* is a technical term for illicit heterosexual sexual intercourse.

Biblical Incidents of Sexual Intercourse Using 'nh

Several biblical incidents of sexual intercourse need to be investigated to find out (1) if *'nh* automatically indicates rape, as many scholars assume, (2) if bonding or lack of bonding is an issue in its use and (3) if the verb *'nh* indicates the shame associated with sexual intercourse that violates or does not lead to marital, family or community bonding and obligation.

In Deut. 22.23-24[13] within the city (i.e. within hearing or vision of the community), a man finds and lies (*škb*) with a young woman (*bᵉtûlâ*) who is engaged or bonded. There is sexual intercourse between the man and the already bonded young woman, with no use of force and no cry of help from the woman in a place where it would have been heard. This does not qualify as rape; there is no cry for help and no use of force.[14] But, since the young woman is already bonded, this intercourse violates the existing bonding and obligation. For this, both the man and the woman are to be taken to the city gate and stoned to death. The issue is the violation of the existing bonding and obligation. The woman is to die because she did not cry for help, and does not value her social bonding and obligation. Her wilful sexual behavior is threatening to the cohesion of the group and should be eliminated. The man is to die because he has humiliated (*'nh*, v. 24) a bonded young woman. Despite the fact that there is no rape, the sexual intercourse is shameful because it threatens the social bonding of the community. Note that in this case the word *'nh* follows *škb*, which seems to be the case when rape is not involved.

In Deut. 22.28-29 a man finds and takes hold of or touches the heart of (*tpś*)) an unbonded young woman (*bᵉtûlâ*) and lies (*škb*) with her. There is no cry for help from the woman and no violence on the part of the man. There is voluntary sexual intercourse between two unbonded people, but with no prospect of bonding and obligation. This too does not qualify as rape. In fact, the man has touched the heart (*tpś*) of the woman, as Shechem does to Dinah. But there is no request for future bonding, and therefore, he has humiliated (*'nh*, v. 29) her. Again, note

---

13. The correspondence between some Genesis material and the laws of Deuteronomy has been pointed out and investigated by Carmichael (*Women, Law, and the Genesis Tradition* [Edinburgh: Edinburgh University Press, 1979]).

14. Freedman ('Dinah and Shechem: Tamar and Amnon', p. 54) finds consensual sexual relations here and in Deut. 22.28-29.

that, with no rape involved, *'nh* follows *škb*. To erase the shame and establish bonding the man is obligated to give the father of the young woman fifty pieces of silver as a bride gift,[15] to marry her and never divorce her. Despite the fact that there is no rape, the sexual intercourse between these two people is shameful, and the verb *'nh* is used.

In contrast, in Deut. 22.25-27, in open country (outside the vision and hearing of the community), a man finds and overpowers (*ḥzq*) a bonded young woman and lies (*škb*) with her. The young woman cries out for help (*ṣ'q*), but there is no one to rescue her. There is protest from the woman and obvious use of force. This certainly qualifies as rape. The text states that the woman has acted correctly; she has cried out for help, so this sexual intercourse is not voluntary and is not considered a violation by her of her existing bonding and obligation. Consequently, there is no shame for her, and the verb *'nh* is not used to describe the rape. It is simply a hostile, exploitative crime against a woman and the community, for which the man deserves to die.[16] There is rape, but no shame, the verb *'nh* is not used.

In 2 Sam. 13.11-14, Amnon, the brother of Tamar, overpowers (*ḥzq*) her and commands her to lie (*škb*) with him, but she refuses, saying,

> No, my brother, do not humiliate me (*'nh*) because such a thing is not done in Israel. Do not do this foolish thing (*nᵉbālâ*). For I, where shall I take my shame (*ḥerpâ*) and you, you shall be like one of the fools (*nᵉbālîm*) in Israel... But he was not willing to listen to her voice, and he overpowered (*ḥzq*) her, humiliated her (*'nh*), and lay (*škb*) (with) her (vv. 12-13, 14).

This qualifies as rape because of Tamar's protest and Amnon's use of force. The forcing (*ḥzq*) precedes intercourse (*škb*), and it is with the forcing (*ḥzq*) that the *'nh* (humiliation) is linked. The rape is shameful

---

15. For a discussion of the *mōhar* (bride gift) for a man who has sexual intercourse with an unbonded virgin, see R. de Vaux (*Ancient Israel: Social Institutions*, I [New York: McGraw–Hill, 1965], pp. 26-27). Otwell (*And Sarah Laughed*, pp. 37-40) stresses that daughters are not sold into marriage, that they are not disposable property and that the giving of a gift does not imply a subordinate status for the bride.

16. The woman's cry for help in open country cannot be verified, so the man would be condemned to death on the strength of the woman's uncorroborated testimony. But as policy rather than actual binding legislation, this example speaks more to the need to honor social bonding and obligation than it does to the acceptance of a woman's uncorroborated testimony.

because it is carried out by a member of her family, a person with whom there is bonding and obligation that precludes such sexual activity. This rape violates the existing family bonding and responsibility, and it is described as both humiliating (*'nh*) and a reproach (*ḥerpâ*) to Tamar. In addition, Amnon becomes one of the fools (*nᵉbālîm*) of Israel. Fools are those who are ignorant or insensitive[17] to societal ideals and customs. Within a shame-culture the reference to 'shame' (*ḥerpâ*), 'humiliation' (*'nh*), 'foolishness' and the expression 'such a thing is not done in Israel' (a common expression in shame-cultures),[18] all point to the sense of inadequacy that an individual should feel for violation of the societal ideals and customs, which should produce an emotional response of shame. So each of these words or expressions is fundamental to the experience of shame/shaming.

These examples both involve rape, yet in Deut. 22.25-27 the rape is not humiliating, and *'nh* is not used, while in 2 Sam. 13.11-14 it is humiliating, and *'nh* is used.

Genesis 34 and the Issue of Rape

Now we return to Genesis 34. In light of the four passages discussed, does the description of the sexual intercourse between Dinah and Shechem qualify as rape? Shechem sees (*r'h*) Dinah, and he takes (*lqḥ*) her, lies (*škb*) (with) her, humiliates (*'nh*) her, his whole being bonds (*dbq*) with her, he loves (*'hb*) her and he speaks to her heart (vv. 2-3). The sexual intercourse involves two unbonded people, with no mention of violence on the part of Shechem or of a cry for help on the part of Dinah. But Shechem is an outsider, a 'prince' of the Canaanites, so there is no possibility of marital and family bonding and obligation with this outsider. Since Shechem's 'whole being' (*nepeš*) bonds (*dbq*) with Dinah, it is like the situation in Deut. 22.28-29. So from the point of view of the Jacobites Shechem humiliates (*'nh*) Dinah. And as in Deut. 22.23-24 and 28-29 where there is no rape, *'nh* follows *škb*.

Scholars have suggested that the verbs preceding *'nh* contribute to its meaning of 'rape'. This too needs to be tested. Before Shechem has intercourse with Dinah, he sees (*r'h*) her, using the same verb as her going forth to see (*r'h*) the daughters of the land. In neither case is there

---

17. Driver, *The Book of Genesis*, p. 303.

18. See D. Daube, 'The Culture of Deuteronomy', *Orita* 3 (1969), pp. 27-52, for a discussion of this phrase.

violence implied. Then Shechem takes (*lqh*) Dinah. When rape is assumed, scholars claim that *lqh* (to take) designates physical force.[19] Yet, elsewhere in the story *lqh* has no inherent connotation of physical force. For example, it is used most often in the expression 'to give (*ntn*) and take (*lqh*)' wives (vv. 4, 9, 16), which is a part of the proposed 'giving and taking'[20] between the Shechemites and the Jacobites, an interplay intended to foster bonding and cooperation, but not carried out by physical force. It is only in vv. 25-26 where violence is described in association with *lqh* (taking [*lqh*] the sword and killing all the males). Without a similar association of force in v. 2, there is no indication of rape in Shechem's 'taking' (*lqh*) of Dinah. Finally, the verb *škb* designates sexual intercourse, but it too has no inherent suggestion of force.

Then, the text goes on to emphasize Shechem's bonding (*dbq*) with her, his love (*'hb*) for her and his speaking to her heart. *Dbq* (to bond) is the same word that is used in Gen. 2.24 to characterize the process of becoming 'one flesh', a marital bonding that is both sexual and psychological.[21] 'To speak to the heart' is an expression that connotes 'reassurance, comfort, loyalty and love'.[22] It is used to describe one person's professing of love for another or God's professing of love for

19. Some scholars assume that the string of expressions here (to see, to take and to lie) is a sign of the combining of sources, though 'perhaps not rightly so', says von Rad (*Genesis*, p. 331). Others have pointed to the accumulation of verbs as evidence of force and rape, with the verbs of endearment that follow not cancelling out the rape, e.g. Sternberg, *Poetics of Biblical Narrative*, pp. 446-47; *idem*, 'Biblical Poetics', pp. 473-77; Jeansonne, *The Women of Genesis*, p. 92; Rashkow, 'Hebrew Bible Translation', p. 226. In contrast, Fewell and Gunn ('Tipping the Balance', pp. 195-97) recognize the extraordinary quality of these verbs.

20. The Jacobites are the subject of 'giving' five times (vv. 8, 9, 12, 14, 16) and 'taking' seven times (vv. 9, 12, 16, 17, 25, 26, 28) and the Shechemites are the subject of 'giving' four times (vv. 11, 12a, 12b, 21) and 'taking' three times (vv. 2, 4, 21). The 'giving and taking' is not proportionate; the Shechemites do more giving and the Jacobites do more taking.

21. See L. Bechtel, 'Rethinking the Interpretation of Genesis 2–3', in A. Brenner (ed.), *A Feminist Companion to Genesis* (The Feminist Companion to the Bible, 2; Sheffield: Sheffield Academic Press, 1993) for the use of *dbq*.

22. P. Trible, *Texts of Terror: Literary-Feminist Readings of Biblical Narratives* (Philadelphia: Fortress Press, 1984), p. 67. Speiser (*Genesis*, p. 264) says it is done to persuade Dinah and to ask her forgiveness. Rashkow ('Hebrew Bible Translation', p. 227) interprets these verbs as words of 'permanent bonding' and strong emotion that are spoken deviously.

Israel (e.g. Judg. 19.3; Hos. 2.16). Sociological studies reveal that rapists feel hostility and hatred toward their victims, not love.

In addition, after seeing Dinah, taking her, lying with her, humiliating her, bonding with her and professing his love for her, Shechem goes immediately to speak to his father about asking for Dinah as his wife. In this request he makes no mention of rape, force or hostile intentions. He longs for (*ḥšq*, v. 8), delights in (v. 19) and wants Dinah as his wife (v. 4). Shechem's desire for bonding stands in tension with the lack of potential for bonding, at least from the point of view of the Jacobites. Hamor then 'goes forth' to speak to Jacob, declaring publicly that Shechem wants Dinah as his wife. There is no apology for a rape or suggestion of force or hostile intentions. Instead, the text stresses that these are honorable men.

For Shechem, Hamor and the Shechemites the motive for interaction is to unite, bond and cooperate. The overall action of Shechem (and his community) is one of honor. Shechem is described as the most honored (*kbd*) in his family (v. 19),[23] and he wants to 'find favor in the eyes of' the Jacobites (v. 11). The expression 'to find favor' is not casual language, but carries considerable significance in a shame–honor society.[24] It is an attempt to establish a reciprocal relationship between the Shechemites and the Jacobites. All of this diminishes the likelihood that rape was seen to have occurred.

Because Hamor is negotiating the marriage of a *nāśî'*, a prince or chief of a tribe, this marriage is more than a private affair; it is both the bonding of two individuals and two groups. When kings or princes take wives, it can be for political alliance and economic cooperation as well as mutual attraction and love, so it is a public affair. Thus, Hamor puts his emphasis on 'uniting', which is spoken of in terms of mutual marriages that will create a bonding between the two groups, to the advantage of both parties. This 'trusting' city[25] (v. 25) wants to begin a process of 'give and take'—of intermarrying, dwelling and holding property peace-

23. Jeansonne (*The Women of Genesis*, pp. 93-94) observes the incongruity of rape for such an honorable man, as well as the incongruity of his not apologizing or expressing remorse.

24. See Bechtel, 'Shame as a Sanction of Social Control in Biblical Israel'. See also Daube, 'The Culture of Deuteronomy'.

25. Westermann (*Genesis 12–36*, p. 534) interprets *bṭḥ* (trust) as modifying Simeon and Levi rather than the city folk.

fully together with the Jacobites.[26] As Shechem and Dinah have bonded (*dbq*) together, likewise, the Shechemites can bond with the Jacobites, and undo the 'shame'. In v. 9 Hamor negotiates an alliance, but it is not aggressive or demanding. The emphasis is on the initiative of the Jacobites, accentuated by the use of '*you* give your daughters to us and *you* take our daughters for yourself', not 'I' or 'we' will take your daughters. These are not people who feel vulnerable, inferior or lacking in control, so that they need not create the illusion of power, control, dominance and superiority through rape.

After an agreement appears to be reached, Hamor and Shechem speak to the men of their city and discuss the public aspect of the agreement, the 'uniting'; that is, after all, what is relevant to the group. They stress that the Jacobites are peaceful people that can be allowed to dwell and move about freely in the land and with whom they can exchange daughters as wives (v. 21). The speech to the Jacobites and the one to the Shechemites form an inclusio, with 'you [the Jacobites] giving and taking' in v. 9 and 'we [the Shechemites] taking and giving' (reversed) in v. 21. The motive for this alliance is economic growth and peaceful coexistence (v. 23). But to become 'one people' all the Shechemite males will have to be circumcised as the Jacobites are circumcised. The Shechemites must have some concept of the group bonding inherent in circumcision, because they agree to be circumcised.

The final clue regarding the issue of rape comes in the last sentence of the story. Simeon and Levi say, 'Should he have made our sister like a harlot?' (v. 31). Some exegetes point to Shechem's offer of a bride gift (*mōhar*) (v. 12) as proof that Shechem has treated Dinah like a harlot—paying her for her 'service'.[27] Yet the text makes plain that Shechem, in asking for Dinah as a wife, agrees to give even more than the customary *mōhar* (v. 11). Shechem is honoring the customs of the Jacobites and seeking to find favor in their eyes. Since Shechem and Hamor are suggesting that they exchange daughters in marriage and live together peacefully, this sounds more like an attempt at alliance than a way of

26. Shechem and its fortress-temple, El-Berit, are associated with a tradition of covenant making (Josh. 24) between a variety of groups that will eventually make up the nation of Israel. See further, E.F. Campbell, 'Shechem (City)', *IDBSup* (Nashville: Abingdon Press, 1976), p. 821.

27. E.g. Sternberg, *Poetics of Biblical Narrative*, pp. 445-75. Westermann (*Genesis 12–36*, p. 534) states that Shechem is paying to atone for his crime.

paying a harlot. Simeon and Levi's comment in v. 31 must refer to something other than Shechem's bride gift.

Harlots engage in sexual relations for business purposes; there is mutual consent. Harlots are not raped. Their sexual activity is considered marginal because it is conducted outside the bonding and obligation of the marital/family unit, outside the central social structure of the society.[28] They potentially threaten the cohesion of the social structure. By saying that Dinah has become like a harlot, the sons of Jacob show that they do not regard Dinah as having been raped. Instead, they are pointing to the fact that she has become a marginal figure by engaging in sexual activity outside her society and without the possibility of bonding, since the sons are unwilling to give their sister to an uncircumcised outsider. For them the relationship threatens the cohesion of the tribal structure. It is to this threat that the sons react.

The emphasis in the text on wanting to get acquainted, nonviolent 'giving and taking', bonding, professing love, honoring and cooperating cannot be ignored. Throughout the text there is no indication that Dinah is raped.[29] The description of Shechem's behavior and attitude does not fit that of a rapist. It is not the correct psychological context for rape.

The Image of Dinah ('To Go Forth')

If Dinah is not raped, how does she function in the story? The image of Dinah revolves around the initial term used for her—she 'went forth' (*ys'*, v. 1). To understand the implications of this term, the function of 'going forth' has to be studied elsewhere in the story. In v. 6 Hamor goes forth (*ys'*) from his city on a diplomatic mission to talk to Jacob. In v. 24 all the men of the city, who 'go forth (*ys'*) from the gate', listen to

28. See P. Bird, 'Images of Women in the Old Testament', in R.R. Ruether (ed.), *Religion and Sexism* (New York: Simon & Schuster, 1974), pp. 41-88; 'Harlot as Heroine: Narrative Art and Social Presupposition in Three Old Testament Texts', *Semeia* 46 (1989), pp. 119-39; C. Newsom, 'Woman and the Discourse of Patriarchal Wisdom: A Study of Proverbs 1–9', in P.L. Day (ed.), *Gender and Difference in Ancient Israel* (Minneapolis: Fortress Press, 1989), pp. 142-60.

29. Although at that time their interpretation may have been colored more by the negative image of Jews in Renaissance England than an understanding of the Hebrew text, Rashkow ('Hebrew Bible Translation', p. 228) points out that English Renaissance biblical translators (she refers specifically to the Rheims–Douay translators) did not interpret the situation as rape, but focused on Shechem's loving attention and Simeon and Levi's vitriolic qualities.

Hamor and Shechem. In v. 26 Simeon and Levi take (*lqḥ*) Dinah from
the house of Shechem and go forth (*yṣ'*). In each of these cases, people
pass through an entrance/exit and cross over the *boundary* of a group.[30]
When Dinah goes forth to see, to get acquainted with, the daughters of
the land, she exits and crosses her group/tribal boundary. For the sons of
Jacob her crossing the boundary threatens the unity of her tribal community and threatens their identity. The notion of her 'going forth' and
crossing her tribal boundary forms the foundation of what evolves in the
story. Dinah is both a figure who 'goes forth' and crosses her group
boundaries and a marginal figure who engages in sexual activity outside
the group.

The Idea of Pollution, Circumcision and Shame

The Jacobites view the sexual intercourse between Dinah and Shechem
in a very different way than Shechem and Hamor. When Jacob first
hears of the sexual intercourse, he keeps silent until the whole group
hears. When the sons of Jacob hear of it, they 'become indignant (*'ṣb*)
and very angry (*ḥrh*) because he has done a foolish thing (*neḇālâ*) in
Israel by lying (with) the daughter of Jacob. Such a thing is not done'
(v. 7). The sexual intercourse is called 'pollution' (*ṭāmē'*) in vv. 5 and 13
and 'a foolish thing' (*neḇālâ*) in v. 7. The use of 'pollution'[31] in vv. 5
and 13 is tied to and literally frames the description of the sexual intercourse as a 'foolish thing' in v. 7. Each description brings with it a
particular variation in meaning. This sexual intercourse is considered
pollution because Dinah has been tainted with 'outside stuff'. Shechem
is an uncircumcised, impure outsider. This outside pollution or outside
impurity defiles the whole Jacobite community. It is considered 'a
foolish thing' that 'is not done' because it violates the ideals and customs of the tribal group that attempt to preserve the group boundaries
and continue the existence of the group (cf. 2 Sam. 13.12-13). Sexual

---

30. Cf. Speiser (*Genesis*, p. 265), who suggests that those who 'go forth' may
be defenders of the city who participate in the city council. Sheres (*Dinah's
Rebellion*, pp. 6-7) maintains that 'going out' entails a process of 'self-discovery'.

31. *ṭāmē'* ('defiled', vv. 5, 13, 27) is a normal term for the 'ritual impure'
(Lev. 5.2; 11.25, 28; 12.2, 5; 15.18; 22.8), but it is not found elsewhere in Genesis.
Cf. von Rad, *Genesis*, p. 332, and Sternberg, *The Poetics of Biblical Narrative*,
pp. 449, 471.

intercourse is only acceptable if it follows the customs of the community and is done in the proper way within the group.

Even after Hamor and Shechem ask for Dinah as a wife and want to 'give and take' wives between the two communities, the sons of Jacob continue to interpret the situation as 'pollution' (v. 13). If there is a marriage, Dinah will be given to an outsider, and the sons say, 'We are not willing to do this thing, to give our sister to a man who is not circumcised, for it is a shame (*herpâ*) to us' (v. 14). Dinah's marriage to an uncircumcised outsider means that her sexual power, which continues the existence of the group, is leaving the tribal group and building an outside, unbonded (uncircumcised) group. Both the loss of power and the violation of tribal ideals are shameful.[32]

The sons of Jacob must now 'save face' for their shame. So they deviously suggest that the Shechemites be circumcised. Although at one time circumcision may have been part of a male's sexual and social maturation and a rite of passage in marriage,[33] for the Jacobites circumcision functions as an act of initiation into the covenant community which creates blood bonding or a 'mark of belonging'[34] for those whose allegiance is inside the group. As a 'mark of belonging' it forms a strong boundary that distinguishes the circumcised insiders from the uncircumcised outsiders. The Shechemites seem to know and willingly embrace this function since it leads to their goal of 'giving and taking' and becoming 'one people'. But for the Jacobites the suggestion of bringing these impure outsiders into the group through circumcision is as much of a violation of the community ideals as Dinah's marrying an outsider.[35] The requirement of circumcision is only a clever pretext to render the Shechemites defenseless,[36] so they can take revenge for the shame of the pollution of their group. They are 'saving face'. The shame and threat have made them feel vulnerable, inferior and without control,

32. Pointed out by Geller, 'The Use of Typology', pp. 2-3.

33. I.e. the 'bridegroom of blood' in Exod. 4.26. For a discussion of primitive circumcision, see H. Eilberg-Schwartz (*The Savage in Judaism: An Anthropology of Israelite Religion and Ancient Judaism* [Bloomington, IN: Indiana University Press, 1990]).

34. Westermann, *Genesis 12–36*, p. 540.

35. This story reflects a time when circumcision forms strong societal bonding, and there is a societal ideal, at least within some circles, that prohibits exogamy and general interaction with outsiders.

36. Skinner, *Genesis*, p. 419. See also Carmichael, *Women, Law, and the Genesis Traditions*, p. 33.

so Simeon and Levi act with cunning, which is often the last recourse for an inferior person in relation to a superior one. They retaliate by slaying, plundering and taking the strength of Shechem, Hamor and the Shechemite community. The fact that the revenge is carried out against the entire Shechemite community shows that from the sons' perspective the pollution has affected the entire Jacobite group. As a community concern, it warrants revenge on the entire Shechemite group.

Their vengeance, although it is generated by the group-oriented motive of preserving group integrity, actually jeopardizes its wellbeing and existence. The Jacobites are few in number, and now a larger, more powerful group may take vengeance against them. Their behavior has made social intercourse and peaceful coexistence impossible. In the long run this kind of behavior violates group-oriented ideals and is condemned by Jacob, and the text, in Gen. 49.5-7.

Ironically, if there is a rape in this story, it is Simeon and Levi who 'rape' the Shechemites. It is their behavior that is violent and hostile, carried out for the purpose of exploitation.[37] It creates the illusion of dominance, control and superiority, in order to silence their feelings of vulnerability and inferiority. From a modern individual-oriented perspective, exegetes, although they condemn the methods, often support the action of Simeon and Levi because they are punishing the assumed guilt of Shechem and defending the rights of the 'individual', Dinah.[38] They have missed the group-oriented perspective.

---

37. Brueggemann, *Genesis*, p. 278.

38. Caspi ('The Story of the Rape of Dinah', pp. 30-32) and Rashkow ('Hebrew Bible Translation', p. 230) claim that the vengeance is justified because Simeon and Levi are only paralleling the actions of Shechem. Brueggemann (*Genesis*, p. 276) proposes, 'The response of the sons of Jacob (vv. 13-17) is one of religious zeal, but not an unreasonable zeal'. Sternberg (*Poetics of Biblical Narrative*, pp. 446, 472-73, 468; cf. 'Biblical Poetics', pp. 483-88) takes Simeon and Levi as the real heroes because of 'their idealistic and uncompromising stances'. The massacre is justified because of the 'enormity of the rape'. Although they become the victimizers, he suggests that the reader has complete identification and sympathy with them as victims. Westermann (*Genesis 12–36*, p. 544) argues that the killing is necessary in order to satisfy honor. Von Rad (*Genesis*, p. 334) comments that Simeon and Levi are 'proud and implacable' characters who the ancient reader would not have called wrong.

Jacob's Behavior and Response

Jacob's actions in the story are limited. He 'hears' of the pollution, is 'silent', waits for the return of his sons and after the massacre reprimands Simeon and Levi for their threatening, exploitative behavior. Jacob's behavior stands in contrast to the deceitful and explosive reaction of his sons, particularly Simeon and Levi. He displays the proper group-oriented behavior. He is quiescent, passive, dependent on his community and cooperative. He does not carry out independent action, but waits for mutual support. He cooperates with Hamor; he is willing to listen. From an individual-oriented perspective, modern exegetes are either puzzled by the behavior of Jacob or critical of his quiescence and passivity[39]—they are, after all, 'feminine' traits in modern society. But from the perspective of the story Jacob is the ideal group-oriented person!

Jacob is also willing to include outsiders who honor the group values, customs and ideals. 'Outsiders' can become 'insiders' on the basis of allegiance.[40] On the surface this attitude appears to threaten the existence of the group, but in the long run it promotes the wellbeing and longevity of the group.

The Mediating Figures

Dinah and Jacob, Hamor and Shechem are mediating figures between the inside group (the Jacobites) and the outside group (the Shechemites). Dinah and Hamor both 'go forth'; they both cross their group boundaries. Dinah and Shechem actively engage one another and bond sexually. They are an example of one kind of interaction between inside

39. For example, Speiser (*Genesis*, p. 267) declares that 'Jacob is presented in an unimpressive light'. Von Rad (*Genesis*, p. 332) comments that Jacob 'cannot pull himself together' and 'form a clear opinion'; his role is weak and his censure a mere peevish complaint. Sternberg (*The Poetics of Biblical Narrative*, pp. 448, 473-74; 'Biblical Poetics', pp. 481-88) sees Jacob as an inert, neglectful or indifferent parent and the story's least sympathetic character once his cowardice has been revealed. He does not protest the 'offenses', but acts pragmatically, which is most incongruous. He is 'the voice of egocentricity and self-preservation' which finds itself 'opposed by the voice of idealism' in Simeon and Levi.

40. See the conclusions of Rowlett ('Inclusion, Exclusion and Marginality', pp. 15-23) regarding the determinants of inclusion.

and outside groups: private, active sexual/family bonding and obligation. Hamor and Jacob negotiate and compromise, trying to settle things honorably; their aim is to bond, cooperate and live together. They are an example of another kind of interaction: public, passive, community bonding and obligation. And as a mediating pair Dinah and Jacob fit together nicely. Dinah has no voice, only action in the beginning of the story; Jacob has no action, only voice at the end of the story.

Conclusion

The Jacobites value a strong sense of bonding, obligation and focus on the overall wellbeing of the group, yet there is dissension within the community concerning how best to accomplish these values. One element (Dinah and Jacob) is interested in interacting with outsiders (Shechem, Hamor and the Shechemites) that show allegiance to their group values and customs. The other element is made up of militant folks (Simeon, Levi and the sons of Jacob) who are threatened by the impure outsiders and want to maintain strict group purity and absolute separation. The story seems to be challenging this attitude by showing the potential danger in which it places the group.

JSOT 63 (1994), pp. 89-104

'A STRONG WOMAN, WHO CAN FIND?'
A STUDY OF CHARACTERIZATION IN GENESIS 24, WITH SOME
PERSPECTIVES ON THE GENERAL PRESENTATION OF ISAAC
AND REBEKAH IN THE GENESIS NARRATIVES

Lieve Teugels

The present study is an inquiry into the presentation of character in biblical narrative. I have chosen Genesis 24, the account of the betrothal and marriage of Isaac and Rebekah, for three reasons. First, Genesis 24 is, by Pentateuchal standards, an exceptionally long, coherent narrative, and thus the presentation of the characters is relatively developed. A second reason is the interesting but intricate characterization of both Isaac and Rebekah, as compared to the other patriarchs and matriarchs. A third reason for selecting Genesis 24 from among the narratives about Isaac and Rebekah[1] is that it initiates Rebekah as a full character, and the couple Isaac–Rebekah as a unity.

The present study divides into four parts. Since characterization in Genesis 24 can only be fully understood when the surrounding patriarchal narratives are taken into consideration, we will start with the literary context—in more technical terms, the 'co-text'—of the narrative (Section 1).[2] An overview of the general narrative structure of the text

---

1. I consider as the Isaac–Rebekah narratives, those passages in Genesis where Isaac and Rebekah appear together, or at least in relationship to each other. The texts under consideration are: Gen. 22.20-24 (as an introduction on Gen. 24), Gen. 24, Gen. 25.19-32, Gen. 26, Gen. 27–28.9. The narratives about Isaac alone (his birth, the Aqedah-story etc.) will be called the Isaac-narratives.

2. For a precise definition of the notion 'co-text', as opposed to 'context', see A. Goldberg, 'Zitat und Citem', *Frankfurter Judaistische Beiträge* 6 (1978), pp. 23-26 (24): 'Kotext bezeichnet den Textzusammenhang in der literarischen Einheit im Unterschied zum Kontext, zu dem auch alle für das Verständnis

itself will follow (Section 2), then the characterization in the text will be analysed (Section 3). Finally I will outline a study of a fascinating but largely ignored problem, namely the comparatively meagre presentation of the second patriarch. Here we will take a broader view of the presentation of Isaac and Rebekah in Genesis as a whole (Section 4).

1. *Genesis 24 in its Co-Text*

Coming as it does at the end of the Abraham cycle we would expect this story to be a transition to an Isaac cycle. It is, however, hard to discern such an Isaac cycle. Only in the two stories in ch. 26 is Isaac an active protagonist, and even these narratives are not unique, but have been related twice before, with some variation, about Abraham.[3] In the other Isaac stories, he appears as a kind of acted-upon anti-hero, the 'passive patriarch'. The account of his marriage is frequently and more properly referred to as 'The Wooing of Rebekah'.[4] Indeed, we shall see that it is Rebekah, not Isaac, who, alongside Abraham's servant, plays the role of protagonist in this story.

Though it is hard to speak of a well-defined Isaac cycle, it is clear that the Genesis 24 narrative is situated in a co-text, made up of Abraham, Isaac, and Isaac–Rebekah narratives, from which it derives part of its meaning. These narratives are found in Gen. 21.1-19; 22.1-19, 20-24; 23.1-2; 25.19-26 and 27–28.9.

notwendigen Text- und Sinnzusammenhangen gehören'.

3.   The first part of ch. 26, the story about the patriarch who passes off his wife as his sister when endangered in a foreign place, is also found in Gen. 12.10-20, and in Gen. 20.1-18. The second part of the chapter (vv. 12-33) is a continuation and a partial repetition of the account of the covenant between Abraham and Abimelech related in Gen. 21.22-34. Different opinions are voiced about the chronological relationship between the three stories of the endangered matriarch. Refer for this question to n. 19.

4.   See e.g. K. Aitken, 'The Wooing of Rebekah', *JSOT* 30 (1984), pp. 3-23; A. Rofé, סיפור אירוסי רבקה (Studies in Jewish Thought, 1; Beer Sheva, 1976), pp. 42-67; W. Roth, 'The Wooing of Rebekah', *CBQ* 34 (1972), pp. 177-87; 'The Wooing of Rebekah', in M. Sternberg, *The Poetics of Biblical Narrative* (Indiana Studies in Biblical Literature; Bloomington, IN: University of Indiana Press, 1985), pp. 131-36; B. Jacob, 'Die Werbung um Rebekka', *Das erste Buch der Tora: Genesis* (New York: Ktav, 1974 [= Berlin, 1934]), pp. 513-34; C. Westermann, 'Werbung um Rebekka', *Biblischer Kommentar. II. Genesis 12–36* (BKAT, 1.2; Neukirchen–Vluyn: Neukirchener Verlag, 1981), pp. 462-80.

We start with the passage most directly connected with our narrative. In the genealogy of 22.20-24, the birth of Rebekah is announced to Abraham, and the genealogy seems to be specially written to introduce Rebekah.[5] In most cases daughters are not mentioned in genealogies, but here she is the only one of the third generation to be named (v. 23), while her brother Laban, who plays an important role in the following chapters, is not mentioned. Why did Rebekah have to be identified? The answer is found in the narratives surrounding this passage.

In his chapter on readers' perspectives, which he illustrates with the Rebekah stories,[6] Meir Sternberg states that the reader, driven 'by an internal knowledge built into the reading process', expects at this point of the course of events, that is after the Aqedah, related in Gen. 22.1-19, the introduction of Isaac's future wife. This expectation is created by the analogy between Abraham's two sons.

> Ishmael's career shows three landmarks: late birth (16.16), mortal danger averted by a timely divine intervention (21.14-19), and marriage to a compatriot of his Egyptian mother (21.21). Isaac having likewise gone through the first two stages (21.1-8; 22.1-12), the third is now due by compositional logic.[7]

This reasoning seems to fit, although the announcement of Rebekah as Isaac's future bride in 22.20-24 is somewhat veiled. Not until ch. 24 is it clear that Rebekah is indeed the one chosen as Isaac's wife.

The link between 22.1-19 and Rebekah's birth (vv. 20-24) was already forged in the rabbinic literature, for instance in Genesis Rabbah:[8] 'When Abraham was still standing on Mount Moriah, trembling with fear from what he had just gone through, they came to tell him that the wife of his son was born'. Here the 'gap' in the biblical text opened by the genealogy is filled. Then, the crucial point in the dramatic development of the story is made: 'while Abraham was standing there, he was thinking

---

5. The link between Gen. 22.20-24 and Gen. 24 has been explicitly accentuated by traditional Jewish commentators. See Ibn Ezra's Commentary on the Pentateuch, Gen. 22.20: להזכיר יחס רבקה and Rashi's Commentary on the Pentateuch, Gen. 22.23: כל היחוסין הללו לא נכתבו אלא בשביל פסוק זה. See also Ramban, *Commentary on the Pentateuch*, Gen. 22.23.

6. M. Sternberg, 'Viewpoints and Interpretations', in *idem, The Poetics of Biblical Narrative*, pp. 129-152.

7. Sternberg, 'Viewpoints', p. 132.

8. *Gen. R. 57 Bereshit Rabba mit kritischen Apparat und Kommentar* (ed. J. Theodor and C. Albeck; Jerusalem: Wahrmann, 1965).

about what could have happened. If Isaac had died on Mount Moriah, he would have died childless'. Isaac, the only heir of the blessing, is also the only means of continuing the sacred line. He too needs an offspring, and Rebekah is to ensure the continuation of the blessing. Furthermore, immediately afterwards (ch. 23), Sarah's death is recorded. As Benno Jacob stresses, Rebekah is to be Sarah's substitute and successor. Before the first matriarch died, the second is already born.[9] Gen 24.7 finally makes this explicit.

Of the chapters following Genesis 24, two episodes are of particular significance for certain aspects of the marriage narrative. In 25.22-23 Rebekah goes and inquires of YHWH, and is answered by means of an oracle which informs her of the future of the twins in her womb. Already the rabbis had noticed that Rebekah is the only woman in the Bible of whom it is related that God spoke directly to her:[10] not the father, as in the case of Abraham (Gen 17.15-21; 18.1-15), but the mother is told of the destiny of her children, and in ch. 27 Rebekah's knowledge influences her actions directly when she deliberately favours her younger son Jacob above his brother Esau. She does not even shrink from deceiving an old and blind Isaac.

2. *The Textual Representation of the Events:*
The Structure of Genesis 24[11]

Genesis 24 is a clear and simple narrative having four main parts: an introduction (I), two middle parts that form the corpus (II and III), and a

---

9.   Jacob, *Das erste Buch der Tora*, p. 505.

10.   Midrash (on the psalms) *Shoher Tov* 9,7 (ed. S. Buber; repr. Jerusalem, 1966 [Wilna, 1891]), pp. 83-84.

11.   I follow Shlomit Rimmon-Kenan in the distinction she makes between the three components of a narrative: story, text and narration. Cf. S. Rimmon-Kenan, *Narrative Fiction: Contemporary Poetics* (London: Methuen, 1983). The narration component falls beyond the interest of this paper. Because the text is the only means by which the reader can acquire knowledge of the story, the text is always primary to the story. For this reason we will not treat story separately but immediately focus upon the composition of our narrative as a text. Rimmon-Kenan distinguishes within the text between 'time' and 'characterization'. 'Time' is defined as *the textual arrangement of the events in the story*, and 'characterization' is *the representation of the characters in the story*. Instead of the (in my opinion) too restrictive term 'time', we will use the more general term 'structure'. Characterization will be dealt with in the following paragraph.

conclusion (IV). Parts I and IV make up the frame of the narration in the form of an *inclusio*. The two parts of the *inclusio* form a chiasm. One element is Abraham's commissioning of the servant (IA) and the success of the mission in the marriage (IVA). The other element is the journey of the servant to (IB) and from (IVB) Aram Naharaim.

Genesis 24.1-67: A Schematic Representation of the Structure of the Narrative

    I. Verses 1-10. Commissioning and journey of the servant

        A. 1-9. Abraham gives his servant an order

            1. The title: introduction to the narrative (Abraham)

            2-4. Abraham gives his servant an order and makes him swear an oath. The order is the following:

                a. to find a wife for Isaac in Aram Naharaim

                b. to bring the woman to Canaan

            5. Objection and question of the servant

            6-8. Reply of Abraham to the objection and the question of the servant

            9. The servant swears the oath

        B. 10. The journey of the servant to Aram Naharaim

    II. Verses 11-27. The servant at the well, or: How do I find the fit woman? (first stage of the mission)

        A. 11. Arrival in the city of Nahor—the waterdrawers

        B. 12-14. The prayer of the servant to God (His aim: How will I meet a fit woman? His strategy: The servant imposes an omen upon God)

        C. 15-22. The meeting with Rebekah:

            a. 15-20. Rebekah passes the test, the omen is fulfilled—the first stage of the mission seems to be fulfilled

            b. 21. Reaction of the servant: Wonder about God's intervention

            c. 22. The servant gives gifts to Rebekah

        D. 23-27. The last doubt subdued—definitive confirmation that a fit woman has been found:

            a. 23. The decisive question: Is she indeed the fit woman?

            b. 24-25. The confirming answer: She is the fit woman

            c. 26-27. Prayer of thanks

    III. Verses 28-60. The servant in the family, or: How do I get the woman back to Canaan? (second stage of the mission)

        A. 28-32. Arrival in the house of Rebekah's family

        B. 33-49. The account of the servant to the family (His aim: To take Rebekah to Canaan. His strategy: The rhetoric of his report)

        C. 50-53. The family convinced:

            a. 50. The family is convinced—also the second stage of the mission seems to be fulfilled

            b. 52. The reaction of the servant: Thanks for God's involvement.

c. 53. The servant gives gifts to the family
D.   54-60. The last difficulty overcome—definitive confirmation that Rebekah will join him:
        a. 55-56. Retardation—the success of the journey in danger for an instant
        b. 57-58. The confirming answer of Rebekah herself: She will join him
        c. 59-60. Farewell blessing of Rebekah
IV.   Verses 61-67. The meeting between Rebekah and Isaac—the mission of the servant is fulfilled.
B.   61. The journey back
A.   62-67. The meeting between Rebekah and Isaac
    62-65. Isaac and Rebekah meet
    66. Account of the journey to Isaac
    67a-d. The marriage
    67e. Conclusion of the narrative (Sarah)

Verses 1 and 67e respectively make up a title and conclusion for the whole narrative, but also fulfil a function beyond the boundaries of the text. They confirm its position in the co-text by invoking two situations and two main figures from the foregoing narratives. Verse 1 refers to the wealth that Abraham has attained (Gen. 12.16; 20.14-16; 21.22-34; 23), and to his old age (17.17; 18.11; 21.5-7). Verse 67 reminds us of the recent death of Sarah (23.2).

Encompassed by the narrative frame (I and IV) is the actual kernel of the story: II and III. Here the action takes place, with the servant the main actor in both central parts, absent from the scene only in the last verse. One notices a striking parallelism between II and III, both in content and form. As to content, the two respective parts recount the two stages of the servant's mission. In part II he succeeds in *finding* a fit wife for Isaac, and in part III in *taking the woman home with him*. In both parts a strategy for success is also described. In II this consists of an omen which he himself prescribes to God; in III it lies in his presentation of the situation to Rebekah's family. In both situations the servant succeeds in shrewdly manipulating the objects of his address, God and the family.

The formal likeness between II and III is represented in the schema by A–D and a–c. Each item denotes a step in the unfolding of the plot. Note that the parallelism is quite rigid:

A: *Arrival in a new place.* In IIA the servant arrives at the well of Nahor's city; in IIIA he is received by Rebekah's family.

B: *Development of the strategy.* In IIB the omen; in IIIB the account of the journey given to the family.

C: *Apparent success of the mission.* In IIC he meets the girl who at first view fulfils all the requirements: exceptional hospitality and beauty; in IIIC the family appears convinced that the marriage should proceed. Development *inside* the two C parts is also parallel: in a. the servant's goal seems to be reached; in b. the servant's reaction to God's intervention is formulated, and in c. gifts are given out.

D: *An element of doubt and its resolution.* In IID the decisive question still has to be asked, that is, concerning the identity of the girl. Success depends on the answer (a slave-girl would be unfit). It is a positive answer: the girl is the niece of Abraham; in IIID the family has second thoughts about its decision, and want to retard the events, but Rebekah herself takes the final step: she will go with the servant. The two D-parts thus also show a parallel structure: a. consists in an element of doubt that functions as a retardation; in b. doubt is removed by means of a positive answer from Rebekah. Both c.-elements reach a poetic conclusion, first in the form of a prayer of thanks, formulated by the servant, and second in the solemn farewell blessing of Rebekah (I admit that the parallelism between these two c-parts is less obvious than between the other parts).

The foregoing analysis of the composition of our text reveals an elaborated parallelism between the different parts as the most striking characteristic which, together with *inclusio*, chiasm and the frame-narrative, creates a well-constructed literary composition, elevating the betrothal story into narrative art.

3. *Characterization in Genesis 24*

Characterization in narrative is built up by the use, along the text-continuum, of two kinds of indicators,[12] namely direct definition and indirect representation. The first sort are rare in our text. Here character is chiefly drawn indirectly. Of Rimmon-Kenan's four strategies of indirect character representation—action, speech, external appearance and environment—the first two are apparent in our text. Rebekah is

12. Rimmon-Kenan, *Narrative Fiction*, p. 59.

largely characterized by her action, and the servant by his speech. Isaac, by contrast, is inactive, also indicative of his character.

The role of the servant in the narrative should not be underemphasized. An extensive study of his character requires a separate paper;[13] to be noted here is the strategy concealed in his long report of the journey to Rebekah's family (vv. 34-49) and his cunning, even towards the deity (see how the prayer in v. 27 is distorted in v. 48). But here we want to focus on the characterization of Rebekah and Isaac and their relationship.

Rebekah

Even though the presentation of Rebekah in Genesis 24 is rather complex, it can hardly be called deeply psychological. In this regard the story does not differ from other Torah narratives. Detailed description of the inner life of the characters is not the interest of the authors of such narratives. They prefer, on the contrary, to display character through outer appearance, action and speech.

Direct Definition: The Ideal Marriage Candidate. There are two direct descriptions of Rebekah by the narrator. Both serve the same purpose, namely to indicate that Rebekah is a good, and even very desirable, marriage candidate for Isaac. The first description concerns the girl's descent: in v. 15. she is said to be a direct relative of Abraham. The explanatory note in v. 15 clearly refers back to 22.20-24, where the birth of Rebekah was announced. This revelation by the narrator is directed toward his audience; the servant remains unsure about the identity of his 'find'. The reader, however, informed by the preceding narratives, and especially by 22.20-24, understands at once the appearance of this girl as predestined. She has been prepared by God, announced to Abraham, and will now be provided as a wife for Isaac. The conception of Rebekah as a divine gift will be very important throughout the following narratives. We will return to this in the final section.

The second description is found in the following verse (16), as very beautiful and, important in the context, as a virgin (בתולה). The latter,

---

13. See L. Teugels, 'The Anonymous Matchmaker. An Enquiry into the Characterisation of the Servant of Abraham in Genesis 24', *JSOT* 65 (1995), pp. 13-23. An elaborate study of the characterization of the servant by means of the expressions used in the text to denote him, viz. העבד, האיש and אדון, was presented by P. Mandel, העבד האיש והאדון. רטוריקה של פרק בבראשית, in *Jerusalem Studies in Hebrew Literature* 10-11 (1987–88), pp. 613-27.

like the family background, is directed to the audience. The servant cannot have known it. These characteristics, with what the reader already knows about her descent, supply her with the minimum conditions required from a marriage candidate for Isaac.

Indirect Representation: Not Words but Deeds. Before considering Rebekah's actions, I want to draw attention to one more point in the text where, in line with the above descriptions, another trait of Rebekah as the ideal wife is depicted, not through direct definition but indirectly through action. In vv. 64-65, informed of his arrival, she makes her way to her future husband. Rebekah glides from her camel and covers herself with a veil. Both actions demonstrate the humility of a wife towards her husband. This action reveals a trait that fits the biblical image of a good wife.

I referred above to the complex characterization of Rebekah. This emerges in this chapter but is fully developed in the following narratives, and especially in ch. 27. I want to demonstrate that, besides being an ideal wife—and in this context we should add her exemplary hospitality towards human and beast—some of Rebekah's traits reveal the roots of future hidden and overt tensions between her and Isaac, culminating in her deception of him in ch. 27. Her decisiveness and purposeful behaviour deserve special mention here.

The characterization of Rebekah in Genesis 24, as has been said, is chiefly attained through description of her actions. She is a 'doer', one who acts rather than speaks. Rhetorically this trait is conveyed by the large number of action-verbs used of her—in particular the verbs 'to hurry' (מהר), and 'to run' (רוץ), but also descending, drawing water, giving to drink. The many actions bespeak an intention to represent Rebekah as an active person. The prescription of the omen by the servant in v. 14 underlines this idea, functioning as a sort of character test.

Rebekah's behaviour generally points in the same direction. In her decision to marry Isaac, she has to repeat the step once set by Abraham, to leave her family, her home town and her country. The link between the two events is clearly present in the four times repeated variation on Gen 12.1: 'Go out (לך לך) from your land and from your kindred and from your father's house', in vv. 4, 7, 38 and 40. Rebekah is to be ready to leave her family forever for a place and a man she does not know. Like Abraham (12.4, וילך), she takes this irreversible decision in

v. 57 with a simple and unconditional אֵלֵךְ[14]. Is Rebekah's decisiveness a confirmation to Abraham of the choice made? Is it a condition for being the new mother of the chosen? Such a condition could explain why the arrangement is made through an intermediary. Total, unconditional faith is expected of Rebekah, as it once was expected of Abraham, and of Sarah who came with him. Even the man she is going to marry remains unknown until they are inside the borders of Canaan. She is the אֵשֶׁת חַיִל of Prov. 31.10.

The exceptional behaviour of Rebekah and her parents emerges in vv. 57-58. Unusually for a biblical marriage (cf. Gen. 29 and Exod. 2),[15] not only is Rebekah asked for her approval, but she has the last, decisive, word. The importance of this is accentuated by an extra structural marker, namely, an anticipation in the first part of the story. In v. 5 (repeated in v. 8) the servant raises the following objection: 'Perhaps the woman will not be willing to go after me to this land'. Such an anticipated objection, that *the girl* might not want to follow him, is improbable in a society where arranged marriages were the rule. His remark can only be fully understood in relation to the question raised in v. 58.

A final aspect of the remarkable attitude of this unmarried girl in biblical narrative is that, when confronted with a total stranger at the well, she shows no sign of shyness or unsureness. In vv. 17-21 she gives drink both to him and his animals. In vv. 24-25 her response is again firm and decisive as she invites the unknown man to stay overnight in her parents' home.

But if Rebekah is a 'doer', she is certainly not a 'talker'. Her answers are limited to the necessary. She never initiates a conversation. In this she is the counterbalance of the servant, who hardly ever stops talking. But even he ceases speaking when Rebekah shows herself as an indefatigable whirl of action, and merely watches her in silence (v. 21). Rebekah's laconic speech is completely in line with her all-prevailing

---

14. The rabbinic elaboration of Rebekah's answer is significant in this context: 'And she said, I will go, of my own accord, even though you do not consent' (*Gen. R.* 60.12, see also Rashi on this verse).

15. The three stories are often considered as three variations on the so-called betrothal type-scene. On this subject see e.g. J.G. Williams, 'The Beautiful and the Barren: Conventions in Biblical Type-Scenes', *JSOT* 17 (1980), pp. 107-19, esp. p. 109 on the betrothal type-scene; R. Alter, *The Art of Biblical Narrative* (New York: Basic Books), pp. 47-62, esp. 51-57; C. Gilead, לִיד הַבְּאֵר בבראשית ובשמות פניישה, *Beit Mikra* 22 (1977), pp. 220-23.

action. An exemplary speech-act of Rebekah is found in v. 58, where the shortness of her answer 'אֵלֵךְ' demonstrates her decisiveness. She does not have to think things over; she decides and she acts. Similar brevity of speech occurs at vv. 18 and 24-25. The narrator's stress on her actions rather than words is imparted in v. 28, where, in contrast to the full report of the servant's words, Rebekah's own words to her family are rendered: 'And she told all this to the household of her mother'.

Isaac

Direct Definition: The Son of the Master. Throughout ch. 24, Isaac is named in three ways. Abraham, in his command to his servant in the first part of the narrative, calls him 'Isaac' and 'my son'. In the third part, he is called 'Isaac' by the narrator, and once 'my master' by the servant. In the central part, however, where the deal between the servant and the family is described, he is consistently referred to as 'the son of my/your master'. Hence, according to the narrator, the family apparently does not even know the name of the future husband of Rebekah. The anonymity of Isaac serves to underscore his general portrayal throughout the narrative.

Only once in the report of the servant is direct attention given to Isaac himself, namely in v. 36, where the reference to him serves precisely the strategy of the speech by describing 'the son of the master' as a rich man. Yet his wealth is explicitly linked to his inheritance, and so the only quality of the groom-to-be that is mentioned is really a quality of his father: Isaac himself is again less than a full person in his own right.

Indirect Indicators: The Absent Bridegroom. As pointed out earlier, Isaac in this chapter is characterized negatively by the absence of action and speech. But moreover he is largely absent from the story, an absence all the more significant since the subject of this narrative is his own marriage! By thus treating Isaac, the narrator portrays him markedly as an anti-hero. In the comparable scenes in Genesis 29 and Exodus 2, Jacob and Moses undertake the journey to find their wives. Here this possibility is not raised, although Isaac was already an adult and his father too old to travel. Instead, Isaac receives his wife from a servant.

Even the surrounding narratives provide scant material about Isaac. When he is mentioned at all, he is presented as a humble, weak and passive character. Exemplary in this regard are the Aqedah, where he is depicted not as a hero or martyr but as an object of his father's (and God's) will, and ch. 27, where, old and blind, he is deceived by his wife and younger son. Isaac is a largely silent victim.[16]

4. *The Problematic Portrayal of Isaac (and Rebekah) in the Genesis Narratives, and some Narrative Perspectives that Could Furnish an Answer*

The questions raised in this final part of the paper follow the characterization of Isaac and Rebekah in Genesis 24 as analysed above, but extend to Isaac, Rebekah, and their relationship in the entire Isaac–Rebekah narratives. The portrayal of Isaac must have historical or ideological reasons. These reasons, however, are hard to define.[17] It is even harder to decide whether there is a connection between the (quantitative) scarcity and the (qualitative) modesty of the biblical portrayal of Isaac.

A coherent tradition-historical explanation of the unequal division of material between the patriarchs was given by Martin Noth.[18] In his

16. The picture of a strong Rebekah versus a very weak Isaac should, however, not lead us to disregard all indications of a patriarchal viewpoint. In a recently published study of Mary Shields on 2 Kgs 4, I found a frame of interpretation that also fits the Gen. 24 narrative. Cf. M.E. Shields, 'Subverting a Man of God, Elevating a Woman: Role and Power Reversals in 2 Kings 4', *JSOT* 58 (1993), pp. 59-69, esp. pp. 66-69. Like the Shunammite in 2 Kgs 4, Rebekah, and not the patriarch Isaac, is the dominant character of the two, so that one can speak of a 'reversal of gender roles'. This dominance is accentuated by a textual indicator, viz. the fact that in the main part of the text Rebekah is named while Isaac is not. The last four verses of the narrative should, however, not be overlooked. Here the gender roles are in turn again 'subverted by the patriarchal perspective'. Verses 62-67 contain in a nutshell the main characteristics of a patriarchal relationship between man and wife: she puts on a veil and falls to the ground for him; he 'takes' her. The fact that Isaac's name is mentioned for the first time in v. 62 supports this idea. See also L. Teugels, 'A Matriarchal Cycle? The Portrayal of Isaac in Genesis in the Light of the Presentation of Rebekah', *Bijdragen* 56 (1996), pp. 61-72.

17. I should remark that in many critical commentaries on the book of Genesis, no serious attention is given to this problem. In most cases a mere establishment of the fact that there is a problem seems to suffice. If treated, mainly the quantitative viz. traditio-critical problem is concentrated upon, while the qualitative problem remains ignored.

18. M. Noth, *Überlieferungsgeschichte des Pentateuch* (Stuttgart: Kohlhammer, 1948), p. 112-27. A recent overview of the different opinions concerning the history of traditions of the Isaac narratives is presented in H. Schmid, *Die Gestalt des*

view, the Abraham and Isaac stories originally developed independently around local cultic places established in the name of the two forefathers at neighbouring localities in the south of Israel. In the growth of the national tradition, the older stories, establishing Jacob as the forefather of the twelve tribes, were supplemented by Isaac traditions, thereby identifying Isaac as Jacob's father. Later, a third generation was added by the Abraham narratives. During this process, the more 'modern' Abraham gained dominance over Isaac, whose stories atrophied. A good deal of the material now in the Abraham tradition once belonged to the Isaac tradition, for example the triple narrative of the 'endangered ancestress' (Gen. 12, 20, 26). Against many other scholars,[19] Noth defended the antiquity of the ch. 26 version, which, in his view, stands closest to the *Urform* of the story.

Whatever the historical value of such explanations, they do not explain why the remaining traditions about Isaac portray him as such an anti-hero. When one takes the strong characterization of Rebekah into consideration, the problem intensifies. If most of the Rebekah material passed away together with the Isaac traditions, then why did *her* image remain strong and influential by comparison with Sarah, Rachel and Leah? I want to contribute some narrative perspectives to an answer. These ignore the possible historical development of traditions, and consider Genesis 24 and its co-texts as they are found in their final form in the Masoretic text. This procedure is justifiable since the Isaac–Rebekah texts form a single narrative, not without some obstructions, but with a

Isaaks: Ihr Verhältnis zur Abraham und Jakobtradition (Erträge der Forschung, 274; Darmstadt: Wissenschaftliche Buchgesellschaft, 1991), p. 26-34. Schmid's study focuses on Gen. 26. He, however, also ignores the problem of the weak characterization of Isaac in comparison with that of Rebekah. The characterization of Isaac in Gen. 24 is in this study not referred to as being meaningful for the presentation of Isaac in general (on Gen. 24, see pp. 64-67).

19. Gunkel for example considers Gen. 26 as the latest version (See Gunkel, *Genesis*, p. 225). Wellhausen, on the other hand anticipated Noth in his judgment that Gen. 26 was the oldest form. S. Sandmel, 'The Haggada within Scripture', *JBL* 80 (1961), pp. 105-22 (esp. pp. 109-12), is convinced that the Gen. 12 narrative is the oldest one, and that Gen. 20 and Gen. 26 are narrative (haggadic) expansions and variations on the former story. Likewise, but for different reasons, E. Blum claims antiquity on the part of the Gen. 12 version. Both Gen. 20 and Gen. 26 presuppose knowledge of Gen. 12. Among the two other versions, Gen. 26 is the latest in his view. See E. Blum, *Die Komposition der Vätergeschichte* (WMANT, 57; Neukirchen–Vluyn: Neukirchener Verlag, 1984), pp. 301-311, 406-410.

continuous plot from the birth of Isaac, through the Aqedah, birth of
Rebekah, death of Sarah, marriage and the birth of Jacob and Esau, to
the blessing of Jacob in Genesis 27. A synchronic approach to the text
assumes that the text in its final form is, *on principle,* meaningful, since
the biblical redactors were authors in the full sense of the word, and not
mere compilers.

By human standards, a weak man and a strong woman are united in
the Isaac–Rebekah couple. What binds them to each other, is the line of
descent associated with the promise and the covenant.[20] It is significant
that the divine blessing on Abraham concerning his line in 22.17, and
the blessing of Rebekah by her family concerning her line, in 24.60, are
similar in both wording and content. Isaac, Abraham's descendant, is the
bearer of the divine covenant/blessing/promise, which, as derived from
the Isaac–Ishmael and Jacob–Esau conflict, could, at this stage of the
patriarchal history, only be carried by one person (see Gen. 17.18-19;
27.35-37). The significance of his birth, of his mere existence, is, following biblical literary standards, indicated by the exceptional circumstances surrounding it. It is important to note, however, that God's
promise to Abraham that he would bless his descendants (22.17) *is not
repeated to Isaac himself but to Rebekah* (24.60).[21] The presentation of
Isaac and Rebekah in the narratives as a whole is in accordance with
this.

Isaac has difficulties in carrying the blessing and passing it on to the
next generation. In Genesis 22, the blessing is endangered beyond his

20. See J. Scharbert, 'ברך', *TDOT*, II, pp. 306-307. I do not want to overlook
the difference between the three notions: blessing, promise and covenant. In the
context of this paper we will not dwell, however, on this theological difficulty. When
the patriarchal narratives are considered as a narrative continuum, it is clear that the
three ideas are united, and that one and the same line, that of the blessed
descendance, runs from Adam through Seth, Enosh...(see Gen. 5), Noah, Shem...
(Gen. 11.10-32), Abraham, Isaac, to Jacob. The different accentuation of the three
notions is probably due to the theology of the subsequent redactions. As for the final
redaction, no clear and substantial difference is noticeable.

21. For the last remark I am indebted to M.D. Turner. In an article named
'Rebekah: Ancestor of Faith', she develops the idea that the period between
Abraham and Jacob should be reconsidered from a new perspective. Not Isaac, but
Rebekah, is the dominant *ancestor* in this generation. Consequently, she pleads that
we lay aside the exclusive designation 'patriarchal narratives' and use the more
neutral term 'stories of the ancestors' instead. (See M.D. Turner, 'Rebekah Ancestor
of Faith', *Lexington Theological Quarterly* 20 (1985), pp. 42-50).

will (compare *Genesis Rabbah*: 'If Isaac would have died, he would have died without a descendant...'). In Genesis 27 the same blessing is almost passed on to the wrong son, this time, in principle, within Isaac's will. In short, as the bearer of the divine blessing, Isaac is presented as exceptionally valuable, but at the same time a dangerous 'vessel' for the blessing. It is, so to speak, not safe in his hands since he attracts bad fortune.

Rebekah is the divinely sent helper. Her role is to pass the blessing on to a fit bearer of the next generation. The 'divine hand' is noticeable at several crucial points in her life. When she is born (Gen. 22.20-24), Abraham is informed. In the betrothal story she is the divine answer to the prayer/omen of the servant (24.15). When pregnant she asks and receives an answer from God in which she—not Isaac—is informed about the identity of the new blessed son, the youngest one, Jacob (25.22-23).

On an abstract, 'semiotic' level, then, Isaac is the passive bearer of the blessing, a mere precious vessel. Rebekah, on the other hand, although herself not the bearer of the promise, is the active helper, the one in charge of passing it on to the right heir. On a more concrete textual level, however, several tensions between the so-called 'divine' and a 'human' levels come to the fore. From the 'divine' perspective, Isaac is the bearer of the promise, and both promise and bearer are more than once endangered. Rebekah is the providential intermediary who will pass the promise on. At this level it is the tension between promise and the threat to it that dominates. From the 'human' perspective, on the contrary, Isaac appears as weak and helpless, a plaything of his father and his wife, one who cannot even acquire his own bride and is fooled by wife and son. Similarly, Rebekah appears as an unnatural mother and wife. She is decisive, uncompromising, deceives her husband and favours one son over the other. Here is a tension: what is fit and predestined from a 'divine' point of view does not appear so from a 'human' point of view (cp. Gen. 22 and 27).

This tension recurs throughout the Torah, even throughout the Tanach (e.g. Job). Where it appears critical exegesis should not reconcile or explain away. It is to be discovered and brought to the fore, and as such reveals a fundamental issue of biblical theology and anthropology that needs to be addressed.

JSOT 64 (1994) 33-55

BEASTLY SPEECH:
INTERTEXTUALITY, BALAAM'S ASS AND THE GARDEN OF EDEN*

G. Savran

'A healing tongue is a tree of life' (Proverbs 15.4)

Introduction

Speech, according to the writer of Proverbs, is the handmaiden of wisdom, and its proper use is crucial in determining one's lot in life. Beyond its obvious importance in wisdom literature, the pre-eminence of spoken language is conspicuous throughout biblical literature. The exclusive position of speech within the complementary worlds of prophecy and prayer emphasizes the verbal quality of the relationship between God and humans, each calling the other to responsiveness and responsibility. Biblical narrative as well is characterized by a high proportion of direct address relative to third person narration, deployed through a wide range of narrative strategies. To choose but one example, subtle variations in quoted and repeated speech often serve as crucial indicators of hidden intentions, whether on the part of the narrator or on the part of the characters themselves.[1] Insofar as direct discourse is so central to

---

*   I would like to thank Dr Marc Bregman and Professor Edward Greenstein for their helpful comments on an earlier draft of this essay.

1.   Representative analyses of direct speech (and quotation) in biblical narrative can be seen in M. Sternberg, *The Poetics of Biblical Narrative* (Bloomington, IN: Indiana University Press, 1985), pp. 131-52, 286-308; R. Alter, *The Art of Biblical Narrative* (New York: Basic Books, 1981), pp. 63-87; G. Savran, *Telling and Retelling* (Bloomington, IN: Indiana University Press, 1988), pp. 77-108; A. Berlin, *Poetics and Interpretation of Biblical Narrative* (Sheffield: Almond Press, 1983), pp. 64-72. See also the articles by Alter and Sternberg in J.P. Rosenblatt and J.C. Sitterson (eds.), *Not in Heaven: Coherence and Complexity in Biblical Narrative*

the definition of human identity in biblical narrative, it is not surprising that speech is rarely attributed to non-humans. In only two cases are animals endowed with the capacity to express themselves articulately,[2] and here too the impact of their speech is central to the understanding of these texts. While a great deal has been written about the words of the serpent in Gen. 3.1-5,[3] relatively little has been said about the significance of the speech of Balaam's ass in Num. 22.22-35,[4] and even less on the possibility of a connection between the two narratives.

The episode describing the interaction between Balaam and his ass

(Bloomington, IN: Indiana University Press, 1991), pp. 12-57.

While Martin Buber's notion of the 'spokenness' (*Gesprochenheit*) of the Bible refers to biblical poetics in general, it nonetheless owes a great deal to the prominence of direct speech. See M. Buber, 'Biblical Humanism', *On the Bible: 18 Studies* (New York: Schocken Books, 1968), pp. 214-16, as well as the discussion by M. Fishbane, in *The Garments of Torah* (Bloomington, IN: Indiana University Press, 1989), pp. 81-90.

2.   While metaphoric personifications of nature in poetry (Ps. 19.1; Job 38.7, 35) or in parable (Judg. 9.8) may also include the ability to speak, such discourse is not in direct dialogue with humans, as in the examples of animal speech we will discuss.

3.   On the speech of the serpent in the garden story, cf. T. Boomershine, 'The Structure of Narrative Rhetoric in Genesis 2–3', *Semeia* 18 (1980), pp. 113-29; U. Cassuto, *A Commentary on the Book of Genesis* (Jerusalem: Magnes Press, 1961), pp. 138-47; F.M. Landy, *Paradoxes of Paradise* (Sheffield: Almond Press, 1983), pp. 241-44; J. Rosenberg, 'The Garden Story Forwards and Backwards', *Prooftexts* 1 (1981), pp. 1-27; L. Alonso-Schökel, 'Sapiential and Covenant Themes in Genesis 2–3', in J.L. Crenshaw (ed.), *Studies in Ancient Israelite Wisdom* (New York: Ktav, 1976), pp. 468-80; T. Walsh, 'Genesis 2.4b–3.24—A Synchronic Approach', *JBL* 96 (1977), pp. 161-77; C. Westermann, *Genesis 1–11* (Minneapolis: Augsburg, 1984), pp. 239-40; H.C. White, 'Direct and Third Person Discourse in the Narrative of the "Fall"', *Semeia* 18 (1980), pp. 91-106.

4.   Recent discussions of the literary aspects of the Balaam narrative include: Alter, *Biblical Narrative*, pp. 104-107; G.W. Coats, 'The Way of Obedience', *Semeia* 24 (1982): 53-79; J. Licht, *Storytelling in the Bible* (Jerusalem: Magnes Press, 1978), pp. 69-64, M. Margoliot, 'The Connection of the Balaam Narrative with the Pentateuch', *World Congress of Jewish Studies* 6 (1973), I, pp. 279-90; D.T. Olson, *The Death of the Old and the Birth of the New* (Chico, CA: Scholars Press, 1985), pp. 153-64; A. Rofé, *Sefer Bil'am* (Jerusalem: Simor, 1982); J.D. Safren, 'Abraham and Balaam', *VT* 28 (1988), pp. 105-13. A fuller bibliography can be found in M.S. Moore, *The Balaam Traditions: Their Character and Development* (Atlanta: Scholars Press, 1990), pp. 124-36, with special attention to the role of the seer in the ancient Near East and to the Deir 'Alla texts.

itself is characterized by a tension between repetition and transformation.
Three times in 22.22-27 Balaam's ass turns aside to avoid an angel in
her path, upsets her master and suffers a beating. The climactic interchange in 22.28-35 breaks the above pattern in accordance with a well
established folktale pattern: a series of repeated experiences, described in
similar (if not identical) language, culminates in a final encounter that
departs from the formal aspects of the preceding, and brings the narrative to a climax.[5] Suddenly the ass is changed from the passive recipient
of punishment to the articulate defender of her own actions, and as her
mouth is opened in speech (22.28-30), Balaam's eyes are opened to a
different perception of his reality.

As I have argued elsewhere,[6] this vignette plays a pivotal role in interpreting Balaam's story. Within the confines of Num. 22.2-38, Balaam's
encounter with the angel (מלאך) functions as a counterpoint to Balaam's
interactions with Balak's messengers (מלאכים) in 22.2-21.[7] In the context
of the larger story in Numbers 22–24, the episode foreshadows Balaam's
encounters with Balak in Numbers 23–24, and serves as an integrating
element in the entire Balaam narrative. As with Balaam and his ass,
Balak leads Balaam to a number of different places (although the one
being led is really in control). Sight is of crucial importance here: the ass
sees the angel before her, whereas Balaam perceives it only in 22.31.
Correspondingly, Balaam is directed to locations from which he can see
Israel and thus curse her,[8] but he himself achieves insight only in 24.1.[9]

---

5. The repetitive pattern of X + 1 is found in the ancient Near East (Gilgamesh
Epic 11.140-47, 148-54, 210-29; Keret text, *CTA* 14.III.106-108, IV.205-209) as
well as in the Bible. See, for example, the account of Samson and Delilah in Judg.
16.6-20, or Elijah and the emissaries of King Ahaziah in 2 Kgs 1. Cf. Y. Zakovitch,
'Al Shelosha V'Al Arba'a (Jerusalem: Magnes Press, 1979), as well as his treatment
of Judg. 16.6-20 in *Hayei Shimshon* (Jerusalem: Magnes Press, 1982), pp. 171ff.
More elaborate uses of the pattern can be seen in Gen. 1 (3+3+1—cf. Cassuto,
Genesis, pp. 17ff.) and in the plague cycle of Exod. 7–11 (3+3+3+1—cf.
M. Greenberg, *Understanding Exodus* (New York: Behrman House, 1969),
pp. 172-77).

6. Cf. G. Savran, 'The Structure of the Balaam Narrative' (forthcoming).

7. Note that Balaam's consultations with God in the first part of the chapter take
place at night, at Balaam's initiative. This is given an ironic twist in 22.22-35, where
God instigates the encounter with the angel in the daytime, yet the seer himself is
unable to sense this divine presence.

8. While the offering of sacrifices seems to be an integral part of both the
sorcerer's and the diviner's rituals (see Moore, *Balaam Traditions*, pp. 104-106;
J. Milgrom, *Numbers* [Philadelphia: Jewish Publication Society, 1990], pp. 471-73),

Balak's accusations of bad faith (23.11, 24.10) mirror the ass's charge against Balaam in 22.28; the ass protests to Balaam for having beaten her three times, and Balak accuses Balaam of having duped him three times.[10] As the ass is elevated from a senseless beast to a model of obedience, so Balaam is transformed from a mercenary sorcerer into an exemplary prophet.

But our central concern here is a broader Pentateuchal context, in which a number of significant parallels between Numbers 22–24 and Genesis 2–3 reveal a reworking of the notions of blessing and curse as seen in the story of the Garden of Eden. The fact that Numbers 22 and Genesis 3 are the only narratives in the entire Bible in which an animal communicates in human speech invites a closer look at the intertextual relationship between the two stories. In the broadest sense, the expression 'intertextuality' implies a general recognition that 'every text is constrained by the literary system of which it is a part, and that every text is ultimately dialogical in that it cannot but record the traces of its contentions and doubling of earlier discourses'.[11] But the term also has a more limited significance which will inform our discussion, namely an examination of the interaction between the specific text which is the object of study, and one or more additional texts (the intertext).[12] In biblical studies this interrelationship is generally measured according to the canons of source criticism, where establishing the prior existence of one text over another is essential to the larger aims of interpretation. (In

animal sacrifice itself is a clear expression of human domination of the animal world. In this sense there may be an indirect connection between the reversal of Balaam's superiority over the she-ass and the failure of Balaq's sacrifices to affect the fate of Israel.

9.   Cf. Alter, *Biblical Narrative*, pp. 105-106; Moore, *Balaam Traditions*, pp. 102-103; Rofé, *Sefer Bil'am*, pp. 30-34, and below.

10.   Moore, *Balaam Traditions*, pp. 102-103, suggests a further reversal: 'Balaam beats his she-ass using a "rod" (מקל) as a riding crop, not as a source of power', pointing to the magical connotations of the rod in Exod. 4.2-4, 20; Num. 17.23; Hos. 4.12; and possibly Ezek. 20.37 (pp. 52-53).

11.   D. Boyarin, *Intertextuality and the Reading of Midrash* (Bloomington, IN: Indiana University Press, 1990), p. 14.

12.   See the discussions of intertextuality in J. Culler, *The Pursuit of Signs* (Ithaca, NY: Cornell University Press, 1981), pp. 100-107; L. Jenny, 'The Strategy of Form', in T. Todorov (ed.), *French Literary Theory Today* (Cambridge: Cambridge University Press, 1982), pp. 34-63; M. Riffaterre, 'Intertextual Representation: On Mimesis as Interpretive Discourse', *Critical Inquiry* 11 (1984), pp. 141-62.

our case this might mean a discussion of the J (or JE) writer, or of his relationship to the P source).[13] While more recent discussions of inner-biblical exegesis are somewhat less concerned with the extraction of individual sources from the redacted text, there is still a marked prefer-ence for determining earlier and later texts as developmental markers for the history of the religion of Israel.[14]

Intertextuality, on the other hand, focuses on the interpretative pro-cess itself, preferring a synchronic approach to the reading of texts over the traditional diachronic model. A recent essay on 'Intertextuality and Ontology' explains this distinction in the following way:

> Intertextual analysis is distinguished from source criticism both by this stress on interpretation rather than on the establishment of particular facts, and by its rejection of a unilinear causality (the concept of 'influence') in favor of an account of the work performed upon intertextual material and its functional integration in the latter text.[15]

Accordingly, our discussion of Numbers 22–24 and Genesis 2–3 will emphasize the synchronicity of their relationship. This is due in part to the difficulty of determining the vector of influence in biblical texts,[16] but more importantly, it is a response to the need for a more flexible interpretative framework to deal with the multi-leveled texture of biblical narrative.

Both the ass and the snake speak in a surprisingly natural manner, without the formulaic speech patterns common to personifications of

13. E.g. Rofé, *Sefer Bil'am*, pp. 7-9, 53-58; J.T. Greene, *Balaam and his Interpreters* (Atlanta: Scholars Press, 1992), pp. 35-68.

14. M. Fishbane's volume on *Biblical Interpretation in Ancient Israel* (Oxford: Oxford University Press, 1985) addresses the relationship of traditio and traditium as reflections of the dialectic of revelation and tradition in the biblical text (see pp. 1-19). But his primary purpose is to examine this tension within the framework of the history of exegesis; cf. the critique by L. Eslinger, 'Inner-Biblical Exegesis and Inner-Biblical Allusion: The Question of Category', *VT* 42 (1992), pp. 47-58. A more interactive model of textual relationship is offered by T.B. Dozeman, 'Inner-Biblical Interpretation of YHWH's Gracious and Compassionate Character', *JBL* 108 (1989), pp. 207-33.

15. J. Frow, 'Intertextuality and Ontology', in M. Worton and J. Still (eds.), *Intertextuality: Theories and Practices* (Manchester: Manchester University Press, 1990), p. 46. Cf. Boyarin, *Intertextuality and the Reading of Midrash*, p. 135 n. 2, who uses the terms synchronic and diachronic to describe this difference.

16. Eslinger, 'Inner-Biblical Exegesis', pp. 51-53.

nature in the Bible.[17] Neither creature offers any introductory comment to explain its verbal ability, and this talent is accepted unquestioningly by the human counterparts in the story. Indeed, the ease with which human and animal enter into dialogue contrasts sharply with the extraordinary nature of the interchange. In the garden story, the serpent and the woman engage in a dialogue of interpretation about the correct meaning of the divine prohibition in Gen. 2.16-17, as if this were a normal topic of discussion between them. In Numbers 22, Balaam responds to the she-ass's opening words ('What have I done to you to make you beat me three times?') by cursing her and threatening her with death, much as he might speak to a rebellious servant. When the ass tries to provide some perspective to assuage her master's anger ('Aren't I your trusty she-ass? Would I do something like that to you?'), Balaam's mono-syllabic response seems to indicate that he is persuaded by her reasoning. In both texts, the dialogue takes place between a lone individual and the animal, which by itself might suggest that the person was simply 'hearing things'. But the narrator backs up the claim of animal speech with his most authoritative source: In Num. 22.31-33 the angel verifies the ass's perceptions; and in Gen. 3.14 God himself curses the serpent. Stylistically, the irruption of animal speech into the human world is treated in similar fashion, yet the content of the speeches is contrasted in a number of significant ways.

Both the ass and the snake use interrogatory statements to persuade the listener, but their questions have different rhetorical intent. The snake opens his words with a deliberate misquotation of the divine command in Gen. 2.16-17, which serves to confuse the woman and set the stage for the snake's argument in 3.4-5. His question cannot be answered by a single word, but requires some explanation—hence the woman's lengthy

17. Compare the speech of the trees in Jotham's parable, Judg. 9.15, and the moralistic comments of the cedars of Lebanon in Isa. 14.8. Outside the Bible, we find dialogue between animals (and trees) in Mesopotamian literature almost exclusively in fables. In these texts animals and trees communicate only with one another, never with humans. See 'The Ox and the Horse', 'The Fable of the Willow', 'The Date and the Tamarisk', 'The Fable of the Fox', in W.G. Lambert (ed.), *Babylonian Wisdom Literature* (Oxford: Oxford University Press, 1960), pp. 150ff.; and the story of the serpent and the lion in the epic of Etana (*ANET*, pp. 114-18). On the other hand there is dialogue between animals and humans in Egyptian tales such as 'The Doomed Prince', in M. Lichtheim (ed.), *Ancient Egyptian Literature* (2 vols.; Berkeley: University of California Press, 1976), II, pp. 156-59, and 'The Tale of the Shipwrecked Sailor' (*ibid.*, I, pp. 211-15).

response in 3.3.[18] The deployment of the question at the beginning of the snake's dialogue with the woman serves as a point of entrance into discussion. By contrast the ass's speech is straightforward and honest, aimed at clarifying Balaam's confusion rather than complicating it further. Her first question in Num. 22.28 is a partial protest against Balaam's brutality, and her second in 22.30 is entirely rhetorical in nature. In contrast to the confused reply of the woman of Genesis 3, Balaam's response is a clear 'No', despite his inability to comprehend what is going on.

Of great importance is the question of the source of the animals' verbal abilities. The snake speaks of its own accord, yet the text offers no explanation for this other than the snake's exceptional cleverness. In a worldview in which words are charged with creative power, this capability may point to a source of power outside of God, whether it be a whittled down representation of those forces which oppose God in creation,[19] or an allegorical representation of the independence of the human mind in confrontation with God.[20] The very fact that the snake has the capacity for articulate speech, together with the subversive use to which it has been put, challenges the hierarchical order of the universe as it has been created.[21]

---

18. See the discussion of deceptive quotations in Savran, *Telling and Retelling*, pp. 63-64; P. Trible, *God and the Rhetoric of Sexuality* (Philadelphia: Fortress Press, 1978), p. 109; J. Rosenberg, 'Kinship vs. Kingship: Political Allegory in the Bible' (PhD dissertation, University of California at Santa Cruz, 1978), pp. 115-16.

19. H. Gunkel, *Genesis* (Göttingen: Vandenhoeck & Ruprecht, 1917), p. 15; B.S. Childs, *Myth and Reality in the Old Testament* (London: SCM Press, 1960), pp. 48-50; J.A. Soggin, 'The Fall of Man in the Third Chapter of Genesis', in *Old Testament and Oriental Studies* (Rome: Pontifical Biblical Institute, 1975), pp. 94-100; J.L. McKenzie, 'The Literary Characteristics of Gen. 2–3', *TS* 15 (1954), pp. 563-64. Cf. Pss. 74.12-17; 89.9-13; Isa. 51.9-10; Job 7.12; 9.13; 26.7-14; 38.8-11.

20. I.e. the entire dialogue with the woman takes place intrapsychically, and the wish to eat from the tree springs from the woman's own desires. Cf. M. Fishbane, *Text and Texture* (New York: Schocken Books, 1979), pp. 22-23; Cassuto, *Genesis*, pp. 139-43, and the discussion in J. Rosenberg, *King and Kin* (Bloomington, IN: Indiana University Press, 1986), pp. 29-30. A. Kariv, *The Seven Pillars of the Bible* [Hebrew] (Tel Aviv: Am Oved, 1968), pp. 50-51, suggests that the speech of Balaam's ass is likewise the product of his own imagination, reflecting the seer's internal dilemma about going to curse Israel.

21. 'By permitting the transgressive thought to originate in the neutral arena of the animal world by means of a singular instance of speech by an animal, the source

The ass also has independent powers of judgment, but her motives are not so dark as those of the snake. In her case the gift of speech is divinely endowed; we are told unambiguously that 'The Lord opened the mouth of the ass', and only then 'And she said to Balaam' (Num. 22.28). The God of the Balaam story controls prophetic human speech (at least regarding Israel), and animal speech as well results only from divine intervention. The theological world of Balaam is much less murky than that of the Garden of Eden; as the extent of the ass's free will is limited, so the prophet's freedom of speech is restricted as well.

In addition to the phenomenon of speech, there are a number of interesting similarities in the role played by each animal within the narrative. Both animals lead people astray, the snake figuratively and the ass literally. But while the snake's action results in the imposition of mortality, Balaam's ass saves the life of her master. As noted above, the motives of the snake are not stated explicitly, but its ambiguous status and contrary advice present the serpent as an alternative to the divinely-controlled universe described in Genesis 2. The she-ass, on the other hand, acts out of her concern for Balaam, even though her actions cause her to receive a beating from her master.

In both texts the animals exhibit a deeper understanding of the relationship between the human and the divine than do their human counterparts, and they reveal their knowledge in the course of 'educating' the figures involved. The snake asks an imprecise question with the intent of deceiving the woman. As a result of his efforts human mortality is decreed, and angels with a fiery sword are set in place to prevent access to the garden and the tree of life (Gen. 3.24). By contrast the ass asks two straightforward questions (Num. 22.28, 30) with no deception intended, and acts to save its master from an angel with a sword who stands in its path (22.32ff.).[22]

The interconnections that we have traced between the speech of the

of evil is rendered totally ambiguous' (White, 'Direct and Third Person Discourse', p. 97).

22. Additionally, the angels of Gen. 3 are stationed there to prevent a return to the garden, while Balaam's angel tries to prevent Balaam's departure.

The phrase הכרובים והחרב המתהפכת is unique to Gen. 3.24. The expression in Numbers 22—וחרבו שלופה בידו—occurs twice elsewhere: in Josh. 5.13-14 it describes the angelic figure who is the leader of the hosts of Israel, and in 1 Chron. 21.16 it refers to the angel sent to destroy Jerusalem. In Joshua and Numbers the angel speaks, but with different intentions: Joshua's angel is supportive and encouraging, while Balaam's angel actually threatens his life.

snake and the words of Balaam's ass point to a larger set of correspond-
ences, or contrasts, between the narratives in which they are embedded.
All these elements taken together—the nature of animal speech, their
roles in relation to the humans in the story, and the threat of the angel
with the sword—suggest that the Balaam story be read in complement
with the story of the Garden of Eden. The garden story establishes,
through a series of curses, an interlocking chain of desire and domination that sets man, woman and the natural world at odds with one
another. By contrast, the Balaam account describes the frustration of
Balak's desire to curse and to dominate Israel, reflecting a harmonious
relationship between Israel and God.

Blessing and Curse

Among the most significant themes deployed in the narratives is that of
curse and blessing. In the garden story, the perfected universe described
in Genesis 2 is undone by the snake's efforts in the subsequent chapter,
and the dissolution of this harmony is concretized in the curses of Gen.
3.14-19. Enmity is 'established' between the human and the animal
world, between humanity and nature, and between people as well. The
final stage in this process of cursing is expulsion from the sacred center,
exile from a place of stability and rootedness to wandering and vulnerability. The Balaam story moves in the opposite direction: after the
Exodus from Egypt Israel is still wandering, but is moving towards a
permanent location. Israel is vulnerable to attack from Balak as well as
from other peoples whose land passes through. As Balaam is saved from
death at the hands of the angel by the actions of the she-ass, so he in
turn protects Israel from curse and destruction at the hands of Balak.
But beyond the sense of divine protection that is brought out in Numbers
20 and 21, Balaam offers blessing to Israel. Whereas the narrative sections of chs. 22–24 speak primarily of protection from danger, Balaam's
oracles hold out the promise of positive elements such as progeny,
protection from sin, rootedness, and military success.[23]

---

23. H.C. Brichto, *The Problem of 'Curse' in the Hebrew Bible* (Philadelphia:
Scholars Press, 1963), pp. 86-87, 99-100, argues that the use of ארור in Gen. 3.17
and Num. 22.6, 12 carries with it a sense of being under a spell, and suggests that
ברך in 22.12 means 'immune to a spell'. Contra C.W. Mitchell, *The Meaning of
BRK 'To Bless' in the Old Testament* (Atlanta: Scholars Press, 1987), pp. 63-64,
91-93. Moore (*Balaam Traditions*, p. 98) suggests that נרש in 22.6 contains the

One implementation of this theme of blessing can be seen in the extended simile in Balaam's third oracle, where Israel's good fortune is likened to a tree planted in a garden (Num. 24.5-7a).

How fair are your tents, O Jacob,	Your dwellings, O Israel.
Like palm-groves that stretch out,	Like gardens beside a river,
Like aloes planted by the Lord,	Like cedars beside the water.
Their boughs[24] drip with moisture,	Their roots have abundant water.[25]

The language used here shares in the complex of imagery found in Jer. 17.7-8, Ezek. 47.12, and Psalms 1 and 92. Whereas this symbolism does not originate with Balaam, or even within Israel,[26] the present context provides some interesting contrasts with less positive images in Genesis 2–3. The trees in Genesis are a source of life and knowledge, yet they are forbidden to humankind. Rather than offering protection and rootedness, they are the cause of strife between God and his creatures. Ironically, they generate not blessing but irretrievable losses. The tree of knowledge leads to the forfeiture of innocence and the dissolution of trust, while the tree of life brings with it only exile and mortality. Balaam's use of arborescent imagery owes something to the well-watered garden of Gen. 2.8-10, planted by God (כאהלים נטע ה') and set beside flowing rivers (כגנת עלי נהר). But whereas the trees in the garden were unapproachable, now Israel itself is likened to them, towering over the waters, firmly rooted in the primal deep.[27] Israel returns to a state of

---

notion of exorcism as well as physical departure. We note the use of the same term in Gen. 3.24 to describe the expulsion of the man and the woman from the garden.

24. Ibn Ezra derives this from דליות 'branches' in Jer. 11.16.

25. Cf. S. Morag, 'Layers of Antiquity—Some Linguistic Observations on the Oracles of Balaam', *Tarbiz* 50 (1981), pp. 14-16.

26. Compare 'The Instruction of Amen-em-Opet', ch. 4:

(But) the truly silent man holds himself apart.
He is like a tree growing in a *garden*
It flourishes and doubles its yield;
It (stands) before its lord.
Its fruit is sweet; its shade is pleasant;
And its end is reached in the garden... (*ANET*, p. 422).

See further T. Frymer-Kensky, 'The Planting of Man', in J.H. Marks and R.M. Good (eds.), *Love and Death in the Ancient Near East: Essays in Honor of Marvin H. Pope* (Guilford, CN: Four Quarters Publishing, 1987), pp. 129-36.

27. On the meaning of the pairs גנת // נחלים and אהלים // ארזים, see Morag, 'Layers of Antiquity', pp. 14-16. On מים רבים, see H.G. May, 'Some Cosmic Connotations of "Many Waters"', *JBL* 74 (1955), pp. 9-21.

harmony with nature, a harmony initially undone by the curses of Gen.
3.14-19.

As the tree changes from a symbol of blessing to a source of travail in
Genesis 2–3, so the image of dust undergoes a similar transformation. At
the beginning of the narrative, dust is associated with creation, for it is
the material from which the man has been formed (Gen. 2.6). But this
positive sense is overshadowed by the unfavorable connotations of dust
in the curses of Gen. 3.14-19. Dust is to be the serpent's lot, reflecting
the change in his place in the cosmos. Beyond this symbolic meaning of
abasement is its signification of death in the final curse in Gen. 3.19—
'Until you return to the dust from which you were taken, for dust you
are, and to dust you shall return'.[28] Man's reversion to his original dust
foreshadows God's undoing of his creation, a process of 'anti-blessing'
which reaches its climax in the flood story.

In the Balaam narrative this process of transformation is reversed. At
the beginning of the story, the vast numbers of the Israelites are seen by
Balak as a threat—not unlike the response of the Pharaoh in Exod.
1.8.[29] Balak uses language that recalls the image of the locust plague in
Exod. 10.5—They cover up the 'entire' earth, and threaten to devour
everything in their path. The comparison of Israel with dust in
Num. 23.10 inverts this negative imagery, moving from the dust of death
in Gen. 3.19 to a metaphor of exceptional birth and regeneration: מי
מנה עפר יעקב—'Who can count the dust of Jacob?' While the use of
dust as a symbol of the proliferation of Israel is not unique to Balaam, its
presence in Num. 23.10 can be read as a response to the curses of the
garden. Dust is not only the raw material of the creation of humans, but
it is the symbol of Israel's proliferation as well.[30]

---

28. On dust and humility/humiliation, see Gen. 18.27; 1 Sam. 2.8. The
association of dust with death occurs frequently; cf. Pss. 22.16, 30; 30.10; 104.29;
Job 7.21; 17.16; 21.26; 34.15, as well as the linkage of dust and mourning in Josh.
7.6; Ezek. 27.30; Job 2.12. See also D.H. Hillers, 'Dust: Some Aspects of Old
Testament Imagery', in Marks and Good (eds.), *Love and Death in the Ancient Near
East*, pp. 105-109.

29. Compare further the distress of the Moabites—ויקץ מואב מפני בני ישראל
(Num. 22.3) with that of the Egyptians in Exod. 1.12—ויקצו מפני בני ישראל.

30. Dust is associated with the blessing to the Patriarchs in Gen. 13.16; 28.14 (cf.
2 Chron. 1.9), and is used as an image of abundance in Ps. 78.27 (manna) and Job
27.16 (silver); cf. Hillers, 'Dust', pp. 106-107. Compare the use of celestial imagery
in Gen. 15.5, 22.17, 26.4; Exod. 32.13; Deut. 1.10, 10.22, 28.62; Neh. 9.23; 1
Chron. 27.23; cf. C. Westermann, *The Promises to the Fathers* (Philadelphia:

The significance of cursing in both texts is brought out by the use of the root ארר. In Genesis, the complete breakdown of the blessed state of the garden is manifested in the curses that are pronounced in Gen. 3.14-19, two of which are introduced by ארור. In 3.14 the status and stature of the snake are reduced, and eternal enmity is placed between the snake and humankind. In 3.17 the ground is cursed with diminished fertility, in contrast with the natural productivity of the garden. Where the man's task was previously designated as mere 'tending and keeping', he must now labor strenuously to bring forth food. The ultimate judgment is the extension of this curse to include mortality in 3.19; the once-fertile soil has been exchanged for the dust of the grave.

In Numbers 22–24, Balak wishes to have Israel cursed (ארור) by means of human intervention, though it is not entirely clear what type of curse he is seeking.[31] The blessings described, on the other hand, fall into familiar categories: numerical superiority (23.9-10), fertility and longevity (the well planted tree in 24.6-7), and divine protection reflected in kingship and military success over its enemies (23.24; 24.7-9). To Balak's dismay, Balaam not only rejects the idea of cursing Israel, but he substitutes blessing in its place. As opposed to the depiction in Genesis of a God who curses what he had first blessed, Balaam's God will not change his mind: לא איש אל ויכזב/ובן אדם ויתנחם (23.19—'God is not man to be capricious/Or mortal to change his mind'), and the blessing initially bestowed upon Israel will not be changed.

This profound reversal of blessing and curse can be seen in the paired use of ברך/ארר in two complementary verses. In 22.6 Balak appeals to

---

Fortress Press, 1980), pp. 148-55. See further the discussion of רבע = 'dust cloud' in S. Gevirtz, *Patterns in the Early Poetry of Israel* (Chicago: University of Chicago Press, 1963), pp. 63-65. On מנה as 'fate', see Morag, 'Layers of Antiquity', pp. 8-9.

31. Cf. Brichto, *The Problem of Curse*, p. 100, who suggests the casting of a spell to incapacitate Israel; Moore, *Balaam Traditions*, pp. 98, 104-109, posits Balaam in the role of a Mesopotamian *asipu*-exorcist, but also sees support for the earlier theory that Balaam's behavior fit that of the baru priest, a type of seer. See S. Daiches, 'Balaam, a Babylonian *baru*', in *Assyriologische und archaeologische Studien Hermann von Hilpricht gewidmet* (Leipzig: J.C. Hinrichs, 1909), pp. 60-70; Mitchell, *The Meaning of BRK*, pp. 90-93; R.R. Wilson, *Prophecy and Society* (Philadelphia: Fortress Press, 1980), pp. 90-98; 132-33. Milgrom (*Numbers*, pp. 471-73) argues that the entire story revolves around the tension between these two roles: 'Balaq hires Balaam as a sorceror, but Balaam…can act only as a diviner'.

Note also the personal element ('for me') in Balak's request to curse Israel— ארה לי (22.6; 23.7); קבה לי (22.11,17; cf. 23.13, 27).

Balaam with an expression designed to flatter:

כי ידעתי את אשר תברך מברך ואת אשר תאר יואר

> For I know that whomever you bless remains blessed, and whomever
> you curse is cursed

This phrase is 'reformulated' by Balaam in the oracle in 24.9—מברכיך
ברוך וארריך ארור ('Blessed be those who bless you, and cursed be
those who curse you'), but the emphasis has been changed from subject
to object.[32] In Balak's formulation, Balaam's blessing or curse was
primary, but in 24.9, the fate of the 'blesser' depends entirely upon his
treatment of Israel. Not only is Balaam's autonomy limited, as we have
seen before, but now the object itself—Israel—determines the fate of the
one who would presume to control it. Ironically, Balak's words in 22.6
set in motion a process that results in the blessing of the very people
whom he sought to curse.[33]

As mentioned earlier, the image of an angel armed with a sword is
common to both stories. In Gen. 3.24 angels are placed at the entrance
to the garden to obstruct human passage, thereby preventing the
attainment of eternal life. In this way they are guardians of immortality,
but guarantors of death to humankind. The angel in Numbers 22 is sent
by God to frustrate Balaam's journey to Balak, and is clearly menacing
to both Balaam and to the she-ass, but he represents a temporary danger
rather than a permanent deterrent. Despite his hostile intention as described in 22.33 ('I would have killed you'), his role turns out to be primarily cautionary, warning Balaam not to deviate from the message he
will receive (22.35). This provisional threat to Balaam's life is turned to a
more positive purpose: to prevent harm from being done to Israel in the
form of curse, and ultimately to guarantee life to Israel in the form of
blessing.[34]

Vision and Understanding

In both narratives a distinction is made between ordinary human sight,
which is limited to surface perceptions, and 'enhanced' vision, which

---

32. Compare Gen. 12.3; 27.29; cf. Mitchell, *The Meaning of BRK*, pp. 29-36.
33. Cf. Savran, *Telling and Retelling*, pp. 91-92.
34. On the different functions of angels in the prophetic stories, see Rofé, *Sefer Bil'am*, pp. 57-58; *Sippurei Hanev'im* (Jerusalem: Magnes Press, 1983), pp. 150-54.

reveals nuances of meaning otherwise unavailable to the beholder. The source of this extraordinary vision is divine in both texts, but it is attained by different means, and its achievement leads to opposite results. In the garden story, the recurrent use of the root ידע brings out this tension between what is apparent to the eyes and what is truly known. The fruit of the tree of knowledge (עץ הדעת) is forbidden (2.17) yet visually desirable (Gen. 3.6; cf. 2.9), constituting a temptation before which the woman cannot stand. Enhanced vision (= knowledge) is obtained only by violating what is commanded, by trespassing upon the realm of the divine. Partaking of the fruit opens their eyes, but the understanding they receive is of an unexpected nature: 'Then the eyes of both of them were opened and they knew (וידעו) that they were naked'. The anticipation of knowing everything (טוב ורע as all knowledge) is reversed by their sudden recognition of human limitation (טוב ורע as the faculty of distinction, moral and otherwise).[35] Their eyes have been opened at their own initiative—just as the serpent has spoken by its own volition—and they must bear the consequences of their actions. The very process of obtaining knowledge has brought curse upon humanity and the natural world. The final mention of דעת in Gen. 3.22 makes it clear that their acquisition of knowledge is the reason for the expulsion from the garden.

For Balaam, this discontinuity between what is immediately apparent and what is actually present is developed in two distinct but interrelated ways. Within Numbers 22, the discrepancy between the visual abilities of Balaam and his ass is heightened by the repeated mention of what she sees (22.23, 25, 27—ותרא האתון) over against Balaam's reputation as a seer (22.9, 20; cf. 22.6). Only after his eyes are opened ('And the Lord opened the eyes of Balaam and he saw...' 22.31) does Balaam discern the angel and realize something of the limits of his own vision (22.34—כי לא ידעתי). Like the man and the woman in the garden there is an immediate change in his perception, but instead of moving toward sin, Balaam bows down in obedience and acknowledges his error.

Despite this realization, Balaam remains ignorant of the real nature of his mission, and the narrator makes use of his lack of awareness to

35. This is a deliberate play on the ambiguity of the phrase 'the knowledge of good and evil', which can be taken generally to refer to all knowledge, or more specifically to the capacity of discriminating judgment. See the fuller discussion of the phrase in J.A. Bailey, 'Initiation and the Primal Woman', *JBL* 89 (1970), pp. 144-48; H.N. Wallace, *The Eden Narrative* (Atlanta: Scholars Press, 1985), pp. 116-28; Westermann, *Genesis 1–11*, pp. 241-45.

refine the connection between seeing and the pronouncing of blessing or curse. As Balak looks upon Israel in 22.2 (וירא בלק) and wishes them cursed, so he claims that it is essential for Balaam to see Israel in order to curse them.[36] In his initial dealings with Balak, it is not clear if Balaam actually intends to curse Israel, but even before the first oracle the text hints at the reversal of the king's expectations. Elsewhere Balaam speaks about what God will tell him,[37] but in 23.3 he states that he will reveal to Balak whatever God will show him (23.3—דבר מה יראני).

The linkage of seeing and understanding is further unfolded in Balaam's oracles. In the first (23.7-10), there is an implicit relationship between his *seeing* Israel (אראנו...אשורנו) and his perception of its unique situation (23.9—הן עם לבדד ישכן). In the second (23.18-24), God sees no wrongdoing in Israel (23.21—ראה, הביט),[38] and its state of blessedness therefore remains unaffected. Just prior to his third oracle Balaam finally grasps the connection between God's blessing of Israel and his own words: וירא בלעם כי טוב בעיני ה' לברך את ישראל (24.1). The usual introductory formula for each oracle, וישא משלו—'He took up his oracle' (23.7, 18; 24.3,15) is replaced by a statement about Balaam's perception in 24.2—וישא בלעם את עיניו—'He lifted up *his eyes*'. Balaam now speaks with an enhanced quality of vision which is simultaneous with his looking directly at Israel in 24.2 (וירא את ישראל). This newly found understanding spills over into the oracle itself, as reflected in the use of three distinctive epithets which describe Balaam's exceptional powers of vision: נפל וגלוי עינים, אשר מחזה שדי יחזה, שתם העין.[39]

---

36. W. Zimmerli (*Ezekiel* [Philadelphia: Fortress Press, 1979], I, pp. 182-83) suggests that a connection between visual contact and cursing can also be seen in the phrase שים פניך in Ezek. 4.3; 6.2; 13.17, etc., and both he and Milgrom (*Numbers*, pp. 193-94) relate this to the notion of the evil eye. Additionally, the descriptions of the three sites to which Balaam is taken are all associated with seeing; cf. Moore, *Balaam Traditions*, p. 101 n. 19.

37. Num. 22.28; 23.12, 26; 24.13; cf. 22.20, 35.

38. So KJV, following *Targum Onqelos*; alternatively, NJPS translates 'No harm is in sight for Jacob/No woe in view for Israel'. For עמל and און as 'woe' rather than sin, cf. Ps. 90.10.

39. The ancient versions understood this variously as he whose eye is open or 'perfect' (following the sense of the LXX, *Targum Onqelos*, and the Peshiṭta), or as the one whose eye is closed (following the Vulgate), where the physical absence of an eye in Balaam's visage would contrast with the quality of his 'inner vision'. W.F. Albright, following Wellhausen, sought etymological support for the former by suggesting the reading *shettam ha'ayin*, or *shettama 'eino* ('The Oracles of

The last of these harks back to Balaam's earlier revelation of the angel in
22.31—וַיְגַל ה' אֶת עֵינֵי בִלְעָם ('And the Lord opened Balaam's eyes'):
As Balaam's eyes were opened to the immediate vision of the angel
standing in his path, now he is privy to a more profound revelation.
Whereas the actual blessing of Israel in the first two oracles was restricted
to the last line of each poem (23.10, 24), the third oracle consists entirely
of promises for Israel's success and wellbeing.

The final stage in the process of Balaam's enlightenment can be seen
in his fourth oracle. In 24.15-16 the three epithets of 24.3-4 are repeated,
but with a significant addition: וְיֹדֵעַ דַּעַת עֶלְיוֹן ('Who obtains knowledge
from the Most High', 24.16). Here Balaam describes himself as having
achieved the highest level of perception, in which his clairvoyant eye is
completely attuned to divine intentions. Reflecting the shift in perspective
from seeing to knowing, this last oracle speaks of a type of sensitivity
that surpasses his immediate vision—אֶרְאֶנּוּ וְלֹא עַתָּה/אֲשׁוּרֶנּוּ וְלֹא קָרוֹב
(24.17—'What I see for them is not yet/What I behold will not be
soon')—describing Israel's blessing as something which transcends the
present moment. In sharp contrast to the garden story, knowledge in the
Balaam narrative leads first to Balaam's awareness that he is unable to
curse Israel, then to his perception of the interrelationship between
Israel's situation and God's approval of it, and finally to the blessing of
Israel itself.[40]

Disobedience and Divination

Genesis 2–3 and Numbers 22–24 each contain two interrelated contests
of wills—one between the human and the divine, and the other between
the human and the animal. In both cases the protagonist is granted the
freedom to act as she or he wishes, but there is a great distance between
the woman's disregard for higher authority in the face of temptation
(eating from the tree), and Balaam's deliberate consultations with God
despite his desire for the reward offered by Balak. The woman briefly

---

Balaam', *JBL* 63 [1944], p. 216). Morag, ('Layers of Antiquity', pp. 12-13) offers
evidence for the latter reading by taking שָׁתַם to mean 'dug out' (*m. 'Abod. Zar.* 5.3,
t. Abod. Zar. 7.13, 14, 15; cf. also *b. Sanh.* 105a). In either case Balaam seems to be
describing the extraordinary nature of his vision.

40. The use of the phrase 'to do good or evil' in Num. 24.13 resonates with the
similar expression in Gen. 2–3, but the immediate referents in Balaam are blessing
and curse.

expresses hesitation about defying the command against eating from the tree (Gen. 3.3), but she is quickly persuaded that the reward will outstrip the punishment. The man, for his part, shows no compunction whatso-ever about taking the fruit offered to him by the woman (3.6). Obedience to the voice of the snake entails the rejection of divine authority.

In marked contrast to this are Balaam's continual protestations that he cannot go against the command of the Lord (22.13, 18, 38; 23.12, 26; 24.13), as well as his firm stance in the face of Balak's enticements of silver and gold. Noteworthy in this regard is Balaam's ultimate objection in 24.13:

לא אוכל לעבור את פי ה' <u>לעשות טובה או רעה מלבי</u>

> I could not do anything *good or bad of my own accord*, contrary to the Lord's command.

The man and the woman eat willingly of the tree of good and evil, while Balaam rejects the possibility of making an autonomous decision when it conflicts with a direct command from God. Unlike the garden story, Balaam's defiance of authority takes place primarily on the human level, as he disobeys Balak's order to curse Israel. When Balak challenges him with the phrase מה עשית לי (23.11), it recalls God's accusation of the woman in Gen. 3.13—מה זאת עשית, as God confronts the woman with her deed.[41] In both texts the expression carries with it a sense of finality, of an action taken which can never be undone. The woman's response in Gen. 3.13 is to point the finger at the snake, denying her own respon-sibility just as the man tried to acquit himself by blaming her. Balaam, on the other hand, answers in words that are consistent with what he has said before—'I will speak only what the Lord has placed in my mouth' (23.12; cf. 22.18, 38; 23.26; 24.13).

In the light of all these interconnections, it cannot go unremarked that the root נחש occurs in both Genesis 3 and Num. 23.23; 24.1. As the snake is crucial to the garden story, so the theme of the superiority of a direct divine–human relationship to the techniques of divination is central to the Balaam narrative. While the נחש of Genesis and the נחש of Balaam

---

41. The phrase has two primary connotations: When the verb used is in the first person, the speaker protests innocence, like the words of the ass to Balaam (cf. 1 Sam. 17.29; 20.1, 32; 28.18; 29.8; Mic. 6.3). In the second person it is a statement of confrontation, an accusation in the form of a rhetorical question, as in Gen. 3.12 and Num. 23.11 (cf. Gen. 4.10; 12.18; 20.9; 26.10; 29.25; Jon. 1.10).

are clearly not identical,[42] the occurrence of the root in both texts is more than fortuitous, and functions as something of a key to this intertextual reading of the Balaam narrative. If this were the only point of contact between the two texts it would be little more than gratuitous coincidence. But given the scarcity of the talking animal motif, and the common concern with the issues of blessing/curse and life/death, the reader's search for the intertext leads naturally to the garden story, and to a consideration of the root נחש as a 'connective' between the text and the intertext.

Among the different types of connectives, or 'ungrammaticalities', which alert the reader to intertextual activity, Michael Riffaterre's understanding of syllepsis is of particular interest here:

> ...syllepsis consists in the understanding of the same word in two different ways at once, as contextual meaning and as intertextual meaning. The contextual meaning is that demanded by the word's grammatical collocations, by the word's reference to other words in the text. The intertextual meaning is another meaning the word may possibly have, one of its dictionary meanings and/or one actualized within an intertext. In either case, this intertextual meaning is incompatible with the context and pointless within the text, but it still operates as a second reference—this one to

---

42. There are various indications that ancient Near Eastern magical traditions may lie behind the image of the serpent of Gen. 3. Note the use of snake omens in Mesopotamia (R.M. Whiting, 'Six Snake Omens in New Babylonian Script', *JCS* 36 (1984), pp. 206-10), and see the comments of W. Robertson Smith, 'On the Forms of Divination and Magic Enumerated in Deut. XVIII. 10, 11', *Journal of Philology* 14 (1885), pp. 113-28. (My thanks to Avigdor Hurowitz for this reference). Most noteworthy in this regard is the copper snake of Num. 21.4-9, dubbed the נחשתן in 2 Kgs 18.4. But beyond this, little textual evidence has been offered to support a philological connection between נחש 'serpent' and נחש 'divination'. The primary exponent of this view was T.C. Vriezen, whose views are discussed by Childs, *Myth and Reality*, pp. 46ff. and by Westermann, *Genesis 1–11*, pp. 237-38. While its proximity to the Balaam story is tempting, the copper snake seems to have more to do with sympathetic healing than with divination. Cf. K.R. Joines, 'The Bronze Serpent in the Israelite Cult', *JBL* 87 (1968), pp. 245-56; M. Haran, *Encyclopaedia Biblica*, IV, cols. 826-27. The suggestion of a connection with Canaanite fertility cults is more widely accepted; cf. F. Hvidberg, 'The Canaanite Background of Genesis I–III', *VT* 10 (1960), pp. 285-94; Soggin, 'The Fall of Man', pp. 94ff. See also the comments of K.R. Joines, 'The Serpent in Genesis 3', *ZAW* 87 (1975), pp. 1-11.

the intertext. The second reference serves either as a model for reading
significance into the text...or as an index to the significance straddling
two texts...[43]

Thus, while נחש in Genesis 3 can only mean 'snake', and in Numbers
22–24 it can only mean 'divination', the presence of this particular
syllepsis in both texts highlights the intertextual connection and points
toward a deeper relationship beyond the philological issue. What do
divination as represented by Balaam and 'serpent speech' as spoken by
the נחש have in common?

I suggest that the homophone נחש can be seen to reflect contrasting
aspects of the relationship between the human world and God. As
divination constitutes an indirect approach to understanding the will of
the divine, so the counsel of the snake in Genesis 3 bespeaks a desire to
control the divine by human means. The transition of the man and the
woman from obedient creatures to rebellious individuals results from the
subversive efforts of the serpent. Prior to its appearance there are no
indications of a human urge for autonomy and control, but the snake
provides the means to encourage human desire, resulting in sin and
banishment.

In Balaam, the situation is reversed. The ass is the exemplar of obedience and submission to divine authority, while Balaam himself is initially
reluctant to accept the dictates of God. Only by means of his encounter
with the ass is he brought to an awareness of sin. That episode, coupled
with Balaam's understanding of the nature of Israel's blessedness (24.1-
2), results in a submissiveness to, and a unity of purpose with, the divine.
Balaam's confrontation with the ass brings him to reject divination as a
path to knowledge and as a means to control the future.

Instead of addressing the question of broader human knowledge, the
Balaam narrative condemns only a certain modality of understanding—
divination. The text does not go so far as to deny the efficacy of
divination, since it is acceptable in certain forms elsewhere in the Bible.[44]

43. M. Riffaterre, 'Syllepsis', *Critical Inquiry* 6 (1980), pp. 637-38; cf. *idem*,
'Compulsory Reader Response: The Intertextual Drive', in M. Worton and J. Still
(eds.), *Intertextuality: Theories and Practices* (Manchester: Manchester University
Press, 1990), pp. 56-78. This is one manifestation of Riffaterre's notion of the 'dual
sign' (*Semiotics of Poetry* [Bloomington, IN: Indiana University Press, 1984],
pp. 81ff.), a concept that has been used productively by Boyarin, *Intertextuality and
the Reading of Midrash*, pp. 57-79.

44. On divination in Israel, cf. B.O. Long, 'The Effect of Divination upon

Rather, the central issue is whether or not such techniques can affect a future that has been dictated by God. Whatever the possible philological connection between 'divination' and 'serpent', the narrative association is clear: the serpent urges the woman to try to control her own future by 'knowing' all things, advocating human self-sufficiency over dependence upon the divine.

Balaam's quest for knowledge in the form of divination is nowhere near as far-reaching as the drama in the garden, but it too reflects an attempt to control the outcome of human affairs by means of a quasi-magical influencing of the divine. The issue is no longer the right of humans to 'know', but the proper application of that knowledge by means of divination, when it conflicts with the intentions of the divine. The garden story describes a situation in which knowledge empowers the individual to defy God, and in which humans must be limited by curse and by expulsion from the garden. The Balaam narrative affirms the power of a different kind of knowledge, exemplified by Balaam's realization in Num. 24.1-2. This type of understanding goes hand in hand with blessing for Israel.[45]

Conclusion

The echoes of Genesis 3 which we have traced in the Balaam narrative reveal a constellation of images and themes unique to these texts, but we can also discern larger patterns of interpretation found elsewhere in the Pentateuch. If we read the two texts diachronically, within the narrative outline of the Pentateuch, then the basic outlines of this design involve the reapplication of cosmic or universal notions of origins to Israel's

Israelite Literature', *JBL* 92 (1973), pp. 489-97; Wilson, *Prophecy and Society in Ancient Israel*, pp. 150, 161; Moore, *Balaam Traditions*, pp. 46-65, 98-104; J. Lust, 'On Wizards and Prophets', in D. Lys, *et al.* (eds.), *Studies on Prophecy* (VTSup, 26; Leiden: Brill, 1974), pp. 139-42.

45. We can see similar principles at work in other Pentateuchal transformations of 'precedents' from Gen. 1–11. For example, God's decision to destroy all humankind with a flood (כי נחמתי...וינחם—Gen. 6.6, 8) and his subsequent promise not to repeat such a punishment (Gen. 8.21) are reflected in God's threat to destroy all the Israelites in the wake of the Golden Calf and Moses' successful intercession in Exod. 32 (הנחם...וינחם—32.12-14). These are the only two uses of the verb הנחם with respect to God in the Pentateuch (but cf. Num. 23.19). As in the case of Balaam, the perspective changes from the universal (the fate of humankind) to the national (the fate of Israel).

national self-understanding.[46] Thus, for example, the peril to which the paradigmatic man and woman in Genesis 2–3 are exposed is transformed into a threat to the entire community of Israelites. But when we read the texts synchronically, this difference becomes not one of reinterpretation or influence, but a representation of the profound tension between universalism and the particular fate of Israel. The universal curses of Gen. 3.14-19 are countered by Balaam's specific blessings toward Israel. This recalls, to a certain extent, the tension between the primordial history of Genesis 1–11 and the Abraham narratives: all humankind is cursed and dispersed, but Abraham is the sole recipient of the promises of Gen. 12.1-3. According to Balaam, others are to be blessed (and cursed) in accordance with their relationship with Israel, and we again note the similarity between Num. 24.9, מברכיך ברוך וארריך ארור ('Blessed are they who bless you, accursed are they who curse you'), and Gen. 12.3, ואברכה מברכיך ומקללך אאר ('I will bless those who bless you and curse him that curses you').

Similarly, the allusion to Exod. 10.4-5, 15 in Num. 22.5, 11 recalls the comparable distinction between Israel and the Egyptians in the plague narrative. While the Egyptians suffer through the plagues, the Israelites remain unaffected. In Numbers 22 Israel itself embodies a threat to Balak—like the locusts in Egypt they 'cover the entire land', and threaten his hegemony. As opposed to the fate of all humankind described in Gen. 3.14-19, Israel's fate is described in a blessing that accentuates its separateness: 'There is a people that dwells apart, not reckoned among the nations' (23.9). Herein lies the strange irony of the Balaam narrative: the presence of a foreign seer recalls the inclusiveness of the early chapters of Genesis,[47] but that same seer blesses Israel with a promise that emphasizes the particular at the expense of the universal—

46. Fishbane, *Biblical Interpretation in Ancient Israel*, p. 426, describes such a rhetorical strategy in terms of a 'nationalization of content'; cf. also pp. 354-57; 372-73. The stress on the national character of Israel's blessing is also reflected in Balaam's predictions of Israel's military success in Num. 24.17-19 (cf. also 23.24; 24.8-9).

47. Cf. Olson, *The Death of the Old*, p. 163; G.B. Gray, *A Critical and Exegetical Commentary on the Book of Numbers* (Edinburgh: T. & T. Clark, 1903), p. 317, and the more extravagant claims of anti-exclusiveness made by R. Mackensen, 'The Present Literary Form of the Balaam Story', in W.G. Shellabear (ed.), *The Macdonald Presentation Volume* (Princeton, NJ: Princeton University Press, 1933), pp. 276-91.

Israel's exodus from Egypt, its distinctiveness in relation to the world, and the defeat of its enemies.

Another facet of this shift is revealed in the handling of the question of evil. In contrast to Genesis 3, where the source of evil is ambiguously located between the cosmic and the intrapsychic, the cause of Israel's misfortune in Numbers 22–24 is fixed entirely in the person of a foreign king. As Balaam's ass is unmistakably good, so Balak is unequivocally bad. This reworking of the source of evil recalls the recrudescence of elements of the creation story in Exodus: Pharaoh is placed in the role of the 'snake' as the cause of Israel's troubles; the Israelites' remarkable growth as a people (Exod. 1.7) is expressed in the same language of pro-creation as Gen. 1.28, 9.1; the splitting of the sea is less a cosmic battle with the forces of chaos than a struggle with an enemy of Israel.[48]

In one sense the intertextual interplay of the Balaam narrative tends to 'clear up' certain overt ambiguities in the garden story by projecting the concerns of that text into a new setting: evil is associated with a foreign ruler, and not with a divinely created animal; the animal speaks only by divine initiative, and has no special powers of its own; the achievement of knowledge/understanding is entirely positive, and leads to blessing instead of curse. In complementary fashion, the Balaam story awakens the reader to other, latent ambiguities in Genesis 2–3, such as the matter of whether or not God is entitled to change his mind.[49] But as much as

48. Cf. Ezek. 29.1-12 on the identification between Pharaoh and the Nile. On the application of creation language to the Exodus, see F.M. Cross, *Canaanite Myth and Israelite Epic* (Cambridge, MA: Harvard University Press, 1973), pp. 134-44; B. Anderson, *Creation versus Chaos* (New York: Association Press, 1967), pp. 37-38; J.S. Ackerman, 'The Literary Context of the Moses Birth Story', in K.R.R. Gros Louis *et al.* (ed.), *Literary Interpretations of Biblical Narratives* (Nashville: Abingdon Press, 1974), I, pp. 74-79; B.S. Childs, *The Book of Exodus* (Philadelphia: Westminster Press, 1974), p. 2.

49. In the garden story, the question is implicit in the serpent's challenge to the woman's statement about the mortal consequences of eating from the tree. He is correct in that they do not die immediately, though the imposition of human mortality does result from this. The issue has to do with God's original intentions, and the significance of a divine change of heart—a theme that carries through Gen. 1–11. Cf. G. von Rad, *Genesis* (Philadelphia: Westminster Press, 1972), pp. 95-96; R.W.L. Mowberly, 'Did the Serpent Get it Right?', *JTS* 34 (1988), pp. 9-19. In Balaam the issue is presented more explicitly: In Num. 22 God clearly changes his position and allows Balaam to accept Balak's offer, yet in 23.19 he is described as not being fickle like human beings. While the immediate referent of the latter text is God's intention to bless Israel, the larger question remains, both in Num. 22 and

the Balaam narrative 'interprets' the Garden story, it also serves as material to be interpreted by other texts which are part of the Balaam traditions in the Bible. Indeed, a consideration of the relationship between the pious Balaam of Numbers 22–24 and the hostile character of Numbers 31 and elsewhere might lead us to identify Balaam with the devious serpent rather than with the obedient ass.[50]

throughout the wilderness narratives. Cf. further the discussion of 1 Sam. 15.29 in D.M. Gunn, *The Fate of King Saul* (Sheffield: Almond Press, 1980), pp. 72-73, and R. Polzin, *Samuel and the Deuteronomist* (San Francisco: Harper & Row, 1989), pp. 140-44.

50. Despite Balaam's acceptance of divine authority in Num. 22–24, he is portrayed in a negative light elsewhere in the Bible—cf. Rofé, *Sefer Bil'am*, pp. 45-49; Liver, 'The Figure of Balaam', pp. 97-100; Milgrom, *Numbers*, pp. 469-71; Moore, *Balaam Traditions*, pp. 109, 116-22; G.W. Coats, 'Balaam: Saint or Sinner', *BR* 18 (1973), pp. 21-29.

Targum Pseudo-Jonathan describes Balaam quite literally as a 'snake in the grass', translating וילך שפי in 23.3 as ואזל נחון כטויא 'and he went, bending like a snake'. While this is probably based upon נחש // שפיפון in Gen. 49.17, the use of the verb שוף in Gen. 3.15 suggests an implicit comparison between Balaam and the serpent of Gen. 3. For fuller treatments of Balaam in Rabbinic literature, see E.E. Urbach, 'Homilies of the Rabbis on the Prophets of the Nations and the Balaam Stories', *Tarbiẓ* 25 (1955–56), pp. 272-89; J.R. Baskin, *Pharaoh's Counselors* (Chico, CA: Scholars Press, 1983), pp. 75-113; G. Vermes, *Scripture in History and Tradition* (Leiden: Brill, 1961), pp. 127-77. Most recently, J.T. Greene has discussed reflections of the Balaam story in Qumran and in Samaritan literature in *Balaam and his Interpreters*, pp. 83-135.

JSOT 64 (1994) 57-81

THE DEATH OF ISAAC:
STRUCTURALIST ANALYSIS OF GENESIS 22

Seth Daniel Kunin

This paper is titled the 'Death of Isaac' in order to highlight one of the primary problems developed in Genesis 22. Whether Isaac is sacrificed is a question depending not only on the interpretation of this specific text, but also on the relation of the structural elements found in Genesis 22 to those characteristic of Genesis in its entirety, and of biblical mythology as a whole. This problem will be addressed on three related levels. First, the structural oppositions within the specific myth will be described and analysed; secondly, these oppositions will be examined in the context of biblical structure as a whole; thirdly, the oppositions will be analysed in regard to their diachronic development in midrashic texts. The development of three related oppositions is charted through their diachronic development both within the text and in time. These oppositions are: Israel and the nations; inside and outside; and divine and human. Each one of these oppositions is included within a specific mytheme: Ishmael, Sacrifice, and Rebirth.[1]

We are concerned not only with the specific structural elements found in these texts, but also with the broader question of the structural

---

1. Mytheme is the term used for 'a basic structural building block'. Mythemes usually have as their centre a relation between two types of structural elements, e.g., 'Ishmael' stands for the horizontal relation between Isaac and Ishmael. These relationships, and the mytheme as a whole can have three types of qualitative valence: positive (+), neutral (=) or negative (–). The valence may be different depending on how the mytheme is used in relation to other mythemes. The three valences are not distinct types. They are points on a continuum. Thus, a mytheme can be considered as valenced +/= (i.e. as generally positive but leaning towards neutral).

continuity of Rabbinic and later texts with biblical or Israelite mythology.[2] Do these texts transform structural elements, and thus reflect changes in the cultural foundations of the community, or are the transformations primarily at the level of emphasis or mediation, indicating areas of cultural continuity?

No attempt is made in this paper to present an analysis of either structuralist theory or methodology. It is necessary, however, to examine certain implications of the approach, and to highlight the differences with the traditional application of structuralist theory. The approach applied in this paper finds its roots in the work of Lévi-Strauss and Leach.[3]

There are, however, several key areas that distinguish the approach taken here. One primary area of difference lies in the understanding of diachrony both on the intertextual level or the extratextual level, that is both narrative development *within* a specific text, and diachronic development *between* texts. Traditional structuralism was primarily concerned with the paradigmatic level of the text. It sought to identify the key structural elements of the text and to categorize them in overall sets of oppositions based on formal characteristics rather than meaning. This categorization was not interested in the placement or order of the elements in the text. Terence Turner has developed a modification of this approach which adds into the analysis the syntagmatic, or combinatory level.[4] He shows that within a mythological text there is often a progressive development of structure, whereby different episodes of the myth will play off structures against each other in order to develop the structural logic.[5]

---

2.   The definition of mythology used here is a synthesis of the work of Roy Wagner and structuralist theory. Mythology is defined as: the logical framework, or metaphor, through which society views, or creates, its past, present and future—it is a creator of ontology. A myth then is a text, historical or otherwise, which has been shaped by (and shapes) this logical framework.

3.   See for example: E. Leach and D. Aycock, *Structuralist Interpretations of Biblical Myth* (Cambridge: Cambridge University Press, 1983); C. Lévi-Strauss, *Structural Anthropology* (New York: Basic Books, 1963); *idem*, *The Raw and the Cooked* (New York: Harper & Row, 1969).

4.   See, for example, T. Turner, 'Animal Symbolism, Totemism and the Structure of Myth', in G. Urton (ed.), *Animal Myths and Metaphors in South America* (Salt Lake City: University of Utah Press, 1985), pp. 49-106; and *idem*, 'Narrative Structure and Mythopoesis: A Critique and Reformulation of Structuralist Concepts of Myth, Narrative and Poetics', *Arethusa* 10.1 (1977), pp. 103-63.

5.   This is found in the biblical text, especially in regard to Gen. 17. Gen. 17, 'the

A second level of diachronic analysis is also useful in discovering the structural logic of a system: the analysis of the developments of structure over time. Analysis of diachronically later material (e.g. rabbinic and midrashic texts) may reveal aspects or transformations of the cultural grammar as yet not uncovered in the synchronic level of analysis. The ways in which the myths are transformed can illuminate earlier structural patterns. This methodology is especially useful where there is a long history of textual development.

Aside from this deviation from traditional structuralism, it may be useful to highlight certain implications of structuralist analysis that have a bearing on the arguments developed in this paper. Structuralism suggests that myths from a single culture will deal with a limited set of culturally specific oppositions, which relate to resolving the same structural problem. Owing to the nature of myth, which functions to cloud and obscure crisis, individual myths will reveal these structures with varying degrees of clarity. Thus, a myth may include only a few elements of the structure, elements may be doubled or repeated in other ways, mediators may be placed in between elements, or structural elements may be inverted. This has two implications. First, studying one myth on its own will only reveal a small/incomplete picture of the structural grammar; a complete picture requires the analysis of a large body of myth. Secondly, other myths within the same cultural context can be used to help explain ambiguous or missing elements in the myth being analysed.

The problem of inversion is also explained by this understanding of myth. One way of obscuring structure is to reverse or invert the structural elements. The structural relationship, however, is retained, because it is through the relationships of the elements that the myth works on the problem. In order to maintain the relationship all elements of the myth must be equally inverted. Thus the general principle is: where a mythological text is in inverted form, all elements will be inverted or transformed in the same way. This theorem can be expressed in the

covenant of circumcision', is the centre of a clear pattern of parallel texts in which structural elements are progressively developed. The texts presented prior to Gen. 17 are recapitulated and structurally developed—emphasizing the structural elements—after Gen. 17. Thus structural analysis must work on the two related levels, the synchronic presentation of structural elements, and the diachronic development of structure.

following equation A:B :: $A^{(-)}:B^{(-)}$.[6] Research on Genesis suggests that this theorem can be extended to all transformations, leading to the equation: $A:B :: A^{(t)}:B^{(t)}$.[7]

A few final points need to be made in regard to the biblical text. Although it is clear that Genesis is composed from texts coming from at least four strata, it should not be thought that the text will have four independent structural logics. If the strata were composed within the same culture then they should all have identical structure. Differences in time or place of composition, or ideological perspectives, should not effect the structural logic. Even if the structures of the strata were originally different, or if external material was imported into the text, it is likely that the text before us would still evince consistent structure. When the text was redacted, the redactor would have unconsciously tailored the texts to fit the present structural needs. Thus, any analysis of the structure of the Bible must view the structures found as revealing an editorial present of the text, rather than revealing previously embedded structures. Structures are not artifacts, they live in a living textual tradition.[8]

Genesis 22: The Death of Isaac

The initial mytheme developed in the text is an opposition that works on the horizontal plane between Isaac and Ishmael. Ishmael, however, is not mentioned by name in ch. 22, and thus the opposition is implicit rather than explicit. In v. 2 God tells Abraham, 'take now your son, your only son Isaac, whom you love'. The text is clearly comparing Isaac to Abraham's other son, Ishmael, since the terms are used to single out Isaac. Rather than using a single term to describe Isaac, the text uses

6.   The signs in the equations should be interpreted as follows: ':' expresses 'is to'; this expresses a relationship, often an opposition between two structural elements; '::' is 'as'; this sign states that two equations are based on an identical structural pattern; '$^{(-)}$' expresses 'inverted' and '$^{(t)}$' expresses 'transformed'; these two signs state that the relationship between the structural elements has been changed in some specified way.

7.   See S.D. Kunin, *The Logic of Incest: A Structuralist Analysis of Hebrew Mythology* (Sheffield: Sheffield Academic Press, 1995), pp. 270-71.

8.   Detailed analysis of the structural elements found in the four biblical strata reveals that all four (as defined by E. Fohrer in *Introduction to the Old Testament* [Slough: SPCK, 1986]) contain all of the key structural oppositions (Kunin, *The Logic of Incest*, pp. 269-70).

three. Each of these terms establishes Isaac as ideologically positive, and by implication Ishmael as ideologically negative (i.e. he is the opposite of the terms used to describe Isaac). By characterizing Ishmael as structurally opposite to Isaac, the myth creates ideological distance between the two, overriding the genealogical closeness.

The text goes a step further, describing Isaac as Abraham's only son. Although it is clear that this is not true on a narrative level, it is an essential point on the mythological or structural level. It is the logical outcome of the opposition already established. The initial opposition created ideological distance between Isaac and Ishmael. This statement creates the logical possibility of genealogical distance as well.

Although Ishmael is not mentioned by name in this text, there is a clear pattern of opposition developed in the narratively earlier sections of the myth. Ishmael is born prior to Genesis 17, in which Abram is reborn as Abraham. Isaac is born after Genesis 17. The texts after Genesis 17 recapitulate the earlier events of Abraham's life. The recapitulated events are presented as the completion of the previous events, and as ideologically positive in relation to them. There is also a clear ideological distinction between the respective mothers of Ishmael and Isaac. Whereas Hagar is identified as an Egyptian concubine, and therefore structurally outside, Sarah, at the very least, comes from Abram's family in Haran, and is therefore comparatively inside. This ambiguous status of Sarah, however, is clarified in Genesis 20, where the text states that Sarah is Abraham's sister and therefore structurally inside.

The mytheme is also developed in regard to God's rejection of Ishmael, and acceptance or choice of Isaac. Ishmael is rejected by God as the bearer of his blessing in Genesis 17, this rejection is identical to that of Eliezer in Genesis 15, making Ishmael and Eliezer structurally equivalent. This equivalence is seen again below in regard to the discussion of Genesis 22 in the wider context of Hebrew mythology. Isaac, however, is specifically chosen to be Abraham's inheritor. And finally, upon Isaac's birth, geographic distance is created between Isaac and Ishmael, with the expulsion of Hagar (and Ishmael) from Abraham's household. Thus, both in Genesis 22 and the preceding chapters there is a clear pattern of opposition between Isaac and Ishmael.

The second mytheme developed in the text is a generational opposition primarily between Abraham and Isaac. This opposition works on the vertical level, that is, between generations rather than within a generation. This mytheme centres around the sacrifice (or attempted sacrifice).

Abraham is opposed to Isaac through being the principal actor in the sacrifice. In effect, Abraham symbolically reverses his role as parent—killing rather than creating a child. This opposition is weakened through the imposition of the ram which prevents the sacrifice from occurring. The text, however, does not completely remove the possibility of Isaac's death. In v. 6 the text describes Abraham and Isaac's ascent up the mountain, it states that they went יחדו, that is 'together'. However, when the text describes Abraham's descent from the mountain, Abraham goes alone and Isaac is never mentioned. The text forces the careful reader to ask, 'Where is Isaac?'[9]

The opposition between Abraham and Isaac, like that between Isaac and Ishmael, also has its roots in earlier texts. This opposition, however, is of a different kind from the previous opposition. The myth does not create ideological distance between Abraham and Isaac; rather it serves to remove Abraham from his parental role—opening the possibility that Isaac was of divine origin rather than human origin.

Throughout the texts leading up to Genesis 22 there is a continual process whereby Abraham's role or possibility of being a parent is denied. In ch. 17 Abraham is symbolically castrated through the covenant of circumcision. Circumcision should be taken as a symbol for castration because it is part of a structural set denying human fertility. It is parallel to barrenness in women. Throughout Genesis the myth develops a paradox: natural, uncircumcised, uncastrated is barren, while divine, castrated and circumcised is fruitful. He himself articulates the unlikelihood of his having further children in Gen. 17.17. And in several places his advanced age is mentioned, further emphasizing the fact that birth of a future child was naturally unlikely. A similar pattern is developed in regard to Sarah. Throughout the text her barrenness is emphasized. And as in the case of Abraham she denies the possibility of bearing a child at the age of 90 years. The final denial of Sarah's role in Isaac's birth comes after the sacrifice of Isaac. Prior to Isaac's symbolic rebirth (discussed

---

9. The sacrifice is seen as a mytheme (a structural component) for several reasons. The sacrifice is central to the text (on the narrative level), being the primary focus of the action. Although no actual human sacrifice occurs, a sacrifice is performed. The ram is sacrificed specifically in Isaac's place. The text uses the word תחת, 'in place of', to describe the replacement of Isaac in the sacrifice. This word is often used to mean 'replace' with the implication of taking the status or role. Thus the ram should be seen as the structural replacement for Isaac, and therefore as structurally equivalent to Isaac.

below) Sarah dies, emphasizing that she had no part in the rebirth. The death of Isaac (or the symbolic death of Isaac) is necessary in order to enable him to be symbolically reborn. Rebirth or divine birth is the third mytheme developed in the text. It is precisely the element of rebirth (the reverse of the sacrifice) that is the structural centre of the text. And, with the progressive denial of his physical parent, his spiritual parent comes to the fore. In Gen. 21.1, the text suggests that God played an important role in Isaac's birth: 'the Lord did to Sarah as he had spoken'.

This denial of human parenthood is tied directly to the question of sacrifice. The sacrifice (or in this case the abortive sacrifice) removes Isaac from the line of human descent. His parents have been symbolically removed, and thus his rebirth can be solely through divine agency rather than human agency. Thus the opposition between Isaac and Abraham is really the opposition of two types of birth, that is, Human birth : Divine birth. This opposition can then be tied to the initial opposition, Isaac : Ishmael—thus Isaac : Ishmael :: Divine Birth : Human Birth. And as in the initial opposition the ideological value of Ishmael and human birth relative to Isaac and divine birth is (–).

The opposition can then be taken to a higher level. In Genesis, heroes tend to have a corporate rather than a purely individual identity. This phenomenon is best illustrated in the use of the name Israel for Jacob, and the names of the twelve tribes for his sons. Thus Isaac structurally stands for Israel (i.e. the people of Israel) and Ishmael for the Ishmaelites (and most likely the other nations as well). Thus the final equation, which brings together all three mythemes, is, Isaac : Ishmael :: Divine : Human :: Israel : The Nations.

There is a second opposition (or in this case transformational set) which finds its centre in the sacrifice: between Isaac prior to the sacrifice (a), and Isaac after the sacrifice (b). The text, however, imposes a mediator between these two. In mythological texts, mediators are figures that share attributes of both elements of the opposition, and thus, by their similarity to both, cloud the opposition. In this text the ram mediates between Isaac (a) and Isaac (b). The ram is inverted in relation to Isaac. Prior to the sacrifice Isaac is a product of natural birth; after the sacrifice he is the product of divine birth. The ram mirrors these elements. It is initially given by God (divine birth), but in its essence it is natural. Thus the ram, in mediating between the two, is the logical replacement for Isaac in the sacrifice.

The opposition between the two aspects of Isaac is tied to a transference of blessing from Abraham to Isaac—passing of the divine seed from one to the other. Earlier in the text, Genesis 12, 15 and 17, Abraham went through a similar process of rebirth. And, after the final rebirth Genesis 17, the divine seed becomes fruitful and Isaac is born. With the sacrifice of Isaac, Isaac is symbolically reborn, and becomes the bearer of the divine seed and blessing in the place of Abraham.

It would be structurally illogical for both Abraham and Isaac to be carriers of the seed simultaneously, because the system is based on a single line of descent. If both carried the seed then two lines of descent could develop (or would be logically possible). The transfer of blessing is highlighted in Genesis 25. In Genesis 25 Abraham, as in Genesis 17 before his final rebirth, has children with a concubine. These children are clearly structurally opposed to Isaac. The opposition of Abraham's second set of children with Isaac is highlighted further on in Genesis 25 by a list of descendants of Ishmael—structurally equating the two groups. The opposition is completed in v. 23 where the birth of Isaac's sons is described.

In regard to the initial mytheme it was suggested that ideological distance was created between Isaac and Ishmael, to overcome genealogical closeness.[10] The equation presented above adds a second level of distance. It suggests that Isaac is of divine origin, rather than human origin, and therefore creates genealogical distance as well as ideological distance. These two levels of distance are necessary to overcome a paradox created by Israelite ideology.

The text creates a paradox which is based on two mutually exclusive structures. On the one hand, if one God created the world, and people are descended from a single couple, then all nations are related and therefore, if not the same, they are at least similar. On the other hand, the text develops the ideology of endogamy which suggests that peoples are naturally distinct from one another, supporting the requirement to marry within. This paradox is reflected in the two types of genealogies found in Genesis: linear genealogies detailing the origins of Israel reflect the ideology of exclusivity, and segmentary genealogies outlining the

10. The pattern of using ideological distance indirectly related to genealogical closeness is most clearly found in regard to the genealogies of Israel and the nations found in Genesis. My research indicates that the closer a nation is genealogically to Israel the greater the ideological distance between the two (Kunin, *The Logic of Incest*, pp. 178-204).

origins of the nations reflect that of universality or single origin.

The paradox is resolved initially by the imposition of ideological distance, and then by the denial of genealogical relation by bringing in the element of divine descent in regard to Israel. Genealogical closeness is dangerous, because it challenges the ideology of difference which is the basis of endogamy. If other nations are said to be your brothers, then in effect they are almost you (at least relative to those nations genealogically more distant). Mechanisms must be developed to overcome or cloud the similarity.

Thus, although Genesis 22 on a narrative level does not include an actual sacrifice, through making the sacrifice the centre of the text, it creates the structural possibility that the sacrifice actually occurred. And by creating this possibility it serves the structural needs of the system. The element of death and rebirth is examined again below in regard to the structural set in which Genesis 22 is included. This text leaves two ambiguous elements. The ambiguous nature of the sacrifice is already mentioned. The second is found in the two unnamed young men whom Abraham takes with him to mount Moriah. Both these elements are clarified when Genesis 22 is examined in regard to the structures found in Genesis as a whole.

Genesis 22 is part of a broader structural set which is found throughout the book of Genesis. The same structural patterns of oppositions are found in: the murder of Abel and the birth of Seth in Genesis 4, the myths about Abraham centring on his rebirths in Genesis 12, 15, and, with special emphasis, in Genesis 17, the myths about Jacob with their centre in Genesis 32, in which Jacob wrestles with an angel and is reborn as Israel, and the myths about Joseph with their centre in Genesis 37. They are also partially found in Genesis 3, 6 and 48 (in regard to Adam and Eve, Noah, and Ephraim and Manasseh respectively). The oppositions are also found in texts relating to Moses, and in the New Testament in texts relating to the birth, death and rebirth of Jesus.

In each of these texts the central mytheme is the denial of human, natural birth in favour of divine rebirth. In several of the texts the sacrifice/murder is actually carried out, in other texts the sacrifice and associated rebirth is symbolic. This pattern resolves one of the initial questions: was Isaac sacrificed? Structurally, he was.

Comparison of Genesis 22 with Genesis 37

It is through comparison with an inverted version of the myth that the second ambiguous element of Genesis 22 can be clarified. The basic structural elements of Genesis 22 can be diagrammed as follows. On the horizontal are three points: A, the father (Abraham); B, the son (Isaac); b, the ram; and C, the two young men (the unknown radical). The text also has a vertical axis, representing the direction of movement, in this case (+) an upward movement. The upward movement is illustrated in two ways: the mountain where the sacrifice is to occur; and the word for sacrifice itself: להעלות 'to raise up'. In Genesis 22, A (the father) raises (+ movement) B (the chosen son), leaving C (the two young men) behind, b (the ram) is killed in the place of B (Figure 2).

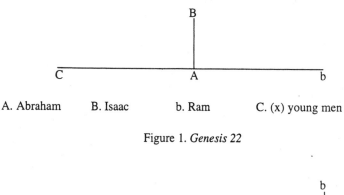

A. Abraham   B. Isaac   b. Ram   C. (x) young men

Figure 1. *Genesis 22*

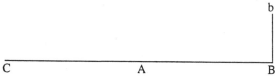

Figure 2. *The Structure of Genesis 22*

Genesis 37 is an inverted version of Genesis 22. In Genesis 37 Joseph is sent to the fields by his father, who remains behind. When Joseph arrives his brothers place him in a pit, and discuss whether to kill him. Eventually he is removed from the pit and sold to the Ishmaelites or Midianites. The Ishmaelites and the Midianites should be regarded as mediators between the Israelites and the Egyptians. On the one hand, the Egyptians are completely outside in respect to Israel. They became genealogically distinct from the line which led to Israel in Genesis 11. On the other, the Ishmaelites and the Midianites are half in and half out.

They are descended from Abraham (inside) and Hagar and Keturah (outside). Thus they are a perfect conduit to move Joseph from inside (his family) to outside (Egypt). The brothers kill a goat and use its blood to prove that Joseph was dead.

The structural elements of the text can be diagrammed as follows. On the horizontal axis are three points: A1, the father; B1, the son (with b1 being the goat) and C1, the other sons of Jacob. The vertical axis in Genesis 37 is (–) because it involves a downward movement (Figure 3). In Genesis 37, C1 (the sons) lowers (– movement) B1 (Joseph), leaving A1 (Jacob) behind; b1 (the goat) is killed in the place of B1 (Figure 4). In Genesis 37 the positions of the radicals are reversed from the positions found in Genesis 22, and the movement in the text is reversed.

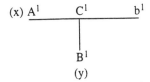

A. Jacob   B. Joseph C. Joseph's Brothers   b. Goat

Figure 3. *Genesis 37*

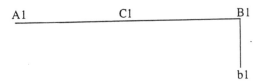

Figure 4. *Structural Elements of Genesis 37*

The inversion is clearest in reference to the structural positions of A and C in Genesis 22 and A1 and C1 in Genesis 37, and on the y axis, the direction element in the text. The four radicals, the fathers', the slaves' and the brothers' roles in the two texts are exactly inverted. In Genesis 22 the father sacrifices the son, while the young men remain behind. In Genesis 37 the father remains behind while the young men kill their brother. The y axis is also inverted, Genesis 22 moving in an upward direction, and Genesis 37 downward.

Thus the relationship between the two texts is: A = C1, B = B1, C = A1, and b = b1 (see Figure 5). If the Genesis 37 is re-inverted then C can be see as being structurally identical with C1. This suggests that since

C1 is Jacob's other sons, it is structurally likely that C fills the identical structural role, that is, Abraham's other sons: Ishmael and Eliezer.[11] The structural equations of the texts are therefore: A : B :: $A1^{(-)}$: $B1^{(-)}$ and B : C :: $B1^{(-)}$: $C1^{(-)}$.

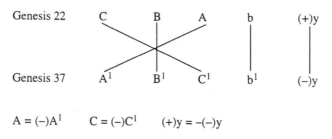

$$A = (-)A^1 \qquad C = (-)C^1 \qquad (+)y = -(-)y$$

Figure 5. *Structural Relationship Between Genesis 22 and 37*

Eliezer is mythologically equated with Ishmael (as a son) due to their structurally equivalent positions in Genesis 15 and 17 respectively, in which they are rejected by God from becoming Abraham's inheritors. This identification is also supported by the absence of Ishmael from Genesis 22. Although that text implicitly opposes Isaac and Ishmael, the opposition is weakened by the absence of Ishmael himself. If the young men are structurally identified with Eliezer and Ishmael, the structural logic of the text becomes much stronger.

The two directional elements of the texts are also significant. Both the mountain and the pit are liminal spaces. They are the points were opposing domains meet. The mountain joins earth with sky, and the pit joins the world with the underworld. The liminal aspects of the movement enhance the danger of the movement and equally strengthen the symbolic equation with death. The upward movement is more explicitly tied to death, 'to raise up' actually being the word used for sacrifice. The downward movement is tied to the Israelite conception of death—which involved going down to Sheol, a cave where the bones of the dead were gathered. Thus the two directions become structurally equivalent in Genesis 22 and 37.

The type of symbolic death described in the two texts is also inverted. In Genesis 22 Abraham symbolically sacrifices Isaac. Sacrifice should be considered a positive death which purifies rather than defiles. In Genesis

---

11. It is not suggested that the two men were considered to be Abraham's other sons by the text, the author or the community that heard the myth; rather it is suggested that they fill the same structural position.

37, on the other hand, the brothers symbolically murder Joseph. Murder is clearly a negative death which defiles rather than purifies. Based on this final element it is likely that Genesis 37 is the inverted version of the structural pattern developed in Genesis 22.

The two types of death are also connected with the ideological valence of the two axes of Israelite myth (see Figure 6). In these texts murder is associated with the horizontal axis, that of Joseph and his brothers, while sacrifice is connected with the vertical axis, that of Abraham and Isaac. This suggests that there is a qualitative distinction between the two. If the axes are generalized within the mythological context, the distinction can be clarified. On the one hand, the horizontal axis, which is ultimately Israel and the nations—Inside : Outside—has a strong negative component, the murder. On the other hand, the vertical axis, which is within the chosen line—Inside : Inside—contains a positive or at least in this context neutral component, sacrifice.

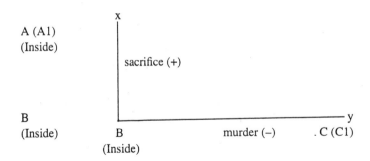

Figure 6. *Sacrifice and Murder: Vertical and Horizontal Qualitative Markers*

These texts are part of a broader pattern of creating a logical distinction between Israel and the nations. The opposition of natural and divine is also developed through the concept of choice. Throughout Genesis there is a pattern in which natural choice is opposed to divine choice. In almost every case individuals who would normally carry on the line of descent, who by birth were the natural leaders, are set aside in favour of divine choice.

This characteristic pattern is seen in the choice of Isaac over Ishmael, of Jacob over Esau, of Joseph over his brothers, of Judah over Reuben, and, possibly, of Shem over his brothers. The age of Shem given in the text suggests that he was not the eldest son.[12] It is also found in regard

12. The question regarding Shem's genealogical position is based on Noah's age

to Samuel and David in the historical books, both of whose stories also conform to most of the structural elements described above. The element of divine choice is found on a tribal level with Saul. Saul is said to come from the tribe of Benjamin, the smallest and youngest tribe. This opposition is mirrored in the broader concept of chosenness. Chosenness should not be seen as a separate ideology from endogamy, but rather as the theological expression of endogamy.

All of the oppositions that were developed in Genesis 22 are part of the overall structure of Genesis and Hebrew mythology. Genesis itself works to resolve the paradox alluded to above. It uses both mythological text and genealogical material to create both ideological and genealogical distance, thereby resolving the paradox in favour of endogamy, which is the cultural choice.

The first half of this paper has traced the presentation of several key mythemes of biblical mythology as they are found in Genesis 22. Three mythemes are explicitly depicted in Genesis 22 and a fourth is implicit. The two related mythemes of sacrifice/murder and rebirth (albeit only in symbolic forms) are the central focus of the myth. In Genesis 22 both of these mythemes are tied to a further mytheme, generational opposition within the chosen line. This mytheme is developed in the form of Abraham's willingness to sacrifice Isaac. The element of sacrifice, a positive act, emphasizes that this opposition is not negative; rather it is a transfer of blessing (and procreative power within the line) from one generation to the next. The implicit mytheme is the horizontal opposition between brothers. Since Ishmael (and Eliezer) are not mentioned in the narrative the opposition is never fully developed.

The horizontal opposition between Isaac and Ishmael is never fully developed in Genesis. Throughout the text Ishmael retains ambiguous or positive elements. It is possible that he is qualitatively neutral owing to his genealogical relation to Isaac. Although they share a father they have different mothers. Some texts suggest that children of different mothers

---

when his first child was born. The text states that Noah was five hundred years old when he began to have children (Gen. 5.32), and that the flood occurred in the six hundredth year of his life. Therefore at the end of the flood his oldest son would have been one hundred years old, and thus could not have been Shem—who would only have been ninety-eight. Therefore his oldest son must have been either Yaphet or Ham. One other indication in Genesis itself that this may be the case is found in Gen. 10. In Gen. 10, the table of nations, the descendants of Shem, rather than being enumerated first, are listed after those of Yaphet and Ham.

could marry and thus may be considered genealogically distinct.[13] In the rabbinic texts, which were written at times when this type of marriage was prohibited, Ishmael's role is much less ambiguous.

The same mythemes are shown to be found in the inverted version of Genesis 22, Genesis 37. In Genesis 37, however, the horizontal opposition is brought to the fore. The opposition between Joseph and his brothers is clearly negative. This is developed by the use of murder rather than sacrifice. This negative valence fits in with a general pattern in Genesis. Whereas the vertical opposition is inside–inside, the horizontal opposition is inside–outside. The negative valence of the opposition emphasizes the ideological impossibility of bridging the opposition.

The mechanisms of transformation found in comparison of the two narratives raises an interesting theoretical point. Most structural analyses have focused on transformations of myths between communities rather than in a single synchronic body of myth. It is suggested that where transformations occur within a body of myth two processes may be occurring. First, the original message of the myth may be too clear and thus culturally problematic—such a structural pattern would require obscuring or clouding, which is one of the functions of myth. Secondly, the inverted version could work on other mythemes equally part of the system.

In the myths examined here we find both processes at work. It seems likely that the structures developed in the 'Sacrifice of Isaac' were culturally problematic. This process is already found to be at work in Genesis 22 in which a mediator, the ram, is placed between Abraham and Isaac. The second process is also found in Genesis 37 where the inverted version of the myth is used to work on the horizontal opposition, as opposed to the vertical opposition that was the focus of Genesis 22. It is likely that within a mythic tradition, in all similar transformations to that discussed here, both of the processes will be at work.

Rabbinic Transformations of Genesis 22

The rabbinic texts discussed span the period including Amoraic midrashim, for example, *Genesis Rabbah*, to the period of the compilations, for example, *Yalkut Shim'oni* and *Midrash HaGadol*; that is, from c. 400 to c. 1300 CE. The oppositions presented above are reflected with clear areas of continuity in all the rabbinic texts examined regardless

13. See for example, Gen. 21 and 2 Sam. 13.

of time of composition. Although only a few of the texts are presented here, they are characteristic of the majority of rabbinic texts that have been analysed.

The rabbinic texts focus primarily on the key areas of opposition: Did the sacrifice occur? Why did Sarah die? What was the nature of the ram? Who were the young men? All these questions are answered and developed in structurally consistent ways. The transformations in the texts can be tied, in many cases, to historical events and to changes in cultural norms and forms. In order to highlight the diachronic development of mediation and transformation within the oppositions, texts from three midrashic periods will be surveyed, and significant texts will be examined in detail.

Genesis Rabbah

Genesis Rabbah is an Amoraic midrash written (or compiled) possibly as early as the fifth century, though there is a continuous development in textual tradition after the fifth century.[14] The texts are attributed to different rabbinic figures, and often are (at least explicitly) independent of each other. The texts are also (as in many exegetical midrashim) fragmentary in nature. There do, however, seem to be consistent patterns of transformation within *Genesis Rabbah* as a whole. This consistency is most likely due to the selection and editing process.

In its exegesis of Genesis 22, there are five significant texts that develop the oppositions described above. The first two texts develop the opposition between Isaac and Ishmael. *Gen. R.* 55.1 presents a discussion between Isaac and Ishmael—they are competing for who is more beloved. Ishmael states that he was circumcised in his thirteenth year, Isaac counters that he was circumcised on the eighth day (as is prescribed by Jewish Law). Ishmael states that he is better because he could have protested against being circumcised while Isaac could not. Isaac responds that he would be willing to give to the Lord one of his limbs. To which God replies, offer yourself to me as a sacrifice. This midrash has an explicit opposition built into it, Isaac and Ishmael with their argument set up the opposition themselves. The final distinction is made when Isaac offers himself, and Ishmael has no response.[15] The text

---

14. J. Neusner, *Genesis Rabbah: The Judaic Commentary to the Book of Genesis* (3 vols.; Atlanta: Scholars Press, 1985), p. ix.

15. An identical text is found in *b. Sanh.* 89b.

also adds a new element to Genesis 22. Isaac becomes an active participant rather than merely a passive one.

The second midrash (*Gen. R.* 55.7) similarly distinguishes between
Isaac and Ishmael. Versions of this text are found in all the midrashim
discussed. This text presents a discussion between God and Abraham
based on Gen. 22.2. The midrash is based on the three terms that God
uses to describe Isaac. It states,

> And He said to him: take...your son; he said to Him: which son; He said
> to him: your only one; he said to him: this is only son of his mother and
> this is the only son of his mother; He said to him: the one you love; he
> said to Him: I love both; He said to him: take Isaac.

Although this midrash appears to equate Isaac and Ishmael, a subtle
distinction is developed. On one level, like the above text, Isaac is identified as ideologically (+) in relation to Ishmael because in the end Isaac is
chosen rather than Ishmael. On a second level, no equation of Isaac and
Ishmael is possible. It is God who describes Isaac using the three terms
(son, only one, and whom you love), and all Abraham's disclaimers
which he uses to save Isaac are of no avail. The terms used by God in
the end can only apply to Isaac. And by disclaiming them Abraham
emphasizes them and therefore strengthens the opposition between Isaac
and Ishmael.

There is a consistent pattern of intensifying the negative valence of the
Ishmael mytheme. This is found not only in the two texts quoted here
but also in several narratively earlier texts in *Genesis Rabbah*. In
Gen. R. 53.11, for example, the words 'making sport' are interpreted in
four different ways—fornication, idolatry, murder and claiming the
inheritance—each one qualitatively negative.[16] This pattern of transformation is also found in the latter midrashic texts.

Gen. R. 55.7 concludes with an interesting association. It connects the
sacrifice of Isaac with Abraham's (Abram's) leaving his father's house.
The rabbis observe that both texts include the word לך לך. And further,
that in each case God uses three words to describe the point of transformation in the text. In Genesis 22 the three terms describe Isaac, who
is structurally transformed from human origin to divine origin, while in
Genesis 12 they describe Abram's father's house—which structurally is
transformed from inside to outside. On a structural level both texts
describe the process of divine rebirth.

---

16. This interpretation is based on words in Gen. 21.9.

Several texts in *Genesis Rabbah* focus on and thus emphasize the centrality of the sacrifice. This is seen in *Gen. R.* 56.6 where it states that the two (Abraham and Isaac) went together, the binder and the bound, the slaughterer and the slaughtered. And again in 56.12 it discusses whether Abraham drew even a drop of blood from Isaac. Both these and other texts, while not admitting to actual sacrifice, continue to keep the possibility of sacrifice in the fore.

The final significant text in *Genesis Rabbah* is 56.19, which addresses the biblical statement that Abraham returned alone. The text offers the possibility that Isaac was sent to study Torah with Shem. This separation is one step away from death. Although mythologically Shem was still alive at the time of the binding of Isaac, his Yeshivah (school) has other-worldly elements, emphasized by the fact that Shem lived ten generations before Abraham. Thus this text creates the possibility of a death (and subsequent rebirth) without describing an actual sacrifice (thus materially transforming the biblical text). All the texts described are typical of *Genesis Rabbah* as a whole. It tends to explore oppositions developed in the biblical text, without adding significant transformations or mediators.

Pirke Rabbi Eliezer

The opposition between Isaac and Ishmael is developed in similar ways in *Pirke Rabbi Eliezer* (*PRE*), a midrash from the eight/ninth century. We find a similar midrash to that found in *Genesis Rabbah* with, however, several significant additions. The text is introduced by a statement that just prior to the events (of Gen. 22) Ishmael returns from the wilderness, thus making explicit his structural opposition to Isaac by bringing Ishmael in person into the myth.[17]

The midrash continues with an expansion of the first few verses of Genesis 22: the midrash portrays Abraham as bargaining with God, stating that each term might apply to either Isaac or Ishmael, until God finally singles Isaac out by name. The primary difference between this version and those found in other midrashim (see the version from *Genesis Rabbah* quoted above) relates to an additional way of

17. The additional element of wilderness can also be seen as ideologically negative in respect to Ishmael. The element of wilderness is also used in the biblical text regarding Esau. Thus the structural equation Isaac:Ishmael :: Jacob:Esau :: Culture (the camp): Nature (the wilderness) :: (+):(−) is implied.

distinguishing between Isaac and Ishmael which is introduced by Abraham. Abraham asks God 'Which son, the one born prior to the circumcision or the one born after circumcision'. This emphasizes the importance of the covenant of circumcision, and Genesis 17 as a whole, in distinguishing between Isaac and Ishmael—developing the opposition: Prior to Circumcision : After Circumcision :: Natural : Divine. The force of this element as well as the other expansions of this part of the text emphasize the opposition between Isaac and Ishmael (and implicitly the opposition between Israel and the nations). This is further accentuated by the rationale given for Abraham's questions: Abraham's exceptional love for Isaac (*PRE* 31).

The second means of developing the opposition between Isaac and Ishmael is also found in several different midrashic texts.[18] This text describes a discussion between Ishmael and Eliezer—who are identified as the two young men brought by Abraham to Mount Moriah. Ishmael tells Eliezer that with the upcoming sacrifice of Isaac, he will become Abraham's beneficiary. Eliezer challenges this, citing Ishmael's expulsion from Abraham's camp, stating that in fact he will inherit his master's property. At this point a voice from God tells them that neither one nor the other will inherit. This text works on several levels. On the one hand, it inserts Ishmael and Eliezer into the myth, strengthening the opposition of Isaac to both of them as well as strengthening their structural equation, making clear that Ishmael and Eliezer are structurally identical. The text therefore exactly corresponds with the structural analysis of the role of the young men in the biblical text and the projected identification of the two. On the other hand, it strengthens the opposition by clearly stating that neither Ishmael nor Eliezer shall inherit. Neither could take the place of Isaac as bearer of God's blessing (*PRE* 31).

This opposition is further developed on the spiritual level. Abraham asks Ishmael and Eliezer if they see anything on the mountain. They say that they see nothing, whereas Isaac is said to have seen a pillar of fire. Abraham tells them to remain with the donkey—'because just as the ass saw nothing, likewise you saw nothing'. This ties into the opposition already developed: Ishmael and Eliezer, the products of natural birth, are equated with the ass, a product of nature, whereas Abraham and Isaac, products of divine birth, are equated with the divine. This text is also found in *Genesis Rabbah*, however, with one significant difference. In

---

18. Also found in *Sepher Yashar*, Vayera 44b; and *Midrash VaYosha* 37.

Genesis Rabbah the two young men are not identified as Ishmael and Eliezer (*Gen. R.* 56.2; *PRE* 31).[19]

Whereas in *Genesis Rabbah* the only hint of the death of Isaac was that he went to study with Shem, in *Pirke Rabbi Eliezer* we find a clearer reference to death. Towards the end of the texts discussing Genesis 22 it states,

> When the sword touched Isaac's throat, terrified, his soul fled [he died]. Immediately his [God's] voice was heard from between the angels, and he said 'do not lay your hand on the boy', thereupon his soul returned to his body... And Isaac knew of the resurrection of the dead from the Torah, that all the dead are destined to be resurrected (*PRE* 31).

This text openly includes a death and resurrection, albeit in a short space of time. Although it might be thought that this merely refers to fainting or unconsciousness, the inclusion in the text of material referring to the future resurrection implies that this was an example of this phenomenon. This ties into the logic discussed above, emphasizing both the structural elements of sacrifice and of rebirth.

There are several texts in *Pirke Rabbi Eliezer* which develop the opposition of natural and divine birth—especially in regard to the denial of Sarah's parental role. These texts tie the death of Sarah directly to the sacrifice. Thus in ch. 32 the text presents the following story. After Satan found that he could not convince Abraham and Isaac to be unfaithful to God he went to Sarah. He told Sarah that Abraham had killed Isaac, whereupon Sarah died in grief. This text emphasizes a connection already built into the narrative structure, the placement of the death of Sarah immediately after the Akedah, and it attributes her death directly to the Akedah.[20] The death of Sarah, as suggested above, is part of a logical

---

19. The pattern of increased negative valence is strongly developed in *PRE*. On 37b the text focuses on the future troubles that will be created by Ishmael. It lists 15 evil things that the descendants of Ishmael will do in the land of Israel. It also lists three wars that the descendants of Ishmael will wage on the earth. As discussed below, it is likely that this increased negative valence reflects the rise in Islamic power.

20. Akedah is the Hebrew word meaning 'binding'. It is the traditional name of the text. It has become popular in recent years to use this name, or the English translation of it ('The Binding of Isaac') when referring to the text, rather than the other title 'the Sacrifice of Isaac'. Perhaps this indicates that today the concept of sacrifice is once again problematic.

structure in which the natural parents are progressively denied, leaving only the divine parent as the agent of the rebirth.

Pirke Rabbi Eliezer is much freer in regard to developing oppositions found in the biblical text. It clarifies and emphasizes connections made, for example by tying the death of Sarah to the sacrifice, and by recalling the similar structural and narrative elements in Genesis 12, Abraham's first rebirth. It also expands upon the structural elements, transforming the biblical text to emphasize the logical oppositions. It strengthens the opposition between Isaac and Ishmael through bringing Ishmael directly into the narrative. It also strengthens the element of sacrifice through including the death and resurrection of Isaac—albeit in a slightly weak form, since Isaac dies of fright rather than actually being sacrificed. All the oppositions developed, however, remain consistent with those developed in the biblical text. They are also consistent with structuralist projections in regard to the development of the myth; for example, *Pirke Rabbi Eliezer* agrees with the structural identification of Abraham's young men, identifying them as Ishmael and Eliezer.

The Midrashic Collections

These oppositions are developed in a variety of ways in later midrashic texts. The opposition between Isaac and Ishmael remains consistent with the earlier texts. As in *Genesis Rabbah* and *Pirke Rabbi Eliezer* the Ishmael mytheme continues to become more negatively valued than in the biblical text. *Lekach Tov* (an eleventh-century collection) includes a similar text to that in *Genesis Rabbah* presenting the argument between Ishmael and Isaac. The text in *Lekach Tov* includes a subtle transformation.

In *Genesis Rabbah* Isaac offers a limb to God, while in *Lekach Tov* he offers himself as a sacrifice. This midrash continues a development already seen in both *Genesis Rabbah* and *Pirke Rabbi Eliezer*, for example, that Isaac was a full partner in the sacrifice (perhaps to reduce Abraham's culpability). The same text also creates a further opposition between Ishmael and Isaac. While Ishmael is circumcised against his will, Isaac goes to the altar willingly.

The midrashic collections all include various texts emphasizing the opposition between Isaac and his brothers (Ishmael and Eliezer). These include variations on the text in *Yalkut Shim'oni* in which Ishmael and Eliezer argue as to who will inherit Abraham's property, and those texts in which they are associated with the donkey (*Yalkut* 100; *Midrash HaGadol* [*MHG*] on Vayera, Gen. 22.3). There are no significant transformations in these texts.

The death of Isaac is developed in several ways in differing texts. In midrashim from all periods emphasis is placed on the description of the events leading up to the sacrifice. They describe how Abraham placed Isaac on the wood (*Tanh.* on Vayera). They describe the discussion between Abraham and Isaac, often making Isaac a full participant in the events (*PRE* 31; *MHG* on Vayera, Gen. 22.8). These elements focus the mythological centre on the sacrifice, emphasizing the logical possibility of sacrifice. This logical possibility is further focused on in several midrashim in which Abraham and Isaac discuss the outcome of the sacrifice; for example, in *Midrash HaGadol*, which is a thirteenth-century collection, Isaac asks Abraham not to tell Sarah when she is on the wall in case she should fall and die (*MHG* on Vayera, Gen. 22.11). This both focuses on the possibility of the sacrifice occurring, and creates logical connections between the death of Sarah and the sacrifice. It is primarily in regard to the sacrifice that significant transformations or developments are found.

One text in *Yalkut Shim'oni* (a thirteenth-century midrash) further enhances Isaac's participation in the sacrifice. The text states,

> The two of them came to the place, and the two of them brought the stones, and the two of them brought the fire, and the two of them brought the wood...[Isaac said to Abraham] 'Father quickly do the will of your creator. Burn me well and bring my ashes to my mother' (*Yalkut Shim'oni* 101).

This and similar texts focus the mythological centre on the sacrifice, emphasizing the structural possibility of sacrifice.

In a text in *Midrash HaGadol* the death and resurrection is emphasized by a midrash which states that Isaac spent three years in Paradise before returning to his home. The midrash also directly ties Abraham's returning alone to the death of Sarah. Sarah dies when she sees that Abraham arrives without Isaac (*MHG* on Vayera, Gen. 22.19). Sarah's death is structurally necessary to emphasize the divine aspect of Isaac's rebirth.

In *Lekach Tov*, the text states that Isaac died and was revived by dew drops of resurrection (*Lekach Tov* on Vayetze, Gen. 31.42). In *Shibbole Ha-Leket* (quoted by Spiegel), a thirteenth-century text, it says that Isaac was reduced to dust and ashes, after which he was revived by God who used life-giving dew.[21] Thus in these later texts the trend begun with the Bible and *Genesis Rabbah* finds its logical conclusion. The structure develops from a suggestion of sacrifice in the biblical text, to a literal sacrifice and resurrection in the midrashic texts.

The midrashic texts also turn their attention to the mediator, the ram, attributing to it all types of miraculous connections. One interesting text in *Midrash HaGadol* states that the ram's name was Isaac (*MHG* on Vayera, Gen. 22.13). This text highlights the connection of the mediator with Isaac. The closer the ram is to Isaac the greater its potential as mediator. In connecting the ram with miraculous events the aspect of mediation is weighted in favour of the divine aspect of Isaac. Thus in several texts the ram is said to be resurrected, emphasizing the logical possibility of Isaac's resurrection. In other texts the ram is said to be taken from Gan Eden—Paradise—also being Isaac's temporary home (*Yalkut Shim'oni* 101). In a seventeenth-century collection the identification of Isaac and the ram is even closer. Isaac's soul, upon departing his body is said to have been transferred to the ram, and the ram itself is miraculous, being created during the six days of creation (*Yalkut Reubeni* 200).[22] This texts makes many of the elements discussed here explicit.

> Isaac's soul departed and was hidden in the ram. The explanation: at the time of the binding his soul went out and came into the ram which was created between the days [of creation]. 'This is the goat for sacrifice my son' it is indeed my son.

All of these texts strengthen the ram as a mediator, and, by strengthening its identification with Isaac, strengthen the logical possibility that he too was sacrificed.

Transformations occur on three levels. First, on the level of emphasis: in the early texts the question of sacrifice is left to the realm of logical possibility rather than actuality, while in most late texts Isaac actually dies and is reborn. It is possible that historical events led to the sacrifice being perceived as less problematic and thus textually acceptable.[23] The

---

21. S. Spiegel, *The Last Trial* (New York: Behrman House, 1979), p. 33.

22. *Yalkut Reubeni* quotes the source of this text as *Asara Ma'amarot*.

23. See, for example, Spiegel's *The Last Trial*, where this question is examined in detail. He suggests that with the persecutions of Jews in the Middle Ages, death (sacrifice) for the sake of heaven had become a central theme in Jewish thought. It is also likely that with the degradation of the Jewish community in the periods in which these midrashim were written the mytheme of sacrifice and divine rebirth became

death of Isaac was, however, structurally acceptable and implicit even in the biblical texts.

Secondly, transformations occur on the level of mediation. This type of transformation is seen primarily in relation to the ram. In the later texts (and to some extent in the earlier texts) the ram is much more closely identified with Isaac than in the biblical text, strengthening its role as mediator, and strengthening the logical structure.

Thirdly, the role and ideological value of Ishmael is transformed. In the biblical text, although Ishmael is implicitly opposed to Isaac he is never specifically mentioned in the context of this narrative. In general, in Genesis, Ishmael is ideologically neutral rather than being strongly positive or negative. This neutral or mediating role is mentioned above in respect to Genesis 37. In the midrashic texts, however, Ishmael becomes progressively more ideologically negative.

This trend is found not only respecting the Binding of Isaac, but also in regard to all other biblical accounts of Ishmael. This transformation in ideological valence is probably traceable to the rise of Islamic power—since the Islamic powers were associated with Ishmael. With the Ishmaelites' increasing importance, ideological distance was needed to counteract their genealogical closeness. Thus Ishmael's ideological value becomes increasingly negative.

In all the midrashic texts surveyed, although there were areas of transformation, there were also areas of significant structural continuity. This continuity is found on two levels—the relationships between structural elements, and the patterns of thought upon which those structural relations were built. This suggests that there are aspects of cultural continuity between the community that created the biblical text and that which created the midrashic texts. This is not to say that the Israelite culture remained static, or that biblical culture was the same as rabbinic or mediaeval culture, but rather that while it developed and went through transformations many key elements of its structural foundation remained constant.

In this journey through the diachronic development of Genesis 22 several consistent mythemes have been presented. The mythemes centre around the symbolic sacrifice and subsequent symbolic rebirth of Isaac. As the text developed, and the aspect of sacrifice became less culturally

---

even more significant in order to emphasize the divine origin and role of Israel in comparison to its materially and politically stronger neighbours.

problematic, it was made progressively more explicit in the text. The sacrifice functions on a structural level to emphasize the distinction between natural birth and divine birth, and, through that distinction, the opposition of the nations to Israel. This opposition was supported by two related oppositions also developed in the midrashic texts: between Ishmael and Isaac, which created ideological distance to supplement genealogical distance, and between human parenthood and divine paternity. These oppositions serve to create a logic whereby endogamy is perceived as the natural and logical choice, and it is precisely the role of mythology to prove that cultural choices are also natural choices.

JSOT 65 (1995), pp. 25-36

THE ANTHROPOLOGY OF CLOTHING IN THE JOSEPH NARRATIVE

Victor H. Matthews

Cloth has been both an economic commodity and a social marker throughout human history. Its physical properties are generally determined by environmental as well as social and aesthetic factors. Humans address themselves, their community and the world by the choice or style of their clothing.[1] Its weave, its color(s), its decoration and its style have all contributed to clothing's desirability as a trade item and as an indicator of membership within a defined community.

Cloth and clothing have a variety of cultural uses which are indicative of the human desire to define and maintain identity of persons and groups. It serves as a form of language which reflects societal norms of beauty, modesty, fashion.[2] As Schwarz[3] notes, 'more than any other material product, clothing plays a symbolic role in mediating the relationship between nature, man, and his sociocultural environment'.

Thus clothes can be a simple indicator of gender in which men and women are identified and restrictions are placed on cross-dressing to prevent sexual or social confusion (Deut. 22.5). At this basic level, clothing can also be a sign of employment (2 Sam. 20.8—'soldier's garment'; Exod. 28.31-42—priestly vestments). However, on the symbolic level, clothing always serves as a means of visual communication. The message conveyed may be artistic ('many-colored' cloth: Ps. 45.14; Ezek. 16.10; 26.16; or embroidered material: Exod. 26.36; 39.29), but

---

1. R.A. Schwarz, 'Uncovering the Secret Vice: Toward an Anthropology of Clothing', in J.M. Cordwell and R.A. Schwarz (eds.), *The Fabrics of Culture: The Anthropology of Clothing and Adornment* (The Hague: Mouton, 1979), pp. 24-25.

2. M.E. Roach and J.B. Eicher, 'The Language of Personal Adornment', in Cordwell and Schwarz (eds.), *The Fabrics of Culture*, p. 7.

3. Schwarz, 'Uncovering the Secret Vice', p. 31.

very often it is also relevant to power relationships.[4] For example, the lack of clothing in the Near East, in contrast to ancient Greece, distinguished social classes and conditions as well as shame (Gen. 3.7, 10-20) and powerlessness.[5] Day laborers (Exod. 22.26-27; Amos 2.8) gave up their cloaks as collateral for their hire and prisoners of war were distinguished by their lack of clothing (Isa. 20.2-5).

The particular weave of the fabric may mark it as rural or urban, domestic or imported, cultic or common (Lev. 19.19). Its decoration may contain rank insignia and its cut may indicate its owner's age, fashion sense or social standing, such as Tamar's 'widow's garment' in Gen. 38.14 (see also Jdt. 10.3). Quality of manufacture, color or design, and the age/physical condition of clothing (Gibeonites in Josh. 9.5, 13) may all contribute to establishing the identity, prosperity and rank of an individual or group. In some cases, it can also serve as a disguise, combined with other 'style-of-life symbols' such as grooming, facial expression and speech pattern.[6] This is the basis for the deception of Joshua by the Gibeonites in Josh. 9.5-13, who masked their true identity in dusty, ragged clothes and a story of a long journey.

A bit of cloth, with its distinctive physical qualities serving as an identifier, may be used to sign a document, as it is in *ARM* 10.7, where a male cult prophet (*assinnu*) becomes ecstatic and sends the message of the god to the king. The prophet signs a clay tablet by impressing the hem of his garment into the message. Undoubtedly, the mark of its weave and perhaps its decoration was unique to the cult community in which the prophet lived and the social class to which they belonged.[7] By using this indicator of the clothing style of his professional community, the prophet not only pledges his own honor but also that of his community to uphold his message to the king. Such distinctions within the cloth were also used to designate membership in the community of Israel (the blue threads in the tassels in Num. 15.38-39).[8]

Special occasions also demand proper attire. In the parable of the wedding banquet in Matt. 22.11-13, those guests who are not wearing

---

4. J. Schneider, 'The Anthropology of Cloth', *Annual Review of Anthropology* 16 (1987), p. 409.

5. L. Bonfante, 'Nudity as a Costume in Classical Art', *American Journal of Archaeology* 93 (1989), pp. 544-46.

6. Roach and Eicher, 'The Language of Adornment', pp. 11-12.

7. *CAD*, A.II (1968), '*assinnu*', p. 341.

8. J. Milgrom, 'Of Hems and Tassels', *BARev* 9 (3, 1983), pp. 61-65.

'wedding robes' are summarily dismissed from the banquet. Such careful attention to proper attire is found in Yahweh's recital of his care for the 'bride' Jerusalem.[9] First, her nakedness is covered (Ezek. 16.8), restoring her to honorable status among the nations,[10] and then she is clothed in 'embroidered cloth and with sandals of fine leather' (Ezek. 16.10). This solicitous care is then contrasted to the city's infidelity to Yahweh.[11] The mood is set by such attention to fashion or 'proper attire'.[12] The detailed recital of priestly garb in Exodus 28 is designed to distinguish the priest when engaged in official duties and thereby set a tone of difference between the secular and the sacred.

On several occasions, a portion of clothing or a special garment, such as the mantle, is used to designate legal responsibility when it is laid over another person. For instance, the expression 'spread your cloak over your servant' is used in Ruth 3.9 when Ruth petitions Boaz for help. Similarly, in Ezek. 16.8 Yahweh recites his care for Jerusalem, using what is very probably a legal expression: 'spread the edge of my cloak over you'.[13] In both cases the act of covering the woman with a cloak (*kānāp*) is a reference to marriage.[14]

Cloth can also be used to dub a person as one's successor.[15] In what is effectively an investiture ceremony (1 Kgs 19.19), Elijah designates Elisha as the one who will inherit his prophetic power. This demonstrates the power of the cloth as a symbol of continuity, binding together two generations of prophets and providing legitimacy to Elisha's claim to be Elijah's successor.[16]

Seizing the hem of a garment sometimes serves as a legal euphemism. For instance, a person can be taken into custody or claimed as payment

---

9. Compare the robes of the princess-bride in Ps. 45.13-18.

10. Bonfante, 'Nudity as Costume', p. 544.

11. W. Zimmerli, *Ezekiel. I. A Commentary on the Book of the Prophet Ezekiel, Chapters 1–24* (Philadelphia: Fortress Press, 1979), p. 341, and J. Blenkinsopp, *Ezekiel* (Louisville: John Knox, 1990), p. 78.

12. Roach and Eicher, 'The Language of Adornment', pp. 9, 18.

13. A. Kruger, 'The Hem of the Garment in Marriage. The Meaning of the Symbolic Gesture in Ruth 3.9 and Ezek. 16.8', *JNSL* 12 (1984), pp. 79-86.

14. A. Viberg, *Symbols of Law: A Contextual Analysis of Legal Symbolic Acts in the Old Testament* (Stockholm: Almqvist & Wiksell International, 1992), pp. 138-44.

15. Viberg, *Symbols of Law*, pp. 127-35.

16. J. Schneider and A.B. Weiner, 'Introduction', in A.B. Weiner and J. Schneider (eds.), *Cloth and Human Experience* (Washington, DC: Smithsonian Institution Press, 1989), p. 3.

for a debt through the grasping of the hem.[17] Power roles can be defined by that same action. In 1 Sam. 15.27, Saul pleads with Samuel to reverse his condemnation of the royal house by seizing the hem of the prophet's robe. This supplicative act marked the king as submitting to the authority of a prophet and asking for mercy.[18] Similarly, touching the clothing of a person was considered to have power, being able to infuse into the supplicant a transference of strength. This includes the belief in healing by the woman 'suffering from hemorrhages' in Mt. 9.21 and Mk 5.28: 'If I but touch his clothes, I will be made well.'

Test Case: The Joseph Narrative

It has long been recognized that dream interpretation serves as a structural device in the Joseph narrative which provides unity to a plot which contained a number of digressions.[19] Additionally, the episodes include a number of familiar folklore themes: Youngest Son Triumphant, the Wise Courtier, Spurned Wife, and Magician.[20] The structural unity of this novella remains intact despite its digressions, with only a few examples of later redaction.[21]

There is another motif found in the Joseph cycle which has not received a great deal of attention, the garment motif.[22] Based simply on the received text, two stages of development might be posited. In the first stage of the story, Joseph receives a garment from his father and later is divested of it by his brothers. Then at the conclusion of the narrative he once again receives a garment which also marks him as the favorite of

17. *CAD* 16.223, '*subatu*'; Waterman Bus. Doc. 74.7.

18. See *ARM* 6.26: 'I seized the hem of my lord's garment, may my lord not brush off my hand'.

19. D.B. Redford, *A Study of the Biblical Story of Joseph (Genesis 37–50)* (Leiden: Brill, 1970), pp. 68-71, and J.R. King, 'A Pattern for Making a Healthy Existence: An Interdisciplinary Examination of the Biblical Story of Joseph' (PhD dissertation, Florida State University, 1977), p. 38 n. 92.

20. On these see King, 'A Pattern', p. 46; W.L. Humphreys, 'The Motif of the Wise Courtier in the Old Testament' (PhD dissertation, Union Theological Seminary, New York, 1970), pp. 205ff., and E.C.B. McLaurin, 'Joseph and Asaph', *VT* 25 (1975), pp. 29-35.

21. See G.W. Coats, *Genesis, with an Introduction to Narrative Literature* (Grand Rapids: Eerdmans, 1983), pp. 264-65, for discussion of these elements.

22. See C. Westermann, *Genesis 37–50* (Minneapolis: Augsburg, 1986), pp. 37, 43, 66-67.

an authority figure, the pharaoh. An ironic touch, which balances the narrative, is found at the end when Joseph gives clothing to the same brothers who had once taken away his.

A second stage can then be posited which added the material describing Joseph's time in Potiphar's service and his imprisonment (Gen. 39.1–41.23). If these episodes are regarded as embellishment of the narrative which originally only included detailed accounts of Joseph's life until his sale as a slave and his rise to power in pharaoh's court, then this would explain why the garment motif is not an explicit part of the story. What I wish to suggest, however, is that the motif serves as an *inclusio*, with the material in between serving as logical digressions which both heighten the tension in the narrative and provide a foundation for Joseph's introduction at pharaoh's court.

Where the motif does appear in the text, it highlights the theme of Joseph's rise to a position of favor, his precipitous fall and the manner in which he will save Jacob's household from extinction by rising once again to a position of power and influence.[23] Clothing explicitly serves within the framework of the narrative as a device signalling these status changes. However, it also serves as a socially implicit element in the transitionary material. The social realities of the setting, based on social custom and the practicalities of identifying persons according to status and social condition, allow for the assumption of clothing-based events even when they are not explicitly described in the text. The continued appearance of explicit or implicit scenes involving clothing thus add to the argument that this transitionary material is part of a well structured narrative,[24] not one that has been expanded later.

Garments are central to Joseph's position within his family and to his role as a high official in Egypt. In each case he is given a distinctive garment. In the first case he is clothed in a robe which marks his favored position within Jacob's household. After his brothers sell him into slavery, Joseph must leave his robe behind, thereby initiating a status change. The second example, which completes the *inclusio*, includes another transformation, this time when he exchanges his clothing for the robes of office given to him by the pharaoh. In the final episode of the narrative, when he has revealed himself to his family and is preparing to bring them to Egypt, Joseph reverses the pattern originally set by his

23. G.A. Rendsburg, *The Redaction of Genesis* (Winona Lake, IN: Eisenbrauns, 1986), p. 92.

24. See Coats, *Genesis*, pp. 279-82.

brothers and gives garments to these brothers (Gen. 45.22), marking the final status change in which he becomes the master, thereby fulfilling the prediction of his dreams.

Episode 1: Joseph's Robe

The rendering 'coat of many colors' in Gen. 37.3 is based on a mistranslation of *kᵉtōnet passîm* in the LXX which was then perpetuated in the Vulgate and the KJV. This item, expensively made, whether enhanced with dyes or not, was used to mark Joseph as his father's favorite son and, along with his ability to interpret dreams, created a tension with his brothers that eventually led to his first change of status. Its distinctive style ('long sleeves' in NRSV) is a good parallel to the 'long robe with sleeves' noted as a garment worn by the 'virgin daughters of the king' in 2 Sam. 13.18. In both cases, persons are set aside as special by their costume, and all others recognize the power relationship symbolized by this garment.

The giving of a garment is a well known theme in cultural studies[25] and a standard item in royal correspondence from Mari.[26] Messengers, foreign ambassadors, military leaders and local administrators are all rewarded with one or more new items of clothing. Yahweh begins the practice by giving Adam and Eve garments of animal skins in Gen. 3.21. The importance attached to garments as gifts or prizes is also found in the story of Samson's riddle (Judg. 14.10-19).

In the face of a mounting cycle of shame and anger caused by their envy of Joseph, his brothers relieve the tension by an act of physical violence.[27] They take advantage of the opportunity afforded by his visit to their encampment, seizing him and selling him as a slave to Midianite traders (Gen. 37.12-28). His robe, however, remains behind.

Initially, his brothers divest him of this symbol of 'privileged social position' as a display of their anger and perhaps as a prelude to his murder.[28] Redford[29] suggests that this is an afterthought on the part of the brothers. In the heat of their anger, they initially plan to kill Joseph.

---

25. Schneider and Weiner, 'Introduction', p. 2.

26. See *ARM* 1.8.31; 10.17; 29.10; 46.15.

27. T. Scheff and S.M. Retzinger, *Emotions and Violence: Shame and Rage in Destructive Conflicts* (Lexington, MA: Lexington Books, 1991), p. 126.

28. King, 'A Pattern', p. 51.

29. Redford, *A Study*, pp. 142-43.

Reuben and/or Judah convince them to relent and the Midianites offer an alternative means of disposing of the unwanted sibling. Once they begin thinking again, some of them must come to the realization that Jacob will want proof that Joseph has been killed.[30] The blood stained robe thus serves as the prop they need to make their case.

However, the stripping of Joseph's garment from him could be described as a reversal of the investiture ceremony in which his father clothed Joseph in his special robe. Precedent for this is found in the systematic disrobing of Inanna as she makes her way through the levels of the underworld.[31] As each garment is removed, her power and life force is drained from her until in the end she becomes 'a corpse, a piece of rotting meat' hung from a hook in the underground storehouse.[32]

Thus once Reuben/Judah talks the brothers into holding him until they discuss Joseph's fate, the cloak takes on a new importance. It is used as evidence of his demise (Gen. 37.31-33), the *corpus dilecti*,[33] convincing Jacob that his son has been killed and eaten by wild animals. The loss of the garment, like the stripping away of insignia from a soldier who is being 'drummed out' of the military, transforms Joseph from an honorable person to a shamed person. He is subsequently relabelled from 'son' to 'slave'.

Episode 2: The 'Livery' of Potiphar's House (Genesis 39.12-18)

During the time that Joseph serves as a slave in Potiphar's household there is an implicit use of clothing as a status marker. It is quite likely, although the text does not provide this detail, that he would have been given a garment distinctively marking his entrance into this Egyptian official's service. Its weave or color would have proclaimed to all his bond to that household.[34] Naturally, it would have also clearly marked him as a slave, but within that context his clothing, like that of every

30. This is a stark reminder of Jacob's deception of his own father, Isaac, wearing Esau's garments and an animal skin to simulate Esau's hairiness—Gen. 27.15-26.

31. *ANET*, pp. 52-57, and D. Wolkstein and S.N. Kramer, *Inanna, Queen of Heaven and Earth: Her Stories and Hymns from Sumer* (New York: Harper & Row, 1983), pp. 57-60.

32. T. Jacobsen, *The Treasures of Darkness: A History of Mesopotamian Religion* (New Haven, CT: Yale University Press, 1976), pp. 56-57.

33. Westermann, *Genesis 37–50*, p. 43.

34. Schneider and Weiner, 'Introduction', p. 2.

person of every social condition, would have indicated his social role and responsibilities.[35] Eventually, when he was elevated to the position of 'overseer' (Gen. 39.5), the clothes would have become a 'form of power', an outward sign of his authority and his enhanced role within the household.[36]

Although it is not described in the text, Joseph's garment would have probably consisted of a gown worn over the tunic, which was the 'common dress of all classes of men above the very lowest'.[37] It is most often depicted in Egyptian art 'with a short and comparatively close-fitting sleeve on the nearer side, but on the other the garment hangs loosely from the upper arm and is gathered in at the waist.'[38]

When Potiphar's wife attempts to seduce him, Joseph refuses her invitation, realizing both its honor-shattering implications and the 'dependence' position sexual relations with his master's wife would create.[39] He is only able to escape her clutches in the end by pulling out of his livery and leaving it in her hands. Again, he is stripped of his status-marker and the symbol of his role within that community.

Subsequently she uses this robe, which had visually marked him as slave-overseer, as evidence of Joseph's attempted rape. Joseph's status, and presumably his clothing, are exchanged once again to reflect his new role as a prisoner (Gen. 39.20).[40] The garment, which has provided an element of honor to Joseph's status as a slave, now becomes the basis for his shame. In the face of indisputable physical evidence and the fact that his word as a slave may not be accepted in judicial proceedings, Joseph cannot deflect the charges and is relabelled for a second time, from 'servant' to 'prisoner'.

The similarity between this stripping away of honor along with the garment in this episode and the similar occurrence in Episode 1 is not coincidence. It is an artful use of a societal element to reinforce a literary theme. The *inclusio* remains intact and one of its prime elements is re-enforced in this transitionary material.

35. H.J. Drewal, 'Pageantry and Power in Yoruba Costuming', in Cordwell and Schwarz (eds.), *The Fabrics of Culture*, p. 190.

36. W. Brueggemann, *Genesis* (Atlanta: John Knox, 1982), p. 315.

37. N. de G. Davies, *The Rock Tombs of El Amarna*. I. *The Tomb of Meryra* (London: Gilbert & Rivington, 1903), p. 11.

38. Davies, *Rock Tombs*, p. 11.

39. L. Abu-Lughod, *Veiled Sentiments: Honor and Poetry in a Bedouin Society* (Berkeley: University of California Press, 1986), p. 148.

40. See the fleeing 'young man' in Mk. 14.52.

Episode 3: 'Robes of Office' in Pharaoh's Court (Genesis 41.42)

After spending an unspecified period of time in prison and distinguishing himself there, Joseph becomes a 'trustee' (Gen. 39.21-23). Although the text does not mention that Joseph was given a special prison garment, it seems likely that he wore something that marked him as a prisoner, replacing the garment taken from him by Potiphar's wife. This practice of supplying prison attire is suggested by 2 Kgs 25.29 in which king Jehoiachin is described as putting 'aside his prison clothes'. Additionally, when Joseph became the 'trustee' for the prison, his costume may have been enhanced with a chain of office or an additional fringe.

This narrative serves as a transition to the episode in which Joseph successfully interprets the Pharaoh's dreams. It is linked to that episode with a series of catchwords,[41] but more importantly it provides an episodal link and narrative logic. Joseph's skills as a 'sage' in the interpretation of dreams will be his key to freedom and personal survival. It will also be the means for insuring the survival of his family.

Thus his accomplishment is magnified in the narrative, providing him with the public opportunity to not only interpret the pharaoh's dream but also to surpass the skills of all of the Egyptian 'magicians' (*ḥarṭummîm*) and 'sages' (*ḥᵃkāmîm*).[42] The result is that he is given a high-ranking position and his status change is marked by the presentation of Pharaoh's signet ring, garments of fine linen, a gold chain, and a retinue. This investiture ceremony (Gen. 41.42-43) completes the *inclusio* initiated by the scene in which Joseph's father had clothed him in his special robe (Gen. 37.3). In substance, it is similar to those graphically portrayed in the El Amarna tomb paintings of Meryra[43] and those

---

41. Rendsburg, *The Redaction of Genesis*, pp. 95-96, provides a number of examples of catchwords which connect the episodal units of this narrative. For example, among the catchwords that link unit C (Reversal: Joseph guilty, Potiphar's wife innocent, Gen. 39.1-23) with unit D (Joseph hero of Egypt, Gen. 40.1–41.57) are six occurrences of *bêt hassōhar*, 'prison house', in Gen. 39.20-23 and two in Gen. 40.3, 5.

42. See R.J. Williams, 'The Sage in Egyptian Literature', in J.G. Gammie and L.G. Perdue (eds.), *The Sage in Israel and the Ancient Near East* (Winona Lake, IN: Eisenbrauns, 1990), p. 95, and W.L. Humphreys, *Joseph and his Family: A Literary Study* (Columbia, SC: University of South Carolina Press, 1988), p. 160.

43. See Davies, *Rock Tombs*, Plate XXX and pp. 35-36.

described in a number of ancient Near Eastern documents, although most are from the first millennium BCE:[44]

1. 'I clad him in linen and in garments with multi-coloured trim (and put rings on him).' Sargon II (722–705 BCE) in *CAD*, 'B' 258, '*birmu*' from H. Winckler, *Die Keilschriftexte Sargons*, pl. 45 F1.10'.

2. 'I made a (treaty) with him, (protected by) oaths which greatly surpassed (those of the former treaty). I clad him with a garment with multicolored trimmings, placed a gold chain on him (as the) insigne of his kingship, and put gold rings on his hands.' Ashurbanipal (668–633 BCE) in *ANET*, p. 295, ii, from M. Streck, *Assurbanipal und die letzten assyrischen Könige bis zum Untergang* (Leipzig, 1916).

3. '...and Daniel was clothed in purple, a chain of gold was put around his neck and a proclamation was made concerning him that he should rank third in the kingdom' (Dan. 5.29). This last example serves as one of the many parallels between Joseph and Daniel.[45]

The radical change in appearance effected by these new robes of office, and the other gifts given to him by the pharaoh (his new name, and his Egyptian wife) transforms Joseph from a prisoner into a courtier.[46] They also extinguish all signs of his origin as a 'Sand-Crosser'. This is a term used in the 'Tale of Sinuhe' for bedouin or persons from Syro-Palestine,[47] which would have marked him as completely outside of Egyptian society.

Joseph's physical transformation into an Egyptian makes him acceptable at the Egyptian court and it reflects his own acceptance of a new identity within the power structure of a foreign culture.[48] It also aids in his deception of his brothers when they come to purchase grain during the famine. In fact, it is difficult for him to convince them of his identity when he finally reveals himself (Gen. 45.3-4).

He has adopted not only the costume, but also the mannerisms of an Egyptian of high social status and authority, thereby distinguishing him-

44. Redford, *A Study*, pp. 225-26.

45. Humphreys, *Joseph and his Family*, pp. 210-12, also notes the similarities with the stories of Esther.

46. See Humphreys, *Joseph and his Family*, pp. 155-57, 161, for the correlation between the court investiture theme and both tomb inscriptions and the story of Sinuhe.

47. *ANET*, p. 22, ll. 290-95.

48. E.J. Langdon, 'Siona Clothing and Adornment, or You Are What You Wear', in Cordwell and Schwarz (eds.), *The Fabrics of Culture*, pp. 297, 311, and Roach and Eicher, 'The Language of Personal Adornment', p. 16.

self in their eyes as a foreign ruler.[49] This demonstrates how behavior is a reflection of and a reaction to social action and social understanding. Because Joseph is dressed as an Egyptian and acts like an Egyptian, he is unreservedly taken to be an Egyptian and the brothers do not even consider the possibility of a deception.

For them to believe that it is truly Joseph, several things are required (Gen. 45.1-15). First, all non-Israelites are removed from the room. This insures that there will be no witnesses to Joseph's 'non-Egyptian' actions, and it removes the aura of power associated with an official surrounded by his advisers and servants.[50] In addition, the brothers will have no Egyptians present to measure Joseph's costume or manner against. It could even be said that by removing the attendants, Joseph removes his costume.

Secondly, Joseph instructs them to come closer, breaking down the barriers associated with 'court behavior'.[51] He then uses a self-revelatory formula (Gen. 45.3, 5) and a series of theological reflections for all previous events in this family's history. Some commentators see this as a theodicy, taking the events out of human control and portraying Yahweh as the driving force throughout.[52] In any case, his intent is to humble himself, weeping and calling on his brothers not to be afraid or ashamed of their previous actions (i.e. selling Joseph into slavery). Finally, through repetition of his message, a break with his former manner, and his demonstrated knowledge of their family, Joseph is able to re-establish his kinship role while at the same time retaining his position as a 'ruler over all the land of Egypt'.

Once they have been convinced of his true identity, Joseph gives them each gifts of new garments as evidence of his forgiveness and favor toward them. This final step brings the story full circle and provides one final use of garments as a status marker. Joseph is now in a position to give clothing to his brothers. He gives each brother one set of garments, but, like his father before him, Joseph shows his favoritism (by giving

---

49. U.R. von Ehrenfels, 'Clothing and Power Abuse', in Cordwell and Schwarz (eds.), *The Fabrics of Culture*, p. 401.

50. Westermann, *Genesis 37–50*, p. 142.

51. Westermann, *Genesis 37–50*, pp. 142-43.

52. Coats, *Genesis*, p. 293, and G. von Rad, *Genesis: A Commentary* (Philadelphia: Westminster Press, 1961), p. 393. Compare this to Westermann, *Genesis 37–50*, p. 143.

Benjamin five sets of garments, Gen. 45.22).[53] Their acceptance of the gift marks them as his clients and also as persons who are subject to the rule of the Egyptian pharaoh for whom Joseph works.

Conclusion

Clothing and other forms of personal adornment have an important social function in every human community. Their appearance, shape, decoration and style are all part of a symbolic language which expresses personal identity, group membership and social status. In the Joseph narrative, clothing or the lack of it provides one of several structural elements. An *inclusio* is formed by the two investiture ceremonies in the narrative (when Jacob gives Joseph his robe and when the pharaoh vests him in robes of office). In the transitionary material between these two events, clothing continues, although sometimes implicitly, to serve as a signal of status change and favor within the setting of the story. By applying the principles of the anthropology of clothing to these narratives, its social context is better revealed.

53. See the similar action in Gen. 43.34.

INDEXES

INDEX OF REFERENCES

OLD TESTAMENT

NEW TESTAMENT

OTHER ANCIENT REFERENCES

INDEX OF AUTHORS

THE BIBLICAL SEMINAR